Thatcher and Sons

A City at Risk
Landlords to London
Newspapers: the Market for Glory
The Companion Guide to Outer London
Images of Hampstead
The Selling of Mary Davies
The Battle for the Falklands (with Max Hastings)
Accountable to None: the Tory Nationalisation of Britain
England's Thousand Best Churches
England's Thousand Best Houses
Big Bang Localism

SIMON JENKINS

Thatcher and Sons

A Revolution in Three Acts

ALLEN LANE
an inprint of
PENGUIN BOOKS

ALLEN LANE

Published by the Penguin Group

Penguin Books Ltd, 80 Strand, London WC2R ORL, England

Penguin Group (USA) Inc., 375 Hudson Street, New York, New York 10014, USA

Penguin Group (Canada), 90 Eglinton Avenue East, Suite 700, Toronto, Ontario, Canada M4P 2Y3

(a division of Pearson Penguin Canada Inc.)

Penguin Ireland, 25 St Stephen's Green, Dublin 2, Ireland (a division of Penguin Books Ltd)

Penguin Group (Australia), 250 Camberwell Road, Camberwell, Victoria 3124, Australia

(a division of Pearson Australia Group Pty Ltd)

Penguin Books India Pvt Ltd, 11 Community Centre, Panchsheel Park, New Delhi – 110 017, India

Penguin Group (NZ), 67 Apollo Drive, Mairangi Bay, Auckland 1310, New Zealand

(a division of Pearson New Zealand Ltd)

Penguin Books (South Africa) (Pty) Ltd, 24 Sturdee Avenue, Rosebank, Johannesburg 2196, South Africa

Penguin Books Ltd, Registered Offices: 80 Strand, London WC2R ORL, England

www.penguin.com

First published 2006

1

Copyright © Simon Jenkins, 2006

The moral right of the author has been asserted

Set in 10.5/14pt Adobe Sabon
Typeset by Palimpsest Book Production Limited, Grangemouth, Stirlingshire
Printed in Great Britain by Clays Ltd, St Ives plc

A CIP catalogue record for this book is available from the British Library

ISBN-13: 978-0-713-99595-4
ISBN-10: 0-713-99595-5

Contents

Acknowledgements

My interest in politics began when I worked on a project for the Redcliffe-Maud commission on local government in 1970 and in travelling and talking to people in every corner of the United Kingdom ever since. The conclusions of this book are the outcome of that experience and as a columnist for *The Times, Evening Standard, Guardian* and *Sunday Times*.

My sources are reflected in the notes and bibliography. Conversations and interviews with participants are mentioned where appropriate. I would like to thank Stuart Proffitt of Penguin, who has been a spur and encouragement through the project. Others who were generous with stimulus, advice or argument include Leon Brittan, Robin Butler, Christopher Foster, Jonathan Freedland, Peter Hennessy, David Howell, Martin Ivens, Kate Jenkins, Jeffrey Jowell, Tim Lankester, Andrew Likierman, Nick Raynsford, Adam Ridley, Richard Ryder, Andrew Turnbull, William Waldegrave and David Willetts. I acknowledge the groundbreaking work of David Marquand, Gerry Stoker and Anna Randle on localism. Tony Travers has been a constant source of inspiration and advice. He and my assistant, Charlotte Dewar, read and commented constructively on the text.

Introduction

Margaret Thatcher was Britain's most famous prime minister since Church-ill. Over eleven years she transformed her nation and gave birth to an -ism in use to this day. She was not widely loved, but she was admired even by those who disagreed with her. Her Conservatism was controversial, yet it showed that democratic leadership could both prescribe and administer unpopular medicine and win elections in doing so.

A quarter of a century is a good span of time from which to re-examine any historical movement or event. Thatcher was a truly revolutionary leader. She was dissatisfied by what she saw round her and set herself to change it utterly. She saw socialism and wanted the opposite, freedom from the state. She was no conservative, other than in an emotional attachment to a certain sort of Britishness, but proselytized ceaselessly for change. In the process she bred a generation of politicians all of whom took her as their reference point and all of whom dedicated themselves to the cause of reform. Unlike most radicals who end by running before the wind of events, merely nudg-ing an occasional course correction, Thatcher headed straight into oncoming gales. Though her form of economic liberalism was not new, her will to implement it against the grain of politics was unique. Hers was never going to be a quiet revolution.

The test of any revolution is, did it work and did it last? When on 20 Novem-ber 1990 Thatcher's cabinet colleagues trooped into her Commons room and told her to go, the world gasped. What had they done? The answer is that they had decided that Thatcherism could best be preserved if its progenitor were removed from the scene, and they were right. After the fall, the legacy was carried forward by John Major, Tony Blair and his powerful Chancellor, Gordon Brown, to become the ruling consensus of British government. These three men, Thatcher's 'sons', were convinced disciples, going where even their mistress had feared to tread. She treated them, with varying degrees of faith, as her heirs. For more than a quarter of a century Britain was in the grip of a concept of government at first wholly untried but soon established and exported round the world. Such milestones in a nation's history are rare.

I witnessed the Thatcher era from the start. I worked on the fringes of the Conservative party before the 1970 general election as it sought a new direction in Opposition under Edward Heath. Harold Wilson's 1964 Labour government, of which so much had been hoped, was a disappointment. The post-war welfare consensus known as Butskellism (after the Tory, Rab Butler, and Labour's Hugh Gaitskell) was in disarray. The economic ideas underpinning Thatcherism can be found in embryo in debates in the 1950s and 1960s, first in the Institute of Economic Affairs and increasingly within the Conservative party itself and in such think tanks as the Bow Group. At the time they were espoused by a minority. Conservatism was still essentially what it said, a reluctance to depart radically from the ruling consensus, even when it was that of post-war welfare socialism.

Heath's undoubtedly radical ambitions, many of them proto-Thatcherite, did not long survive his arrival in Downing Street, dying in the industrial chaos of 1973–4. A year after the party's early exit from power came the backbench putsch that brought Thatcher to the leadership. The then Labour governments of Wilson and James Callaghan proved, for the last time, that the prevailing view on how to manage the economy did not work. British politics was seldom so miserable as between the IMF crisis of 1976 and the 'winter of discontent' of 1979. The nation seemed lost to defeatism and its government to impotence. Editorials referred hopefully to the spirit of Dunkirk as if history might yet replay 1939 and after. But the much-debated 'British disease' seemed incurable.

Like most observers at the time, I at first viewed Thatcher's Tory leadership as transitional, a rightist rebellion, possibly shock therapy, probably a mistake. The Heathites, reverting to Butskellism, would somehow resume control. Thatcher had come to power at the head of a 'peasants' revolt' and did not seem a natural leader, let alone a prime minister. Her voice was shrill and her manner hectoring. She was a bad listener and responded to any suggestion with a cantankerous right-wing tick. Her four years as leader of the Opposition were unhappy for her and for her party, and her early years in office hardly less so. Thatcher before the Falklands

War of 1982 never seemed other than a passing phenomenon.

The war proved a turning point. It made Thatcher famous world-wide and gave her the elixir of military victory. She was emboldened, though only slowly, to confront previously intractable forces ranged against her: the trade unions, Europe, local government and enemies within her own party. Previously averse to foreign policy she strutted the world stage, 'punching above her weight' alongside her friend, Ronald Reagan. She brought to peacetime leadership qualities normally associated with war, above all those of emphatic, decisive rule. Thatcher post-Falklands was a prime minister in a position to get things done. She was ready to honour Machiavelli's dictum that it is better to be feared than loved: 'Men love as they please but fear when the prince pleases. A wise prince should rely on what he controls, not on what he cannot control.'

Thatcher enjoyed only the briefest of real ascendancy. It lasted from the defeat of the miners in 1985 to the poll tax revolt of 1989. Only then was she able to bring the full force of her '-ism' to bear on public administration. Her style was that of battle rather than debate. Her bossiness made her few friends and her treatment of subsidiary institutions was brutal. Though she had a sentimental attachment to the more dignified elements of the constitution, such as royalty and parliamentary procedure, she could show a fierce contempt for civil servants, academics, nationalized industries and civic leaders. 'None of you can be any good,' she told the British Rail Board over lunch, 'or you would be in private industry.'[1] She did not suffer fools gladly, indeed she suffered few gladly. When at last she tried to curry electoral favour by abolishing the rates, she fell into the poll tax trap and found herself without friends or allies. Her party rose up and sacked her. Like Al Capone she was brought down by an act of tax evasion.

The fall of Thatcher left the nation stunned. Nanny had been thrown out by the inmates of the nursery. What would they do now? The Tories' hope was that a softer version, 'Thatcherism with a human face', would be carried forward by John Major. As after any revolution, its heirs tried to retain the good and discard the bad. Thatcherism was seen as a comet that had raced across the sky and burned itself out. A set of essays on the concept published in 1988, two years before Thatcher's fall, saw it as so idiosyncratic that it could not survive her departure.[2] It was a style of leadership rather than a change of political direction. When Thatcher was gone British politics would surely return to the *status quo ante*.

This limited view was mistaken, distorted by Thatcher's eccentricity and political solitude. We can now see her departure in 1990 as the end of the beginning. It reinforced rather than undermined Thatcherism by separating the -ism from the lady herself. Had she survived, the Tories might well have lost the 1992 election and an as yet unreformed Labour party would have reversed much of what she did. In the event, Major's leadership gave momentum to her legacy while the 1992 victory blew away old Labour and created the phenomenon that was Tony Blair. He was Thatcher's most devoted follower, progenitor of what deserves to be termed Blatcherism.

The word Thatcherism is elusive because it appears to embrace so many contradictions. These reflect the paradoxes in Thatcher's own character, a Hayekian liberal contending with a Methodist nanny, a small statist with a strong statist, laissez-faire with 'more must be done'. These paradoxes mirror those in the British constitution, where a tradition of strong Crown pre-rogative contends with a supposed respect for pluralist democratic institutions. They run as two strands through the story of Thatcherism. They are ideologically distinct, so distinct as in my view to merit analysis not as one revolution but two.

The first revolution set out to liberate the 'supply side' of the British economy and give new spirit and confidence to private enterprise. Taxes were cut, labour markets freed through employment law reform and com-petition enforced, notably in financial services. The private sector was also invited to reinvigorate the public sector, and the boundary between the two was blurred and, under Blair, transformed beyond recognition. Thatcher and her successors tore up the rulebook of British government. Her distaste for convention, for officialdom and for the old ways of doing things became her unique offering to high office. Her addiction to the BBC satire *Yes, Minister* was not to its humour but to its moral message. It showed how the system would defeat attempts to change it. This first revolution was a revolution of political will. It assaulted the modern state in order to 'roll back its frontier' and assert the supremacy of the individual.

The second revolution arose from the management of the first but led in a quite different direction. It was a revolution not of will but of power. Thatcher centralized government, enforced Treasury discipline and regu-lated both public and private sectors to an unprecedented degree. Where state ownership retreated, state control advanced in the form of an unprece-dented volume of new legislation from both Westminster and Brussels.

The British state did not roll back its power in the late twentieth century. Today its size and cost is as great as it was in 1979 and its intrusion into the lives of its citizens is probably greater. The chief casualty has been the British constitution. Political leadership is less subject to institutional restraint and is closer to being an elected dictatorship than in any other western democracy.

As these two revolutions enveloped British politics in the 1980s and 1990s, their impact was dramatic. The Conservatives under Major made no attempt to undo either of them, quite the reverse. More remarkable was the total conversion of Tony Blair and Gordon Brown. Their 'project' after 1994 may have been sold as tactical, 'to make Labour electable', but its consequence was to render Thatcherism irreversible. Labour's election victories in 1997, 2001 and 2005 saw no return to high income tax rates, nationalization or employment protection. They saw no rush to European corporatism. Blair drove privatization into every corner of the public services. He signed up to the first Thatcher revolution in Opposition and to the second as soon as he was in power. He first refashioned the Labour party to end its constitutional pluralism and then refashioned the British constitution in much the same way. He took to the second Thatcher revolution as eagerly as he had taken to the first. He emerged as one of the most authoritarian prime ministers of modern times. As the tabloids often said of him, 'To Thatcher, a son'.

The story begins with a remarkable woman whose political personality dominates this book, continuing long after her dramatic fall. Thatcher's image was never fuzzy, always sharp, that of a confident, dominant, unwavering woman. Hardly a week passed during her time in office when she was not in the news, commanding headlines, losing, winning, chiding, arguing, battling. She was loved and loathed. She never won a popular majority at the polls and for much of her time ranked as the least supported prime minister since the Second World War.[3] Her name still evokes a fierce reaction in people over the age of forty. Yet there is no point in complaining that Thatcher was not somebody else. She appeared on the scene of history when someone like her was needed, and she did the job. A different Thatcher might have been a nicer person, but she would not have been Thatcher.

Brenda Maddox remarked in her personal biography, *Maggie*, that 'Iron

Ladies are not born, they are made'.[4] I believe in both nature and nurture. The qualities which a leader brings to power are embedded in his or her parentage and background. Perhaps a consensus politician, going where the wind blows, need not draw on some distant gene pool or upbringing. Conventional leaders such as Heath, Wilson and Callaghan reacted similarly to the trials of the 1970s, despite widely differing personalities. Thatcher's leadership was not conventional. Her radicalism had to draw on something other than those round her, and it drew naturally on her past. For that reason her leadership cannot be fully understood without an account of her background, education and early career.

Thatcher's mannered public confidence was rooted in a provincial Methodist upbringing. Her Toryism was that of a girl yearning to escape Grantham and better her position in life. The towns of the East Midlands lack the hold the Welsh valleys or Scottish lowlands have over their political alumni. Thatcher hardly ever returned to Grantham. Yet throughout her career, she claimed to hear messages from her past. 'Voices' called from her father, Alderman Roberts, from the Oxford chemistry lab and from the suburban drawing room. Others called from supposed soulmates whose spirits she tried to honour through her career, Milton Friedman, Friedrich von Hayek, Michael Oakeshott and Sir Keith Joseph. Their destinations (by no means all the same) she felt should be hers. They were her familiars, flapping round her head even when events dragged her in the opposite direction. Students of Thatcherism need to hear these voices.[5]

Politicians play up their deeds and play down their inheritances. Historians, blessed beneficiaries of hindsight, lean in the other direction and regard the continuities of history as more significant than its discontinuities. Revisionists have suggested that Thatcher did not depart greatly from the post-war consensus, certainly not as much as Blair was to do after 1997. She retained the welfare state more or less intact. She was at best a late and partial convert to privatization. She shrank the boundaries but not the size of the state. To these critics, she was just another Conservative prime minister.[6]

Yet every revolution takes time to unfold. Only two leaders in the twentieth century, Lloyd George and Churchill, are regularly compared with Thatcher. Both came to office during the turmoil of war, when the nation was in peril. Thatcher's leadership was certainly salvaged by a war, in the Falklands, but she had to establish her ascendancy amid economic travail, when she could call on few of the loyalties that war inspires. Her transformation of politics emerged from the Heath U-turn of 1972, the IMF crisis of 1976 and the subsequent inflationary spiral. Previous governments tried to muddle through such troubles, hoping that something would turn up to save them and their policies from disaster. The Keynesian and social welfare settlements were always incorrigibly optimistic.

The experience of the 1970 Heath government left Thatcher a brutal realist. Her two talented chancellors, Geoffrey Howe and Nigel Lawson, tore up Keynes and her successors tore open the welfare state. Battles with the miners and with local councils destroyed any agreed concept of how Britain should be governed. After decades of Downing Street pusillanimity, Thatcher reasserted the prime duty of democratic leadership, which was to lead. She expanded the concept of what could be done by modern government. As Churchill said of Joseph Chamberlain, she 'changed the weather'.

The nineteenth-century sociologist Max Weber described what he called the 'ideal leader' of the future, one who could handle Europe's emergent democracies and the countervailing force of its elitist bureaucracy. Weber's leaders had to be romantic, charismatic, activist figures with whom whole peoples could identify. They should speak the language not of policies but of values and convictions, vague generalized ideals. They should be 'occasionalists', able to seize on passing events and turn them to advantage. To them a crisis was always an opportunity. They needed above all to convey the Nietzschean concept of will. Weber's thesis was much in evidence in twentieth-century leadership, not always with benign consequences. Both Thatcher and Blair displayed many of Weber's required features.[7]

The Thatcherite settlement has survived seven general elections, three prime ministers and (roughly) three economic cycles. This book traces the story of Britain's domestic government over this time. It relates the political context in which Thatcherism was born, that of Britain in the 1970s, and notes the rise to power of its three prime ministerial exponents, Thatcher, Major and Blair. It is not a general history of the period. Headline events such as riots, strikes, crime and terrorism plague all governments and are described, like the Falklands, Europe and Iraq, only insofar as they intrude on the developing revolution. Detailed analysis is devoted to the customary business of government, the financing and administration of the public sector. It is a business much neglected by the theatrical conventions of Westminster reporting. Yet only in health, education, police, the law and public services generally, can the inner character of a government be traced and the choices supposedly embraced by democracy laid bare. If the narrative sometimes delves into the undergrowth of waiting time contracts, rail regulation or the rate support grant I make no apology. These are, to most citizens, the stuff of government rather than the fluff.

All three prime ministers were total politicians. They had inconsiderable careers outside Westminster when they came to office. Their *Who's Who* entries were starkly barren of achievement. None showed any deep awareness of Britain's past or experience of its present. None read much or were given to cultural references outside politics (except for Major's love of cricket). Blair's ignorance of history, including Labour history, could be startling. He once told Edward Heath how lucky the latter was to have missed Suez (when Heath was chief whip). Such ignorance of the world can be an aid to radicalism, but it is dangerous when the going becomes tough and a sense of the past might shine light on the future.

Perhaps as a result all three were remarkably cavalier towards their parties and party politics generally. Whether the party emperors really had no clothes or whether they were merely threadbare is a question to which I return. But Thatcher, Major and Blair were able to convince their parties to go to places that would have provoked mutiny two decades before. In doing so they established a new consensus. After the initially bitter struggles of the 1980s, British politics seemed to drain of ideological argument. By the turn of the century no titanic forces seemed to be in contention. Manifestos were emptied of substantive content. Labour and Conservative (and even Liberal Democrat) parties were like Hazlitt's stagecoaches, splashing each other with mud as they raced towards the same destination.

The word 'revolution', though of seventeenth-century origin, is nowadays customarily associated with the left. As such it arose from Marx's dialectic struggle between competing class forces, with mankind progressing through historical tensions, intellectual, political and economic. This battle between thesis and antithesis, said Marx (echoing Hegel), was unstable, resolved only by reaching a synthesis. At that point, as Isaiah Berlin put it, 'A sudden leap takes place to a new level, whereupon the tension between a new cluster of forces begins once more.'[8] Thus one ideal, human equality, is challenged by the inequality implicit in the class struggle, leading in turn to revolution.

There is an echo of this dialectic in Britain's experience over the past quarter century. Both Marx and Thatcher saw politics as rooted in economics and in class. Both were obsessed with change. Having little vested interest in roots or property or group or professional interest, both saw the future as theirs to upheave and to that extent were optimists. Marx regarded it as a fallacy to hold that humans 'under suitable conditions will voluntarily give up the power which they have acquired by birth or wealth or ability for the sake of a moral principle'. Political allegiance was a matter of self-interest which the reformer had to harness. Conflict would be eliminated only when the class struggle ended in an economic utopia, in his case communism. Marx's synthesis required the 'dissolving of the state itself, hitherto the instrument of a single class, into a free classless society'.[9]

Thatcher's outlook was not dissimilar. Her dialectical struggle, if we call it that, was an inversion of Marxism-Leninism. Her thesis was the ruling ethos of post-war socialism. Her antithesis would be an uprising of the bourgeoisie followed by her own highly personal dictatorship. Her synthesis was uncannily like Marx's, an economic utopia in which the state would roll back its frontiers and, at least ideally, wither away. Thatcher would not have quarrelled with Marx's maxim that philosophers may interpret society but the real task is to change it. She would not claim a better epitaph than Berlin's on Marx:

With an inner tranquillity based on clear and certain faith in a harmonious society of the future, he bore witness to the signs of decay and ruin which he saw on every side. The old order seemed to him to be patently crumbling before his eyes.[10]

Thatcher believed in a revolution aimed at a society where class was overwhelmed by the benign, equilibrating forces of a free-market economy. In a much misquoted phrase, she said there was 'no such thing as society', but a free market of competing individuals, families and, perhaps, communities. The modern Marxist historian Eric Hobsbawm understood this better than many Thatcherites. He cited Thatcher's 'determination to break with the traditional British ruling-class', to confront labour and to wage war on 'the enemy within'. The pillars of the British establishment, wrote Hobsbawm, 'rightly regarded Thatcherism not as a continuation of the old ways by other means, but as a striking and worrying innovation'.[11] Thatcher herself described her seizing of power in her party as a 'shattering blow delivered to the Conservative establishment. I felt no sympathy for them. They had fought me unscrupulously all the way.'[12]

Neither Marx nor Thatcher saw their utopias achieved. Marx's state did not dissolve, nor did Thatcher's roll back its frontiers. In my rare meetings with her, she sometimes showed a flash of recognition of this failing, though it did not seriously worry her. Like all leaders she would claim to have needed power only to conquer her enemies, in her case socialists, before 'handing it back to the people'. But she was no Ronald Reagan, whose antipathy to big government led him to devolve to subordinate state governments the management of American welfare, such as it was. Thatcher was, by nature and nurture, a nanny statist and did not try overmuch to disclaim it. She showed no interest in dismantling the authority of her office, any more than did Major or Blair. That is why *Thatcher and Sons* must be the story not of one revolution but two.

Any observer of revolution tends to set it not just against its objectives but against his own. As will be apparent I am an admirer of Thatcher's first revolution and deeply fearful of her second. I see the first as liberating Britain at a time when liberation was needed and the second as authoritarian. I believe in liberal democracy in a minimalist state, as did Thatcher. But I am more of a conservative than she was, seeing with such students of British politics as Michael Oakeshott, John Gray and Roger Scruton some virtue in the continuity of institutions and loyalty to people, places and communities, a virtue that extends beyond nostalgia to the underpinning of democracy. Such continuity is a bulwark against the second revolution, possibly the one truly lasting one. In any reasonably prosperous and stable polity the onus must be on the revolutionary to prove his case. The sceptic should always put the onus of proof on the utopian.

In Britain a diminution of state power is as far as ever from being realized. Hence in the final chapters I return to Thatcher's original goal, to pursue a possible synthesis to her antithesis. How in the twenty-first century is a true 'rolling back' of the state to be achieved, assuming it is desirable? What form might a third Thatcherite revolution take? Hegel remarked that 'governments never learn from history, or act on principles derived from it. They thus condemn themselves to repeat its mistakes. Thatcher was careful not to repeat the mistakes of her predecessors, indeed she was obsessed with avoiding them. This was her greatest strength. Yet she ushered in a state which, while liberating its economy to competitive forces, spent a quarter of a century intervening in the lives and liberties of its citizens more than any of its forebears, be they conservative or socialist. It imposed more taxation, more laws, more regulations, more forms and more inspectors. Thatcher's state may have helped create more wealth, but that is not the sole purpose of democracy. It should also promote liberty and self-reliance and devolve risk to individuals. It should seek self-government in all senses of the word.

The historian of politics should not be 'a celestial chief justice, sentencing the guilty and setting free the innocent'.[13] Yet all history is selective and is thus in some sense judgemental. It is the supreme expression of reason. It seeks out the mistakes of the past so as to help the present avoid them. To me, reason is the tool of opinion. It is history as argument. Such history is not simply a lamp on the stern of the ship, illuminating a disappearing wake. It lights the sea all round us. History offers the only rational explanation of who we are and why we act as we do. Without it, we cannot steer a course ahead.

PART ONE

The Revolution in Embryo

I

Climbing the Ladder

Myth clings to the foothills of any great career. It clings peculiarly to Margaret Thatcher, née Roberts. Britain's first woman prime minister came to office a bizarre bundle of contradictions. She presented herself as poor girl turned rich, lower, then upper, middle class. She was a Midlander yet a Southerner. She was a successful career woman yet not a feminist. John Campbell, the most thorough of Thatcher's biographers to date, tried to pick his way through the fog and record the 'rebranding' that took place when she was in sight of high office. Besieged by profile-writers and instant biographers she presented her life story as a rise from humble origins, an 'improving morality play, illustrating the rewards, personal and national, of hard work, self-reliance, family values and practical Christianity'.[1] Over a dozen biographies have accepted this authorized version of Thatcher's origins. It is only partly true.

Thatcher was born in 1925, the younger of two daughters of Alfred and Beatrice Roberts, then shop-owners. Roberts was neither impoverished nor working class. His career from shopkeeper to merchant was a classic of middle-class upward mobility. He moved into local politics as an Independent with Liberal leanings, and for twenty years was chairman of Grantham's Finance and Rating Committee. After service as a councillor he was elected by his colleagues an alderman (now a defunct office), and in 1945 he served a term as mayor. In addition, Roberts was chairman of the local branches of the Chamber of Trade, the Rotary Club and the local Workers Education Association. He was director of the Trustee Savings Bank and governor of both of Grantham's secondary schools. As a prominent figure he was much reported in the local press.

This activity ended in 1952 when an incoming Labour council voted the sixty-year-old Roberts off the aldermanic bench after twenty-seven years. He retired with dignity and, he said, with 'no medals, no honours but an inward sense of satisfaction'. The removal of Roberts was a partisan act, but it came at a time when Independents were disappearing and aldermen with them. Thatcher herself had long left Grantham when it occurred. Yet she later exploited the incident to illustrate all that was wrong in Labour local government, indeed in public life generally. At the height of her battle with Ken Livingstone and the Greater London Council in 1985 she referred to it on television with tears in her eyes. When discussing Thatcher's fall from grace in 1990, Alan Clark recalled that the supposed fall of Roberts 'was a subject to which she adverted several times'.[2]

For all that, Alfred Roberts passed on to his daughter the idea of a fixed moral framework rooted in Methodism (though she later switched to her husband's Anglicanism). Roberts was a lay preacher and expected his children to go to church three times on Sundays. He was ambitious for their advancement, paying for them at the fee-paying Kesteven and Grantham Girls' School and instilling in them a culture of relentless hard work. Their lives were dominated until Margaret was ten by a Victorian grandmother, Phoebe, her father's mother. She ordained an upbringing that seems to have been regimented, inhibited and joyless. While Margaret's mother, Beatrice, emerges from the memoir photographs as a warm, approachable woman, the grandmother might be an Amish matriarch.

The absence of Beatrice from Thatcher's accounts of her past has been much remarked. She is not mentioned in Thatcher's *Who's Who* entry and is almost lost from her memoirs, amid eulogies of her father.[3] One acerbic biographer, the Labour MP Leo Abse, even wrote a book explaining Thatcher's politics as a reflection of her starvation of maternal love and her Freudian eagerness to live up to her father's ambition.[4] Feeling such pressure is allegedly common among second daughters of fathers who have no sons. Certainly in Thatcher's case, energy was channelled into competitive achievement. When she won a recital prize at the age of nine, she was complimented by a teacher on her good fortune. She instantly replied, 'I wasn't lucky. I deserved it.' In her memoirs there is no trace of girlish frivolity. The American historian Charles Dellheim has compared Thatcher harshly with the Victorian mercantilists whom she so admired, characterized by extremes of 'individualism, materialistic philistinism, insensitivity to the plight of the poor and a distrust of the state'.[5] He points to the similarity with a traditional Hebraic upbringing as explaining Thatcher's lifelong affinity to

Judaism. It contrasted with her distance from the 'Hellenistic' Tory moderates who initially opposed her.

Margaret Roberts felt she needed to escape Grantham. Everything in her youth suggested an eagerness to leave the provinces behind. After going up to Oxford she seldom involved her family or Grantham associates in her success. They appear to have been an embarrassment. After her marriage to Denis, her parents rarely visited them or the grandchildren in London. Visitors to the Roberts house in Grantham when the father was still alive noted not a single photograph of Margaret later than of her graduation, and not one of Denis or the grandchildren. In her memoirs Thatcher wrote how proud her parents were when she entered the House of Commons, implying that they were there. They were not. They 'saw' her only because 'the press contained flattering photographs of me in my new hat'.[6] Their absence was surprising for a new MP with a still active, formerly politician father who must, on any showing, have been proud of his daughter. Campbell concludes with the 'inescapable impression that Margaret was very much less devoted to her wonderful father while he was alive than she became to his sanctified image after he was dead.'[7] The piety and hard work of her upbringing were genuine; its implied family cohesion was not.

The Robertses and Grantham offer what must be an important backdrop to Thatcher's politics, even as she fled south to escape them. She brought with her a Roundhead view of how society should be run, a mix of rugged individualism for oneself and a readiness to intervene in the lives of others. Thatcher took comfort in such old Puritan maxims as 'cleanliness is next to godliness', 'hard work harmed no man' and 'if it's worth doing, it's worth doing well'. Her ambition and harsh treatment of those round her was so aggressive, so angry, that much of Abse's thesis rings true. Denied the childish pleasures that others enjoyed, Thatcher sought all her life to vindicate that denial. The qualities she could not handle were tolerance and love.

No gate into the British establishment was so pearly in the middle decades of the twentieth century as Oxbridge. For those lucky or clever enough to gain admission, it was a launch-pad for any career. Oxford projected Wilson, Heath, Thatcher and Blair into the networks of power. It was a citadel of meritocracy. For a humble provincial girl, the first few months might seem a horror of loneliness and insecurity. But once feet were found, once friendships were formed, Oxbridge wiped away all past and offered the world. She arrived at Somerville College in 1943 without a scholarship and at her father's expense. She confessed to finding it 'cold and strangely forbidding'. She lacked the personal and social skills to make friends easily. Her chosen subject, chemistry, required long hours in the laboratory while other undergraduates were jostling in lectures and swapping badinage in tutorials. She turned to the enthusiasms she had brought with her from Grantham, to music and politics. She joined the university's Bach choir and, as if rejecting her father's independent liberalism, joined the Oxford University Conservative Association (OUCA).

Such a decision was odd for a girl from a provincial grammar school. The left would have been her natural habitat, especially with post-war Britain beckoning as testing ground for socialism. The Conservatives under Churchill were still the party of Empire and opposition to the welfare state. A contemporary at Oxford, the novelist Nina Bawden, recalled meeting her on firewatch duty and chiding her for being a Tory when 'people like us' should be trying to build a newer, better world. Thatcher replied, in what would still have been a Midlands accent, that 'she meant to get into parliament and there was more chance of being "noticed" in the Conservative Club just because some of its members were a bit stodgy'.[8]

This was the patois of an Oxford political career. Her father had advised her to 'ignore the crowd', perhaps to protect her from social slights. To Janet Vaughan, left-wing head of Somerville at the time, she stood out as 'so set in steel as a Conservative. She just had this one line.'[9] To her, Thatcher was always sure she was right and could not deal with those who thought they were right too. But she never shut off an argument. She was a one-woman, right-wing Militant Tendency. Oxford alone may not have made her an intransigent arguer but it must have reinforced her psychological carapace.

Though excluded by her sex from the Oxford Union, the university's facsimile parliamentary playground, Thatcher rose through the ranks of the more open-minded OUCA. Those who recall her at the time remember her as 'brown' and uncharismatic, struggling to change her voice and appearance. Her views appear to have been on the liberal wing of the party. She espoused individualism against an overpowering state, yet admitted in her memoirs that she 'had not yet fully digested the strong intellectual case against collectivism'.[10] She described her first party conference, in 1946, as nothing short of an epiphany, her first encounter with the party rank and file. 'So often in Grantham and in Oxford it had felt unusual to be a Conservative. Now suddenly I was with hundreds of other people who believed as I did and who shared my insatiable appetite for talking politics.'[11] She returned to Oxford invigorated and achieved the remarkable ambition of becoming OUCA president, a distinction that made a career in politics not just possible but probable.

The thesis that Thatcher had to fight her way up from humble beginnings is nonsense. The presidency of OUCA offered a gilded path to the top, with privileged access to the most senior party figures. She rubbed shoulders with Robert Boothby, David Maxwell Fyfe, Peter Thorneycroft, Lord Hinchingbrooke and the future Lord Home. She met as contemporaries Tony Crosland, Edward Boyle and Tony Benn and received a crash course in the language and habits of politics. What Oxford did not give Thatcher was also significant. An exclusively scientific education was narrow and she left university having read no history or literature, a shortcoming Tony Blair also regretted after reading law. To Methodism's moral certainty her study of chemistry seems to have added the intellectual fixity of the foothills of science. Campbell concluded that she 'left Oxford as she went up, devoid of a sense of either irony or humour, intolerant of ambiguity and equivocation.'[12] To many this might seem a shortcoming, a weakness. In the circumstances in which Thatcher found herself it was probably a strength. Oxford transformed an ambitious but insecure girl into an acolyte at the altar of power. She avoided Oxford's social life and casual friendships. No memoir or biography contains any hint of a boyfriend, let alone of sex. Thatcher was not ready to claim a passage into the upper echelons of the Conservative party, but she had sniffed the air of politics and found it exhilarating. Oxford had taken nature and nurture and shown them the uplands of political leadership.

The tale of Thatcher's political evolution after Oxford goes cold. She had to find a job. Politics had nothing to offer a penniless chemistry graduate. The thirteen years between graduation and arrival in the House of Commons occupy just 39 of the 1,468 pages of Thatcher's memoirs. She never considered returning north but passed seamlessly from working as a laboratory assistant for a plastics firm in Essex to the caterers, J. Lyons, in Hammersmith. It was at the 1948 party conference in Llandudno that she had what proved to be a crucial break. An old Oxford associate introduced her to the chairman of Dartford Conservative Association, then looking for a candidate for their certainly unwinnable seat. She won the nomination at the tender age of twenty-three and moved into lodgings in Dartford.

Thatcher fought the Dartford elections in 1950 and 1951 and showed the first sign of a distinctive political personality. Her manifesto was patriotic, calling for independence from American aid and more reliance on home production and imperial preference. It opposed Labour's nationalization programme and championed individual enterprise against 'a soulless socialist system'. She promised when in parliament 'to vote as my conscience not the party line dictates' and would allow herself 'no rest until the duties which fell to my lot were complete'.[13] She lost the 1950 election honourably. Edward Heath won the adjacent Bexley seat and Thatcher recalls finding him 'aloof and alone'.

During the election she met and in 1951 married a member of the Dartford association, a divorced paint manufacturer named Denis Thatcher. He was ten years her senior and seems to have offered security and an income. Their daughter, Carol, remarked in her account of her father's life that the marriage was of 'mutual convenience rather than a romance'.[14] A sign of Thatcher's upward mobility was that the wedding did not take place in Grantham but in London. Her dress was a political blue and the reception was hosted not by her father but by her Dartford sponsor, Sir Alfred Bossom, in his house in Carlton Gardens. The speech was given by her local party chairman. She subsequently attended only one of Denis's beloved rugby matches but enjoyed the Paint and Varnish Manufacturers Annual Dance.

Thatcher often claimed that marrying Denis was 'the best decision I ever made'. In old age he came close to secular sainthood, softening her image and linking her, however tenuously, to a recognizable world of directorships, golf clubs, rugby and gin. Marriage and the birth of twins caused Thatcher's career scarcely to miss a beat. She abandoned the laboratory and read for the Bar. When she returned to Somerville for a gaudy and was invited to speak, contemporaries already noticed the loss of her Midlands accent. She was called to the Bar in early 1954 and began work in chambers immediately. Yet the search for a parliamentary seat became obsessional. She recalled that, 'Once you have been a candidate everything else palls.'

If workaholism were a clinical condition, Thatcher would merit a thesis. Work was for her like pumping iron to a bodybuilder. She never 'put the family first', as she later said all women should do, and referred to being 'lucky' in having a wealthy husband to pay for nannies, as if every woman should go out and find such luck. Unlike Denis, who left for work waving to the children at their window, she left with head already buried in papers.[15] She appears not to have enjoyed the law any more than she enjoyed science. She did not use the Bar to advance her career, as did most politician/lawyers, but turned her back on its conviviality and networking. Then in 1958, aided by a Central Office eager for women MPs, Thatcher was selected for the safe seat of Finchley. A year later she campaigned under Macmillan's claim that the British people had 'Never Had It So Good' and won. She summoned the press to photograph her arrival in parliament, one of just 25 women MPs out of 630. By luckily winning third place in the first private member's bill ballot she was able to make her maiden speech introducing her own bill, to let the press into council meetings. Though such bills rarely pass into law, she spoke for half an hour without notes and was praised to the skies. Within weeks there was talk of her getting early promotion into office.

Thatcher revolted early against her own government, in favour of the return of corporal punishment in 1961. Rab Butler, Home Secretary at the time, recalled the trouble he had 'with Colonel Blimps of both sexes', but in other respects she swung with the Tory wind. She spoke on the budget, worried that 'the system of control of government expenditure is very dangerous in that it gives all the appearance of control without the reality.' At a Woman of the Year lunch she and others were asked which character from history they would like to have been. She astonished the gathering by choosing Anna, the royal governess in *The King and I*, who had gone to Siam 'not merely as a job but with a sense of destiny'. She could often seem beyond parody.

Most intriguing was Thatcher's attitude to Macmillan's 1961 application to join the Common Market. She later played down her support for it but at the time she argued passionately that joining was not a detraction from sovereignty but a 'reinforcement of it'. She continued, 'We should be failing in our duty to future generations if by refusing to negotiate now we committed this country to isolation from Europe for many years to come.'[16] Thatcher remained fiercely pro-European up to the moment when she became prime minister. Blair, as we shall see, was fiercely 'anti' until that moment.

Whatever Thatcher's social insecurities they were masked by her gift for self-confidence. She never seemed less than in command, not always considered an appealing quality in the male-dominated world of politics, especially to Tories of both sexes. Thatcher was unashamedly feminine, immaculate in New Look dresses, never wearing trousers or suits to work. The then Labour MP Shirley Williams recalled her remarking in the Lady Members Room, 'We have to show men we are better than they are.'[17] To Williams she exuded a 'strong sense that men were agreeable, playful and, in the end, not very serious creatures'. There seemed no chink in her armour.

Within two years, in October 1961, Thatcher won a government job as junior minister for pensions and national security, the first of the 1959 intake to win promotion. It was an advancement she admits she owed to being a woman. Macmillan was determined to have at least three in his government. Thatcher's account of her interview with him spoke volumes of their respective worlds:

I sorted out my best outfit, this time sapphire blue, to go and see the Prime Minister. The interview was short . . . He said: 'Ring the permanent secretary and turn up at about 11 o'clock tomorrow morning, look around and come away. I shouldn't stay too long.' He said the job involved just turning up for a part of each morning, signing a few letters and then going home.[18]

Thus did a statesman schooled in gentlemanly Edwardian government address raw ambition. Thatcher gazed at him in amazement. After her first meeting, her ministerial boss, John Boyd-Carpenter, told his permanent secretary, 'She's trouble'.[19]

Thatcher now rebranded herself. So far she had rejected her past, changed her voice and settled down as 'just an ordinary Chelsea housewife'. As the spotlight turned towards her, she brought Grantham and Alderman Roberts from the cupboard. She referred to them often in interviews as paragons of simple, provincial virtue. The closer she came to power the more she felt the need of a hinterland. Her path from Oxford to political office had, by most standards, been free of serious struggle. Now she needed struggle. Like populist leaders the world over, she cast herself as an outsider and many, of a snobbish turn of mind, were happy to oblige. There is no evidence that Thatcher was conscious of what she was doing. Certainly she never admitted it. But the outsider temperament was one she exploited to the full throughout her career. She lacked a warm or sympathetic personality, though she could show sudden, intense concern for subordinates in distress. She was infatuated with her son, Mark, yet could not see how this damaged him or her relations with his twin, Carol. In six years at the Inner Temple and moving among aspiring politicians of both parties, she formed few friendships. She confined her social life to the well-modulated relationship with Denis.

Towards the world beyond she showed restless hostility. Like a girl seeing demons at the foot of every bed she created a stage army of opponents whom it would be her life's work to overcome. She went about, said one of her colleagues, 'looking for enemies instead of making friends' – a strange habit in a politician. Social gaucheness remained with her throughout her life. Grantham and the apparently bleak Roberts home of her childhood became a sort of comfort blanket. Her father's original shop took on the iconic role of Lincoln's log cabin, a psychological and political reference point sought out by journalists (and briefly made a restaurant in her honour).

The Ministry of Pensions was housed in a grim, 1930s building off the Strand, from where it ran a giant nationalized industry. I briefly served there as an undergraduate intern and agree with Thatcher's account of its duties as 'more technically complicated than those falling to any other branch of government'.[20] She defied Macmillan's account of the job, working furiously and involving herself in minute details of policy. She loved correcting officials whenever she caught them out. Letters were challenged and sloppy presentation interrupted. She read everything and dominated other ministers in the department, who resented it. Her every suggestion was resisted because of its 'repercussions'. She recalled, 'How I came to hate that word repercussions.' She was furious when a change to an earnings rule which she had proposed and the office opposed was effected as soon as Labour followed her into power.

In the Commons Thatcher was equally combative. She was accused by the Opposition of nannying and 'schoolmarm-ism', jibes that were to echo throughout her career. Had her experience of life and the failings of others been wider, she might have been more accommodating, but she would not have been Margaret Thatcher. Already in this Indian summer of post-war Toryism, she was identifying the weak points in her party's armour. She supported the chancellor, Selwyn Lloyd, in his 'pay pause', precursor of later

disastrous attempts at pay restraint in the 1970s. But she told her constituents that 'we are approaching the time when trade union laws ought to be
revised.' She complained often that the country was paying itself more than
it earned. 'Good housekeeping' should be the test of sound policy, she
said.

The year 1964 was not a happy one for Thatcher. The Tories finally
lost power after thirteen years in office. Her upward trajectory was halted
and she faced the appalling prospect of nothing to do. Denis was experiencing trouble with his family firm and rarely saw his wife. That year he
seems to have had a breakdown and vanished to South Africa for three
months. Margaret, with the twins at boarding school, had been 'totally
absorbed in her career' and, according to Carol, was 'the last person he
would have discussed [his illness] with'.[21] After Christmas Thatcher herself
became, for the first and only time in her life, seriously unwell with
pneumonia. She could not even attend the funeral of her hero, Winston
Churchill, in January 1965.

Yet few things in Thatcher's career were not turned to good account.
The Tory defeat was the making of her. Opposition cleared out the old
guard and opened up opportunities for a younger generation. In 1965 Sir
Alec Douglas-Home was bundled out of the leadership as ruthlessly as were
his successors. Thatcher's response was instructive. The choice of replacement was between Reginald Maudling and her neighbour in Kent, Edward
Heath, with the maverick Enoch Powell as an also-ran. While her 'outsider'
affinity seems to have been with Powell, an imperialist free-marketeer of
sound right-wing credentials, something in him deterred Thatcher. She had
upset her constituency by inviting him to speak in Finchley and his opposition to Common Market entry proved too much for the loyalist in her
to bear.

Of the two main contenders Thatcher admitted to liking Maudling's
'combination of laid-back charm and acute intellect'. Heath, with whom
she had 'never risked developing a friendship', was admirable and serious-
minded, 'but he was not charming nor, to be fair, did he set out to be'.[22]
She wrote, 'I did not either then or later regard amiability as an indispen-
sable or even particularly important attribute of leadership.' Future
colleagues would say amen. Yet charm ranked high in Thatcher's opinion
of men and she developed a bizarre, even flirtatious, weakness for
Westminster's matinee idols. Speaking for the Opposition in 1965, she

complained of the dashing Niall McDermott that, whenever the government wanted to say no, it 'always puts up the handsomest man to say so'. She boasted of his gallant riposte that she was 'the Opposition's most attractive representative'.[23] Thatcher later confessed that her decision in the leadership contest was made for her by her future mentor, Sir Keith Joseph. Though she had been inclined towards Maudling, Joseph persuaded her otherwise. Heath was as much a free-marketeer as Powell, and had pushed through sound competition legislation at the Board of Trade. He was also pro-Europe. He had, Joseph assured Thatcher, 'the passion to get Britain right'.[24]

If Thatcher hated Opposition, Opposition did not hate her. Over the six years of the 1964 and 1966 Wilson governments she held six shadow portfolios: pensions, housing, economics, power, transport and education. It was a formidable list but essentially an apprenticeship. Thatcher dabbled. She considered reforming the rating system and shifting more of the burden to central government, but she concluded that councils should not be stripped of too much accountability, 'otherwise the whole basis of local government is undermined for good and all'. Given later events it was an intriguing insight into her earlier good judgement.

The burst of liberal legislation sponsored by Roy Jenkins at the Home Office left Thatcher floundering. She supported easier abortion and homosexual law reform but opposed easier divorce and the abolition of capital punishment. Looking back on these issues, Thatcher felt it had been important that 'the law should be enforceable and its application fair to those who might run foul of it.' Hence her views on abortion and homosexuality, claiming acquaintance with people touched by both. She was liberal when friends were involved, yet stereotypically right-wing when life had kept its distance. As a mother of teenage children, she had no affinity with the liberation felt by young people in the Sixties. At her tenth anniversary ball as an MP in 1969, she spoke out against the past decade. Asked by the *Finchley Press* what she most wanted for the future, she called for 'a reversal of the permissive society'.[25] *The King and I* still lived.

In 1966 Thatcher joined Iain Macleod's Opposition Treasury team, concentrating on tax. It was the first time she had worked closely with her fellow politicians and Macleod's leadership made a deep impression on her. *The Times* remarked that she deployed 'every female weapon short of a rolling pin'. Her self-taught accent was 'beginning to hammer on Labour ears like some devilish Roedean water torture'.[26] Campbell uncovered an ironic jibe which she hurled at the government's new selective employment tax. It was, she said, 'this particular poll tax'.[27] She found that she thrived on battle.

Richard Crossman remarked that the two most difficult tasks in politics are finding a seat and getting into the cabinet. Government jobs are available to a hundred and fifty MPs, the cabinet to just two dozen. Thatcher's first opportunity came after three years in Opposition. The only woman in the shadow cabinet, Mervyn Pike, retired. Heath's aversion to Thatcher is attested in the memoirs of them both but, as she openly admitted, he had no option. She was the only available woman.[28] Once again Thatcher's sex was crucial to her advancement. It made the attainment of cabinet rank in a future Tory government all but inevitable.

Thatcher's performance in the shadow cabinet was not a success. She was now in the big league, covering first energy and then transport. She had no experience of man-management and little of committee work. She could not stop talking, though none of the talk was 'small' and her lack of social graces grated on those round her. To Woodrow Wyatt's informants she was 'a niggler not a debater . . . the sort of thing that happens if you allow women to go into politics.'[29] Others commented that she had 'a voice like a dentist's drill'. So far Thatcher had been able to control her immediate environment. As the junior member of a team this was no longer possible. It was nothing to do with being a woman, only with being Thatcher. It was said that no one who worked with her in the shadow cabinet at this time eventually voted for her as leader. They could not face it.

The conventional view is that Thatcher came to Thatcherism relatively late, perhaps not until after she took office as prime minister. Yet her speeches in the late 1960s contain clues as to where her mind was moving. Already the fault lines in post-war Conservatism were forming. The Institute of Economic Affairs was pushing out pamphlets advocating privatization and free markets to solve every public-sector problem. Many young Tories were eager for a new approach to Britain's poor economic performance in the 1960s, including Joseph, Howe, John Biffen, David Howell, Nicholas Ridley and Thatcher herself. As shadow energy minister she was convinced of the evils of nationalization and inquired into the possible privatization of electricity generation. She rejected it as unpopular.[30]

In 1968 Thatcher gave the Conservative Political Centre lecture at the party conference in Blackpool, a platform in the gift of the party leader. Thatcher assumed that Heath was looking for some feminine slant on politics but she grabbed the opportunity of a wider remit. An armful of books went down to her weekend retreat at Lamberhurst and gave her a crash course in political theory, possibly her first. What emerged was remarkable. Asking 'what was wrong with politics?' she said simply, 'too much government'. It should stop meddling in people's lives and stick to 'the control of the money supply and the management of demand'. It should exercise the same discipline on itself that it constantly imposes on others. The message was unmistakeable. This was a voice from the right, and one spoiling for a fight. Thatcher even declared consensus politics 'fundamentally subversive of popular choice'.[31] She was always to detest consensus. Conservatives fundamentally disagreed, she said, and should not hide their disagreements. Let argument bleed and, above all, act on the outcome. Thatcher was obsessed with doing, not just saying.

When the liberal Sir Edward Boyle decided to leave politics in the autumn of 1969, Heath appointed Thatcher as education spokesman in his place. This was not considered ideologically significant, and indeed the appointment was regarded by the press as a sign that he had 'resisted pressure from the right to appoint a dedicated opponent of the comprehensive system.'[32] As one of Boyle's researchers at the time, I remember the anguish with which he departed politics. The issue was not education but the treatment meted out to him by his Birmingham constituents on race and immigration. Thatcher was opposed to Boyle on immigration and agreed with Powell, but she was content to follow his and the party's line on secondary education. MPs were reporting that it was examination selection to separate local schools at eleven, the 'eleven-plus' of Butler's 1944 Education Act, that had cost them the 1964 election. Of the two-thirds rejected, many were the children of Tories who were no longer able to get into their local grammar school. Labour was committed to ending the eleven-plus. There might be a debate as to what form of comprehensive schools should follow. But getting rid of selection was vital.

Thatcher's brush with educational controversy was her first real testing in the fire. She had not opposed comprehensives in her local borough of Barnet, 'where appropriate'. She merely deplored the loss of 'good' grammar schools. This dodged the issue, which was to do away with any form of selection. She promised not to reverse existing comprehensive schemes and oppose only 'botched' ones, but she was unable to explain what this meant.[33] As education spokesman at the 1970 election she never suggested reversing what was then a major revolution in school structure and, to a large extent, in the class basis of local Britain. The paradox was to haunt her in office.

2

The Sorry Seventies

The Seventies have a reputation in twentieth-century British history as second in gloom only to the Great Depression. Most generations look back on their youth as a time of comfort, security and hope. Those whose youth lay in the Seventies tend to the opposite view. Whatever excitement had been generated by the 'swinging Sixties' was dissipated. Whatever post-imperial Britain had hoped to achieve had come to nought. Throughout her ascendancy, Thatcher would rouse her audiences to crusading fervour by crying, 'Remember the Seventies ... the three-day week ... the social contract ... the winter of discontent.' She would recall rulers (never mentioning Heath) who asked the electors, 'Who governs Britain?' and received the derisive answer, 'Not you!' The Seventies became political aversion therapy. Their defining art forms were brutalist architecture, nihilist drama and punk rock. To Thatcher they were ugly and transient, the last dying gasp of the post-war crypto-socialist consensus. Yet to Tory politicians at the start of the decade it was the 1960s that were years of missed opportunity. In preparing for power Heath knew that radical treatment was needed. He was no Tory traditionalist and his background was remarkably similar to Thatcher's. From a middle-class family he won a scholarship to Oxford, and thence into the army and politics. He rose swiftly to become chief whip to Eden during Suez and trade minister under Douglas-Home. Happier with the minutiae of policy than with the 'grip and grin' of the hustings, he saw government as a Rolls-Royce. The driver should only need to press the buttons and the machine would respond.

It has become a truism that Heath's plans for government were more 'Thatcherite' in 1970 than were Thatcher's in 1979. Many of his colleagues had been active in refashioning Conservatism, in returning to their ideological roots and dabbling in think tanks. The Institute for Economic Affairs under Ralph Harris and Arthur Seldon had kept alive the spirit of 'Manchester liberal' economics of the Mont Pelerin society, founded in 1947 as a counterbalance to what they saw as the spreading socialist conformity. The IEA offered a London platform during the 1950s and 1960s to such Pelerin alumni as Friedrich von Hayek and Milton Friedman. While avowedly not of the right, its appeal at the time was predominantly to the free-market strand of Tories.

When Heath's team were preparing their programme for the 1970 election, this intellectual right was already hovering in the background. The IEA and the new Bow Group, set up by Geoffrey Howe and a group of friends from Cambridge, proved a fertile source of ideas and research. Inspiration widened from Oxbridge to the London School of Economics and St Andrews and to the Conservative college at Swinton in Yorkshire. Support came from journalists on *The Times* (Peter Jay), the *Financial Times* (Samuel Brittan) and the *Daily Telegraph*. It was in the last in 1969 that Sir Keith Joseph published a series of pro-market articles under the tutelage of a mentor of his, Alfred Sherman, a talented and intellectually fearless former communist. A young party official close to Heath, David Howell, published a pamphlet in May 1970 advocating a slashing of the size of government and something he called by what he admitted was the 'ugly word', privatization.[1] The IEA and others had high hopes of a new Tory government. This was reflected in the pre-election Sundridge Park conference of shadow ministers to prepare a document called 'The New Style of Government'.

Just how deeply this 'new right' influenced Heath is hard to judge in view of the trauma of the 1972 U-turn in favour of economic interventionism. The manifesto had espoused free markets and a more competitive economy, echoing Heath's personal crusade to end resale price maintenance when at the Board of Trade. It rejected government support for 'lame ducks', planned a more efficient Whitehall and anticipated the 'cold douche' of Common Market entry. All this was derided by Harold Wilson as ignoring the poor and benefiting only 'Selsdon man', named after the suburban hotel at which he thought (wrongly) that the Tory manifesto had been written.[2] Wilson referred to Heath's programme as 'an atavistic desire to reverse the course of a years of social revolution . . . a deliberate return to inequality.'

Whatever truth lay in this jibe it recognized Heath as a forerunner of

Thatcherism. One of the many right-wing Tory ginger groups to spring up in the 1970s was called the Selsdon Group to honour the caricature. At Heath's first conference as prime minister, he was anything but conservative. He promised prophetically 'a change so radical, a revolution so quiet and yet so total that it will go . . . far beyond the decade, and way into the 1980s.'[3] His ambition, and most lasting monument in office, was Britain's entry into the European community. But the reason he gave was not a quest for a protectionist economy or an easy, collectivist life. It was to galvanize, discipline and transform Britain. Heath's tragedy was never to see in Thatcher a disciple of his own 1970 call to a new British revolution.

The Heath government immediately cut income tax, cut public spending, refused to intervene in a dock strike and abolished the interventionist Prices and Incomes Board. Unions were made subject to a controversial Industrial Relations Act and special court (later abandoned). The government also instigated a carefully prepared programme of public-sector reform. Consultants were employed to introduce an American-style Programme Planning Budgeting System (PPBS), with a unit in Downing Street. Waste was to be cut and services outsourced or tested against private-sector comparators.

The impact of events soon devastated these ambitions. Howell, charged with reforming the civil service, watched as each change ran into union or professional opposition which the cabinet lacked the collective will to overcome. Reflecting on his efforts in 2005 he remarked that 'we were just too early.'[4] Unshackled from incomes policy, unions drove wages upwards and inflation doubled in a year. In the winter of 1971/2 came a miners' strike and an energy crisis. Unemployment broke through the million mark for the first time since the Depression. The pressure of all this on Heath was appalling. Campbell remarked that January 1972 must 'rate as the most dreadful short period of concentrated stress [on government] ever endured in peacetime.'[5] Downing Street buckled and, in the early months of 1972, did one of the most stark U-turns in history. The miners' demands were met and Heath introduced an interventionist Industry Act. Lame ducks, including Rolls-Royce and Upper Clyde Shipbuilders, were rescued with large subsidies.

More dramatic, Heath abandoned his belief that free markets should determine personal incomes. He created a statutory Pay Board to fix pay 'relativities' over a three-phase period. It was, wrote Thatcher in retrospect,

'the high point of the Heath government's collectivism'.[6] The implementation of the new pay policy was often bizarre, as if a Conservative government
was distastefully having to do something that only a Soviet one would
normally have contemplated, yet doing it with British efficiency. I remember
a civil servant arriving at the newspaper where I worked to vet the annual
salary increases of individual journalists. It was a regime more statist (we
fumed that it was more fascist) than anywhere in the western world. Under
further pressure from the miners and power workers and a doubling of the
oil price at the end of 1973, the government introduced a state of emergency and a three-day working week. The country saw rolling black-outs as
traffic lights went dead and citizens ate dinner by candlelight. It was an
eerie, uncertain time.

In all this Thatcher acted as a loyal bystander. The election had propelled
her into national prominence as education secretary and she did not enjoy
it. Education was a subject of which she had no real understanding. It meant
conflict with a corner of the constitution of which she had no experience,
local government. County and city education authorities were beyond her
control and she found them difficult to manage. 'The ethos of the DES was
self-righteously socialist', she wrote later. 'It was soon clear to me that on
the whole I was not among friends.'[7] She was certainly not, but the task of
a minister is to win friends, especially in the emotive world of education.
This was never Thatcher's strong suit. Though she worked hard at her briefs,
hearts and minds eluded her. Her permanent secretary, Sir William Pile,
later told Campbell he found her 'narrow-minded, emotional, difficult to
argue with, driven by passions which he found abhorrent ... always
wanting to do things which he had to tell her she could not do'.[8] It was a
foretaste of what Downing Street was to experience a decade later. Thatcher
pre-formed a view on any evidence before her, and if anyone present
demurred, she became instantly aggressive and dismissive. If she felt she
was losing a point she switched to another. This sign of insecurity she
regarded as her 'will'.

At the height of Heath's battle with the miners in early 1972, Thatcher
chose to save money by abolishing free milk in primary schools. The public reaction to the 'milk snatcher' was overdone and, in retrospect,
astonishing. To critics of the Abse persuasion it was a gift, a bossy, middle
class Tory woman withdrawing her breast from the nation's babies in a
fury of unrequited love. Popular resentment against the Heath government

was briefly concentrated on his education secretary. He flirted with the idea of sacking her but rightly judged that this would have been unfair. Free milk was a hangover from wartime rationing and was, anyway, being retained for poor families. For Thatcher it was a case of a socialist entitlement that had to go, and go it did. But she reacted to the public vitriol badly, with tantrums, tears and recrimination against officials. She later referred to the saga as a 'savage and unremitting attack that was only distantly related to my crimes'.[9]

Thatcher at education was the Heath government in microcosm. Whatever ideological radicalism may have lain dormant in her mind, her daily work was the custom and practice of running the welfare state. When Joseph at the industry department asked his mentor, Alfred Sherman, what to do with the department, the abrupt answer was, 'Abolish it.' When Joseph demurred, Sherman accused him of total 'civil service capture'.[10] Thatcher was a conventional 'spending' minister. She fought for her budget and won more than most, being able to boast raising the school leaving age to sixteen. She expanded higher education from 15 per cent of each age cohort to 22 per cent. She even saved the new Open University, which her party had promised to scrap. When a group of right-wingers sent her a 'Black Paper' advocating an end to comprehensives, scrapping the higher school-leaving age and restricting higher education, she rejected it all. The *Guardian* even called her 'a more egalitarian minister than her Labour predecessor'.[11] In her memoirs she blandly admitted that her 1972 White Paper, declaring expansion in every sector of education, was 'the high point of attempts by governments to overcome the problems inherent in Britain's education system by throwing money at them.'[12]

Thatcher withdrew Labour's circular insisting on comprehensive secondary schooling, thus enabling her to claim she had 'saved' ninety-two grammar schools. But she continued to accept new comprehensive schemes when brought to her for approval, confusing many local education authorities as to what she really wanted. The answer is that she did not really know, and yet did not feel strong enough to leave such matters to local councils to decide. Thatcher was uncomfortable with delegation of any sort. She had no experience of business or of managing anything. In her Manichean world, there was no place for subordinate democracy, in this case locally elected councils only half subject to central authority. In a well-ordered world, she believed that ministers should get their way.

33

Her time at education was the germ of her second revolution.

By 1974 the confident Tory army that had set out bright for battle in 1970 was reduced to an exhausted, retreating rabble. The Yom Kippur War had devastated world oil prices and Northern Ireland was in turmoil. The country's lifeblood seemed hijacked by precisely the forces the government had been elected to curb, those of organized labour. The government that went to the polls in February 1974 demanded an answer to a humiliating question, 'Who governs Britain?' The Conservatives had clearly lost control. There is no evidence that Thatcher opposed Heath's U-turns on industrial support or on incomes policy. She supported the bailing out of Rolls-Royce on 'defence' grounds. She was a typical junior cabinet member, protesting when disaster occurred that it was 'not my department' while mouthing a meaningless collective responsibility. At the first 1974 election, her manifesto supported all Heath's actions. She even called for a 'stiffening' of pay and prices policy 'in consultation with both sides of industry'. Her sound-bites were thoroughly Heathite. Britain should be 'united in moderation, not divided by extremism . . . should aim for change without revolution . . . should put aside differences and join in a common determination'.[13]

Thatcher's later denunciation of this period in her party's fortunes was largely a product of embarrassment. During 1972 she had been invited to resign by two anti-Heath rebels, Nicholas Ridley and John Biffen. She declined. She was unmoved by a 1972 letter from a group of IEA economists, including her later aide, Alan Walters, attacking the government's un-monetarist policies. It was only later that she described them as 'brave and far-sighted critics who were proved right'. She offered the coward's defence that her resignation 'would not have made a great deal of difference'.[14] Instead she described the U-turns as 'little by little we were blown off course until eventually, in a fit of desperation, we tore up the map, threw the compass overboard and, sailing under new colours but with the same helmsmen, set off towards unknown and rock-strewn waters.'[15] She added that 'some of us (though never Ted, I fear) learned from these mistakes.'

This sobering view is confirmed by a very different observer, Heath's private secretary at the time, Douglas Hurd. He concluded that the experience of the 1970 government was a vital precursor to what followed. It was 'a necessary first attempt, the rough work of pioneers', a dry run for revolution.[16] Hurd's metaphor was appropriately revolutionary, that before the Bolsheviks could triumph the Mensheviks had to fail. Thatcher herself preferred Kipling: 'Let us admit it fairly, as a business people should, /We have had no end of a lesson: it will do us no end of good.' The question was what lesson and how much good.

Labour's narrow majority in February 1974 led to a second general election in the autumn, and a second Tory defeat. Heath resigned with the worst possible grace and left his party in disarray. Harold Wilson returned to power but handed over to James Callaghan in 1976. My recollection of the time is of Britain's entire political community dazed, tired and bereft of ideas. The Labour party was seeking refuge in its syndicalist roots, in the unions and the public housing estates. It was in collective despair. Callaghan reportedly told Wilson, 'When I am shaving in the morning I say to myself that if I were a young man I would emigrate, except that I cannot think where to.'[17] Britain was the sick man of Europe, with sick humour to match.

Callaghan's three years as prime minister (1976–9) sowed the seeds, but only the seeds, of the dismantling of the post-war consensus. In 1976 the nation faced its worst economic debacle since the Second World War. The chancellor of the Exchequer, Denis Healey, had cut public spending by £1 billion in the spring and promptly faced a seamen's strike, a run on sterling, interest rates at 15 per cent and a desperate and humiliating loan from the International Monetary Fund. This was granted only on condition of another £2.5 billion of spending cuts. In September, Healey dared not leave the country on an intended foreign visit, turning back at Heathrow to reassure the currency markets and save his prime minister from an enraged party conference in Blackpool. IMF monitors arrived in Healey's office at the Treasury. Britain was more a banana republic than a great power.

The 1976 crisis was traumatic in its impact on all in government, especially the civil service and cabinet. It began a distancing of Labour's leadership from its party that became steadily more marked. The 'social market' thinking and monetary discipline associated with the right was championed on the half-left by Callaghan's son-in-law, Peter Jay, in *The Times*. This was signposted in Callaghan's speech to his 1976 party conference, in a passage drafted by Jay:

For too long, perhaps ever since the war, we postponed facing up to fundamental choices and fundamental changes in our society and in our economy. That is what

I mean when I say we have been living on borrowed time ... The cosy world we were told would go on forever, where full employment would be guaranteed at the stroke of a Chancellor's pen, cutting taxes, deficit spending, that cosy world is gone ... We used to think that you could spend your way out of a recession and increase employment by cutting taxes and boosting government spending. I tell you in all candour that this option no longer exists and that, insofar as it ever did, it worked by injecting inflation into the economy.[18]

Welfare socialism had survived half a century of reformulation by the Webbs, Tawney, Beveridge, Crossman and Crosland but found itself at the end of the 1970s in a cul-de-sac. Yet for the time being Whitehall departments knew no other way. They still spent what they thought they needed, and sent the bill to the Treasury. Local councils fixed local taxes and answered to a local electorate. Unions and employers were considered stakeholders in government. The public sector, its managers and workforce, enjoyed a monopoly over the dispensing of services. In all this they knew they could rely on a bedrock of popular support, reflected in such affectionate depictions of the public sector as *Doctor in the House*, *Dad's Army*, *Dixon of Dock Green* and subsidized farming in *The Archers*. A letter in *The Times* during the three-day week told the nation to relax. Britain would survive, 'as it has always done, by muddling through'.

Such naively optimistic Micawberism infused not just the conduct of government. It extended to the constitution, the monarchy, parliament, the cabinet, the courts, the civil service, local government and the universities. If change were needed to any of these, the constitutional convention was to appoint a Royal Commission under a distinguished public figure and see what he said: Robbins on universities, Pilkington on the BBC, Redcliffe-Maud on local government. Each would have a remit to achieve bipartisan consensus. Only then was legislation considered appropriate. This approach to constitutional or institutional reform had itself become a constitutional convention. It was the British way.

As the economy cracked, so did these conventions. Not only politics but the civil service was affected. To Treasury officials the scars of the 1976 humiliation were deep and lasting. Their response was described in a BBC documentary in two words, 'Never again.'[19] Never again would the machinery of government lose command and control. Sound government had in some degree to retreat from the institutions of democracy to sustain its discipline. Some commentators even wondered if democracy could sustain this retreat. If no government could both curb public spending and retain electoral support, which would have to go? What hope was there for fiscal responsibility and consequent economic stability?[20] Perhaps authoritarianism was the only answer. These were turbulent times. I recall discussing at the time whether this was how things felt in Weimar Germany.

The 1976 IMF crisis can be seen in retrospect as heralding the end of the old regime. Two years later the 'winter of discontent' of 1978/9 saw the worst industrial unrest in Britain since the General Strike. Callaghan's negotiated 5 per cent pay policy and his Commons coalition with the Liberals collapsed. The Ford motor company recklessly awarded its workers a 15 per cent pay rise and public-sector wage claims erupted. Strikes broke out in key industries and fuel supplies dried up to hospitals and schools. Garbage piled in streets. Bodies went unburied. Despite his nickname 'Sunny Jim', Callaghan recalled his despair at the time. He remarked in cabinet that he had 'never in fifty years been so depressed as a trade unionist'.[21] The British ambassador to Paris, Sir Nicholas Henderson, wrote a telegram, leaked to The Economist, that Britain's decline was 'so marked that today we are not only no longer a world power, but we are not in the first rank even as a European one.'

The Labour government was in precisely the bind in which the Tories had found themselves just four years earlier. An American commentator on British affairs, Sam Beer, was not considered excessive in ending his study of contemporary British politics with the words that it was 'blighted by pluralist stagnation, class decomposition and a revolt against authority'.[22] The United Kingdom was a country ridiculed across Europe. It had lost its collective capacity to make decisions. Three prime ministers and two political parties had tried to find a new way and failed. Britain seemed ungovernable and broke.

Recent attempts have been made to grant the Seventies a better reputation.[23] Given the 1973 oil crisis, Britain's economic performance was not appreciably worse than that of America or Japan. The state's share of the nation's wealth fell over the decade and inflation was not out of line with the rest of Europe. Indeed the figures on which the 1976 IMF loan was sought were later shown to have been unreliable.[24] Labour unrest was not confined to Britain. As Europe's economy moved from primary and secondary industries towards services, skilled workers naturally sought job protection. The concept of a social contract, of fair incomes and fair taxation, was still widely accepted. Only on the far right was it questioned.

That is probably as far as fairness can go. On the gallows of the Heath and Callaghan administrations were pinned two messages. One was that the monopoly power of organized labour had to be stopped if government was to have any leverage over inflation. Both Heath and Wilson had attempted trade union reform and been forced to retreat. By the end of the decade employment policy was the nation's most intractable political issue. The other message was internal to Westminster. It concerned the allocation of power within the institutions of government. After 1976 it was clear that no course of action could be contemplated without the full consent of the Treasury and its head, the Chancellor. To be effective government had to be collectively disciplined. Only thus could it manage the economy and deliver promises on taxation and public spending.

In accepting his 1976 Nobel prize, Milton Friedman reflected on the ideological war raging worldwide over inflation and unemployment. He pointed out that political change came about not as a result of divergent beliefs. 'It has responded almost entirely to the force of events: brute experience proved far more potent than the strongest of political or ideological preferences.'[25] Brute experience, he might have added, demanded brute leadership. The 1970s had left British politics with the clearest possible remit. It must find a government and a leader with personal authority and political courage. As the last rites were being said over the old regime during the election campaign of 1979, Callaghan remarked to his aide Bernard Donoghue that 'there are times, perhaps every thirty years, when there is a sea-change in politics. I suspect there is now such a sea-change, and it is for Mrs Thatcher.'[26]

Thatcher's own conclusion on the decade was more succinct. The 1970s spelled the end of socialism, she wrote. 'No theory of government was ever given a fairer test or a more prolonged experiment. Yet it was a miserable failure.'[27] She had no doubt that she could do better, but in this self-confidence and optimism she was virtually alone.

3

A Constitutional Coup

Every revolution has its moment of crisis. The serfs rise in revolt, the Bastille is stormed, the Winter Palace is seized. For Thatcherism this moment came at the start of 1975. The catalyst was the loss of control of the Conservative party by its then leader, Edward Heath. Given the later traumas that engulfed Toryism it is hard to recapture 'the trauma of '74'. Loyalty was supposedly the Tories' secret weapon, but in return they expected strong and dignified leadership. Heath offered neither. He behaved in 1974 as if he had been hit by a train, refusing to believe that at fifty-seven his career might be at an end. He was rude to everyone and his party was furious. The incoming Labour government in February had no clear majority and might have been ejected in short order. Yet Heath had lost his ability to command support.

Heath at first thought he might continue as prime minister and attempt a coalition with the Liberals in what was then a hung parliament. When this failed he resigned, and Harold Wilson returned to Downing Street as head of the largest single party but in a minority administration. Heath set about reordering his team for what was bound to be another election soon. He would gladly have dropped Thatcher. She had not been a notable success at education and he and his colleagues were irritated by her brittle presence at the cabinet table. Once again her sex was Thatcher's salvation: any British cabinet had by now to have a woman member, and Thatcher was the only plausible candidate. Heath moved her from education to shadow environment. He denied Sir Keith Joseph the Treasury portfolio, preferring the less ideological Robert Carr. Joseph begged leave of absence 'to examine the causes of the party's defeat'. It was a lethal mistake on Heath's part.

Joseph's post-mortem over the summer of 1974 instigated a painful and flagrant party split. He claimed that the monetarists were right and that the U-turn and fiscal expansion of 1972–4 had caused inflation. Heath violently disagreed and demanded that the party and Joseph stay loyal to his record in government. A frustrated Joseph set up a think tank, the Centre for Policy Studies (CPS), which became an instant focus of dissent from Heath's policies and leadership. As director Joseph chose his old friend Alfred Sherman. The latter had written two articles in the *Daily Telegraph* in 1973 attacking the Heath government's U-turn, which Joseph confessed had 'quite spoilt his summer holiday'.[1] Sherman referred to Joseph as 'a good man fallen among civil servants' but now returned to his patronage. Together they crafted a series of speeches, delivered in mid-1974, which disowned the Heath government and all its deeds.

The speeches caused a sensation. Here was a senior Tory, even a possible leader, savaging everything he had just supported in government. Heathism was portrayed as a betrayal of the true Conservatism that the party had espoused in 1970. Joseph said full employment was a chimera. Lame ducks, institutional, commercial and individual, should go to the wall. Inflation was caused by ministers. Money was too plentiful and government too big. Joseph was undermining his leader and party colleagues when they were about to fight a new election campaign, one which it was conceivable they might win. This was surely no time, said the Heathites, for a senior figure to start asking what Toryism was about? Small wonder Joseph was nick-named the Mad Monk by the party machine.

The Tory right had traditionally been composed of a lunatic fringe of imperialists and nationalists. Its cheerleaders were the League of Empire Loyalists and the Monday Club, whose leading light was Enoch Powell. Neither showed much interest in economic reform, other than Powell himself. The experience of the 1970 government, however, turned the ideological spotlight on to economics. Not just the IEA but a plethora of ginger groups and think tanks came forward to do battle, embracing the Bow Group, the Selsdon Group, the Conservative Philosophy Group and the CPS itself. To Richard Cockett, these groups were 'symptomatic of the realignment that took place in favour of economic liberalism during the mid-1970s. Their activities represented the end of the postwar con-sensus.' They gave a new direction and confidence to those despairing of Britain's economic performance. Above all, they supplied the Tory party with alternative answers and high calibre intellectual champions for them. The most ardent Thatcherites tended to be, like Sherman, defectors from the left.[2] They saw the new British politics as a clash of ideas, not a soci-ety of like-minded souls.

The Joseph/Sherman CPS was briefly central to what became a new Conservative approach to economic policy, despite producing remarkably little by way of literary output. It brought together liberal economics and Conservative history. Thinkers such as Hayek, Maurice Cowling, Robert Blake and Michael Oakeshott injected intellectual thrust into Conservative debate just when the leadership was tottering and received wisdom insecure. The CPS attracted such colourful characters as John Hoskyns and Norman Strauss, like Sherman averse to political expediency and eager to 'think the unthinkable'. They did not care how much they upset the Tory establishment. They had a possible next leader, Joseph, as their friend in court.

Heath's apologists could only make a desperate defence. They protested that they had too little time to implement their 1970 programme. The oil shock had blown their inflation strategy off course. Events, not ideology, had demanded the interventionism and reflation of 1972. To all this, the Joseph faction gave no quarter. It claimed that all governments were profligate and undisciplined, while incomes policy, the philosopher's stone of the previous two decades, was a policy of despair. Seeking to hold down wages when boosting the money supply was like trying to cure a leaking hose without turning off the tap. Britain did not need a crude return to Victorian capitalism but it certainly needed something called a 'social market economy', a free market tamed by redistributive taxation. It was a phrase from which the word social was soon dropped.

The debate, more an open row, culminated in Joseph's most outspoken *mea culpa* speech at Upminster in June 1974. He criticized every quarter of British politics for having 'followed the fashion of socialism' for three decades. Conservatives had not thought it practicable 'to reverse the vast bulk of the accumulating detritus of socialism which, on each occasion, they found when they returned to office.'[3] The challenge to any new Tory administration could not have been clearer. The press and political community loved a sinner publicly repenting. Joseph's star blazed across the political sky.

Thatcher liked and admired Joseph. He was her only soulmate from the former government and, like her, he regarded himself as an outsider. It was hard to imagine them sharing a joke, let alone dining at a Heath dinner table. In May 1974, despite being in the shadow cabinet, Thatcher took a calculated risk and accepted Joseph's invitation to become vice-chairman of the CPS. Her explanation of the move illustrates her state of mind:

Whether Keith ever considered asking any other members of the shadow cabinet to join him at the Centre I do not know: if he had, they certainly did not accept. His was a risky, exposed position, and the fear of provoking the wrath of Ted and the derision of left-wing commentators was a powerful disincentive. But I jumped at the chance.[4]

Thatcher was crystal clear in retrospect: 'I could not have become leader of the Opposition, or achieved what I did as prime minister, without Keith. But nor, it is fair to say, could Keith have achieved what he did without the CPS and Alfred Sherman.'[5] How far she fully grasped what they were saying is moot. She was not a trained economist, let alone an economic historian. She called this a time of listening and learning. She attended think tank lunches and evening seminars. I recall one meeting of the Conservative Philosophy Group at which she sat literally at the feet of Milton Friedman, gazing at him in rapt adoration. But her 1968 CPC lecture showed that she had grasped the essence of monetarism long before. She had criticized government for placing so much emphasis 'on the control of incomes that we have too little regard for the essential role of government, which is the control of the money supply and the management of demand.'[6] If her politics was instinctive rather than taught, it was forceful. She was as ready as Joseph to take aboard the lessons of 1972 as she too bore its scars. She was sufficiently outside the Heathite tent not to feel over-burdened with shame over its volte-face, though unlike Joseph she never did public penance.

Opposition to Heath was wholly absent from Thatcher's public statements. Her loyalty was part instinct, part ambition, but she felt that there would in future be 'no alternative' to a government guided by monetarist principles, expressed as a general self-discipline in all matters of public finance and expenditure. Nor was that all. As Joseph said, 'Monetarism is not enough . . . we are over-governed, over-spent, over-taxed, over-borrowed and over-manned.'[7] Thatcher understood what this meant. She was, like Joseph, a near monastic adherent to political masochism. His message was that to govern was to be unpopular, to endure pain. Not to endure pain was not to govern. It was Joseph's signal contribution to Thatcherism and to British politics.

*

Thatcher in the summer of 1974 had a busy shadow cabinet portfolio to master. Heath had placed his faith in her ability and was content to push her forward as part of a populist platform for a probable autumn election. She was given responsibility for two pledges, to fix mortgages through subsidy and to abolish local rates. She agreed with neither. Subsidizing private housing she regarded as madness as it would cost large sums of money and merely drive up house prices. Nigel Lawson described its insertion in the October 1974 manifesto as 'to my horror'. As for abolishing the rates, she declared that shifting the burden on to central taxes would be 'high-handed and arrogant', not to mention expensive. Anyway, and despite her experience at education, 'local authorities carry out their tasks better than Whitehall could'.[8] Heath none the less insisted and the manifesto declared that rates should be replaced 'by taxes related to people's ability to pay'. It was the only time the Tories espoused anything like a local income tax.

Thatcher went out to sell these policies with apparent conviction. She was undeniably impressed at their apparent popularity. Later in government she was to abandon the pledge of a fixed government mortgage rate, but she did not abandon the principle of a subsidy for mortgage interest, which she defended against all her chancellors. Abolishing the rates was to prove a more dangerous albatross. She could never throw it off, any more than she could find a satisfactory way of honouring it. It became a policy, then a flagship issue and finally an obsession that would destroy her. Rates abolition was the poison pill left Thatcher by Heath and left by her to John Major and then Tony Blair.

Thatcher's hard work and confidence pushed her to the front of the party's platform in the October election. She regularly featured in lists of 'most likely future leaders', though as a wild-card outsider. She began taking advice on her personal presentation. She stopped wearing pearls, wore a hat only on formal occasions and employed Gordon Reece to coach her voice, which he did by taking it down an octave. Her hair seemed to awaken each morning with a life of its own, blonde, immaculate and with a distinctive Sixties wave. She never seemed tired.

The second Tory defeat in autumn 1974 undermined Heath's leadership yet he refused either to accept the danger or do anything to avert it. He might have won a quick vote of confidence had he called one, but instead he hung on, hoping nothing would happen. In doing so he damaged his most obvious successor, William Whitelaw, and gave others time to marshall their forces. Since Heath had not indicated any inclination to resign, it would require a coup to unseat him. The two leading contenders outside the Heath circle were Joseph and the chairman of the backbenchers' 1922 Committee, Edward du Cann. Thatcher informally made herself Joseph's campaign manager.

Joseph swiftly self-destructed. In yet another revisionist speech, in Edgbaston, he strayed beyond monetarism and advocated eugenics to restrain the immigrant population of Britain. The uproar was instantaneous and the tabloids dubbed him 'Sir Sheath'. With the media camped outside his door he found the strain of exposure intolerable and decided he could not stand as leader. When he told Thatcher, she confessed herself despairing, though her reaction showed no hint of hesitation. 'I heard myself saying . . . Look Keith, if you're not going to stand, I will, because someone who represents our viewpoint has to stand.'[9] The die was cast. She would challenge the party leader for his job.

Thatcher rightly felt that she should tell Heath to his face what she intended to do. Depending on the source, his reply was either 'If you must' or 'You'll lose'.[10] At this stage, nobody was greatly disturbed since she was seen as merely a stalking horse. Rules hurriedly revised by the former leader Lord Home required a first ballot win of 50 per cent plus 15 per cent of all Tory MPs. Without such a substantial vote of confidence on the first ballot a second would be triggered. At this point new candidates less bound by loyalty to the leader might feel more free to enter. To lose in the first round was thus not disastrous, provided no strong contender emerged in the second.

Thatcher had no doubt that she was out to topple Heath and his whole point of view. She had been 'convinced that we must turn the party around towards Keith's way of thinking, preferably under Keith's leadership'.[11] But her own intention was no more than to flush out a sympathetic challenger. Her standing would be enhanced by exposure but nobody thought she would win, not even Denis. Rumour had it that when she told him she would be standing as leader he replied, 'Leader of what, dear?'[12]

After Joseph's withdrawal the next sensation came from du Cann. Allegedly fearing press investigation of his financial affairs he too decided not to stand. Whether he would have toppled Heath is doubtful, but he would have neutralized Thatcher. As it was, du Cann turned king-maker, receiving Margaret and Denis in a bizarre interview at his London house, at which they appeared nervously to be seeking his blessing. He compared their demeanour with 'that of a housekeeper and a handyman applying for a job'.[13] He could hardly refuse, as he was himself declining the post, and he duly bequeathed Thatcher his campaign manager, Airey Neave, who loathed Heath and had long schemed his overthrow. Neave had already switched allegiance from Joseph to du Cann and now settled on Thatcher as a stalking horse, to the open scepticism of his co-conspirators. While Heath brooded in his tent, Neave campaigned furiously. Thatcher held personal meetings with waverers and appeared on television with her family, obsessively washing up. She exuded confidence. The idea of a conviction Tory with popular appeal came as a shock to jaded back-benchers.

Subsequent research into the MPs' votes (kept secret at the time) showed that few who opted for Thatcher on the first ballot wanted her as leader. Seventy per cent of Tory voters in the country told pollsters that Heath was their favoured choice.[14] MPs, the bookies and the press overwhelmingly assumed that Heath would survive or that Whitelaw, who did not stand in the first ballot, would win in the second. Neave's tactic with undecided MPs was therefore to imply that Thatcher was merely a vehicle to bring about a proper contest and possible Whitelaw victory. There was no danger of her winning, but Heath had to be forced to a fight. Thatcher must have enough support for that to occur.

The ruse led to overkill. The first ballot, on 4 February 1975, gave Thatcher 130 votes, Heath 119, others 27. This was sensational. Heath had not only failed to secure the overwhelming vote needed to avoid a second ballot, he had not even come first. The former prime minister had been humiliated by a virtual unknown. In her room in the Commons, Thatcher uncharacteristically burst into tears. Tory back-benchers now had to acknowledge that the stalking horse was out ahead. She had won fair and square and, whatever their previous intentions, they felt the ground shifting beneath their feet. The message to Heath was unequivocal. He had lost and had to stand down, which he did. Whitelaw, Geoffrey Howe, Jim Prior and John Peyton stood on the second ballot but with the appearance of men watching a bandwagon fast leaving them behind. Those MPs who had voted for Thatcher seemed to feel that she had honestly won and deserved confirmation. In the seven days between the two ballots Thatcher took on a new personality in the party. She had guts and had grasped her moment. She seemed exciting alongside the tired men of 1970.

On the second ballot on 11 February Thatcher won more votes than all the other candidates together. Against the run of history she who wielded the dagger had indeed gained the crown. Howe, initially a Heathite, recalled her arriving after the announcement to meet her back-benchers, flanked by the all-male officers of the 1922 Committee: 'Suddenly she looked very beautiful and very frail, as the half-dozen knights of the shires towered over her. It was a moving, almost feudal occasion ... By her almost reckless courage she had won their support if not yet their hearts. A new bond of loyalty had been forged.'[15] For the patrician Whitelaw defeat could hardly have been more searing. His service to his party and loyalty to its leadership had been likened to Eden's loyalty to Churchill. It surely entitled him to his day at the top and he was devastated. I watched him speak at a Conservative dinner that weekend in Winchester. He professed continuing loyalty to his party and its new leader. But as he sat down tears were rolling down his cheeks and the audience was in tears with him. I have seldom seen politics so emotional.

What had the Tory party done? Norman Tebbit, a back-bencher who was to be one of Thatcher's close supporters, recalled 'that when we found ourselves with Margaret as leader there were a lot of people who were frankly incredulous.'[16] Thatcher's victory was an unintended consequence, a fluke of circumstance, the outcome of Heath's ineptitude. None of his shadow cabinet and few of his former ministers had voted for her. She would never have emerged from the mystical processes that traditionally chose Tory leaders. Nor at this stage would she have emerged from any electoral college involving party members. Understandably she regarded her election as a 'small earthquake in Westminster'. Her own surprise, she said, 'was as nothing compared to the shattering blow it had delivered to the Conservative establishment. I felt no sympathy for them. They had fought me unscrupulously all the way.'[17]

This remark was a measure of Thatcher's capacity for self-delusion. She had not made herself a popular figure in the upper echelons of her party, in parliament or in the country. Yet the Conservative party had leant over backwards to help her throughout her career because she was a woman and tolerated her cantankerousness because of her sex. Now she had been accorded the highest honour her party could bestow through the support of backbench MPs. To say the party had fought her 'unscrupulously' was an absurd distortion. They did not like her, but that was a different matter.

Distortion continued. Thatcher's success was termed by both supporters and critics a peasants' revolt, or in some quarters a slaves' revolt. Yet in every poll the party's 'peasants' were 70 per cent for Heath, as were the constituency chairmen. The relevant peasants were a coalition of Tory MPs, mostly right-wing iconoclasts and those who, as after any period in government, had been offended by the current leader's treatment of them. Thatcher was the candidate of opposition to Heath. Her support came almost exclusively from MPs on the right, but even they had not intended to elect her. Neave had engineered Thatcher's victory as an accident on which the party should take a gamble. As Campbell put it, 'It was not her convictions they voted for but her conviction.' [18] If she did not work out, she could always be dropped. The whole episode amounted to a reversible constitutional coup.

Thatcher never showed the slightest doubt as to her suitability to be leader. That she had not held high office nor commanded widespread support in the party was of no account. Her assault on the leadership was that of a laser-guided missile locking on to a target. Methodism, science and suburbia had armoured her in self-confidence and self-righteousness. Thatcher had no interests or extraneous achievements, just a massive assurance. Round her she saw male colleagues failing the test. She saw Heath collapsed in a sulk, Whitelaw often close to tears, Joseph tearing himself to emotional shreds and du Cann disappearing in a funk. Could a woman triumph over these men? Of course she could.

The Conservative party duly gave Thatcher its leadership but not its loyalty. Her ascendancy did not begin at any one moment but emerged over time. Tebbit referred to the years of Opposition between 1975 and 1979 as Thatcher's Long March. Yet it began as anything but revolutionary, with her seized with caution, as when education secretary, painfully aware of the pitfalls that had beset her predecessors. From the moment of victory, Thatcher had to secure her position both politically and ideologically. She had to reassure the Heath establishment, which had unanimously opposed her succession, that she understood that the party was a club, not a presidency. Above all, if hers was a peasants' revolt it conspicuously lacked what such revolts need to succeed, which is some barons in support.

Thatcher could not ditch the Heathites as she had no plausible replacements. She offered Whitelaw the deputy leadership, which he accepted. She retained Heath's chief whip, the tall and 'charming' Humphrey Atkins, and appointed the solid Howe rather than the unstable Joseph as shadow chancellor. Figures from the party's left such as Jim Prior, Peter Carrington, Michael Heseltine and Sir Ian Gilmour were all given shadow portfolios. Peter Thorneycroft came back from retirement as party chairman. Nor did Thatcher scare the old guard by bringing on such right-wingers as Nicholas Ridley, John Biffen or Tebbit. She kept them as attack dogs on the back benches. Given the difficulties Thatcher was to experience in power, the modesty of her early appointments can be seen as either wise or foolhardy. She prevented a body of opposition forming on the back benches. Yet by keeping the Heathites in place and in power, Thatcher carried with her an incubus. She had potential opponents in the shadow cabinet room, representing not just the past but, many hoped, also the future. The Heathites were always hovering in the wings, watching and waiting, regarding themselves as custodians of the true Tory faith.

Thus Thatcher might consort with the ideologues of the IEA and CPS and even borrow speeches from them. She claimed always to carry Hayek's *Road to Serfdom* in her bag (though she cannot have read its passage on decentralization). But the sceptics sensed that she was not in full command, expecting always that some crisis would occur and she would be out. Opposition, which she had experienced before, was no fun and the strain it imposed on her was intense. The mask occasionally slipped. An aide entering her Commons office found her unusually exhausted and watering the flowers. 'I don't know how Ted Heath did this for ten years,' she said gloomily. She hated being shown unfavourable press cuttings, telling the young Michael Portillo, 'Just because I'm leader of the Opposition doesn't mean I don't need a bit of encouragement.'[19]

Thatcher's personality steadily broadened. She found set pieces best, especially party conferences. These were staged with panache by a team involving the dramatist Ronald Millar and the Billy Graham alumnus Harvey Thomas. They were professional and American in style but patriotic and British in content. Thatcher offered the public what politics was bad at supplying, a sharp-edged character recognizable from a distance. She travelled the country as a celebrity and began to use television, tabloid newspapers and women's magazines to effect. She was not immediately popular but those who came to ridicule arrayed as publicity. Thatcher as housewife politician grated on her colleagues, but it was fresh, new and made her widely known.

Her international image was immeasurably assisted when the Soviet army magazine *Red Star* reprinted part of a speech she made to the Kensington Tories in 1976. It was ghost-written by a new right-wing think tank, the Institute for the Study of Conflict, and was mostly pseudo-Churchillian waffle. 'The Russians are bent on world domination,' Thatcher declared, 'and are rapidly acquiring the means to become the most powerful imperial nation.' She pointed out that the Soviet politburo could ignore their own public opinion: 'They put guns before butter . . . Let us ensure that our children have cause to rejoice that we did not forsake their freedom.'[20] To the *Red Star* this was outrageous warmongering, clearly from a politician posing as an 'iron lady'. It was meant as an insult.

The phrase was a spin-doctor's dream. Thatcher's knowledge of defence and foreign affairs was near non-existent, so much so that she had brought the elderly Reginald Maudling briefly back into the shadow cabinet to lend her team gravitas. The 'iron lady' sobriquet flashed round the world. With the Cold War dissolving into tedious arms reduction talks, a British politician was telling the world to stay on its guard. She gloried in the phrase and could not stop mentioning it. 'Look at me in my green chiffon gown,' she told one audience, 'face softly made-up, my fair hair gently waved . . . Me? A cold warrior?' Invitations to speak on foreign platforms poured in. Ronald Reagan, governor of California, made a courtesy call and stayed two hours, the start of a firm friendship.

The financial crisis of 1976 made a deep impression on Thatcher. Callaghan's celebrated admonition to his party conference used words she could have written herself: 'We used to think you could spend your way out of a recession . . . I tell you in all candour this option no longer exists.' Thatcher wrote in her memoirs, 'We could now argue that socialism as an economic doctrine was totally discredited . . . even the socialists were having to accept that reality was Conservative.' This posed her a problem as well as an opportunity. She was quick to see that it 'outflanked on the right those members of my own Shadow Cabinet who were still clinging to the outdated nostrums of Keynesian demand management.'[21] But she felt obliged to support the Labour government in crisis measures then being introduced in the national interest. That they came from Labour strengthened what she saw as the monetarist case, but some on the right wondered if it might signal her own prospective 'consensus capture'. Nor was her cause helped by her failure to deliver the breakthrough in public opinion which her party craved. She found the House of Commons a tougher theatre as leader than as aspirant. Platitudes that worked on the hustings offended the more sophisticated ears of the Commons. Healey ridiculed her 'monotonous recitation of disconnected little homilies . . . with all the moral passion and intellectual distinction of a railway timetable.'[22] She could not counter Callaghan's mildly patronizing put-downs at question time.

In truth Thatcher in these early years was behaving not as a revolutionary but as a leader on trial, inheritor of a possibly temporary throne. Previously she had been scrupulous to remain within the establishment of the old Tory party, albeit on its right. It would not have occurred to her to go down the presidential route taken by Blair and his entourage on becoming Labour leader ten years later. Had she been so inclined, her party colleagues would have stopped her. Her greatest asset was her experience of the 1970 government and in this she had a potent teaching aid. Every time her colleagues entered the Commons they saw Heath sitting on the benches below the first gangway, a ghost of the party's all-too-recent past. 'Reading' Heath was the most sensible thing Thatcher did. She told an American interviewer in 1977, 'I have not the smallest intention of failing to learn from experience.'[23] But the lesson was not to be bold but the opposite, to consolidate support and not frighten the electorate with expectations that might presage disappointment. She often remarked that she had to win the argument of power before she could win the argument of policy. Her entire leadership was a conversation between the two.

Hence Thatcher might indulge in right-wing thoughts but not in right-wing policies. She was still the hope of the right, of ideological rebels on the back benches. She was to be their moment, carrying the flag for private enterprise, lower taxes, denationalization and curbs on union power. She would let slip vague assertions that immigration had to be stopped, the union closed shop ended and public spending cut. The welfare state was turning Britons into 'moral cripples' she said in her Macleod Lecture in 1977. No one close to the leader was in any doubt where her private sympathies lay. She even confided to the British ambassador to Iran, Sir Anthony Parsons, that 'there are still people in my party that believe in consensus'. When he assumed this was a good thing she burst out, 'I regard them as quislings, as traitors . . . and I mean it.'[24]

Yet for all this, Thatcher began to disappoint her allies even in specifics. She believed that the British people were not ready for the harsh medicine she thought necessary, let alone ready to vote for it. Tories must above all become electable. (Two decades later, Blair and Gordon Brown were to go forth with the same message for Labour.) Accordingly she ignored the work being done privately by Howe, Lawson, Howell and John Nott on privatization. Ridley had been asked by Joseph to dust off his 1970 papers on the subject. Mild though they were — a hiving-off here, a competitive tender there — Thatcher refused to countenance them. In her memoirs she described privatization at the end of the 1970s as 'revolutionary, all but unthinkable'.[25] On nationalized industries her commitment was to return recently nationalized companies to the private sector but not the giants. She would only 'interfere less' in their management, the oldest cliché in the manifesto book. In the 1976 economic pamphlet *The Right Approach*, there was no criticism of the Heath government and no serious departure from its policies. Thatcher was sounding so moderate that even the Heathite Chris Patten, head of the party's research department, worried that she might be vulnerable to a right-wing coup.[26]

A second stab at economic policy the following year, *The Right Approach to the Economy* (1977), had little more by way of red meat. A Tory government would restrain public spending only 'over the period of a full parliament'. There was no commitment to monetarism or to radical changes in taxes, pensions, benefits or allowances. Even incomes policy, which Thatcher opposed, was not rejected outright since the government might need to come to 'some conclusions' about wages. When asked what this meant, Thatcher hinted at favouring a 'voluntary, not compulsory' pay policy. She must have known this was an absurdity. At first she also refused point blank to advocate anti-union legislation. Speaking in America in September 1977 she said, 'I am afraid we cannot bring legislation against the closed shop as such' as public opinion was simply not ready for it.[27]

Thatcher held to this hypercaution on union reform through to 1978. But that year's 'winter of discontent' and a mild Tory recovery in the polls shifted the balance of power within the debate. The unions were now public villains. Two of Thatcher's acolytes at the CPS, Hoskyns and Strauss, produced a secret paper, 'Stepping Stones', with Joseph and Howe as its sponsors. This unashamedly 'Thatcherite' document was of the kind to thrill and alarm her in equal measure. It argued that 'union reform was at the centre of what we wanted to do; without it the rest of our programme for national recovery would be blocked.'[28] The unions could not be relegated to a subclause of monetarism. To the authors they were an obstacle sitting astride the entire path of supply-side reform which had to be confronted and beaten. The party radicals were throwing down the gauntlet.

Thatcher was at a loss what to do with so explosive a document. She tried to delegate 'Stepping Stones' to Howe and Joseph but realized she could not hide it from the shadow cabinet. There it ran into predictably furious opposition from Jim Prior, whom Thatcher had made custodian of industrial relations policy specifically to reassure the unions. As party chairman, Thorneycroft wanted every copy of 'Stepping Stones' burned. With the nation convulsed with strikes, the Tories' plans were bound to be of intense public interest. Joseph pleaded with Thatcher to move Prior.[29] Thatcher resisted, but every remark from both herself and Prior was being studied by the media for nuances of difference. It was her first test of leadership.

The outcome was a bitterly fought argument over the 1979 manifesto reference to the unions. Most of the document was tame in the extreme, more so than Heath's 1970 one. But on the unions it was specific. Emboldened by the growing unpopularity of the unions, Thatcher sided with Howe and Joseph against Prior and the Heathites. She promised to legislate against secondary picketing, to review union immunities and to seek no-strike agreements in public services, confident that in this she would have public support. The Tories, the Labour government and public opinion were clearly ready for such change. Thatcher was furious that only her shadow cabinet seemed averse. The argument in Opposition over the unions was significant in setting the terms of engagement for battles in government. In truth Thatcher found it hard to concentrate on policy. She had convictions on everything but ideas on little (another parallel with Tony Blair). Policies were the sets and costumes, music and supporting cast for the stage on which her personality was to parade before the electors. She was a politician of instinct and had been in the business long enough to know that events were what dominated the conduct of government, events and a leader's response to them.

Until the actual campaign, victory for the Tories in 1979 was by no means certain. By autumn 1978 they had recovered ground but were only neck and neck with Labour. Worse for Thatcher's morale, the public continued to regard Callaghan as a better party leader and Heath as the more plausible Tory prime minister. Were he still leader, the polls suggested that the Conservative party would be fourteen points ahead.[30] This implied that if she did not win, Thatcher might indeed prove to have been a caretaker leader. As election day approached, though the Tories edged ahead, Callaghan's personal popularity over Thatcher widened. At one point the campaign team suggested that Heath join Thatcher on the platform at the final press conference. She exploded in fury and misery.

On 4 May 1979 Thatcher vindicated the faith her party had placed in her and her strategy. She arrived in Downing Street with 44 per cent of the poll and a working majority of forty-three. The world had turned upside down. A woman had been elected to lead a major western democracy, a woman with a self-styled mission to avenge a mistake and effect a revolution. She felt no humility, just gratification that her tremendous energy was 'for the first time in my life to be fully used'.[31]

4

Civil War

A favourite fantasy of prime ministers is that they are rebels at heart. Wilson would refer to himself as a Bolshevik in a government of Mensheviks. Blair would talk of bearing the 'scars of conservatism' as he battled for reform. Thatcher astonished a Downing Street reception by referring to herself as 'the rebel head of an Establishment government'.[1] Her conference speeches were full of coded attacks on colleagues for lacking radicalism. She remarked that the loneliness of power was exacerbated by the fact that 'I so often had to act as a lone opponent of the processes and attitudes of government itself.' She recalled her portrayal as 'an outsider who by some odd mixture of circumstance had stepped inside and stayed there.' The portrayal, she added, 'was not inaccurate'.[2]

The truth is that a good prime minister must be a rebel inside the cabinet and a focus of unity outside. He or she must wear two hats. Other ministers have the drag of institutions and interests round their necks. Only the prime minister is free of the incubus of a Whitehall department or a specific area of responsibility. Yet only the prime minister has a different and lonelier burden, that of winning elections. We have seen that Thatcher in Opposition was far from being the radical outsider, and was constantly whipping her ideologues, such as they were, into pragmatic line. The question was how far would she continue this role in government. On first arriving on the steps of Downing Street she recited the words attributed to St Francis: 'Where there is discord may we bring harmony', and the world smirked at such implausibility from the most discordant of politicians. It ignored the rest of the quotation, 'Where there is error may we bring truth; where there is doubt may we bring faith.'

Within days of her arrival two things became immediately clear. Thatcher would respect the Tory coalition in the composition of her government, but not in her style of leadership. She would retain most of her solidly Heathite team in office, but she would be hell to work with. This ensured that the strains experienced in Opposition would be multiplied a hundred-fold. Heath had lobbied for the Foreign Office but Thatcher could not face it, leaving him on the back benches as a repelling magnet to all rebels. She was careful to put his former supporters into spending departments but her own into economic ones. She sent Lord Carrington to the Foreign Office, Whitelaw to the Home Office, Michael Heseltine to environment and Mark Carlisle to education. They were to form what came to be termed the 'wet' faction, against the Thatcherite 'dries'. The latter included what she called her 'true believers', Howe to the Treasury with Biffen and Lawson in support. Joseph, whose indecision Thatcher dared not inflict on the Treasury, went to industry, Nott to trade and Howell to energy. The most obvious hostage to fortune was the man who would have to carry out the most contentious pledge in the manifesto, trade union reform. This job she gave to the wet Prior as her 'badge of our reasonableness'. Appointing a more radical figure to this post might have 'provoked a challenge we were not yet ready to face'.[3] Her caution could not have been more explicit.

Thatcher's chief concern at this stage was not revolution but civil war. She was desperate to secure her position internally. If there was to be a war she wanted it inside the tent, eyeball to eyeball. There would be no power bases on the back benches. She gave her foes jobs and 'wriggle-room', but at a distance from the centre of battle. Thatcher loyalists were in a minority but they dominated departments controlling the economy. Alan Clark's observation at the time was typically forthright. Thatcher was surrounded with 'heavy-hitting haters', Prior, Carrington, Gilmour, Heseltine, Peter Walker. Apart from Howe, 'a durable politburo man', the only loyalists he could detect anywhere near her were 'Maude, Biffen, Joseph, the last two so tortured intellectually as to cast doubt on their stability in a crisis.'[4]

Commentators were quick to note the old-fashioned character of Thatcher's team. She brought back Lord Hailsham as Lord Chancellor, Thorneycroft remained as party chairman and Christopher Soames was leader in the Lords. The foreign secretary, Peter Carrington, was a peer. The cabinet contained six Old Etonians, six former Guards officers and five barristers. Just two members had not been privately educated and only one had not been to Oxbridge. Thatcher's weakness for charm was noticeable. She sent her favourite, Humphrey Atkins, to Northern Ireland and appointed the elegantly leftish Gilmour to the cabinet to answer for Carrington in the Commons. Her parliamentary private secretary was Ian Gow, who would prowl the corridors for gossip. His late-night indiscretions to Alan Clark yielded, through the latter's diaries, illuminating glimpses of the early Thatcher years.

Thatcher's addiction to work was maniacal. Considerate to personal staff, drivers and cleaners over whom her supremacy was unquestioned, she was tactless and overbearing to ministers and senior officials. She argued and shouted. She invited them to stand up to her and then battered them with a mix of trivial knowledge and the authority of her office. One aide calculated that she would talk for 90 per cent of the time at meetings. She would state her conclusion at the start and challenge anyone present to disagree. If she risked losing an argument she would veer off to some other point where she might claim victory. Even her close allies, Howe and Joseph, were bullied if they hesitated or made a tiny mistake. Joseph would go off to meet her telling his staff to 'send two ambulances at 3 o'clock'. Whitelaw remarked privately that 'for the first time in my life, politics is not really fun.'[5]

To Thatcher it was not meant to be fun. From the moment she entered Downing Street she was in a hurry to make a mark, as if aware that her reign might be brief. She told Roy Jenkins, over from Brussels where he was president of the Commission, not to try persuading her of something, as 'you know I find persuasion counter-productive'. She interfered in every department and wanted to know of every decision. Clark described her mental processes as having no rational sequence. They were all 'associative lateral thinking, jumping rails the whole time'. She always had to win.

Whenever asked what it was like being a woman prime minister, Thatcher replied, 'I don't know; I've never experienced the alternative.'[6] Yet it was hard not to see her behaviour as desperation to prove herself to her male colleagues. Many of those round her were loyal and wanted the government to succeed. Why be so rude to them? Thatcher's insecurity towards men was sometimes embarrassingly obvious. Her claim to Shirley Williams in the Commons' ladies room, that 'we must do better than them', came to dominate her working environment. When an interviewer told her of admiring gossip that she was 'the best man in her cabinet', she retorted angrily, 'The best woman, you mean.'[7]

Old-style politicians, such as Soames and Carrington, were aghast at any prime minister behaving as Thatcher did. Denis Healey, master of the cutting word portrait, called her 'a mixture of a matron at a minor public school and a guard in a concentration camp.'[8] The clubroom atmosphere on the back benches was more forgiving. Clark saw her in 1980 on a visit to the Commons cafeteria and wrote, 'Goodness she is so beautiful, made-up to the nines but still quite bewitching, as Eva Peron must have been. I do not take my eyes off her.'[9] Some of his raucous colleagues would swap sexual fantasies as they watched her at the dispatch box. Her appearance, morning, noon and night, was a chastity belt which defied all possible unlocking. Her armoured exterior and savage put-downs appealed to the sadomasochistic tendency. Did she? Could she? Would she ever?

We shall never know what role sex might have played in Thatcher's psychological make-up. Maddox has index entries for voice, hair, dress sense, femininity, flirtatiousness, handbags, 'love of flattery' but not for sex. Of her susceptibility there was no doubt. Douglas Hurd recalled her being visited in Opposition by a Spanish foreign minister. Unsure how to handle a woman politician, the Spaniard showed old-fashioned Hispanic gallantry. He declared, 'I had been told, madam, of your formidable intelligence, but no one had warned me of your beauty.' Hurd, who was present at the encounter, assumed she would explode.[10] He misunderstood his mistress. For years afterwards Thatcher would ask any Spaniard she met, 'Whatever happened to that charming foreign minister of yours?'

Thatcher certainly entrusted office to men in whose qualities others saw little more than an engaging elegance. Apart from Atkins, for whom she had a particular partiality, she favoured Cecil Parkinson, John Moore, Paul Channon and Michael Havers. The dashing John Hoskyns, in her private office, commended his colleague, David Wolfson, as 'tall, elegant, with a languid manner and rather mocking, teasing humour . . . prepared to speak plainly to Mrs Thatcher behind the scenes.'[11] Towards Parkinson she was extraordinarily indulgent, even bringing him back into government after his resignation over the pregnancy of his mistress, an affair which privately fascinated her.[12]

Yet everyone, charming or no, operated on a short leash. Those who failed to show valour in battle, as most did, were discarded. Thatcher's fiercely loyal press secretary, Bernard Ingham, would be deployed quietly to mark their cards in the parliamentary lobby. For a while the Commons leader, Norman St John-Stevas, thought he enjoyed a jester's licence, calling her 'the Blessed Margaret . . . she who must be obeyed . . . the leaderene . . . Attila the Hen'. This faith in her sense of humour proved horribly misplaced. Stevas was the first to be sacked, at the end of 1980, and cruelly so. 'I was sorry to lose Norman,' she wrote, 'but he made his own departure inevitable . . . he turned indiscretion into a political principle.'[13] Nobody took Thatcher's humour for granted again.

Cabinet building and man-management showed the two sides to Thatcher's political character. The cautious tactician was positioning her friends and enemies, rolling the pitch for later reform. The cantankerous, domineering leader was making enemies as fast as she defeated them. The first three years of Thatcher's prime ministership have been so obscured by the remaining eight as to have sunk from view. Yet they were important. They were years of hopeless inexperience, of public woe and private despair. Thatcher was charging across no-man's-land, setting off explosions on all sides and with no clear destination in view. She had assumed that by embracing the Heathites in office she might quieten their voice. This did not happen.

The headline events of 1979–81 were a row over British payments to the EEC, the settlement of Rhodesian independence, combating IRA hunger strikes and Howe's three counter-cyclical Budgets. Each tested Thatcher's mettle. The immediate signature of the government was the July 1979 Budget. This had to confront the fact that, during the election, Thatcher had bribed public-sector unions with the promise of large pay rises. It meant more for the NHS, large rises to the police and armed forces and a 3 per cent real increase in defence spending. Howe cut the basic rate of income tax by three pence and the top rate from 83 per cent to 60 per cent, but he had to pay for this with cuts in public spending and a doubling of VAT.

Both Howe and Lawson recall Thatcher 'wobbling' as Howe's increase in VAT added four points to the retail price index and inflation rose back above 10 per cent. Thatcher remarked to Howe that Butler in 1951 had cut taxes gradually; might it not be prudent to wait? He had to persuade her that unpopular changes should always be made at the start of a government, and indeed complained of 'the ambivalence which Margaret often showed when the time came to move from the level of high principle and evangelism to practical politics'.[14] Howe faced similar trouble with his flagship proposal to abolish exchange control, a radical and impeccably market-oriented policy. Thatcher complained that he should surely wait 'until the government's market philosophy was being seen to work'.[15] When he persuaded her to proceed, she said 'on your head be it, Geoffrey, if anything goes wrong'. It was not the most supportive of remarks. By the time of her memoirs she had rewritten history: 'I took the greatest personal pleasure in the removal of exchange controls.'[16] She had not. She was terrified.

By the end of Thatcher's first year in office public expenditure on unemployment and welfare was soaring. Price rises, deepening recession and a further increase in the oil price precipitated a burst of pay claims across private and public sectors. It immediately brought into focus the manifesto commitment to reform industrial relations. The mandate was clear. Secondary picketing was to be outlawed, though closed shops were not (yet) banned. But this was initially as far as Prior was prepared to go. Thatcher also wanted strikers' welfare benefits cut and all secondary strikes stopped. Howe said in public that Prior's bill was just a first instalment, to which Prior vehemently disagreed. Open war now broke out between the two sides. Thatcher regarded Prior as if he were an enemy both in public and in private. Confronting him was a game of bluff and counter-bluff since Thatcher dared not sack him in the short term and Prior knew it. He also knew that if he failed to deliver more reform in the longer term Thatcher would not keep him in post. The employment department at the time was like a British outpost in the Zulu Wars, enduring wave upon wave of spear-throwing attacks from Downing Street. Prior's limited bill was enacted and the sky did not fall. What point this proved was clear to no one. To Prior it showed the virtue of moving softly, to Thatcher the virtue of moving gradually, over and again.

For all this, union reform was a side-show to the great struggle of Thatcher's early years, the longer-term conduct of the economy. Whereas with the unions there was a case for caution, on the economy there was only victory or defeat. The 1979 Budget had been traumatic in itself. Throughout 1980 Howe and Lawson, as his Treasury chief secretary, dabbled with the arcane measures of monetarism, M1, M2, M3 and M4, to increasing ridicule. The effect was to tighten public spending and increase interest rates when the economy was moving into recession. Howe's 1980 Budget reduced spending by £1 billion when unemployment was rising past two million. Thatcher, mesmerized by the parallels with Heath in 1972, dared not gainsay him, even when unemployment reached three million. She shouted at her 1980 party conference, in words given her by Ronnie Miller, 'You turn if you want to; the lady's not for turning.' (How many of the audience got the literary allusion is not clear.) She had faith in her dogged but loyal chancellor and his team if only because the alternative was the unutterable horror of U-turn and failure.

By now the British disease – 'stagflation' – seemed as virulent as ever. Thatcher could go on television and talk about medicine taking time to have an effect but the nation was disinclined to wait. On specific decisions Thatcher's pragmatism was evident in public as well as in private. She went along with Joseph's self-flagellating support for high-profile lame ducks, bailing out British Steel and British Leyland. In early 1981 she capitulated swiftly, against the advice of her energy minister, Howell, to a threatened coal strike. It was her first blatant U-turn and it hurt, precipitating her into meticulous secret planning for another, future confrontation. The predicament was alarmingly similar to that which had confronted Heath in 1971–2. At the CPS Sherman was telling Thatcher what she least needed to hear, that 'history is repeating itself'.[17] The wets were bemused but sensed victory. The pressure on Thatcher to change tack over the course of 1981 was intense, indeed was expected even by the right. Surely she would make a sensible, Keynesian, response to recession and 'reflate' the economy.

If I had to choose a moment in the evolution of Thatcherism when it first matured in the mind of its progenitor, it would be the spring of 1981. 'I shall never forget the weeks leading up to the 1981 budget,' she baldly recalled.[18] Each economic and political weathervane pointed in one direction, to a U-turn and reflation. Clark recalled 'the lady is well and truly beleaguered' with 'party morale never lower'. A cabinet minister told him, 'she is making decisions on a purely day-to-day basis, on impulse and without forethought.'[19] Coffee-room conversation was about whether 'she ought to be pushed'. Yet it was not some sophisticated understanding of monetary aggregates that held her back. Thatcher would always U-turn if politics dictated. What haunted her was simply 1972. She could not bring herself to repeat what she had come to regard as the Great Error, curing the nation's economic failings through capitulating to inflation. Thatcher's memoirs come (uncharacteristically) alive as she recalls herself and Howe preparing for battle. As budget day approached there was a crescendo of opinion pleading for a U-turn, from the press, the back benches, above all the cabinet wets. The prime minister retreated into a cabal of Treasury ministers and personal aides, notably Hoskyns and her new economic adviser, Alan Walters.

Thatcher always said that she never needed to know what to do, only how to do it. She could have spelled that word 'Howe'. With Joseph lost to self-doubt her intellectual reliance on her chancellor was at this point total. She could not have climbed even these foothills of Thatcherism without Howe's dogged presence at her side. His monetary targets, his medium-term financial strategy, his mental resilience and quiet, persuasive manner with colleagues, were foreign to Thatcher. She was clever, but never an economist, let alone a persuader. Howe's clothing of the great deflation of 1980–82 in the droning language of economics reassured her that indeed 'there was no alternative'. Yet she treated him appallingly. She would lash out at him in front of colleagues like a fishwife at a henpecked husband. He was the most often cited victim of her tirades. Thatcher's tributes to Howe were sincere. When talking to a group of MPs about her work she said, 'It's very lonely. It's really Geoffrey and me against the rest of them.' He could only comment, 'It didn't always feel like that.'[20]

With the nation breathless for relief Howe simply ignored all conventional wisdom. His 1979 and 1980 Budgets had been seen as wild gambles. They were anti-egalitarian and reckless, relying on private tax incentives to avert recession. Thatcher sold them vigorously and supported Howe in public, even when in private 'she was always vividly conscious of the political risks ... the last to be persuaded.'[21] The 1981 Budget, introduced with no prior consultation with the cabinet wets, was seismic both intellectually and politically. Howe himself dubbed 1981 the 'most unpopular budget in history'. He proposed further cuts in public spending. An extra £7 billion was to be taken out of the economy in taxes, to reduce public borrowing and hold down interest rates. Howe was adamant that only a ruthless disciplining of the public sector, widespread 'relocation' and shock tactics, would yield economic regeneration.

Howe and Hoskyns both said afterwards that Thatcher once again needed persuading of the virtues of radicalism.[22] But she was now as fearful of appearing weak as she was of being unpopular. The budget seemed monetarism gone mad. In March 1981 *The Times* published a letter from 364 economists saying 'there is no basis in economic theory ... for the government's present policies.'[23] To the critics all that was working was a savage 1930s-style recession. Company bankruptcies were soaring and unemployment figures were greeted each quarter like casualty returns in the Great War. Healey derided Howe's 'sado-monetarism' and Thatcher screeched against 'U-turns'. She talked of guts to see through what she had been elected to do. But with each speech she seemed to be raising the stakes on her survival, making a virtue of sheer bloody-mindedness. The new Social Democratic Party (SDP), formed the year before largely in protest at Michael Foot's Labour leadership, saw its poll support rise giddily over 50 per cent. The Tories slumped to third place in the opinion polls. The tectonic plates of British politics seemed about to shift.

The cabinet now broke into open civil war. Thatcher's cabinet architecture had ensured that the Treasury team would be solid behind the 1981 strategy and the wets isolated beyond the economic pale. Between the two sides the old-style loyalists, Whitelaw and Carrington, acted as occasional go-betweens. This function now collapsed. Prior, Gilmour, Heseltine, Peter Walker and Francis Pym were regularly cited in the press as conspirators. In public speeches Thatcher openly attacked the wets, virtually by name. They had no courage, wanted more expenditure than had been agreed in cabinet and did not want taxes raised to pay for it. Their solution? 'Let's print the money instead . . . the most immoral path of all.'[24]

Thatcher's post-budget concession to the wets was 'greater consultation' on economic policy. This led to what proved a disastrous special cabinet on 23 July 1981 to discuss post-Budget strategy. At the meeting Howe again cast caution to the winds and suggested the need for yet more spending cuts. The room exploded. Not just the wets but even Biffen and Nott thought enough was enough. Thatcher had told Denis that morning that this could be the crunch meeting of her premiership. She recalled afterwards that it was certainly the worst. 'I too became extremely angry. I had thought that we could rely on these people [the dries] when the crunch came', and she attacked them as 'fair-weather monetarists'.[25] Apart from Howe's new chief secretary, Leon Brittan, only Whitelaw and Joseph came to Howe's aid. Thatcher closed the meeting with a sense of defeat and determined that this group of ministers would never meet as a team again.

The wets now felt emboldened to speak out and spread talk of rebellion on all sides. The cabinet rebels made speeches and gave interviews demonstrating varying degrees of disloyalty. As party chairman, Thorneycroft carried particular weight. He mentioned the party suffering from 'rising damp' and called for a 'survival package'.[26] Thatcher knew she had to act fast. The public no longer mattered since her own position was at risk. She had supported Howe's budget. It had been passed by parliament but, apparently, rejected by the cabinet. That cabinet had to go.

In her summer 1981 reshuffle Thatcher was careful, sacking only the weaker members, Soames, Carlisle and Gilmour, but the resulting moves were crucial. Prior was exiled to Ulster and replaced by a red rag to every union bull, Norman Tebbit. Joseph was moved from industry to education, replaced by a Thatcherite, Patrick Jenkin. Lawson went to energy and two dries, Ridley and Jock Bruce-Gardyne, came into the Treasury. Another Thatcher accolyte, Parkinson, replaced Thorneycroft as party chairman. This was a more loyalist cabinet and therefore more comfortable. Whether it would secure Thatcher's survival was still open.

The party conference in Blackpool in October 1981 was extraordinary for a party in government. Normally these occasions are stage-managed banality, but when a party is in trouble the lobbies of the Winter Gardens conference centre and the foyers and bars of the conference hotels seem to have an electric current running through them. The tussle between conspiracy and loyalty is palpable. The 1981 conference saw every speech taken apart and inspected for any nuance of revolt. Potential challengers positioned themselves with meticulous care and every fringe meeting had a frisson of the unexpected. The wets, led by Pym and Prior, openly derided their own government. The dries hit back. Lawson complained that the wet cause was 'nothing but cold feet dressed up as high principle'.[27] Howe quoted back at Heath the latter's own words in 1970, that 'nothing has done Britain greater harm in recent years than the endless backing and filling. Once a policy has been established, the prime minister and his colleagues should have the courage to stick to it.'

Thatcher could claim that she had passed through the valley of the shadow of doubt without flinching. In her conference speech she stood defiant, waving her sword at dragons galore but mostly and manifestly at the wets. She sought to explain high unemployment as due to oil prices. The enemy was 'excessive wage increases, union restrictive practices, over-manning, strikes, indifferent management and the basic belief that, come what may, the government would always step in to bail out companies in difficulty.'[28] In other words, the fault lay with everything that Heath and his followers had refused to tackle, and still refused.

Thatcher recalled later that at the 1981 conference, 'the wets had been defeated but they did not yet fully realise it'.[29] She trumpeted that 'we had already won the second Battle of Britain'. That is not how it seemed at the time. The monetarist prospectus had still not delivered. Interest rates were at 16 per cent and unemployment hovered at three million. Shirley Williams for the SDP wiped out an 18,000 Tory majority in middle-class Crosby in Lancashire. The Tories were down to 23 per cent in the polls and Thatcher was declared the most unpopular prime minister since polling began. The government came through the winter of 1981 with its policy widely discredited, its cabinet divided and little hope of winning a putative election then just two years away. Denis Thatcher mentioned to a journalist that 'she doesn't know whom to trust . . . There are times when she feels like jacking it in.'[30]

Thatcher at the end of 1981 was undeniably in trouble. She had said at the start of her government 'give me six strong men and true, and I will get through', but she now admitted that she did not have six.[31] Only Howe among her senior team was loyally at her side but he brought no party or political support. Whitelaw might fight off a few attackers, but with no conviction. Between her and a small body of back-bench loyalists stood the army of the wets, supported by public opinion, the polls, commentators and the burgeoning SDP. They all fostered a growing conviction that, while she had survived 1981, she could not last much longer. Odds at the Blackpool conference were being placed on her going by Christmas and on the name of her successor. (I remember because I was bet a case of champagne on her fall by a senior journalist, Peter Jenkins.)

Much has been made by Thatcher's supporters of the mild recovery in the economy and the government's poll ratings that occurred in March 1982. The Tories' poll rating rose 10 points to 33 per cent and the economic cycle did begin to turn upwards. But that same month the SDP's Roy Jenkins repeated Shirley Williams' Crosby success, taking the Tories' safe seat of Glasgow Hillhead by storm. The SDP was hugely popular and, in whatever arrangement with the Liberals, seemed likely to command as much as a third of the poll at the next election in 1983/4. On that basis a hung parliament seemed inevitable, in which case it was barely conceivable that Thatcher would continue in Downing Street. She was where Heath had been ten years before. Her worst fears were being realized, of having had no time to put her programme into effect and see it turn to her electoral benefit.

As so often before in Thatcher's career, luck now appeared over the horizon and from a wholly improbable quarter. She was rescued by the one thing she least expected and to which she was, in all honesty, least entitled, a victory in war. It was to make Thatcherism possible after all.

5

Epiphany at Port Stanley

War is the making or breaking of leaders. Victory made Lloyd George and
Churchill. Defeat broke Chamberlain and Eden. Armed combat projects
the business of government into every home. While the general public may
not notice each twist and turn in the state of the economy, everyone knows
if there is a war on. It offers those media staples, violence, death and glory
and makes even politics engrossing. I asked Thatcher's predecessor
Callaghan, towards the end of the Falklands campaign, how he thought it
was going. He answered with a sigh, 'If only I had had a war.'[1]

The events surrounding the invasion and recapture of the Falklands in
the spring of 1982 are extraneous to the main theme of this book.[2] But the
war was critical to Thatcher's future as prime minister. Had it been lost,
she would have been finished. Had it not occurred, it is unlikely that she
would have survived as prime minister after the next election. But while it
lasted it relieved her for the first time from the shackles of internal rebellion
and, when it was over, her premiership had lost its aura of impermanence.
There was no more of the perpetual question in the lobbies, 'How soon
before she goes?'

While the events leading up to the war demonstrated Thatcher's weaknesses, the war itself demonstrated her strengths. The inclination for a busy
prime minister to relegate second order problems to the 'indecision' tray
is understandable. With Europe and the IRA pressing on her non-economic
agenda, Thatcher had little time in 1981 for the hesitant course of Britain's
negotiations at the United Nations over the sovereignty of the Falkland
Islands. Like Gibraltar and Hong Kong, the issue was intractable. The Argentine case was strong in history, but weak by the doctrine of 'prescription',
whereby uninterrupted occupation confers legitimacy. The Falkland
islanders were fiercely British and white, unlike the equally British Chinese
in Hong Kong and Asians on Diego Garcia, both of whom Britain was about
to abandon to alien status. Naturally, less successive governments had been
ready to negotiate a new dispensation with Argentina. There was no denying Britain would like to be rid of the Falklands.

Thatcher's Foreign Office inherited from Labour a policy of transferring sovereignty over the islands to Argentina but of leasing them back to secure the citizenship status of the islanders. Soon after Thatcher came to office, a junior minister, Nicholas Ridley, went to the Falklands to discuss this proposal and was badly received. On his return Ridley none the less persuaded his boss, Lord Carrington, to confront Thatcher with the need to press on with lease-back. The only alternative, he said, was to walk out of the negotiations in New York and fortify the islands against a possible military response from Argentina: the so-called fortress Falklands option. Thatcher's reaction was 'thermonuclear'.[3] She had just 'abandoned' the white Rhodesians to black majority rule and would not abandon the islanders to a military junta. Enough was enough.

Thatcher would never force lease-back on her back-benchers, but her susceptibility to parliamentary pressure was equalled only by her refusal to countenance more expenditure on the Foreign Office, least of all defending distant islands. This reduced policy to Micawberism. A well-oiled Whitehall machine should have gone into default mode. The Joint Intelligence Committee should have been asked for new assessments and reinforced its intelligence in Argentina. The Foreign Office should have demanded the postponement of a decision to withdraw HMS *Endurance*, the one British patrol ship left in the South Atlantic, and insisted that the islands' defences be strengthened, taking the issue to cabinet if need be.

None of this happened. *Endurance* was still to be withdrawn. The South Georgia station of the British Antarctic Survey was to be closed for lack of funds. To crown everything, John Nott's 1981 defence review meant cutting back on the surface fleet, preventing it from staging any major operation in the South Atlantic, a review that brought the Royal Navy close to mutiny. To Argentine intelligence a Britain bound up with Europe, Ulster and its economic woes was clearly not interested in a tiny relic of empire, 8,000 miles across the Atlantic. Talking to Argentinian diplomats after the war, I found them convinced that Thatcher's decision against fortress Falklands was a deliberate ploy to draw them on to her punch and save her office.

The reality was that Carrington, the fulcrum round which these forces swirled, was exhausted in his dealings with Downing Street. His loyalty to Thatcher did not extend to enduring her accusation at meeting after meeting that he was 'soft on foreigners'. Once when he apologized for a trivial error in one of his papers, he was told, 'It's not an error, it's incompetence and it comes from the top.'[4] He had already expended his negotiating capital with the party's right wing over Rhodesia. If the prime minister would not support even one of her trusties, Ridley, over Falklands lease-back, he could do no more.

The iron law of foreign policy is that all crises arise from unexpected quarters. That is why every threat, however small, demands meticulous assessment and every decision be 'joined-up' across Whitehall. Thatcher's style of government at the end of 1981 was ill-designed for such joining. Ministers were terrified for their jobs if they brought her unwelcome news. Nobody talked to anybody, least of all if it meant spending money. The climate was such that a corner of British soil was left unprotected, when a series of simple if expensive deterrents would have secured it. A previous invasion threat to the Falklands in 1976 had been met by a secret submarine deployment quietly communicated to Buenos Aires.[5]

The preliminaries to the Falklands War illustrate the danger that can follow a decay of cabinet government, when an over-dominant Downing Street terrorizes ministers and distorts the information flows round Whitehall. An identical failure was to be repeated in the preliminaries to the 2003 Iraq War, albeit under inverse pressure. In 1981 intelligence was suppressed to play down a threat to Britain in the interests of a Downing Street policy. In 2003 it was exaggerated to play up a threat. In both cases intelligence was polluted, brave advice ignored and bad decisions taken which politicians came to regret.

The threat from Argentina built up in December 1981 with the coming to power in Buenos Aires of General Leopoldo Galtieri, much favoured in Washington for his staunch anti-communism. His arrival led to no new intelligence assessment in Whitehall. Galtieri agreed with the head of the navy, Admiral Jorge Anaya, propagator of Argentina's 'dirty war' against the left, to let his service capture the Falklands. This would be in time for the 150th anniversary in 1983 of Britain's original 'seizure'.[6] The plan was to act in the southern winter of 1982, when Britain could not realistically respond. The Americans and the UN would not object and Britain would accept a fait accompli. Some of this flowed back through the British intelligence machine but became clogged as it neared the top. What analysts call 'cognitive dissonance', a preordained disinclination to believe the truth, set in.[7] Nobody dared alert Downing Street because everyone knew Downing Street did not want to be alerted.

The subsequent Franks Report treated the Falklands invasion as if it were a sudden brainstorm on Galtieri's part. But invasions, especially joint-service ones, require extensive planning and logistical preparation. Had this one proceeded as Anaya planned, in June/July, it would probably have succeeded, but it was pre-empted by freelance elements within the Argentine navy. The covert landing of marines on the South Georgia islands at the start of March compelled the junta to bring forward the operation lest Britain react militarily, possibly by sending submarines south as a deterrent. The South Georgia pre-emption thus brought the invasion into the final window when British naval forces might still be able to respond, before winter, the withdrawal of *Endurance* and the onset of Nott's defence cuts after May.

The South Georgia incident should have rung alarm bells in Whitehall. Yet London did not want to hear even vague warnings from the South Atlantic. Only when the full invasion was finally imminent, on 31 March, did Thatcher realize that she faced the worst catastrophe of her administration, a military invasion and the loss of British territory. She would be remembered not as a Churchill but as a Chamberlain. Her reaction was of complete despair, and for the first time in her career she seemed at a loss. She needed to play for time and she needed help. She tried Ronald Reagan, but he could offer nothing but a futile half an hour on the phone to a drunken Galtieri. Nothing could avert what now seemed an unavoidable national humiliation.

Thatcher was aided at a now-famous 31 March night-time meeting in her Commons office by a bizarre consequence of her defence policy. With an enemy fleet now known to be approaching the Falklands, a bevy of foreign and defence ministers told her, in effect, that there was nothing she could do. Nott was briefed that any naval force sent south ran the risk of having to be used, which was logistically unthinkable. But the meeting was transformed when gate-crashed by the First Sea Lord, Sir Henry Leach, who had raced to the meeting in Nott's footsteps, fearing that his boss would again 'sell the navy short'.[8] Thatcher duly asked whether he thought the navy should be sent to recapture the islands. Leach had already discussed this option with his staff and curtly replied that a force could sail within forty-eight hours. Asked what might happen if such a dispatch did not deter the enemy and had to be used, he replied that the navy would recapture the islands. Thatcher understandably hung on his every word.

Leach offered Thatcher what she most desperately needed, professional approval for her natural instinct, which was to fight her way out of any crisis. In a Commons emergency debate on Saturday, three days later, held in a state of shock with the Falklands now in foreign hands, she had a means of staving off what seemed like her imminent resignation. The strong reservations of the chiefs of staff were overwhelmed by the rush to war. Leach had conducted what an aide described to me as 'one of the most brilliant manoeuvres in naval warfare', both to save his prime minister and to rescue his service from Nott's cuts. He was the answer to Thatcher's prayer. She could at least put a fleet to sea and hope something might turn up.

Had Leach not arrived that Wednesday night it is probable that the defence chiefs would have formed a solid front with Nott and stopped any talk of a task force. Once a diplomatic process was under way the mobilizing of such a force would have seemed unacceptably belligerent and incurred open American hostility. The Falklands would, at best, have passed into a UN limbo and Thatcher been fatally undermined. As it was, a sense of national shame was swiftly converted into one of shared purpose. The navy was plunged into a highly publicized frenzy of preparedness, with servicemen and journalists pouring into Plymouth and Portsmouth in a D-day spirit. Leach had merely ordered his fleet to sea, rightly fearful of a cabinet or joint-services revolt against the Wednesday decision. If his force were told to sail south beyond Ascension Island, all plans would anyway have to be revised. Thus Thatcher was able to present the task force to the world as a fait accompli yet without implying anything as final as war. The cabinet was trapped. Only a withdrawal of the task force would at this stage have forced resignation.

From this moment onwards Thatcher's conduct of the Falklands War was as impressive as her unintended instigation of it was not. She knew that she faced something for which her career so far had not prepared her. She would have to depend on others and this would involve deferring to them. She sought advice from Harold Macmillan, who suggested she suspend normal government and select a small war cabinet, but keep the wider cabinet regularly informed.[9] He advised her never to interfere in military operations, to make sure diplomatic and legal lines were clear and, if it came to war, to back the troops to the hilt. All this she obeyed to the letter.

Thatcher looked back on the Falklands War as her most satisfying period as prime minister. In war the objective of policy is usually clear. There is an accepted way of achieving it, the projection of massive violence. Since defeat is politically cataclysmic, the modalities are straightforward. Above all, money is no longer the dominant governmental concern. Thatcher did not even bother to put Howe in the war cabinet since spending was off the agenda. Howe remarked at the time that for him the war was like a sabbatical. For three months he took no decisions. Whatever damage was done to the public finances would have to wait until the war was over, and could be blamed on it. Even the often sceptical John Campbell accepted, twenty years after the event, that Thatcher was a remarkably good war leader:

While on the one hand she gave her commanders the confidence of her absolute political support and embodied Britain's cause brilliantly to the country and the world, she also recognized her own complete ignorance of military matters and did not interfere in the conduct of operations.[10]

This had not been true of Churchill.

Throughout the task force's voyage south Thatcher had to tolerate parallel attempts to resolve the crisis through diplomacy. She had to keep her mind notionally open to a settlement that might be less than total victory. This meant coping with the inept diplomacy of the American intermediary, Al Haig, and with more subtle Peruvian and United Nations emissaries. Henry Kissinger advised Haig not to attempt a compromise: he would be arbitrating between a Latin and an Anglo-Saxon, two races conditioned not by a tradition of bargaining but by pride.[11] America was opposed to the British operation, as during Suez discarding the bonds of friendship when they did not suit American interests (which were pro-Argentinian). Yet Thatcher knew she could rely on private goodwill from Reagan and might have to turn to him for logistical support, as she did. Since Washington was initially doubtful whether Britain would win, this was high-risk diplomacy on her part, and his.

Thatcher never wavered in her conviction that only victory would rescue her position. She appreciated that most of her colleagues, indeed the political community generally, thought the task force would never have to fight and that some compromise would be reached. She alone sensed that the act of sending the task force made a war of some sort inevitable, since Galtieri would never withdraw voluntarily. Thatcher realized that just as she could not survive anything less than victory, so he could not survive retreat. It was a case of one vulnerable leader reading the mind of another.

Thatcher's leadership now broadened and deepened as never before. She deferred to two groups of advisers. The first were lawyers. She recruited the attorney general, Sir Michael Havers, to the war cabinet and saw that he was fully abreast of every action. When advised that she needed a supportive and unambiguous UN mandate, she assiduously helped her ambassador in New York, Sir Anthony Parsons, to win Resolution 502, never failing to refer to it in her public utterances. It covered her diplomatic flank and, crucially, prevented any new supply of French Exocet missiles to Argentina. When told it would be illegal to shoot down an Argentine reconnaissance plane or bomb the Argentine mainland, she obeyed. The Falklands War saw none of the dodgy legal papers, intelligence dossiers and ambiguity about the UN that preceded the Iraq War twenty years later.

The second group of advisers were soldiers. Thatcher, who had previously shown no interest in defence, was drawn into the minutiae of military planning. It appealed to her cast of mind. She liked sauve, commanding men and admired uniforms. Britain's top soldiers also had a quality she had not encountered elsewhere. They were public servants who snapped to attention before her and did what they were told. In every other walk of government Thatcher had found such behaviour extinct. Here it was novel and most attractive.

The chief of the defence staff, Sir Terence Lewin, on whose advice Thatcher relied throughout the war, was a quiet, able man ideal to the moment. He understood what she wanted and assured her he would do his best to deliver it – a recaptured Falklands. It would not be easy, and would be very expensive. But Lewin, himself a sailor, knew that when Nott's controversial defence review returned to the agenda after the war, Thatcher would sink it without a trace. She did, and Nott with it. Sir Henry Leach had saved the old-style Royal Navy, complete with aircraft carriers, planes, submarines, destroyers and amphibious craft, a navy which Nott (and Thatcher) had been determined to consign to history.

The Falklands operation, from the sailing of the task force on 5 April to the eventual recapture of Port Stanley on 14 June, required little by way of prime ministerial decision. Thatcher visited command headquarters at Northwood in Middlesex only once. What was a huge military and political risk had to play itself out. The collapse of the Haig mission, the British request for American aid to Ascension, the agonizing wait for the break-out from the San Carlos bridgehead and the rejection of Reagan's plea for UN co-sovereignty all required of Thatcher only a steady nerve. The worst moments were not setbacks but casualties. Each ship that was lost reduced Thatcher, so she said, to tears. She wrote a personal letter to every family of a dead serviceman.

The Falklands War was not a political gamble because Thatcher had no realistic option, but it was a big military one. Many of those directly involved, and many observers on both sides of the Atlantic, regarded moving the task force south from Ascension as against every dictate of military caution. A seaborne assault on a defended coast was dangerous, as armies at Normandy and Okinawa had found. With no secure air cover it was even more so. Argentina had big ships, a large army and skilled pilots with modern missiles. Like Thatcher, its leadership also had everything to lose. Had an Exocet sunk the troopship *Canberra*, or had an Argentine submarine run amok in the task force, there could have been no early reinforcement. In the outcome, Britain relied heavily on the professionalism of its own ground forces and the incompetence and cowardice of the Argentinians (other than their pilots) in failing properly to defend what they had captured.

The Falklands War happened because Thatcher had awarded 1,800 intransigent colonials the right to veto her government's received view of the national interest. Having abandoned the Foreign Office policy of lease-back she failed adequately to defend the islands against an increased threat. Thatcher claimed that 'the invasion could not have been foreseen or prevented.'[12] When the Franks Report into the causes of the war arrived in her office six months later she sat down, shut her eyes and asked her secretary to read out only the last paragraph, the exoneration. 'We would not be justified in attaching any criticism or blame to the present government for the Argentine junta's decision to commit its act of unprovoked aggression.' She needed no caveats, just that sentence. 'Fine,' she said, and went back to work.[13]

Certainly no government can be blamed for the reckless aggression of another, but it can be blamed for not defending its own people and territory and for, in some degree, inducing an enemy to chance an attack. The Franks Report was full of criticism and blame but, as with the Hutton and Butler inquiries into the Iraq War, Franks did not feel justified in drawing a 'hanging' conclusion from the evidence. When I interviewed him after publication and put to him the 'whitewash' charge, he paused a long time and told me to remember that he was addressing a nation in the aftermath of victory. 'There is a time and a place for blame,' he said. He then did what whitewashers always do and asked me sternly to read exactly all that he had written, to read between the lines. But politics never reads between the lines. That is the privilege of history.

As defence policy the war was a disaster. The dispatch of a task force did not deter the Argentinians and get them to withdraw, any more than Britain's possession of nuclear weapons deterred the invasion in the first place. It caused the deaths of 255 British servicemen, with another 777 seriously wounded. The cost in lost equipment and subsequent fortification was over £3 billion. The defence review was torn up and aircraft carriers retained. Thatcher's policy had been to retreat from a global to a European theatre. After the war the need for a 'Falklands-style' capability became axiomatic and Downing Street's foreign policy was again able to contemplate out-of-area adventures, precisely the interventionist urge which 'early Thatcher' and the Nott review had hoped to prevent. Its legacy was to be seen in Yugoslavia, Afghanistan and Iraq.

Thatcher later rewrote the history of the Falklands War. She would claim, over and again, that the war was won because she had not allowed Britain to disarm. It vindicated her belief in a 'strong defence policy'. This was nonsense. The war was won because the Argentinians invaded before her 'weak' defence policy had been implemented. The Royal Navy was actually contemplating selling to Argentina ships later used in the task force. Had Buenos Aires invaded when planned, it is near certain it would have succeeded. Thatcher owed much to Galtieri, but even more to Captain Alfredo Astiz, the hothead who seized South Georgia and pre-empted the original plan. She was very lucky.

While the war lasted it was, to Thatcher, a terrifying, draining experience. As soon as it was over she saw it differently, as awakening a slumbering nation to the reality of its greatness. The tabloid press depicted it as the latest in a long tradition of British victories, from the Armada through Waterloo and two world wars. Thatcher relished cartoons comparing her with Churchill, Elizabeth I, even Boudicca. The war was a metaphor for what Britain could do if it had a big enough heart and a resolute leader. It allowed Thatcher to use language which would once have seemed old-fashioned and ridiculous, that of Churchillian Conservatism

The war boosted Britain's self-image at a time when such a boost was badly needed. The nation rediscovered itself, bizarrely, not in realizing some new economic or industrial elixir but in reasserting something archaic, its imperial reach. This created a bond between the nation and its leader not seen in years. To some critics, not all on the left, this was an unwelcome bond. To Campbell it 'exacerbated Thatcher's worst characteristics. . . She used her augmented authority to pursue more self-righteously than before her particular vision of British society. She went on to trample on those groups, institutions and traditions which did not share it.'[14] Nevertheless it was a bond. Alan Clark reflected after the victory that 'the lady's authority is complete. She could make any policy and break any individual.'[15] In short, the war did more than save Thatcher's political bacon. Whereas before she had power only to negotiate, she now had power to command and control.

6

Marking Time

The Falklands gave Thatcher power but how she would use it was still uncertain. Tory popularity soared after the war, rising from an average of 33 per cent in the polls to 43 per cent. The SDP threat was not eliminated but its advance was stopped and thrown into reverse, driving the party into formal alliance with the Liberals. For the first time Thatcher could see blue sky ahead. That July she was exhausted and took a brief holiday in Switzerland. But the effect on her of victory was more energizing than any Alp. It entered her soul as nothing else could do, giving her a dimension which she did not try to conceal. Meeting her shortly afterwards to discuss the Franks findings, I found her exhilarated to the point of intoxication. She knew she had salvaged triumph from the jaws of disaster, but refused to contemplate it. 'We were not to blame and we won,' she incanted again and again.

June 1982 brought a return to normality in government, which Thatcher did not like. At first she seemed reluctant even to dismantle the wartime command structure. The ten weeks of crisis had been a huge stress, a continual round of anxiety and tears, but they had suited her style. There were things about it she knew she did not understand and which she had to delegate to others, to the 'engine room'. But she bore final responsibility and this in itself gave her an aura of being apart, uniquely vulnerable and thus uniquely powerful. People defer to the closeness of victory or disaster in a leader. Enjoyment is the wrong word for war but Thatcher never found leadership so stimulating or obedience so unquestioning again.

She showed no restraint in exploiting the Falklands factor. It was a leit-motif of her speeches for months, indeed years, afterwards. A month after the victory, in July 1982 in Cheltenham, she described the task force as a metaphor for the sort of nation she was determined to create: 'We have ceased to be a nation in retreat ... Britain found herself again in the South Atlantic.' Looking to the future she said that the Falklands' experience had been 'an accurate picture of Britain at war, not yet of Britain at peace ... The spirit has stirred and the nation has begun to assert itself. Things are not going to be the same again.'[1] At her party conference in October she said that 'it would be no bad thing if the feeling that swept the country [during the war] were to continue to inspire us.' Again at the Lord Mayor's banquet in November she recalled that 'the 1970s were racked by doubt ... Those years are over. Doubt whether we shall resolve our problems is giving way to knowledge that we can.'

The equivocation of many of the war's critics was not just swept aside but condemned. A note of conciliation in the Archbishop of Canterbury's Falklands service in St Paul's infuriated Thatcher. It made her a foe of the Anglican hierarchy for the rest of her office. The Falklands was a philosopher's stone, turning political base metal into gold, and she would not have it tarnished by some clergyman. Prime ministers long to wrap themselves in the flag. Thatcher never disrobed. She attended any war-related function and visited the islands, an uncomfortable ordeal, just seven months later. I once heard her iconoclastic adviser Alan Walters, at a Downing Street lunch, suggesting that it would have been cheaper to give every islander a million pounds to vote to resettle in Switzerland or anywhere. Thatcher was incandescent, shouting at him about Judas and 'pieces of silver'.

Nor was the Falklands Factor (which soon acquired a capital F) just a job well done. It offered a template for leadership that suited Thatcher's aggressive, battling style. In fighting the wets in 1980–81, she had been hesitant, giving ground, relying on loyalist advisers to stiffen her resolve. The same had applied to her early union reforms. Now she had a global achievement under her belt something new clicked into place. She no longer wrote 'yes' on decision papers but such lines as, 'I will not tolerate failure on this'.[2] At the end of 1982 there were two scalps hanging on the Downing Street wall, the wets and General Galtieri. Who was to be the next?

Yet as so often before, the politician in Thatcher seemed to hold back the ideologue or revolutionary. There was an election beckoning, her first confrontation with the voters as prime minister. Party aides had considered holding a 'victory' election in the late summer of 1982, but after just three years of a parliament this was thought opportunistic. Spring 1983 was the earliest date that had decorum. It was an election that Thatcher had no expectation of winning before the Falklands War but which now seemed in the bag. Accordingly she felt that nothing should damage that bag. To the open dismay of her supporters, Thatcher exploited the war to boost her personal standing but not to show any policy innovation. She spoke often of 'now let's get down to business', but there was no sign of it.

The remainder of the parliament, from June 1982 to spring 1983, was dominated by Thatcher struggling to extract good news from the economy. Monetarism was in disarray, its targets apparently out of line with the economic process they purported to steer. Sir Ian Gilmour called it the 'uncontrollable in pursuit of the undefinable'. Inflation was falling and growth improving. But this was hardly surprising after the most savage bout of government-induced deflation since the 1930s. In 1983 Britain's domestic product was still 4 per cent below its level in 1979 and official unemployment was still growing. For all Thatcher's references to 'the medicine working', the conventional wisdom was that nanny had merely given a profligate economy an almighty thrashing. Nor was Thatcher immune to this argument. Her sensitivity to the scale of unemployment was reflected both in her responses to Howe's budgetary asceticism and in her unwillingness to tamper with the social security budget. Social benefits rose steadily throughout her reign.

The economy and union reforms had by 1983 expended much of Thatcherism's political capital and for the ragged band of loyalists they offered meagre fare. Of privatization there had been little sign. In 1981 Nigel Lawson, as junior minister at the Treasury, felt emboldened to say that 'no industry should remain under state ownership unless there is a positive and overwhelming case for it so doing.'[3] But Thatcher disliked both the concept of privatization and the term itself, regarding it as an 'ugly word' which for a long time she refused to use, preferring denationalization. She was convinced it would frighten the electorate. She was also concerned at the state losing control over assets such as oil, coal or railways which in some sense belonged to the nation as a whole. For her privatization risked being seen as unpatriotic.

Thatcher had sent her old friend Sir Keith Joseph to the industry department, as if that were sufficient token of her radicalism. He laboured mightily to bring forth a mouse, a form of government stock called Busby Bonds, to raise money for the hived-off telecommunications arm of the Post Office. Thatcher referred to it not as privatization but as popular capitalism. Joseph's successor after 1981, Patrick Jenkin, wanted outright privatization of what became British Telecom but Thatcher stopped him, fearing a private monopoly. She was even more sceptical of the proposed sale of the government's North Sea company, Britoil, which she referred to as 'Britain's oil' or 'my oil'. Howell was initially forbidden to privatize it. Lawson, arriving at energy in 1981, was more determined, overcoming Thatcher's opposition with a promise to retain a 'golden voting share', a device that enabled the government to stop a board decision 'against the national interest'. It was privatization but with the state retaining control, raising £334 million for the Treasury.

Britoil was the only high-profile privatization of Thatcher's first term, though state shares were sold in BP, Cable and Wireless and British Aerospace. But these measures kindled what became a potent Whitehall alliance between the Treasury and 'industry sponsoring' departments. The Treasury was eager for cash from any source and sales in public corporations offered it. Each year the British Rail board was required to deliver assets for sale: cross-Channel ferries, ports, hovercraft, catering, property, hotels (and their wine cellars). While Thatcher had no objection to these assets changing hands, privatization of a core industry was not her intention. If any minister suggested selling the railway itself, as they occasionally did, Thatcher forbad it.

The commentator Samuel Brittan summed up the driving force behind the government at this time as money pure and simple. He wrote that, 'selling public assets was politically much easier and more popular than cutting public expenditure', but only assets that evoked no public affection.[4] The same timidity affected other policies. Having goaded Prior into the most tentative union reforms, Thatcher had unleashed Norman Tebbit on the employment department. Yet Tebbit, like Joseph at industry, was to prove a radical tempered by reality. His crucial innovation was to end a union's immunity from damages if engaged in illegal – mostly secondary – strikes. He baulked at mandatory strike ballots or a ban on strikes in essential services. Thatcher agreed. She was 'convinced that the giant step being taken on the immunity of trade union funds was sufficient for the moment'.[5] She constantly referred to the need to win consent as she felt her way along the frontier between public and private sectors. She was more a Fabian than a revolutionary.

Thatcher's timidity towards the public sector nationally was not reflected in her approach to the one-third of public services still administered locally. As a result it was local government that bore the early brunt of her ideological zeal. Nationally she had torn up the conventional wisdom on economic policy and dipped a toe into trade union reform, but this was Westminster business and it made her nervous. Local government was out of the public eye, the *ultima Thule* of British politics, and Thatcher felt she could use it as a testing ground for Thatcherism. As a result, probably the most radical reform of the first term was to allow council tenants to buy their houses, spurred by a demand that council rents rise towards market rents. This was bitterly opposed by councils, who regarded their houses as part of their charitable housing stock. As we shall see in Chapter 8, Thatcher pushed ahead regardless, releasing large sums to relieve government borrowing. Another emphatically Thatcherite innovation was to force councils to put local services out to competitive tender.

A more visceral antipathy was to any increase in local expenditure. Local rates had risen under Heath, as a result of a surge in spending on education and social services, and because he had attempted a reform to metropolitan government in favour of costly new city regions. This occasioned Thatcher's remit back in 1974 to 'find ways of abolishing the rates'. Yet in 1979 the Tories inherited what was still a relatively disciplined local finance regime. The agreement whereby the amount spent by councils each year was decided informally by their national associations with the Treasury had been broken by only a handful of far-left cities and not so as to affect the overall aggregates. Yet on coming to power Howe ordered all councils to reduce spending by 1 per cent a year in real terms. This feat was near unachievable when the Treasury was conceding inflationary wage settlements to all public-sector workers. Howe then imposed on councils a novel range of penalties, including claw-backs, voluntary referendums and ring-fenced block grants. Local authorities were for the first time given specific spending norms. The concept of the central government target entered the Whitehall lexicon. Libraries were shut, council rents increased, staff were laid off.

In the process one of the most destructive myths of Thatcherism was born, that local government was spendthrift compared with central government. Explaining her attack on the councils, Thatcher wrote that she might 'exhort, bewail and threaten but local government spending grew inexorably in real terms, year after year'.[6] In truth the curb on local spending was successful, far more so than on the centre. When Thatcher came to power local government spent £24.5 billion, or 28.3 per cent of the public sector. By the 1983 election, they were spending (in real terms) £23.9 billion or 26.3

per cent of the sector. Thatcher's accusation was simply untrue.[7] Yet Lawson as junior Treasury minister repeatedly contrasted 'local irresponsibility in exceeding government forecasts' with rising central spending that was due to 'conscious government priorities'.[8] Local electors, by implication, were not entitled to express priorities.

As a result, the Tory establishment in the 1980s lost touch with local government and with the party's traditional roots in the cities and shires. It ignored its 'little platoons'. Though in 1974 Thatcher had protested to Heath against over-centralization, she now found herself pitted against any elected official whose mandate might detract from her own. This included 25,000 local councillors, many of them loyal Tories. She opposed not just councils but devolved assemblies, elected mayors and European parliaments. Beneath the peaks of central government and its benign regulators, she recognized only a rolling plain of individuals, families and a residuum of 'volunteers', which she later characterized as 'not society'.

Thatcher's aversion to localism was attributed to her aversion to the Grantham politicians who had deprived her father of his aldermanic post.[9] Parish pump Grantham was transferred in Thatcher's mind to local government generally. To her upwardly mobile mind, councils were a provincial repertory, where you performed if you could not make it to Westminster. Long after she had left office I asked her about the London mayoralty, then up for election. I suggested she run for the job, as did French ex-presidents, as she would win by miles. What was intended as a compliment evinced an explosion. 'Mayor of London!' she screamed with contempt. 'I was elected prime minister of Great Britain.'

The Tories suffered dearly for her early display of centralization. Over four years they lost half the seats in local government which they had held in the 1970s, and then lost half again. In 1981 they were even stripped of their supposed stronghold of the Greater London Council, fashioned from the old Labour London County Council in the 1960s to be safely Tory. After 1981 London was never Conservative again. Thatcher was duly enraged. She could understand the left's high seriousness, its moral purpose, and even sympathize with its revolutionary ardour. She rather respected the old Labour icon Michael Foot, the 'poor Michael' of her memoirs. But Labour local government was beyond any pale. It had no more public manifestation than Ken Livingstone, who in 1981 had seized the Greater London Council in a left-wing putsch.

Livingstone was ideally cast as a new Galtieri, a mischievous, iconoclastic Londoner of working-class origins. His indulgence of left-wing activism, ethnic and sexual minorities and the frivolous fringe of public life embodied all that Thatcher detested in the left. He festooned the façade of his County Hall headquarters opposite Parliament with the monthly total of London's unemployed. This so annoyed Thatcher that when she finally abolished the GLC she sold the building to a Japanese businessman for a hotel and an aquarium. Tourists and well-fed sharks summed up her view of local politics. She decided to get rid of the GLC and 'cap' all local rates in the 1983 manifesto, one of its few specific pledges.

To many observers Thatcher in the autumn and winter of 1982/3 was 'pausing'. She did not do what she implied after the Falklands and get down to business. Rather she seemed to be taking stock. The wets were in retreat. The economy was at last improving. Yet the prime minister seemed to have lost ideological steam. John Hoskyns, Thatcher's admired policy chief, resigned at the end of 1981, dismayed at her lack of radicalism. She replaced him with a journalist/novelist, Ferdinand Mount. The appointment was greeted by *The Times* as significant, signalling 'the final defeat for the radical approach to government which the prime minister promised but never dared deliver'.[10] This view was reinforced when the Central Policy Review Staff produced a discussion document in late 1982, suggesting radical reforms to the health service, education and public spending generally. It also mooted extensive privatization. Each proposal was of impeccable Thatcherite respectability, and would seem modest today. Thatcher at first advanced the document for discussion, but when it was leaked to the press she professed herself 'appalled'. She shelved it as far too dangerous and even resolved to abolish the CPRS as an accident always waiting to happen.

Hoskyns' resignation and the fate of the CPRS report showed how far the public sector was still untouched by revolution. The prime minister claimed to regard privatization as having gone 'about as far as we can go at this time'. She baulked when Joseph suggested education vouchers and continued her practice as education secretary of allowing grammar schools to close in favour of comprehensives. As for the NHS, she was paranoid about being thought hostile to it; it must always be 'safe in our hands'. Nor did she show any scepticism towards rising expenditure on social security, seeing it as an essential salve to the wounds of monetarism. Thatcher would not tolerate talk of cuts in benefits or steps in the direction of American 'workfare'. Public spending duly rose over Thatcher's first government from 41 per cent to 44 per cent of the domestic economy. The Westminster village shook its head and concluded that Thatcherism must be some figment of think-tank imagination.

With the stark exception of local government reform, the 1983 election manifesto was an exercise in not scaring anyone. It was written elegantly under Howe's direction by Mount and Adam Ridley from the Treasury. Thatcher accepted that the work was 'somehow not exciting', adding that 'tactically I could see that it made sense for us to produce a tame manifesto.'[11] Rather than blame herself she accused Howe of being 'too safe a pair of hands'. Since Howe had long been fearless in pressing for radicalism this judgement was absurd. It was Thatcher who was playing safe. Lawson by way of contrast thought it one of the best of all her manifestos, because of its lack of specificity, a true Treasury view.[12]

Thatcher's caution may have played a part in winning her second election, though more credit must go to Labour's decision to fight under the ineffectual, left-wing leadership of Michael Foot. Despite recession, unemployment, public-service cuts and union reform, Thatcher won 42.4 per cent of the vote to Labour's 27.6 per cent. The intervention of the Alliance (with 25.4 per cent) ensured that although her popular vote was down 2 per cent on 1979, her parliamentary majority was increased. She had done what no one Tory leader had done for half a century and been re-elected for a second full term. She had also proved the potency of military victory to democratic leadership. The 1983 election was one of the first in which the block of Britons defining themselves in the census as working class was no longer a majority of the population, and certainly no longer loyal to Labour. The electoral battle would from now on be over a group of citizens who thought of themselves as middle class, whether upper or lower, occupying the middle ground of the political spectrum. It was the beginning of the end of the old polarity in British politics. As for what that meant for the government of Britain and the policies that it should espouse, all was still largely a mystery.

PART TWO

High Noon

7

The Revolution Takes Shape

'Holy Madness' was the phrase used of the revolutionary fervour that seethed through cosmopolitan London in the nineteenth century.[1] Visionaries and desperadoes, refugees and adventurers, conspired in the garrets and coffee houses of an ever-welcoming city. All shared a romantic allegiance to the left of the political spectrum. From Garibaldi to Bakunin, Marx and Engels their utopianism came to dominate the politics of the late-nineteenth and early-twentieth centuries. But their revolutionary objectives lay not in the host country but in Continental Europe and further abroad. Britons could view their antics with indulgence. Imperial security and the franchise were advancing hand in hand with public welfare. Revolution did not seem the British way.

As the twentieth century progressed, so did a consensus in favour of increased government intervention. In Britain a belief in the virtues of redistributive taxation spread through Labour and Conservative parties. In 1940 Rab Butler could vehemently deny any attachment to laissez-faire. As Thatcherism's most sympathetic exponent, Shirley Letwin, wrote, Conservatives at the time 'were far from clear about the reasons for their quarrel with [socialism] or indeed whether they had a quarrel at all'.[2] An overseas empire was paralleled by a domestic one, that of the welfare state, run in much the same paternalist spirit. It evolved after the Second World War from Beveridge's concept of an insurance safety net to embrace cradle-to-grave universalism. Butskellism was not socialism, but in government practice they seemed much the same thing. When Thatcher came to power at the end of the 1970s, that welfare consensus was overwhelming. The state directly owned 40 per cent of the nation's output and indirectly controlled far more. It ran railways, shipbuilding, car making, coal mining, ports and harbours, airlines and airports, gas, electricity, nuclear energy and arms manufacture. It owned the nation's hospitals, schools, prisons and old people's homes, and ran a national pension scheme. As for the word revolutionary, it had been expropriated exclusively by those who wanted more state control, not less.

Thatcher professed to see things differently. She had said so all her life and couched that determination in overtly revolutionary terms. To her the word revolution was not a mere metaphor for pro-active government, it was a programme for overturning the ruling consensus and replacing it with something else, as yet largely unspecified. Yet after her second election victory in 1983 she had to accept that her upheaval had hardly begun. She had cut some taxes and sold Britoil and half a million council houses. But the great state fiefdoms remained intact. Social security costs were rising faster than ever. As for rolling back the state, it was consuming 3 per cent more of the nation's income than it had under Labour. Thatcher moaned that 'There was still too much socialism in Britain', and especially within government itself, among teachers, health workers, civil servants and even a few ministers. They all had to go, she cried. 'There was a revolution still to be made, but too few revolutionaries.'[3]

Many of Thatcher's supporters were starting to wonder if this was not just talk. Already Hoskyns and Sherman had gone, to brood at the Centre for Policy Studies, replaced by men they regarded as wets. Nicholas Ridley saw the aftermath of the Falklands victory as the most puzzling of Thatcher's reign, referring to 1983–6 as 'the years the locusts ate'.[4] The sympathetic *Economist* wrote constantly of the wasted first term, the years of drift. Thatcher was always a 'front-of-house' politician, never a backroom thinker. She had no book, no grand plan, no *Das Kapital*. The 1983 manifesto was a blueprint for nothing but winning an election, commissioned by a leader of instinct rather than of programme. At this stage she had fought enough battles to know her strength. But if there was to be a revolution it seemed that it would have to emerge from her response to events. This would not come easily. Thatcher's personal relations were dreadful, turning colleagues against her and impeding efficient business. Without these classic arts of politics how could she possibly hope to 'change history'?

Nevertheless there was a new mood to Downing Street after 1983. The defensive prime minister of the civil war against the wets had become an aggressive and confident leader. She had what she craved, confirmation in office. Whitehall and Westminster realized that Thatcher, long seen as the temporary custodian of Downing Street, was there for the long haul, whether they liked it or not. At such times expectations change. Politicians and officials subconsciously adjust their loyalties to accommodate reality. Normal ambition meant that they naturally wanted to be seen, in her notorious phrase, as 'one of us'. Besides, though the prime minister had no plan, she had an approach to leadership, a prejudice, a cast of mind. Her way of responding to the stimulus of events was what shaped policy. Since this approach was so enmeshed in her style critics wrongly saw it not as a revolution but a reaction, merely a harking back to Victorian nannying and self-help. But they were qualities which, if properly directed, could drive the engine of change. Letwin listed the 'vigorous virtues' as uprightness, self-sufficiency, energy, adventurousness, independent-mindedness, loyalty to friends and robustness against enemies.[5] If they were at the expense of 'the softer virtues' of kindness, generosity and forgiveness, so be it.

A talisman of Thatcher's new determination was her post-election reshuffle. From her first arrival in Downing Street Thatcher's casting of ministers had been careful. Even such allies as Joseph, Biffen, Nott and Ridley were judged for their executive and presentational skills and if found wanting dropped. Thatcher now felt strong enough to ignore the wets. She sacked Pym, foreign secretary since Carrington's resignation over the Falklands, remarking that she had 'exchanged an amusing whig for a gloomy one'. She and Pym had disagreed about many things, she said, including 'life in general'.[6] Prior left the government four months later. As always the crucial moves were at the Treasury. Whatever storms might blow, if the Treasury was in safe hands she felt the ship was moving in the right direction. Thatcher felt Howe had, by 1983, done his time and was exhausted. He was not pleased, feeling he was entitled to enjoy the fruits of his titanic effort in steering Thatcherism through its first storm. His replacement was Lawson, Thatcher commenting sardonically that she had 'come to share his high opinion of himself'. Lawson was no politician, more an ideological journalist. But just as Howe had been the perfect chancellor for the macro-economic disciplines of 1980–82, so Lawson was to dominate what was to be her golden age. Even after the painful separation in 1990 Thatcher declared that 'if it comes to drawing up a list of Thatcherite revolutionaries, I would never deny Nigel a leading place on it.'[7]

Howe and Lawson were the twin architects of Thatcher's first revolution. Since the 1960s both had written of the Tories needing to rediscover free-market economics, Lawson as a journalist and Howe as founder of the Bow Group. They were intellectuals, albeit of a different stripe. Lawson had a flash Fleet Street quality to him, while Howe was the epitome of a clubbable advocate. They were loyal to Thatcher and her cause and had the necessary resilience to handle high office, albeit in the lofty turrets of the Treasury. Both had a clear understanding of what Thatcherism might imply and contrived to keep its goals in view even when Thatcher herself was cautious or distracted. That Thatcher came to treat both men so badly was to be her downfall. They were necessary for her success and sufficient for her demise. Thatcher's whole personality seemed to erect a wall between her and her most trusted champions. Her sensitivity to others in distress seemed not to embrace the distress she herself caused. When a Chequers waitress scalded Howe by dropping a bowl of soup over him, Thatcher ignored him in her solicitation for the embarrassed waitress.

Lawson achieved his life's ambition as chancellor. Given a virtually free hand by the prime minister he lit the fuse under Thatcherism's rocket. He built on Howe's policy of shifting revenue from direct to indirect taxes. In 1979 Howe had cut the top rate of income tax from 83 per cent to 60 per cent and the basic rate to 30 per cent. Thresholds for each band were also raised. In 1984 Lawson abolished the 15 per cent 'unearned income' surcharge on investments, which had once taken Britain's marginal rate to a stratospheric 98 per cent. He eventually reduced the top rate to 40 per cent and the basic to 25 per cent. Capital gains and inheritance taxes were reduced to the same top rate as income tax. British incomes overall were now more lightly taxed than any in Europe.

The impact of these cuts was hard to assess, not least because of the balancing rise in indirect, later termed 'stealth', taxes like VAT and that on petrol, and other duties. To Thatcher income tax cuts were essential to enabling the middle classes to build up personal wealth and stem the flight of enterprise and talent abroad. Howe had also attempted to push up local rates to reduce the call on Exchequer grants to local government. One thing was incontrovertible. Thatcher's electoral successes made it an article of faith to both Tory and Labour strategists never to revert to high levels of income tax. If the Exchequer was ever caught short, something else would have to give. Income came to be regarded in Britain as fiscally sacrosanct.

The most immediate beneficiary of this largesse was a world for which Thatcher ostensibly had little sympathy, those earning large sums in the City of London. They were to experience their own first revolution. In 1979 the Office of Fair Trading began to direct its attention to the Stock Exchange, intending to bring the oligopolistic City within the competitive ambit of the Restrictive Practices Court. The City pleaded with Thatcher to be left to regulate itself, meaning to be left alone. The government conceded, but only on terms to be negotiated by Lawson and (briefly) Cecil Parkinson as industry secretary. These terms proved more drastic than anyone expected. Over the course of the 1980s the government relaxed bank deposit requirements and allowed building societies to demutualize and become retail banks. Alongside this came similar pressure to inject competition into the market for stocks, shares and other financial products. These once cosy realms were already being assaulted by transnational computerization. London had either to join this world or be left behind. A new Financial Services Act (1986) faced this challenge head on. It led to the transformation of London's money market to one akin to New York. The Stock Exchange monopoly on share dealing ended. Foreign banks were allowed to operate openly in London both as stock brokers and as merchant banks. It was decided to make the conversion not gradual but overnight, in the celebrated 'Big Bang' of October 1986.

The outcome was spectacular. A London which in the early Eighties was being challenged by Frankfurt, Brussels and Paris as financial capital of Europe found a vitality not seen since the Edwardian era. Family-owned finance houses were swamped in a competitive firestorm. American, German, Dutch and French firms poured into the City to snap up sleepy partnerships or poach their brighter talents. The cult of get-rich-quick linked the Big Bang with what became the 'Lawson boom' of the late Eighties. The associated stereotypes, the yuppie in a black suit, the Cockney futures trader, the 'phone number' bonus, the Porsche and the Cotswold manor became icons of Thatcher's Britain, cruelly contrasted with the unemployed miner and docker. They were satirized in such plays as David Hare's *Secret Rapture* and Caryl Churchill's *Serious Money*, to which yuppies went in droves. Nemesis came a year later on Black Monday, when 25 per cent was wiped off share values. It was a temporary setback. Financial services innovation was a lasting Thatcherite structural reform.

Some of the richest City pickings emerged from another consequence of Lawson's arrival at the Treasury. Thatcher remained persistently nervous about privatization throughout her term of office (though she gave a quite different impression afterwards). In 1985 the elderly Macmillan chided her for 'selling the family silver' to pay for current expenditure. As Campbell commented, the image of ministers, like a lot of dodgy house-strippers, knocking down the nation's heirlooms at a cost well below their true worth, subtly undermined Thatcher's carefully created reputation for thrifty housekeeping.[8]

She herself noted that privatization was never popular in opinion polls. The only attraction in what she firmly called 'denationalization' was that of wider share-ownership.

Lawson pressed ahead, tantalizing Thatcher with the cash that privatization might yield to the Treasury. The first disposal of the 1983 parliament was British Telecom. It raised £3.9 billion and was, at the time, the largest equity offering in history. This whetted the Treasury's appetite for more. In the seven years after 1983 the Exchequer's coffers were swelled by Jaguar cars (£294 million), gas (£5,434 million), British Airways (£900 million), Rolls-Royce (£1,363 million), British Airports (£1,281 million), British Steel (£2,500 million), the water boards (£5,110 million), electricity supply (£5,092 million) and electricity generation (£5,110 million). Every institution nationalized since the war was examined for value. It was the greatest asset sale in history. But the momentum came not from ideology but from the Treasury's eagerness for current revenue and Thatcher's well-founded craving for budgetary rectitude. To her, privatization was the revolution's transitional relief.

As the tempo of asset sales increased, Thatcher constantly intervened. She yielded to the bullying of Sir Dennis Rooke of British Gas to preserve his monopoly when moved to the private sector. She wanted sales to go ahead fast, to avoid closeness to an election or to encourage buyers into thinking they had a bargain. The result was usually a gross undervaluing of the assets. The price set by the government for British Ports meant it was 34 times oversubscribed. British Airways was 23 times oversubscribed, electricity 10 times and Rolls-Royce 9 times. Lucky shareholders were offered get-rich-quick gains. By the end of the decade the National Audit Office was to calculate that Thatcher's break-neck approach to privatization cost the taxpayer £2.4 billion in revenue foregone.[9]

The immediate image of privatization was that of 'fat cat' pay rises which the new boards awarded their chairmen and chief executives, often at the same time as they were laying off staff. As in its treatment of the unions and the City, Thatcherism found it hard to present an attractive face to the world. As the industries passed into the private sector they also carried with them a baggage of regulation that became heavier as the years passed. Although telecommunications, gas, electricity and water were privately owned, they remained in varying degrees monopolistic. They had therefore to be regulated, and the regulatory framework had to be set by ministers and monitored by ministers. Thus the assumptions that ruled the industries when nationalized were often replicated when privatized. Looking over their shoulders were such regulatory acronyms as Oftel, Ofgas, Ofwat and Offer. Industries were ordered by ministers to maintain uneconomic phone boxes, restore Victorian sewers and take their energy from pre-ordained suppliers (such as coal). Regulators vetted prices, and thus could hold a whip hand over corporate profitability. Companies were vulnerable to ministerial direction as laid down in acts of parliament. At the same time the regulators were frequently accused of 'going native'. Ferdinand Mount, formerly head of Thatcher's policy unit, remarked in 1987 that 'the regulators have no teeth and the operators no conscience.'[10] They could reasonably reply that it would take time for them to settle down, as they eventually did.

The upshot was that the end of state ownership did not mean the end of state power. Attlee's nationalizations replaced shareholders with civil servants, usually leaving the old private boards in place and claiming the dividends for the state. Thatcher's privatizations replaced civil servants with shareholders, again leaving the old boards in place. Industry 'sponsoring' departments remained in Whitehall. The state need no longer own what it wished to control. It had only to pass the appropriate statute. Ridley assured a hesitant Thatcher that 'utilities we have privatised or intend to privatise are more easily controlled when they are in the private sector.'[11] Thatcher herself claimed that privatization-with-regulation was more accountable because companies and regulators were more open to public scrutiny than the old nationalized boards. It was not a view shared by many others, who found the regulators unaccountable to anyone other than a limbo called 'parliament'. But privatization there was. Thatcher's first revolution was starting to take off.

If surviving nationalized industries needed any further incentive to welcome their disposal, the Treasury treated them without mercy. The 1940s' arm's-length principle established by Herbert Morrison was discontinued by Lawson. Control over the industries' affairs moved steadily from sponsoring departments to the Treasury. A Green Paper published in December 1984 proposed statutory financial targets for each surviving board, ending their status as autonomous public corporations. It meant that the boards could receive regular instructions from the Treasury, could be milked of money and starved of investment. In particular, they would be subject to something called 'a negative external borrowing requirement', a euphemism for an annual tax on any profits. The as-yet unprivatized board of British Gas protested that it was being reduced 'to the role of a management committee acting at the ultimate behest of the Treasury'.[12] The whole public sector was to take up the same cry in years to come. Though aspects of the Green Paper were diluted, the Treasury treated utility prices as a form of supplementary tax. Gas, electricity, post and rail prices rose rapidly over the 1980s, to such an extent that by 1990 British Rail could envisage moving into operating profit. At the height of the Lawson boom in 1989, the nationalized sector overall was yielding the Treasury a cash surplus. But in most industries investment was starved, with dire consequences in the 1990s.

Most of these reforms were politically painless. They involved stock market operations and manipulation of tax and regulatory regimes. The public noticed them only insofar as it read about them in newspapers or indulged in occasional share-buying sprees. This was not the case with Thatcher's more direct assault on the so-called 'supply side' of the economy, her honouring of the original Stepping Stones prospectus for more radical trade-union reform. If tax cuts and privatization were the crown jewels of the first revolution, fighting the unions was its toughest and most public slog. Making labour markets more flexible to economic change was essential to the industrial restructuring expedited by the 1980s deflation. The resulting conflict did more than anything to brutalize Thatcherism's image, but to a convinced Thatcherite there was no alternative. There had to be another fight and another win.

The miners' strike which began in March 1984 was not an external circumstance requiring Thatcher's reaction, like the Falklands invasion. It was a battle of her own choosing, for which she prepared practically and emotionally. It was the totemic event of Thatcher's second administration, as the Falklands had been of her first, an event with which she regularly compared it. As in the Falklands, victory was by no means predictable. The miners' leader, Arthur Scargill, already had two Tory scalps hanging from his belt, Heath's from 1972 and Thatcher's from 1981. He enjoyed fierce, if mostly emotional, support from the rest of the labour movement, and a potential stranglehold on the strategic resource of power-station coal. He hated Thatcher with a passion, a hatred she richly returned. The conflict evoked all Thatcher's clarity of purpose.

A secret committee had met in Whitehall since 1981 to prepare coal stocks for an eighteen-month stoppage. Many power stations were converted to burn oil or gas. The union reforms introduced by Prior in 1980 had been supplemented by Tebbit in 1982 and Tom King in 1983. These were not drastic, mostly directed at secondary picketing, secret ballots and ending trade-union immunity for damages. But together they were a serious obstacle in the path of any strike. A hardline American chairman, Ian MacGregor, was put into the Coal Board and a competent wet, Peter Walker, into the energy department. When in 1984 MacGregor announced a list of uneconomic pit closures backed by generous redundancy terms, Scargill took the bait and ordered strikes across the industry. The new union laws bit. Only half the pits voted locally to strike and Scargill dared not stage a national ballot. Instead illegal flying pickets were mobilized to intimidate backsliders in non-striking pits. It was war.

The strike saw Thatcher in a state of frenzy. She called it 'Mr Scargill's Insurrection' and referred to him as 'the enemy within'. But she knew that a mishandled pit strike could lead to a general strike, which she doubted she could withstand. She tried not to intervene but soon despaired of MacGregor's inept public statements and inclination to retreat. As the picket violence mounted Thatcher was forced to treat the police nationwide as virtually a national force. She had to be restrained from giving orders direct to chief police officers.[13] Pitched battles took place between strike-breaking miners, police and pickets, involving such medieval weaponry as sticks, catapults, shields, armour and horses. Thatcher was fighting for an abstract principle, the commercial viability of a British industry. Miners were fighting for their communities and way of life. The conflict was emotional and exceptionally bitter, with the strikers enjoying widespread public and media sympathy.

Scargill's failure to seek a national ballot was a crucial win for Thatcher. He authorized violent attacks on working miners and recklessly sought help from Colonel Gaddafi of Libya. He refused all overtures of compromise from intermediaries, much to Thatcher's relief. As for him so for her, this was a case of death or glory. Costly pay rises were even conceded by Thatcher to the railwaymen and pit overseers to keep them at arm's length from the dispute. She also specifically refused to invoke her new union laws

– and discouraged others from using them – lest this encourage a wider labour movement against her. By the end of winter 1984, sufficient coal was reaching power stations to avoid energy cuts. Miners, desperately short of money, were now trickling back to work and in March 1985 the strike collapsed exhausted.

The outcome was a victory for Thatcher's hard-headed and meticulous planning. As during the Falklands so with the miners she showed both strategic and tactical intelligence. But this was a victory she had to relish alone. The strike embarrassed the new Labour leader, Neil Kinnock, who found himself in the same plight as his predecessor, Michael Foot, during the Falklands War, unable to support nor yet fully oppose the government's actions. Scargill remained a hero of the left and was even voted 'person of the year' by a (suspect) BBC poll, while Thatcher ended the strike deeply unpopular. The SDP-Liberal Alliance briefly returned to its pre-Falklands prominence, overtaking the Tories and moving into second place behind Labour. The coal dispute was no Falklands triumph.

Thatcher understood that a fight with Scargill was inevitable if the nationalized sector was to be brought out of subsidy and within the pale of managerial discipline. The victory began a drastic shrinkage of what had been one of Britain's greatest industries, coal, but Thatcher still did not see her victory as a prelude to privatization. Indeed, part of her objection to Scargill was that he had seized as his own what she regarded as the nation's patrimony, its energy reserve. In her memoirs she pointed out, 'I never had regard to the commercial aspects [of the coal industry] alone.' She wanted to smash Scargill, simple as that. After the strike she claimed a particular debt to the working miners, especially in Nottinghamshire, for whom privatization would have seemed a betrayal. 'Where would we be if we had closed pits at which moderate miners had gone on working, and kept more profitable but more left-wing pits open?'[14] Thatcher was never to countenance talk of coal privatization.

Victory was achieved by Thatcher asserting the full power of central government and this she continued to strengthen. She had co-ordinated a national police operation and spent inordinate amounts of public money to buy off other unions that might have spread the strike. She had passed new laws to regulate what were free industrial associations. Britain's trade unions had been a legal eccentricity, traditionally operating under what amounted to charity law. They were now made subject to similar legal controls as other corporate institutions. By the late 1980s employment bills came before parliament almost annually, each one 'tidying up' the law. Acts in 1988 and 1990 extended strike ballots, curbed closed shops and made unions vulnerable to civil suits. The laws were an extension, not a 'rolling back', of state control. They honoured Thatcherism's desire for freer markets, but only at a high cost in regulatory intervention.

This did not go unnoticed. Each union reform was opposed across the political spectrum and Labour pledged itself to repeal every one. A young Labour MP for Sedgefield, newly elected in 1983, fulminated that it was 'unacceptable in a democratic society' for a government to interfere in the affairs of unions, even their enforcement of closed shops.[15] Applying democracy to union affairs, said Tony Blair, was 'self-righteous and sanctimonious pap'. He declared it to be disgraceful that 'an agreement freely entered into by two contracting parties should be torn up or smashed to smithereens in this cavalier fashion'.[16] Perhaps acknowledging some force in this, Thatcher continued to be a cautious labour reformer. Even after 1985 she worried about another miners' strike. She pretended in retrospect to have been on the side of radicalism, but the truth is that her reforms were both gradual and a success, honouring Prior's 'slow-track' approach. With hindsight, even John Hoskyns admitted that slow track was vindicated by the results.[17] At the end of her term in 1990, her regular confidant, Woodrow Wyatt, accused her of running away from further union reform.[18] She replied significantly that 'generalship must often be Fabian rather than Napoleonic.'

The battle with the miners showed a government determined to set an example to management across the economy as a whole, that the monopolistic power of labour could be withstood and the 'supply side' liberated. The example was copied immediately by one industry urgently in need of reform, printing and newspapers. The press was afflicted with near-intolerable management conditions after decades, indeed centuries, of monopoly union power. The unions were able to control the manufacture of a time-sensitive product, a newspaper, to a degree that was unlimited and extra-legal. False names, anarchic conditions and sudden strikes were beyond the wit of management. In 1983 an entrepreneur, Eddie Shah, was the first to make overt use of Thatcher's laws to de-unionize his Warrington plant. He was followed in 1985 by Rupert Murdoch's News International moving its entire Fleet Street production to a new computerized plant in

Wapping. Both operations were met with violence and vilification. But Wapping broke the power of the print unions across an entire industry. It revitalized the British press and brought a close bond between Thatcher and Murdoch.

The union reforms spread their effect across both public and private sectors of the economy. The sceptical Gilmour suggested that this was only because, after a long recession, labour was in a peculiarly weak bargaining position. Thatcher's victory thus 'registered rather than caused the decline in the unions'.[19] Had Gilmour been correct, there would have been a reversion to union power with economic recovery in the late 1980s. This there was not. Union membership fell from 13 million to 9 million within a decade. Days lost to strikes plummeted. British industrial productivity, long the laggard of Europe, began to improve, though not fast enough to save manufacturing from the challenge of the Far East. Britain was soon regarded as a stable, low-cost destination for inward investment. British car manufacturing (albeit not British-owned) went in a decade from being the least to the most efficient in Europe.

Even as Thatcher was girding her loins to fight the miners she was seeking to take the same message to Europe. Overseas was at first a tentative arena for her to show her spurs. She had no experience of foreign affairs. She hated being abroad. For most statesmen foreign trips are an interlude, a sabbatical. Tired and embattled at home, they are cosseted abroad, sleeping in fine rooms and eating exquisite food. Nightly boxes do not arrive and politics gives way to the autopilot of diplomatic protocol. None of this appealed to Thatcher. She had no small talk and hated tourism. She found that foreign leaders, with the signal exception of Reagan, patronized her. Commonwealth meetings were a particular torture and she behaved badly at most of them. Every hour was to her precious. On being told that an aide was on holiday, she is said to have remarked, 'Oh dear, poor man, is he so unhappy with us?'

None the less, domestic and foreign policy maintained a strident conversation throughout her rule. When she came to power, the central structure of foreign policy was the Cold War confrontation with Soviet communism. Dealing with it required no nuance, merely increased spending on defence and keeping close to America. Throughout the 1980s, and especially during the Reagan years, Thatcher's relations with America were 'special'. To her America was not really abroad and in Washington she enjoyed being greeted like a head of state. She could speak power to power and in English. Her later presence on the victors' rostrum at the end of the Cold War might be the luck of history, but she was there as an iron lady, embodying half a century of alliance against tyranny.

The one 'abroad' about which Thatcher had to care was Europe. She had long been an enthusiast, even posing in 1975 in a fiercely pro-Europe T-shirt. She attacked Wilson and Callaghan as not being 'at the heart of Europe'. Now she was to get a taste of the real medicine. Her first encounter with her European partners was over the question of a budget rebate to compensate for the generosity to France of the Common Agricultural Policy. This was then funnelling 90 per cent of the EEC budget to farmers, mostly in states reluctant to reform their agriculture as Britain had already done. Thatcher could not see why British taxpayers should subsidize less enterprising countries. She approached the rebate in 1980 much as Wellington approached Napoleon at Waterloo. She simply had to win, with or without allies. With domestic policy entangling her and the Falklands not yet a factor, she dared not seem weak on Europe. Germany's Helmut Schmidt and France's Valéry Giscard d'Estaing were established Euro-politicians disinclined to appease a female upstart, let alone one challenging their seniority in European affairs. The auguries were not good.

Thatcher battled for 'her money' for four years, breaking all the rules of diplomacy. Schmidt would shut his eyes while Thatcher ranted. Giscard always placed her at the furthest end of any dining table from himself. She wore them down and after a final flurry of aggression won her rebate at Fontainebleau in 1984. Carrington's final verdict was positive, that Thatcher got more money than might a softer approach.[20] She signalled to the rest of Europe that Britain was never going to be a compliant club member. The rebate argument was said by EU supporters to have damaged Britain's influence in Europe, but it was not clear how. It was certainly not an influence that British leaders dared put ahead of British interests.

The effect of Fontainebleau was refreshing. It was one of Thatcher's first post-Falklands foreign policy successes and gave her a glimpse of power on a wider stage. She sensed the ambition that comes to all prime ministers after any European success, that she might be 'at the heart of Europe' after all. She was still, she said in March 1984, 'a European idealist' and was told by her then foreign policy adviser, George Urban, that she might yet become 'Queen of Europe', the sort of language she liked.[21] Thus encouraged,

Thatcher made her one substantive contribution to the new architecture of Europe, the Single European Act. With her impeccably 'dry' Commissioner, Lord Cockfield, she plunged into the minutiae of what she hoped to fashion as a free-trading, market-perfecting measure. She signed up to what the Commission president, Jacques Delors, called the 'four liberties', free movement of goods, services, capital and people. It would create a Europe in which 'by 1992' all national monopolies and protections would end. She even accepted a political dimension, arguing strongly for qualified majority voting as necessary to discipline Europe's more protectionist and corporatist regimes. The act was, for her, a crash programme of Euro-Thatcherism. It was the first revolution gone international.

Thatcher was later accused by anti-Europeans of naivety over the Single European Act, which she signed in 1986. It was stuffed with powers to Brussels and the European Parliament and foretold tax harmonization and monetary union – it had been negotiated against a backdrop of intergovernmental councils seeking 'ever closer' political and monetary union. These features of the act certainly worried Thatcher who was trying to push one form of union, a proper common market, while others had a different agenda. She took the gamble, famously signing the treaty only after a long theatrical pause. Pauses do not negate signatures.

Cockfield's view was that Thatcher never fully understood the single market process, but 'simply deluded herself, believing what she wanted to believe'.[22] Delors and the other European leaders immediately began talks on monetary union. This process was to poison not just Britain's relations with Europe but British politics itself. It bedevilled Thatcher's relations with Howe and Lawson as it did John Major's administration and Blair's relations with Gordon Brown. Thatcher later confessed that she had not realized how far the Single European Act would whet the appetite of her partners in Europe for political union.[23] She should have realized that those who claim power to promote free markets may not deliver the markets, but they always keep the power. It was a tendency to which Thatcher herself was not immune.

After six years in Downing Street Thatcher was beginning to tire. In October 1984 she suffered a trauma that appeared to leave her unmoved, but unquestionably drove her back into herself. Direct rule in Northern Ireland had made 'seeking a solution' to IRA insurgency a longstanding Downing Street obsession. Thatcher had already endured the stress of resisting the 1981–2 Maze hunger strikes. She impressed her advisers by her refusal to countenance concessions or forced feeding. Despite scenes of intense emotion on both sides of the Atlantic, she did not move. After the death of Bobby Sands and nine others, the hunger strikes were called off but the tempo of terrorist bombing increased. This culminated in the attempted murder of the entire British cabinet during the 1984 Brighton party conference.

Today the outcome of the Grand Hotel bomb would have been a mass of retaliatory legislation, with leaders disappearing into bunkers and behind walls. Yet with bodies still being moved to the morgue, Thatcher calmly asked if the local Marks and Spencer could open early for those who had lost their clothes and rewrote her speech for the morning's conference session. I remember foreign journalists in Brighton being incredulous that Thatcher could appear within hours of an assassination attempt with no hair out of place. It was one of the most remarkable acts of personal courage by any prime minister since the Second World War. Thatcher was a rare leader to understand that terrorism was best answered by a studied normalcy.

No less extraordinary, the Brighton bomb caused only a brief hiatus in Thatcher's willingness to press ahead with a Northern Ireland deal. She bonded with a new Irish leader, Garret Fitzgerald, and came up with the Anglo-Irish Agreement of 1985. It was the most substantive attempt yet to square Irish republican aspirations with Unionist majority opinion. In the event it failed, as did Tony Blair's similar Good Friday agreement of 1998 fail to deliver devolved government. Thatcher later regretted it. She had been lukewarm towards Prior's 1982 concept of 'rolling devolution', of a gradual return to provincial self-government. As for genuine devolution to local democracy, she feared it might set a precedent for Wales and Scotland.[24] She approved plans to dismantle Ulster's county and city government, stripping out what might have been a buffer middle tier of political participation. This left an intransigent old guard on both sides of the Ulster divide to dominate politics in the province for a quarter-century of reactionary impotence.

The Brighton bomb left Thatcher both nervous and impatient, the more so when Indira Gandhi was assassinated a few weeks later. Denis gave her a watch inscribed, 'Every moment is precious'.[25] She allowed herself to retreat behind heightened security. Downing Street was gated. Those closest to her in public became bodyguards rather than political associates. A screen was formed between her and not just the public but her own ministers. The MP Emma Nicholson remarked that the bomb 'locked her away in a Nixonian bunker, staffed by overzealous ideological activists and cut off from the voters she needed to see and hear and touch.'[26]

By the mid-1980s Thatcher as prime minister had acquired a specific public persona. It was of a shrill, hard-edged, mercantilist approach to government. The freeing of markets and disciplining of public finances were making Britons rich, but critics tended to fasten on losers rather than winners. They saw white-collar jobs increasing, their incomes growing and taxed more lightly, while blue-collar jobs contracted and were more heavily taxed through duties on expenditure. This dichotomy became a leitmotif of public debate, giving Conservatives an uncaring image they found it increasingly hard to overcome. Thatcherism appeared to many Britons to embody class favouritism, indeed nothing short of an ideology of greed. When Norman Tebbit recalled that his unemployed father had 'got on his bike' to search for work, it was interpreted as a dismissive, Dickensian 'on yer bike' response to the jobless.

This critique made Thatcher ever more determined to be herself. The comparative asceticism of her office was a source of pride. She prevailed upon a Grantham grandee, Lord Brownlow, to lend her some Belton House silver for dinner parties at Downing Street and was televised showing Laurens van der Post round the house. But it would not have occurred to her to moot that something grander was more appropriate to a British leader. Downing Street staff were confined to official duties. There was no butler and only a cleaner for the prime minister's flat. Thatcher returned from an early visit to Balmoral aghast at the ten maids, footmen and other staff assigned to wait on her and Denis during their stay. In Downing Street she had to make her breakfast and supper alone.

Thatcher never exploited her office socially. Her entire career had aspired to a state of bourgeois grace. Yet when she reached the top of the ladder she was immune to its many undoubted delights, continuing to treat 'the whole traditional governing elite as made up predominantly of quislings and appeasers'.[27] Letwin recalled her dismissing 'metropolitan cliques such as the BBC and the toffee-nosed south-eastern establishment of Oxford and Cambridge, the Foreign Office and Athenaeum'[28] She seemed to resent having to stuff her cabinet with Oxbridge graduates. She told an astonished Sir Anthony Parsons, a relatively humble civil servant, 'You know, Tony, I'm very proud I don't belong to your class.'[29] This might be understandable from a proletarian outsider, but by no stretch of the imagination did that describe Thatcher. Her recasting of her image seemed complete.

If the socially gauche Thatcher found being loved beyond her capacity, she had no compunction about being feared. She did not seek out the great and good for company, choosing as her friends only those from whom she could expect agreement, and preferably adoration. There seems to have been no one in her entire circle who disagreed with her. Her insulation from the normal blandishments of office protected her from the pressure for consultation and consensus that comes with lunches, dinners and weekends with friends. She did not care for those who claimed to speak for others. She appointed herself the clan chief of the virtuous, hard-working, home-owning, car-driving upwardly mobile. The working class she regularly and shamelessly described as something from which any sensible person would want to escape.

This cantankerousness always handicapped Thatcher's implementation of her ideas, especially as they moved closer to her home base, the public sector. The chief early impact of the first revolution was on the private sector, on those afflicted by deflation and union reform or advanced by tax cuts and privatization. This was a sector of which, in truth, Thatcher knew little, much as she professed to love it. After 1984 she began to address the subject that was to dominate British domestic politics for the next two decades, the reform of public services. Here she was dealing with potent political and professional interests. They would require of her new reserves of application and, if not of diplomacy, then of aggression.

Thatcher never stopped being angry. She would start each day doing her hair to a chorus of whingeing farmers on the BBC's *Farming Today* programme, leading the agriculture ministry to endure irate early calls from her office. To farmers were added all she saw as guarding some closed shop, privilege or monopoly. They included civil servants outraged at being contradicted; soldiers threatened by defence reviews; state industry bosses dismissed as useless; the media whose scepticism was beyond any pale. Other enemies embraced occupations which had long regarded their income from the state as a right not a privilege – doctors, lawyers, teachers, academics and arts lobbyists. Thatcher's eye was that of a sniper constantly ranging over the plain, seeking a new victim to shoot. Never had a politician seemed less concerned with currying favour. Never had one so spoiled for a fight.

The reality was that Thatcher's colleagues found working for her increasingly stressful and exhausting. In the Westland dispute of 1986 she lost two able ministers, Michael Heseltine and Leon Brittan, as a result of chaotic man-management that brought her close to resigning. 'There were those in my own party and government who would like to take the opportunity of getting rid of me,' she admitted.[30] But it was her fault. Despite working closely with two dozen men for almost a decade, she showed no mellowing towards them, no joviality, no intimacy or social friendship. A number of them would later recall the sheer ghastliness of Thatcher's cabinets, her rudeness to others and her refusal to listen. She revelled in her depiction in the satire *Spitting Image* as a male-suited dominatrix. Dining with her cabinet she is shown ordering 'steak, raw of course'. When the waiter asks about the vegetables she replies, 'They'll have the same.' Lord Hurd criticized her 'failure over the years to make use of the cabinet system . . . which depends on mutual tolerance and support.'[31] I can hear her shouting, 'Tolerance! Support! What did they ever do for me?' It was an attitude that made the first revolution possible. It also made the second inevitable.

8

Enter the Second Revolution

The first revolution unquestionably rolled back one state frontier. By 1990, as a result of a series of industrial privatizations, some 600,000 people were no longer employed by the government. Their managers were called to commercial account as, eventually, were their workers. Cars and ships were no longer made by civil servants, nor were airlines, coaches, railway hotels or telephones run by them. By the end of Thatcher's second term a political and intellectual tide had turned. Alone in Europe Britain had sought a different way of structuring a political economy, by harnessing rather than curbing the dynamics of capitalism.

Thatcher did not hide her light under a bushel. She boasted that by the time she left office she had privatized half the state trading sector. As we have seen, her initial approach to privatization was hesitant and often less than pure. It involved an extension of state regulation, sometimes as interventionist as any public ownership. The frontier between the public and private sectors might have shifted but it was still patrolled by the state. The privatized utilities were quasi-monopolies more akin to Latin American 'parastatals'. Nor did privatization always mean a saving of public money, as the railways were later to prove. The government's failure to use its many powers under statute to curb the remuneration of utilities bosses ensured that the concept, like the word, was for ever associated in the public's mind with greed at public expense. As a result popular capitalism was accepted but never captured the imagination as Thatcher had hoped. Even in the mid-1990s less than a quarter of those regularly polled thought privatization was a good thing.[1] There was never a majority for selling the coal mines, railways or Post Office, which is why Thatcher never dared do so. But while she sold off the easier parts of the government domain, her acolytes were soon turning their attention to the rest. What of hospitals, schools, universities, prisons and asylums? Surely a medicine that was good for part of the state sector was good for all.

Here we come face to face with the persistent handicap to Thatcher's revolutionary zeal, herself. She might plead for the profit incentive as the best way of organizing a human activity, yet she was aware of what she appreciated as its human cost. She worried, 'Were not the attitudes required to get on in Thatcher's Britain causing the weak to be marginalised, homelessness to grow, communities to break down?'[2] Ever sensitive to what the Budgets of 1979–81 had meant to tens of thousands of people, she acknowledged the limits to Thatcherism set by popular consent. She might import into the public sector some of the disciplines that recession had visited on the private sector, but for most public services some means short of privatization must be found. Discipline must not mean loss of control. As always with Thatcher, reform 'must not undermine public confidence'.[3]

On any psychological spectrum from freedom to control there was no doubt where Thatcher stood. She might espouse freedom in theory, but in practice she craved control. Discipline was the necessary precondition of freedom. Her favourite biblical exegesis was on the parable of the Good Samaritan, in which she pointed out that he had to be rich before he could be charitable. Likewise the state had to be controlled and financed before it could dispense liberty. Thatcher's character, her whole body language, was that of an accumulator not a disperser of power. 'I believe in a strong state, strong to break the power of socialism ... I have never believed in letting things be.'[4]

The result was the most intensive refashioning of public services since the 1940s but in a fashion that was the opposite of Attlee's. He sent for whomever he thought the best man for a job – Morrison, Bevan or Silkin – and left him to get on with it. Thatcher had no faith in public-sector management. She appointed ministers and retained cabinet committees but she kept her hand always on the controls. Since she could not be everywhere at once, policy became vulnerable to her shrill interventions. She was a demon for detail but the methodical working through of policy from planning to implementation was not for her. As a result direction veered between radicalism and caution and ministers found it hard to read her mind. In addition, they were constantly afraid of the sack. Reform was blighted by ministers coming and going every few months. Nor did Thatcher allow them the support of political advisers, a breed she never trusted (except for her own). They would give ministers ideas above their station, and become power bases and leak machines. The total number of such advisers, paid for from party funds, was limited to ten.

Thatcher had a similar aversion to civil servants, a hangover from her unhappy time at the Department of Education. She described an early dinner with her permanent secretaries as 'one of the most dismal occasions of my entire time in government'.[5] It recalled to her the reported remark of a former head of the civil service, that its job in modern Britain was the 'orderly management of decline'. She abolished the civil service department, convinced that it was merely a reprise of her favourite television show, *Yes, Minister*. As a result she never got the best out of this cadre of experience and wisdom. She was determined to 'deprivilege' the civil service, expecting from it not advice but obedience, the obedience of an automaton.[6] It was a view Blair was to share.

To Thatcher and Lawson the failure of the public sector to deliver measurable improvements in services was a symptom of ingrained socialism. This had to change. If an activity was not suitable for privatization it must at least be managed by some proxy for it. This was implemented in a series of reforms initiated first by Sir Derek Rayner, then by Sir Robin Ibbs, culminating in a programme to hive off distinct government activities as semi-autonomous agencies, a distant echo of Morrison's 'arm's length' public corporations. These were to see their flowering under Major (see below) until they embraced over half the public sector. Their civil servants were no longer 'secretaries' but became executives, directors and managers. Each was increasingly chained to budgets, targets and performance assessments, quantified so incentives could be generated and rewarded. How else, said the first revolution, would people be motivated other than by money? The result was the introduction into government of tools drawn from the arcane world of management consultancy. They included re-engineering, internal pricing, out-sourcing and virtual markets, for everything from defence supplies to government hospitality. Visitors to Whitehall offices noted that doormen no longer knew the names of their ministers.

Inter-agency 'contracts' were established, usually of short duration. Purchasers had to be separated from providers and everyone defined as a buyer or a seller. This dichotomy, the 'purchaser/provider split', supposedly replicated the free market. Initially the impact was concentrated on Thatcher's favoured test-bed for radicalism, local government. Here the compulsory private tendering of subsidiary services, bitterly contested by the unions, was for the most part a success. Refuse disposal, street cleaning, housing repairs, hospital laundries, public catering, were either contracted out or benefited from the threat of it if kept in-house. The new labour laws and the prospect of privatization induced managers and unions to tighten their work practices. Private-sector disciplines were a success in local government.

These new disciplines produced another paradox of Thatcherism. Both private and public sectors offered services concerned with quality and value for money. But surveys throughout the 1980s and 1990s showed that civil servants were still primarily motivated not by money but by a sense of pub-lic service.[7] They acknowledged an 'ethos' in working for government distinct from that in the private sector. Privatization they could understand. But as we shall see under Gordon Brown, its partial application to public service left them confused. Was their accountability to the public as repre-sented by politicians, national or local, or to a Treasury bottom line? How could the users of a service be termed customers if it was free at the point of delivery? In any public service, who was now the leader and under what banner were they marching? Thatcher presented herself as the answer. But she brought to public service ceaseless upheaval, blood-letting and top-down reorganization. This was informed not by public inquiry or consensus but by consultancy out of ideology. The outcome was always contentious. Almost all the public services discussed below never settled down under later prime ministers. They have remained at the top of the league table of public dissatisfaction ever since, demanding ever more public money with no diminution of central control.

This reluctance on Thatcher's part to let go of any service that Lawson had not emphatically sold reflected a growing centralism towards many of the more formal estates of the realm. If she could not bend them to her will, they were condemned to irrelevance. To start at the top, the monarch's relationship with Thatcher should have been close, as between two women in positions of national leadership. By all accounts it was not. The Queen found Thatcher stiff and humourless and dreaded their meetings.[8] Thatcher regarded the Queen's rank as little short of sacred but its call on her weekly diary was a confounded waste of time. She loathed going to Balmoral, with its long picnics, boring people and cold walks.

To the Church of England Thatcher was less deferential. It was a body for which a former Methodist had little respect and she wielded with glee the powers conferred on her by church establishment. She began interfer-ing in episcopal appointments after years in which Downing Street had considered this wholly inappropriate. She adamantly refused to promote the left-wing Jim Thompson, Bishop of Stepney, and denied Canterbury to the intellectual (and far from left-wing) John Habgood, Archbishop of York, a gross insult to the leading churchman of the day. Downing Street insisted the job go to the evangelical, George Carey, who was never wholly at ease in the post.

Thatcher treated parliament with the respect due to its formal history and its status as her electoral college, but no more. She enjoyed question time as a stage on which she knew she could shine. Early in her office she had allowed St John-Stevas to set up specialist select committees, but she accorded them no power and expected them to remain firmly under the patronage and control of the whips. Thatcher's rare visits to the Commons' tearooms, pressed by her devoted parliamentary secretary, Ian Gow, were described by Alan Clark as terrifying 'search and destroy' missions. At the rumour of her approach, he said, whole rooms would empty, leaving only a handful of sycophantic supplicants for office. As for Thatcher's attitude to the media it was aloof incomprehension. She rarely read newspapers and relied on Bernard Ingham, her press secretary, to relate flattering or important items. Writers supporting her were rewarded with audiences that were hectoring monologues. Thatcher regarded press freedom as like bad weather, something that could not be helped but was never welcome. She was the last prime minister to regard the media as a residue of the democratic process and was unquestionably the stronger for it.

Thatcher's attitude towards the British Establishment was neither that of a constitutional conservative nor of a libertarian, more an irritated eccentric. Though she relished comparison with Elizabeth I – and had her Cecils, Leicesters and Walsinghams – she was far closer to Cromwell. She detested her old university, Cavalier Oxford, and it cannot have been wholly a coincidence that she gradually reduced the preponderance in her cabinet of Oxford men and replaced them with alumni of Roundhead Cambridge. Thatcher was no lover of old institutions, be they constitutional, intellectual, cultural or sporting. The only religion to which she showed unquestioning respect was Judaism. Her court was strongly Jewish and she was the first prime minister to knight and then ennoble the Chief Rabbi.

In examining the public services to which Thatcher directed her reformist attention we should note the many that she left alone. She was timid towards those for which she and her ministers had direct responsibility to parliament. She was bored by defence after (and before) the Falklands War and abandoned further defence reviews. She ignored the scandal of defence procurement, flattered by the courtly deference paid her by its chief beneficiary, GEC's Lord Weinstock. She avoided reforming the police and gave the security services equal protection. In roads and public transport she had no interest, beyond allowing Norman Fowler to privatize long-distance coaches. Farm subsidy was to her a creation of the European devil and beyond her ken or control. Pensions, housing benefit and social security were left untouched by her, even as costs soared and fraud proliferated. Challenged on these lacunae, she would always say, 'I can't do everything at once.' There was no coherent programme of public-sector reform. The revolution depended on the leader's will.

Attention thus fastened on a group of services whose leadership was at some remove from the heart of government, notably the health service, housing, schools and universities, urban renewal and local government. In most democracies these activities were either constitutionally protected or were regional, provincial or municipal in responsibility. Governments legislate for minimum standards and redistribute resources from rich areas to poor, but are little involved in setting priorities. To Thatcher these were just the services most afflicted by socialism, since they were in the grip of such incorrigibly socialist institutions as elected local councils and trade unions. They had to be purged by being brought within the penumbra of her office. Aspects of their delivery might be subject to private-sector discipline but never with loss of control. The purging of public-sector socialism was the engine of Thatcher's second revolution.

THE NATIONAL HEALTH SERVICE

Reform of the NHS has become the holy grail of British politics. For half a century the NHS was a nationalized industry, boasting without irony that it ranked second in size only to the Soviet Red Army. Its founders in the 1940s thought it would shrink in size and expense, since Beveridge had predicted a healthier nation would mean less need for doctors and hospitals. He was wrong. Wrong too was the decision to place the NHS directly in the charge of ministers. Attlee's local government minister, Herbert Morrison, had wanted socialized medicine to be run by local councils, pointing out proudly that London's municipalized hospitals were being imitated across Europe. They had been built and paid for by local benefactors and ratepayers, and should remain under their aegis. The health secretary, Bevan, who loathed Morrison's civic pomposity, nationalized the lot, and famously declared that the noise of 'any bedpan dropped on a hospital floor should be heard in the Palace of Westminster'.

Yet even Bevan did not carry this maxim to its managerial extreme. In setting up the NHS he sought 'a maximum decentralisation to local bodies, a minimum of itemised central approval.' He relied for economy 'not so much on a tight and detailed departmental grip but on the education of the bodies concerned' in the art of delegated management.[9] Local councils remained in charge of day clinics and community health care. Hospitals and GPs administered themselves through local committees, their bills sent to Whitehall for payment on demand. Not until 1974 was this structure seriously challenged. The Heath government began a process of centralization, taking clinics and community health care – as opposed to doctors and hospitals – away from local councils and establishing a new structure of regional and area health authorities under the NHS. This removed the last traces of local government involvement in medicine and began its true nationalization.

Thatcher was terrified of meddling with the NHS. She knew it was the darling of the electorate and could demand money with awful menaces. To her it was, like coal mines and railways, a no-go area for Tory reform. 'I always regarded the NHS and its basic principles as a fixed point in our policies,' she asserted.[10] In 1979 she allowed the health secretary, Patrick Jenkin, a small reorganization, supposedly to cut back on the bureaucracy inspired by the 1974 reorganization. He was determined to push responsibility downwards, with 'a minimum of interference by any central authority'. New health authorities would 'respond to local needs rather than be a conveyor for detailed orders and advice from the centre'.[11] Rudolph Klein, a seasoned observer of health politics, judged Jenkin's objective as a sincere attempt to decentralize responsibility and 'decentralize blame'.[12] It was to be the last such attempt for a quarter of a century.

A feature of Thatcherism's second revolution was always to assert as its objective the exact opposite of what it achieved. Within two years, Jenkin's NHS was accused of being out of control and in need of centralization. Jenkin was replaced by Norman Fowler, who declared that the NHS was not over-bureaucratized but 'under-managed'. The head of Sainsbury's, Roy Griffiths, was summoned. He was scathing about Jenkin's decentralization, concluding that 'if Florence Nightingale were carrying her lamp through the corridors of the NHS today, she would almost certainly be searching for people in charge.'[13]

Griffiths opened the floodgates. He recruited 200 chief executives to take over Fowler's regional and district health authorities, whose lay members were relegated to consultative status. These managers were required to report direct to an NHS board in London, from which emanated Whitehall's first battery of 'performance indicators' in 1983. Geographical authorities remained in place, as did hospital boards and GP committees, supposedly fixing 'clinical priorities'. But London was soon complaining that this control was not enough. It had '191 different National Health Services, rather than one single NHS operating in 191 districts'.[14] As long as the new managers had local boards, especially ones composed of Tory appointees, they would use them to lobby for more money from the centre. Authority chairmen caught between the Whitehall devil and the local deep blue sea naturally opted for the sea.

There now began a process of institutional centralization that took over twenty years and matched nothing outside the Soviet bloc. To deliver ministers some provable 'success' – and often to claim large bonuses – NHS managers were told to log waiting lists, appointments, referrals, lengths of stay, operations, incidents, peri-natal deaths, overall mortality rates, anything to which a number could be attached. The craving for statistics became obsessional, as did that for photo opportunities. Ministers would descend on hospitals like Great War officers inspecting trench accommodation. Edwina Currie would run her finger along a kitchen shelf to see if it was clean. Money was 'ring-fenced' for treatments that had headline value, for cervical smears, Aids tests, hip replacements or heart treatments.

Far from abating, the political hysteria surrounding the NHS increased with each twist in the centralist ratchet. By Thatcher's third election in 1987, health had moved to top of the political agenda. Central spending and monitoring rose to match. The size of the NHS budget increased by a phenomenal 30 per cent in real terms over the first seven years of Thatcher's rule. Yet she received no electoral reward for this, only brickbats. Beveridge could not have been more mistaken. The more care the state offered free, the more was demanded. Thatcher wailed about this 'bottomless financial pit' and even pondered what was anathema to her, a Royal Commission on the NHS.[15] Yet come the 1987 election she still fought shy of change, being 'reluctant to add the health service to the list of areas in which we were proposing fundamental reform'. Only when the election victory brought no relief and the winter of 1987 proved a horror of health scares, did she despair. The Griffiths structure had yielded local health boards 'waving shrouds' the length of Britain. The cabinet threw £100 million at the NHS to silence it over the winter, a straight political bribe, but no sooner was it given than more was demanded.

In December 1987 Thatcher cracked. She told the nation on the BBC's *Panorama* programme, apparently without consulting her health ministers, that the NHS should be totally reformed. She declared a mandate 'for the most far-reaching reform of the NHS in its 40-year history', though there was no such mention in her recent manifesto.[16] A team of ministers and experts was formed, with Thatcher in the chair, meeting in secret. She swiftly dismissed a bid for ideological glory from her then health secretary, John Moore, who offered eighteen options of varying degrees of political explosiveness, including insurance-based schemes with hospitals privatized. To Thatcher anything involving the exchange of money for health was politically unthinkable. She also joined with the Treasury in dismissing a hypothecated health tax. Such taxes either passed direct to the service and the Treasury lost control of them (such as BBC licences), or the Treasury kept control and they ceased to be hypothecated (such as vehicle licences). Thatcher became fascinated by the Treasury's politics, trying to work out what it really wanted as it tried 'to curb any radicalism of which it disapproved'.[17]

By mid-1988 the review was suffering from too many ideas and too little conviction. Thatcher turned to the cautious Kenneth Clarke as new health secretary and was now able to complain not of too much radicalism but of too little, a stance she found more comfortable. Real battle was joined between Clarke and Lawson at the Treasury. Thatcher moved towards a proposal from the American economist Alain Enthoven for an internal market in which 'money followed the patient' from doctor's surgery to hospital treatment. Hospitals would become independent, self-financing 'providers', competing for referral contracts from GPs who would hold cash-limited funds. The Treasury hated any scheme that took hospitals out of its direct control, fearing they would constantly demand money on pain of deaths or bankruptcies. As Lawson put it, human suffering 'will all too often be held to be the direct responsibility, if not the deliberate policy, of the government'.[18] That was true, but Lawson failed to see that this would be the more true the more responsibility was centralized on ministers in London.

Thatcher held fast to GPs becoming 'fund-holders' and hospitals becoming independent trusts. The Treasury, appalled at hospitals enjoying discretion over borrowing, insisted on their respecting Treasury borrowing controls. The resulting, blood-stained White Paper appeared in January 1989, claiming to be 'simulating within the NHS as many as possible of the advantages which the private sector and market choice offered, but without privatisation'.[19] It caused an explosion. Doctors, hospitals, patient groups and the Labour party fought it tooth and nail. Clarke received the brunt of the attack. The abuse from the British Medical Association was apoplectic, describing him as 'a thug and a bully who will be loathed by GPs till time immemorial because he produced a cock-eyed scheme moved by pure political dogma.'[20] GPs had fought Bevan to retain their financial autonomy, and now fought Clarke for daring to offer it back to them.

Hospital consultants had more to fear. Griffiths's managers were now to rule what would become 550 'trust hospitals' nationwide. The ability of a hospital to win referrals from local GPs would hold the key to its prosperity, with managers becoming dominant in fixing priorities and cutting costs to match cloth. They had to make hospitals more efficient and discipline doctors to ration resources. This finally became law in 1990. The Treasury now fought to recover in practice what it had lost in negotiation. It rendered illusory the autonomy of hospital trusts and, to a lesser extent, of GPs. The 'Treasury clauses' in the White Paper bit deep. Hospitals and general practices now found that they had been finally nationalized. As the White Paper had said, there would 'for the first time be a clear and effective chain of management command running from districts through regions to the chief executive and from there to the secretary of state'. All democratic representation on local health or regional health committees ceased. It was replaced by some 700 quangos, requiring 4,000 appointees and straining Tory patronage resources to the limits. Conservative councillors voted out of office in local elections were herded on to health quangos.

The so-called contracts between GP fund-holders and hospital trusts proved unenforceable at law. The Treasury pointed out that the hospital trusts were not corporate or legal entities but part of the NHS. Accident and emergency services had to remain open. Hospitals needed a stable income if they were to offer a 'core' range of treatments, and thus reached informal deals with groups of GPs. Clarke soon admitted that the contract principle, central to the ideology of the reform, was collapsing. Contracts, he told the Commons, were merely 'a different vocabulary in essentially the same bureaucratic environment'. They were another word for administration.[21] This was not the harsh wind of competition. Purchasers and providers, supposed antagonists in this virtual market, were not in contention but in bed.

While Thatcher dabbled in each area of government, the Treasury never slept. It was always 'following the money to its destination'. It retained full control over hospitals' borrowing and thus over investment. This inevitably pushed supposedly independent budgets back under the nose of the NHS. Since all staff pay deals were nationally negotiated, the Treasury claimed the right to vet all staffing matters, including posts and grades. Most astonishing, if any trust made a profit from its transactions the Treasury demanded to seize it and set it aside for future investment. The trusts thus fell into the same category as the still-nationalized utilities examined in the last chapter. They were wholly-owned subsidiaries of the Treasury. One observer, David Hughes, compared the NHS contracts with almost identical ones applied by Stalin to state enterprises under Gosplan.[22] Ten years later the NHS returned to exactly the same battlefield under Blair, with trust hospitals renamed 'foundations'. The arguments were the same and the disputants identical. So too was to be the outcome.

Thatcher's NHS reform traumatized both hospitals and general practice. Like all change it was bitterly opposed by its victims. Like all compromises it had good features as well as bad. It forced a service that had never considered priorities or cost-control to do so. But it lacked the courage to make 'money follows the patient' explicit, to make patients as well as doctors notice how much treatment cost. As both Klein and Lawson predicted, the effect was not just to nationalize responsibility but to nationalize blame. Ministers were held to account in parliament and the media for any and every decision taken throughout the NHS. At every election a waiting list was publicized, a failed operation trumpeted, a patient hauled before the cameras. As targets proliferated so did the expectation that ministers were responsible for meeting them. The prime minister became de facto the chief executive of every hospital in the land.

Ask any doctor whether the 1990 Act liberated or enslaved him or her and there is no doubt of the answer. Yet still the cash drained away, and still health remained at the top of the political agenda. The NHS revolution put in place by Thatcher failed the first test of any reform: as we shall see later it had to be repeated over and again. An attempt at decentralization led to nothing more than a reassertion of control. The first revolution had come to the aid of the NHS, but it had been overwhelmed by the second.

SCHOOLS

No minister was to prove more central to Thatcher's public service reform than Kenneth Baker. He came from the left of the party and was not listed among her loyalists. But he had three qualities essential to service in her cabinet. He was obedient, self-confident and had the hide of a rhinoceros. He was what Thatcher liked, a minister who gave her solutions not problems. When in 1986 she tired of the agonized inertia of her hero, Keith Joseph, at education she took a gamble and gave his job to Baker. There is no evidence that she wanted radical change. As with state pensions, she had been there before and not enjoyed it. Schools were indissolubly public, and privatizing them was unthinkable, yet she was constantly reminded of her failure to save grammar schools. When Baker suggested 'a fundamental reform of the education system' she was nervous, but told him to look into it.[23]

The school system Baker inherited from Joseph was essentially the one created by Anthony Crosland and Shirley Williams twenty years earlier. It no longer separated children at eleven into what were manifestly first- and second-class institutions. The principle of locality, the neighbourhood school, was widely accepted as the basis for primary and secondary state education as well as for post-school technical colleges. The system had bedded down reasonably well. Only in city centres did the social strains of race and deprivation inevitably leave many parents unhappy with the schools to which they were assigned. In these areas left-wing councils also polluted the reform with a vacuous brand of 'progressive' teaching. To Thatcher they were teaching socialism. Something must be done to stop them, something that was to obsess school reform for thirty years.

Thatcher was timid over entering what officials called 'the secret garden' of the professional autonomy of teachers. Callaghan had first mooted a core national syllabus as long ago as 1976. Whitehall had covert plans – the so-called Yellow Book – to take over the curriculum from the professional Schools Council should a minister be so inclined.[24] This was more than Thatcher was prepared to contemplate. With teacher militancy in full flood in 1986 the last thing she wanted was a head-on battle over who owned the curriculum. Besides, such dirigisme was French and 'would not be acceptable in Britain'.[25] The Institute of Economic Affairs concurred. Schools should offer a diverse syllabus and resist 'attempts by government ... to impose a curriculum, no matter how generally agreed they think it to be.'[26]

Thatcher's recollection of what happened next borders on the hilarious. She was unable to control Baker. His Education Reform Bill, to which he added the word great to dub it his 'gerbil', did everything she did not want. In the first place it brought the entire school curriculum within the ambit of central government, backed by a highly centralist testing regime. Thatcher tried to minimize the centralism by chairing the relevant cabinet sub-committee. But every time she turned her back Baker and his officials had seized another block of teaching hours, ending with 90 per cent of the school day ordained in Whitehall. Subject lobbies and teaching unions were soon crawling everywhere. Thatcher wailed that 'the original simplicity of the scheme had been lost'.[27] She found proposals variously 'disappointing ... flawed ... unsatisfactory ... appalling'. The cabinet gleefully obeyed Parkinson's law of triviality and spent hours rewriting the mathematics and history curriculums. Ministers who would agree a billion-pound missile design wrangled over when history began or whether an English adviser was ideologically sound.

The new curriculum was supposedly directed at giving children 'the competitive skills they need for this new world'. In fact the balance was uncannily similar to Whitehall's last attempt to write such a curriculum, the 1904 School Regulations (now with French replacing Latin). That collapsed for being overly prescriptive. The curriculum denied any flexibility or choice, whether for parents, pupils, teachers or schools. It also needed an assessment bureaucracy running to 800 new staff. The new bill was vast, requiring 570 amendments in the Lords alone, and was dubbed by the *Modern Law Review*, 'the high point of elective dictatorship'.[28] Maurice Kogan suggested that no other profession in Britain was subject to such detailed central control over its work.[29]

Thatcher herself let out a final cry, 'I had no wish to put teachers in a straitjacket . . . The whole system was very different from that which I originally envisaged.' She admitted that it was 'my most important centralising measure' and that 'by the time I left office I was convinced that there would have to be a new drive to simplify it.'[30] Thatcher may have been exasperated by the 1988 Act, the biggest of her term of office, but it was a product of her susceptibility to ministers more radical than herself. As education secretary she had not interfered in what had been the preserve of professional teachers and local officials. Now she was dragged by Baker against her instincts towards her apparent beliefs. She found it uncomfortable.

Thatcher's nationalization of the curriculum at least had a Napoleonic coherence to it. Baker's plan for a new framework of secondary education was shambolic. The conventional Tory policy on secondary schools was to espouse some vague concept of parental choice, which in most places outside London was meaningless without long car journeys. Children went to their local school and parents simply wanted it to be good. In the cities, choice could only mean fleeing bad schools by moving house. It was often used as code for selection not of schools by parents but of parents by schools. Since selection had traditionally offered bright working-class children escape from deprived backgrounds, it held iconic attractions to Tory reformers, especially as the memories of the 1960s began to fade.

In her first parliament Thatcher honoured 'working-class escape' by offering state scholarships, known as 'assisted places', to 30,000 children at independent schools. In the event, most were offspring of distressed middle-class parents and the subsidy merely rescued many lesser public schools from closure. Thatcher resisted Joseph's dalliance with the IEA's school vouchers, which critics claimed would lead to ambitious parents cramming to get into one of a few favoured and therefore selective schools. For Thatcher this was a radicalism too far. She was not going to reintroduce selection at eleven in whatever guise (Blair was to prove less fastidious).

Baker now found himself trapped between Thatcher's nervousness of stripping councils of control over 'their' schools and Lawson's determination to 'wrench the schools from the so-called local education authorities'.[31] He duly augmented the assisted places' scheme with a plan for what amounted to Whitehall grammar schools, City Technology Colleges

(CTCs). Baker exempted these institutions from his curricular dirigisme and let them specialize in technology, a subject that could not be entrusted to 'reactionary local education authorities'. Just fifteen were eventually set up at four times their intended cost.[32] Exactly the same was to be true of Blair's imitation CTCs, the city academies.

Next Baker pandered to Lawson's antagonism to local government by legislating for any school to 'opt out' of local control into grant-maintained status. They would join CTCs in what amounted to a parallel, government-run school system. As an inducement to opt out, such schools would receive a gratuitous 15 per cent enhancement in their per capita budgets. Baker's hope (and Thatcher's) was that these would be old grammar schools, expanding in response to demand. They would not be allowed, initially, to 'select' their intake but if they were popular this was unavoidable. Thatcher confidently declared that 'most schools will opt out' of any link with the 'hard-left education authorities and extremist teachers'.[33]

The Treasury was caught in a familiar paradox. It wanted more control over schools but Baker was offering only half control, which was worse than leaving be. Accordingly it fought the proposal for a network of autonomous state schools for the same reason it fought trust hospitals. They would be expensive and render impossible the proper planning of capacity, since such public institutions were not a fluid market. Good ones did not necessarily want to expand and dilute their character, especially with the growth of exam league tables. In the event opting-out, intended as a slap in the face of local councils, was a complete failure. Fewer than 1,000 primary and secondary schools out of 24,000 in England and Wales chose this route, half of them in just eight 'difficult' city areas. Even then the ones that went were those threatened with closure not for being popular but for being under-subscribed, exactly the outcome the Treasury had feared. Since opted-out schools came under Whitehall control, the Treasury duly banned any school, local or national, from expanding if there were spare places in its neighbourhood. This negated the 'free-market' feature of the policy. Meanwhile a sensible reform forced councils to give more budgetary freedom to heads and governors under so-called 'local management of schools'. The success of this devolution further diminished the attraction of opting-out.

Thatcher was aware in retrospect of the paradox of what she had allowed Baker to do. She had not increased parental choice and insofar as grant-maintained and opted-out schools were a return to selection at eleven, they were a return to state direction. The idea that 'the state should select children by the simple criterion of ability' and direct them to specialist institutions was, she wrote, 'far more consonant with socialism and collectivism than with the spontaneous social order associated with liberalism and conservatism. State selection by ability is a form of man-power planning.'[34] One can almost hear the ghosts of the IEA crying out, 'and now you realize!'

As so often Thatcher seemed trapped by her yearning for control. She had allowed Baker to push some schools in the direction advocated by Lawson, towards a national education service. She had let Lawson take control of teachers' pay and conditions of service and turn them, like NHS staff, into de facto civil servants. The theory, fallacious as it turned out, was that Treasury pay negotiators would prove tougher than local author-ity ones. (They were as susceptible to teachers as to doctors and nurses.) The will of central government was thus imposed on education more firmly than under Labour but in a fragmented, unstable fashion. The dichotomy between enhanced centralism and demoralized localism was a mess. Thatcher, the lover of liberty, had struggled with Thatcher, the lover of control, and lost.

UNIVERSITIES

Thatcher half implied that the extension of government control over schools was unintentional. She had allowed Baker his head and his officials relapsed into default mode, bureaucratic imperialism. This had led to 'a confusion'. In higher education there was no such confusion. Britain's supposedly autonomous universities and colleges were nationalized by Baker and brought under direct government control. Here he was pushing at an open door with Thatcher. She hated universities. The few right-wing academics whom she admired, such as Patrick Minford, Maurice Cowling and Michael Howard, were treated as heroic refugees from some totalitarian Colditz. Campbell traced this antipathy to her time at Oxford, but it also reflected her scepticism towards any community of opinionated people beyond her remit. She blamed the universities for what was wrong with Britain, for taking in young people who 'then have every decent value pounded out of them' – and at public expense.[35]

The universities were punished for being left-wing, and severely so. They suffered worse than any public service in Howe's cuts of 1980–82, losing 5 per cent a year from their overall budget in real terms. When in 1985 Thatcher's old university, Oxford, denied her the customary honorary degree she showed an unusually thin skin. It convinced her that higher education too was in the grip of socialism. 'I went to Oxford University, but I've never let it hold me back,' she said in 1989, ignoring its role in launching her career.[36] Tory support among academics at the 1987 election fell to just 18 per cent.[37]

In 1979 state funding of universities was still much as it was after the Great War. The University Grants Committee (UGC), composed of academics, was an independent body in receipt of a Treasury grant, like the Arts Council. The UGC, said its historian, was 'a guarantee that the state itself would not seek to undermine academic autonomy.'[38] The UGC financed a third of university spending, the rest chiefly coming from fees paid by local authorities, reimbursed by the Treasury. Since this fee income was 'demand-led', universities could in theory increase it at will and thus retain their independence. The Treasury refused to permit such fee rises (which it had to finance) on pain of losing UGC grant. This drove universities into ever greater dependence on UGC grants, controlled overall by the Treasury, and on overseas student fees, which soared. Universities might be independent charities, but the state paid the piper even if it did not yet call the tune.

Serious Thatcherites wanted to leave universities alone as independent institutions, free to charge fees and with the state merely financing poor students on demand, a de facto voucher scheme not unlike what had happened in practice. The Treasury opposed this root and branch. It would lose all control over university numbers and planning. Instead it raised overseas student fees, which it did not have to pay, and halved domestic student fees, compensating for this through UGC funds which it could more directly control. The chairman of the UGC, Sir Edward Parkes, could not have been more explicit. Under Thatcher, he said, there would have to be 'a somewhat greater degree of direct intervention in the affairs of individual universities than has been customary or necessary in the past.'[39]

During his time at education (1981–6), Joseph struggled to defend the UGC and the integrity of its decisions, even as it wrestled with Treasury cuts. The impact was dire. Aberdeen and some London colleges came close to bankruptcy. Salford halved in size and staff were forced into early retirement. Lecturers were soon earning less than police officers and nurses. Campbell remarked, with a grain of self-interest, that 'no group in society with the possible exception of trade union leaders suffered a steeper fall in status' under Thatcher.[40] But Joseph at least held to the UGC arm's-length principle, and that of academic autonomy which depended on it.

Baker was having none of this. A White Paper, 'Meeting the Challenge',[41] was the basis of the university clauses of the 1988 Education Reform Act. It had nothing to do with curbing spending, which the Treasury and the UGC had already shown they could achieve under the existing regime. The paper was directed specifically at control and began with a most un-Thatcherite assertion:

The government considers student demand alone to be an insufficient basis for the planning of higher education. A major determinant must also be demands for highly qualified manpower, stimulated in part by the success of the government's own economic and social policies.

This was heading in only one direction. Baker proceeded to abolish the UGC and 'bring higher education closer to the world of business'. He set up a new state funding council, on which academics would be in a minority. It would consider 'employers' requirements for recruits' at differing levels of qualification. If graduate output was not 'in line with the economy's needs ... government will consider whether the planning framework will be adjusted.'

The wording of Baker's paper was extraordinarily statist. The economy's needs were to be expressed in a 'contract' with each institution, a concept then being applied (abortively) to hospitals. More important, grants to universities moved from a five-year to an annual cycle. This would enable 'detailed reviews of particular aspects of universities' work, by subject or otherwise, to be conducted continuously'. The contract stipulated that grant could be withheld by Whitehall if 'the provision contracted for cannot be delivered'. There was no scope for appeal or arbitration, meaning that courses might be cancelled and students laid off in mid-year. As with NHS trusts, this was not so much a contract, more a framework of direction and the word contract was soon abandoned. Baker told Thatcher that universities should answer to 'the nation's needs' as reflected in 'specific policy developments'. It was Leninism. Such was Thatcher's hatred of the sector that she seems, at this stage, not to have minded in the least.

Baker did not stop at universities. He found intolerable the continued existence of a separate local authority sector of higher education, polytechnics and colleges of further education. These comprised 40 per cent of Britain's post-school education, including nursing and teacher-training colleges, art schools, craft institutes, naval, mining and metalwork schools and even colleges for the clergy. Often as old as universities, they were among the jewels of civic pride. Most were explicitly attuned to Baker's 'manpower needs' through their links with local industries. They also offered young people a genuine choice of post-school education, exactly the diversity Tories claimed to want. There was no good reason for breaking the link between these institutions and their local bases (though many principals were certainly eager to break it). Yet Baker's aversion to localism was reinforced by the Treasury's desire to see the 'comprehensivization' of higher education as an aid to resource planning. He accordingly nationalized local colleges as ruthlessly as Bevan had done municipal hospitals. The creations of local benefactors down the ages were simply expropriated. Governors were sacked. Specialism vanished in the face of central targets. Almost any college was allowed to call itself a university.

Baker then delivered his *coup de grâce*. He ended the tradition of academic tenure, considered a bulwark of academic freedom since the Middle Ages. He simply outlawed it and made academics as vulnerable to sacking as any salaried employee. To John Griffith, London University professor of administrative law, this was not just an invasion of autonomy but 'an almost total usurpation, a dissolution of the university system comparable to the dissolution of the monasteries'.[42] Baker was indeed ridding Thatcher of her turbulent priests. Universities were no longer engaged in the disinterested pursuit of learning (any more than were Thatcher's schoolteachers). They were treated like fifteenth-century abbeys, full of corrupt priors and libidinous nuns.

That British universities needed reform was hardly in dispute. But higher education had few of the geographical constraints of schools. They were less susceptible to parental ambition and social classification. As such they would have been well-suited to money-follows-the-student on the American model or money-follows-the-patient in health. Right-wing academics had in 1974 made an effort to establish such an institution, the University College of Buckingham, free of government grant. It became a retreat for distressed Thatcherites and Thatcher herself became its patron. But elsewhere the

Treasury piper could not resist calling the tune. Most extraordinary is that the universities put up so weak a defence of their autonomy. Thatcher appeared to be right. University dons minded less about academic integrity than about losing their grants, and in the end they lost both.

The Education Reform Act contained no trace of Thatcher's first revolution. It turned a decentralized portion of the public sector over to central government, justifying it on grounds of state economic planning. Baker was more interventionist than any socialist had dared be. The phrase, 'the nation's manpower needs', littered his White Paper. Civil servants and economists, not professional teachers or scholars, would in future assess the worth of academic courses and the research needs of the state. As John Ashworth, a former Thatcher adviser and head of Salford University, ruefully remarked, 'They are privatising everyone else and nationalising us.'[43] Many victims of Thatcher's second revolution thought likewise.

As so often, Thatcher herself was alert to these contradictions. She reflected that she had made universities more efficient, but might perhaps have infringed their 'future autonomy and academic integrity'.[44] She conceded that 'many distinguished academics thought that Thatcherism in education meant a philistine subordination of scholarship to the immediate requirements of vocational training.' This, she said, was 'certainly no part of my kind of Thatcherism'. As for whose it was, the answer lay with the Treasury, increasingly the powerhouse of the second revolution. Lawson and his education aide, John Anson, were determined to bring the burgeoning education budget under the same direct control as that of the NHS. It meant bringing to Whitehall's heel a wide range of institutions that had long embodied the pluralism of the British public sector.[45] Thatcher herself remained as hesitant about this as she was about the curriculum. In 1990 she asked her policy chief, Brian Griffiths, to revisit the Baker project. She had been badgered by enough Tory academics to begin to worry if she had behaved in a less-than-Conservative fashion. She asked Griffiths to work up a plan 'to give leading universities much more independence' and thus achieve 'a radical decentralisation of the whole system.'[46] Having grasped power she declared an intention to cede it. She was toppled before such revisionism could be effected.

HOUSING

At the start of the Thatcher era housing rated higher than health or education in the hierarchy of political issues. For Thatcher home-ownership
embodied all the vigorous Tory virtues: secure savings, family values, house-
hold gods, a lifetime of hard work rewarded. If the state had any role in
housing it should be to express those virtues in bricks and mortar. By contrast, council houses symbolized vices: dependency, lack of home-pride,
something-for-nothing and individuals enslaved to the state. Small wonder
home-owners voted Tory in 1983 by three to one, while council tenants
voted Labour by two to one.[47]

The result was to make housing an area in which Thatcher was at her
most paradoxical. She regarded policy as a means to a social end. She was
adamant that the state should use its resources to help people own houses.
The form this took was tax relief on mortgage interest payments. Despite
annual pleadings from the Treasury, she regarded 'middle-class subsidies'
as a fit compensation for years of taxes spent on the undeserving poor. She
was likewise insistent on tax relief for private health insurance (confined by
the Treasury to pensioners) and assisted places at private schools. Thatcher
called this 'socially desirable' expenditure. It was her sort of social engineering, her bourgeois revanchism.

The cost of mortgage interest tax relief under the Tories rose fast. It
increased by 200 per cent in real terms between 1980 and 1990, to stand
at £7 billion. Howe called the relief 'a glaring anomaly, distorting the housing market almost as much as rent control ... and unjustly favouring the
better off.'[48] Thatcher was accused of channelling the nation's savings into
bricks and mortar rather than productive industry. Her retort was astonishing for a champion of popular capitalism: 'However pervasive an enterprise
culture is, most people are not born entrepreneurs.'[49] Whenever Treasury
ministers questioned the subsidy Thatcher became so angry she threatened
to increase rather than cut it – there being no question of a collective cabinet
decision on the matter. Lawson pointed out that home-owners were merely
raising tax-free endowments on their houses to finance luxury consumption.
To him this was inflationary madness. Thatcher did not care.

Needless to say local councils and their tenants enjoyed no such indulgence. When Thatcher was briefly an Opposition housing spokesman in

1974, I offered to show her examples of London's good and bad council estates. She cut me short. 'No, there are only bad ones.'[50] Of all her reforms, the one of which she was eventually most proud was the right to buy a council house. The policy had originated, ironically, with one of her most wet ministers, Peter Walker, but it did not prove easy. When expropriating colleges from their trustees, Thatcher proceeded on the basis that they would remain in the public sector and no compensation was payable, for instance to local sponsors. When ordering councils to sell houses, built partly with local money, she felt she should at least leave the receipts with the locality. The houses served a charitable purpose which would be vitiated by disposal. But Thatcher had no desire to leave local authorities to disperse the money. She meant to control it. She was determined to impose her own view of how the nation's housing stock should be financed and allocated.

From 1980 Thatcher was passing new housing acts virtually every year. They were as furiously contested as her trade union legislation. When some councils refused to sell or advertise for sale, the Master of the Rolls, Lord Denning, remarked that section 23 of the 1980 Housing Act, was 'a most coercive power . . . that enables central government to interfere with a high hand over local authorities'.[51] Even a Tory back-bencher remarked that it was all very well making a Tory minister 'the gauleiter of housing, but on these benches we should remember that the next gauleiter could be a commissar.'[52] It was a fitting comment on many of Thatcher's reforms. As if to show even-handedness, Thatcher passed a law compelling all large private landlords as well as public to offer freeholds to tenants. This secured an exotic alliance of Liverpool's far-left Militant Tendency with the aristocratic owner of Belgravia, the Duke of Westminster. They fought Thatcher hand in hand but only the duke won.

Yet the houses sold. By the end of Thatcher's reign a million and a quarter title deeds had passed to tenants. Most council anger had been directed at Thatcher's insistence on discounts of up to 60 per cent, crudely spending their assets to boost the success of her policy. The loss was to local councils but the cash was real. Sales raised £18 billion during the 1980s, making house sales by far the biggest of Thatcher's privatizations, at 43 per cent of total receipts. The cost of discounting was estimated at £2 billion overall.[53] For its part the Treasury could not bear to see so much money pouring into council coffers. Lawson used his power over local borrowing to restrict the use of right-to-buy revenue for investment, even investment in housing. After 1984, as the balances swelled, he limited their use by councils first to 50 per cent, then 40 per cent, then 20 per cent of what was available. He was determined to treat the money as his own. When in 1987 he boasted a £1 billion undershoot in overall public borrowing he did not mention that it reflected a surge of £2 billion that year in right-to-buy receipts.

The policy withered after Thatcher's departure. Sales proved to have been mostly of houses with gardens on suburban estates. Since they were to sitting tenants who, under the terms of the discounts, could not immediately sell on, the price was in reality an amortization of future rent. Inner-city flats remained unsold until the 1990s when the 1988 Housing Act allowed sales to housing associations and, eventually, to private developers. Thatcher was more interested in giving established suburban tenants a step into the middle class than in some notional freeing of the housing market. In crude terms she appropriated assets that were not central government's, sold them privately to their occupants and used the money as collateral for central government borrowing. Whether or not she understood this, Lawson did.

While council houses were being sold, they were not being built. In the 1970s, local councils built or restored 200,000 units a year. By the end of the 1980s the total was down to 13,000 and falling. A chapter in the history of civic Britain was clearly coming to an end. The government baldly stated in a 1986 White Paper that, as far as housing was concerned, its 'leading policy aim is to encourage home ownership'.[54] This left unresolved the remaining statutory obligation on councils to meet need, including that of homeless, single-parent families and new immigrants. If every house were sold off, how could this requirement be met?

Thatcher's response to this question was intriguing. It was to regard 'my enemy's enemy as my friend'. Charitable housing associations had long complemented local council housing departments, usually more efficiently. Thatcher duly lavished praise on them. Housing associations received 90 per cent of their money direct from central government through a quango, the Housing Corporation. This body could now do no wrong. In 1979 the corporation had 100 staff and a budget of £50 million. When Thatcher left it had 700 staff and a budget of £1 billion. It was sponsoring the construction of three times as many houses as were local councils. The Housing Corporation was, in effect, a state bank lending to the not-for-profit private rented sector. The corporation was boosted by Howe's early insistence that all public-sector rents be at 'market levels'. This had an immediate impact on an area of policy which Thatcher was wary of touching, social security. Poor tenants, whether council or housing association, applied to have their rising rents covered by housing benefit. This doubled under Thatcher, from covering 40 per cent of council rents to covering 65 per cent, while total spending on rent support rocketed upwards.

This in turn led to a remarkable parallelism. Housing figures over the decade (at 1987 prices) showed the two arms of policy almost exactly cancelling each other out. Local council rent subsidies fell from £3.5 billion to £1.4 billion, while personal housing benefit, usually to the same tenants, rose from £1.8 billion to £3.6 billion. Meanwhile subsidies for new building by councils and housing associations together fell from £5.3 billion to £1.3 billion, while mortgage subsidies to private home-owners rose from £2.6 billion to £5.2 billion. In other words public expenditure on housing simply shifted from a cash-limited local budget, which councils had some incentive to police, to a demand-led central one, which no one policed. Though supposedly means-tested, central benefits have always proved harder to control than local ones. In her obsession with freeing an area of policy from local 'socialism', Thatcher left the Treasury more exposed to an ever more burdensome central commitment. When Thatcher left office the government was spending more in real terms on housing subsidy than when she arrived. The second revolution had defeated itself.

In her 1987 election manifesto Thatcher showed some awareness that housing policy had become detached from housing need. She was doing exactly what she had warned Heath might happen in 1974, that intervention risked inflating house prices and then subsidizing the resulting inflation and housing deprivation. Her response to the poor image of inner-city housing was a burst of ad hoc initiatives which came to characterize all Whitehall intervention in this area of the welfare state. The late 1980s saw Housing Action Trusts, Community Housing Trusts, Urban Housing Renewal Units and Priority Estates Projects. Under Major and Blair the pace of such intervention quickened, except that the names were of the 1990s: Estate Action, Rough Sleeper, Tenant Choice.

CIVIC BRITAIN

Civic government in Britain virtually collapsed in the thirty years after the Second World War. While other European cities were struggling to reinvent and revive themselves, urban Britain stagnated. Government by tired party cabals and committees left it vulnerable to domination first by Conservative property interests and then by Labour union activists. Contact with the generality of citizens was lost. Whig historians had long attributed Britain's protection from revolution to vigorous civic autonomy. This autonomy, wrote Tristram Hunt, fuelled the pride that was 'channelled energetically into building the new Jerusalem'.[55] Provincial innovation stimulated most of the early health and housing reforms brought before parliament. The welfare state was led from town halls not parliament.

By the 1970s British cities were symbolized by monotonous, brutalist redevelopment of a bleakness seen elsewhere only in Eastern Europe. Acres of Georgian and Victorian buildings were swept away. Rectangular blocks and towers rose in their place, defacing the centres of Birmingham, Manchester, Newcastle, Leeds and Bradford. There was little sign of the economic renewal led by enterprising mayors in America's rustbelt. There were no elected mayors and scant local initiative. Thatcher's environment secretary, Michael Heseltine, could reasonably protest on taking office in 1979 that as far as urban renewal was concerned, 'Nothing's happening.' He declined to ask why.

Of all 'Victorian values' that a daughter of a Grantham mayor might be thought eager to espouse, civic pride was surely one. In Britain it might be corrupted by socialism, but surely Thatcherism could revive it by cleansing the conduits of local accountability, enforcing privatization and summoning the middle classes to civic leadership. Yet Thatcher reacted as she did to the shortcomings of the NHS and education. She gathered to herself another corner of the public sector and placed it in the lap of central government.

Thatcher had always suspected Michael Heseltine of being after her job and could not bear to attend his popular conference speeches. He was the only one of her ministers to have a genuine personal following in the party. But she could not deny his energy and presentational skill and she shrewdly decided to throw him at the cities. As her first environment secretary he had within six months of taking office invented Urban Development Corporations (UDCs), to bring renewal to Liverpool's and London's docklands. They were followed by nine more for Cardiff, Manchester, Salford, Leeds, Sheffield, Tyneside, Teesside, West Midlands and Bristol. The model was Attlee's new town corporations, appointed by ministers and operating, said Heseltine, 'free from the inevitable delays of the democratic process ... which looked too much to the past and too exclusively to the aspirations of the existing population.'[56]

Heseltine was ruthless. No local councillor was allowed on a corporation board. Any friction between the UDCs and local leaders would be referred to Whitehall and settled in favour of the former. The UDCs were creatures of central government. What was second nature abroad, civic renewal through elected leadership, was to Heseltine beyond the capacity of the British people. He and Thatcher did not reform local democracy, they dispensed with it. The UDCs were given grants not available to elected councils. In Newcastle the council leader, Jeremy Beecham, told me he had no discretionary money to promote any new development, not even to paint the bridges over the Tyne. The only money for his city was available 'down the road' at the UDC offices on the old dockside.

Grants were turbocharged into Heseltine's six urban Enterprise Zones. Here firms not only enjoyed large sums in infrastructure spending but were free of central and local taxes. On London's Isle of Dogs, a huge tower, Canary Wharf, rose into the sky, serviced by Europe's most expensive stretch of road, the Limehouse Link, and the most expensive urban transit system, the Jubilee Line extension. Both were given priority over other metropolitan projects on the personal orders of Thatcher. Canary Wharf, though a totem of Thatcherite private enterprise, had little to do with enterprise and everything with subsidy in the form of grants and tax breaks. It was built by the taxpayer for its first owners, much admired by Thatcher, the Reichman Brothers, whose company still went into receivership building it.

Heseltine's UDCs were in their own terms a success. They did attract new investment to desperate areas. Whether similar sums might have achieved the same goal if targeted through reformed local councils was never tested. British cities were banned from being masters of their own fate. With their revenue and borrowing capped they could raise no money for themselves. Development finance was recast in the form of 'challenge grants'. To rebuild their infrastructure cities had to seek help and permission from Whitehall and place themselves under the leadership of local or national businesses. Thatcher preferred to stimulate local capitalism through central government.

The leadership of most world cities was built on dynamic mayors or governors. Willy Brandt, Jacques Chirac, Ronald Reagan, Bill Clinton and George W. Bush all served their political apprenticeship through local democratic office. They had civic boosterism in their blood. They promoted development by patronage and the manipulation of local finance. The mayor of New York had six separate taxes to manage. When Chirac wanted Paris cleaned as mayor, he raised a tax and cleaned it. Britain was wholly different. Its local leaders emerged from party cabals, usually composed of those unsuccessful on the ladder to national politics. Since rate-capping they had no discretionary resources to barter with local business. As they grew more impotent, they behaved impotently. They acted less as leaders, more as burghers of Calais, poor supplicants to a distant power.

The 1983 Tory manifesto declared a new framework for urban government, set out in a White Paper euphemistically entitled 'Streamlining the Cities'. This claimed that there was 'no basis in need' for the metropolitan authorities created by the Heath government in 1974 and offering regional services to areas such as Merseyside (based on Liverpool), West Midlands (Birmingham), Avon (Bristol) and others. Run by Labour groups in thrall to local trade unions, their passing was mourned by few. The White Paper divided them into their previous city and suburban components. Yet the functions of these metropolitan authorities were not delegated down to the subordinate city councils, but were run by a myriad of ad hoc quangos appointed by London, administering services such as police, fire and transport. It was not less government that Thatcherism wanted, just less local government.

In London the same medicine was administered, but more dramatically. Ken Livingstone's Greater London Council was abolished. Here the relevant minister, Patrick Jenkin, claimed that the abolition of the GLC and its century-old administration at County Hall would mean that local boroughs would take over all its powers. Only 'flood protection . . . and a few minor functions' would stay 'metropolitan'. This was untrue. The powers of the GLC were almost all assumed not by the boroughs but by a government Office for London in Whitehall. This operated alongside an astonishing array of fifty new quangos with an alphabet soup of acronyms

(LPAC, LRT, LTB, LRC, LBGC, LWRA).[57] They ran public transport, the Thames, museums, the arts, sport and even the South Bank Centre. The government set up groups with names such as London Forum, London First and even the ironic London Pride. By 1990 there were some 12,000 laymen and women running London on an appointed basis against just 1,900 elected borough councillors. It was a remarkable constitutional shift from representative to patronage government. Nor did Jenkin trust his quangos. He told parliament in 1983, 'There will remain the need for an overview . . . I shall where necessary give planning guidance to the boroughs and districts.'[58]

Three years later London voters impudently returned a Labour majority on the last surviving pan-London elected body, the Inner London Education Authority. Thatcher promptly abolished it. The whole London saga was crudely dictatorial. In every subsequent poll at least three-quarters of Londoners demanded the return of some elected metropolitan authority. However rotten the GLC had become, there was no demand for its abolition and no cry that Whitehall officials would be an adequate replacement. For all this, after her victory in the 1987 election Thatcher could remark earnestly that 'we must do something about those inner cities'. She seemed unaware that she had been doing something for eight years.

The reform of urban government under Thatcher was bizarre, and was to become surreal under Major. Eventually cities were 'allotted' to individual ministers like problem children. Ann Widdecombe doubled as 'Minister for Sheffield and Hull' and David Curry for an Orwellian construct called 'East Thames'. Some ministers never went near their charges, leaving civil servants to rule them from afar like eighteenth-century bishops. In place of local enterprise was a series of central initiatives with ever grander titles: the Urban Development Group, Inner City Enterprise, Financial Investment Group, Urban Task Force, City Action Team, Urban Programme Management Initiative and City Challenge. Chesterton's satire on London government, 'The Napoleon of Notting Hill', was recast in a pinstripe suit. On this topic Lawson was at his most cynical. Contemplating Thatcher's devastation of local democracy he declared that Britain needed yet more 'sidelining of un-cooperative local authorities ... clearly a field in which there is still much to do.'[59] Perhaps so, but local government had a last kick to deliver its tormentor and it was to prove lethal.

PART THREE

The Fall

9

All Politics is Local

In the ceiling plaster of Uppark house in Sussex is an inscription which reads 'Margaret Thatcher resigned when I was making this.' Eighteenth-century craftsmen traditionally left a personal memento dating their work. Those rebuilding fire-damaged Uppark were true to the tradition. Everyone knew where they were when the Downing Street 'defenestration' occurred on the morning of 20 November 1990. The cause can be found in the preceding chapters. All revolutions eat their children, or in this case their parent. Thatcher fell because she had made too many enemies and too few friends. The catalysts were specific, Thatcher's loss of her two chief lieutenants and her introduction of Britain's first poll tax since the Middle Ages. By then a sort of numb exhaustion had taken hold of her government. When on 11 June 1987 Thatcher realized that she had won an unprecedented third term as prime minister, she did not pause or draw breath. She drove straight from her Finchley constituency to Downing Street and at 2.45 a.m. summoned her aide, Stephen Sherbourne, to begin work. She told him that 'a new day' had already begun.[1] Her energy was phenomenal or demented according to taste.

Thatcherism was entrenched in the mindset of the cabinet and Whitehall. It was no longer merely a hyperactive response to events but was acquiring a programmatic thrust. The economy was approaching the 'Lawson boom', to be followed by a sudden and fierce recession. Taxes had been cut, trade unions transformed, Europe briefly tamed. Thatcher's restlessness knew no bounds. She still had to carry socialism to the political crossroads and drive a stake through its heart. Everywhere she looked, 'Something must be done'. In her post-election conference speech she gave the definitive cry of a recidivist intervener: '"Can't be done" has given way to "What's to stop us!"'[2] Only later did she admit that she had 'embarked on even more far-reaching social reforms than we had originally intended'.[3]

As a result Thatcher's caution, which some might call her political intelligence, deserted her. Campbell observed her at the time, 'driven into an activist, centralising frenzy, at odds with the professed philosophy of rolling back the state'.[4] To Andrew Marr, no area of the public sector seemed immune from her hands-on attention. The years 1987–9 were the 'high-water mark of Thatcherite triumphalism and swagger . . . the years of hubris.'[5] It was as if a third victory had untied her hands and rendered her invincible. In this her outlook was undoubtedly influenced by an increasing absorption in foreign affairs. Although Thatcher's home agenda was always dominant, the impending end of the Cold War exerted an intense appeal to her. For all her early aversion to 'abroad', the jet, the red carpet and the deferential flunkies worked their way into her self-image. She was lucky in that both the American and Soviet leaders at the time, Ronald Reagan and Mikhail Gorbachev, thought highly of her. She treated them as equals, flirting with Reagan and reassuring Gorbachev as he sought to steer his own revolution. She even murmured to herself that she had revived the Yalta triumvirate of Churchill, Roosevelt and Stalin.[6] Such grandeur fed back into her domestic performance, not always with salutary effect.

Thatcher began thrashing about in all directions and with diminishing effectiveness. She sought to end the BBC monopoly on public-service broadcasting, backing down only in the face of opposition from colleagues and the media. She tried to tackle football hooligans by introducing crowd identity cards, which failed. She introduced a state student loans company, which went bankrupt. Next for treatment came the judges. Ministers in every country long to supplant judicial discretion, especially over jail sentences, so as to win public favour. Under the 1988 Criminal Justice Act ministerial discretion was changed to allow the home secretary not only to decide the extent of a 'life' sentence in individual cases but also, in effect, to decide when any murderer would get out of jail. 'I took the greatest satisfaction in this', wrote Thatcher.[7] A talisman of the new policy was the refusal of successive home secretaries to agree parole for the Moors murderer, Myra Hindley, for fear of the tabloid press.

In 1989 Thatcher's Lord Chancellor, Lord Mackay, introduced a Green Paper on judicial reform. It was not based, as was customary when reforming the constitution, on a Royal Commission or similar public inquiry. It was the product of a small group of officials in Mackay's office and the Treasury. They decided that the operation of all courts should be streamlined. As for who should do this, 'The government is not prepared to leave it to the legal profession to settle the principles which these codes [of court practice] should adopt.'[8] The paper proposed to end the barristers' monopoly on appearing in court and, even more radical, proposed a Legal Affairs Commission to reform court procedure. The paper caused outrage from Britain's most powerful lobby. The conservative Lord Chief Justice, Lord Lane, called it 'one of the most sinister documents ever to emanate from government'. A former Lord Chancellor, Lord Havers, said it was 'the first moral issue on which I have felt obliged to vote against my party'. The legal commentator Michael Zander remarked that no single event in the long history of English law 'ever provoked so fierce and so broadly based a negative reaction'.[9] With no ground prepared for battle and few friends in support, Thatcher again backed down.

Next for treatment was the rising number of fatherless families living off the state. Once again a sensible reform was blighted by lack of forethought and by the dominance of the Treasury over its design. Angry at fathers transferring financial support for their children to the state by ignoring court maintenance orders, the Treasury set up a new Child Support Agency with specific targets for recouping the money. These targets encouraged civil servants to concentrate on the easier and wealthier cases, often with scant attention to fairness. The CSA's performance, and its computer, were to blight Whitehall for over a decade. Like so many Treasury measures for saving public money it only increased the cost.

Luck had long been Thatcher's closest ally but now it began to run out. Britain in the late 1980s was afflicted with a strange run of accidents swamping the public's attention. The *Herald of Free Enterprise* car ferry sank in 1987 with 187 deaths. A North Sea oil rig caught fire a year later, with 166 deaths. There were fatal rail disasters at King's Cross in 1987 and Clapham in 1988. The London pleasure cruiser, *Marchioness*, sank with heavy loss of life in 1989. The same year scores were crushed to death at Hillsborough football stadium. Editorials suggested that Britain's infrastructure, starved by 'government cuts', was facing progressive collapse and there seemed some evidence for this, at least in public transport. Blame would once have been diffused, to local authorities, nationalized industries, private operators, even that old standby, acts of God. After a decade of personalized public administration, she who had craved so much of the credit now had to take the blame.

The last straw was the collapse of Thatcher's relations with the two men on whom she had relied most closely, Geoffrey Howe and Nigel Lawson. The issue was one that has torn apart British governments for the past thirty years, Europe. Howe as foreign secretary and Lawson as chancellor took the view that Britain should join Europe's exchange rate mechanism (ERM) as a prelude to joining the common currency. Thatcher too had once taken this view but did so no longer. Thatcher demanded of the Treasury permanent secretary, Peter Middleton, why he was so set on the ERM. Did the Treasury not trust her to discipline the nation's finances? Middleton pointed out that Thatcher would not be there for ever and the Treasury would never forget 1976. Europe was the only secure control.[10] Thatcher did not welcome this intimation of mortality. She had seen her much-vaunted Single European Act turned into a work of treachery by the man whom she had once supported to run Europe, the Gallic president of the European Commission, Jacques Delors. As he carried forward his 'architecture' of political union, even lobbying for it at Labour conferences, Thatcher cried stop. She was ready to use her veto at every opportunity. To Howe this was not just wrong but counterproductive. Constant threats of veto meant that other states saw no point in compromising with Britain. Howe found himself in an intolerable position as a foreign secretary subverted at every turn by his prime minister.

Lawson fared little better. Thatcher feared he might return Britain to inflation which she (and Howe) had suffered so long to conquer. She might revel in Lawson's sensational 1988 Budget, when he brought the top income tax rate down from 60 per cent to 40 per cent (she had wanted to stop at 50).[11] But Lawson's use of interest rates to 'shadow' the deutschmark as a preliminary to joining the ERM infuriated her, a fury in which she was abetted by her economic adviser Alan Walters. When Lawson colluded with Howe to proceed to ERM membership prior to the 1989 Madrid European summit she snapped. She heard of a 'nasty little meeting' between them beforehand and refused either to speak to Howe or to attend any function at which he was present during the summit. Thatcher now retreated behind a clique of aides, her private secretary, Charles Powell, her press secretary, Bernard Ingham, and the engaging but eccentric Walters.

The path to disaster now led through the European elections in June 1989, when Thatcher experienced her first serious rout since taking office. She won just 33.5 per cent of a low turnout, to Labour's 38.7. Labour moved into an opinion poll lead over the Tories and the gilt began falling from Thatcher's crown. There was a smell of the 1970s in the air, when a party leader crosses the magic line that divides her from being an asset to her party to being a liability. An accident seemed waiting to happen. In July 1989 Thatcher moved Howe from the Foreign Office, replacing him with a young and inexperienced favourite, John Major, then a junior minister at the Treasury. Even Major wondered whether this was wise and was soon judged too exhausted to attend evening events. For a bitter Howe, despite the consolation of becoming deputy prime minister and Leader of the Commons, demotion was the culmination of years of public slights and private abuse. Further restless sackings and movements ensued. Thatcher moved Ridley from environment, replacing him with Chris Patten. Baker was moved and Parkinson was moved. The reshuffle seemed without rhyme or reason.

Three months later in October Lawson resigned, having demanded Walters' removal from Thatcher's office and Thatcher refusing. This was a particularly bitter parting. No chancellor had so completely realized the power of the Treasury over British government and Thatcher applauded his abilities, calling him 'a great gambler ... brilliant in concept, brilliant in drafting and brilliant in delivery.'[12] But she could not tolerate his independence. After just three months as foreign secretary Major found himself moved to succeed Lawson, his second great office of state inside a year. He promptly took up Lawson's cry that Britain join the ERM, leaving Thatcher no option. She bitterly complained in her memoirs that Major had gone native and was a 'cracked Treasury record'. Yet she was alone and could no longer resist. ERM entry, like the Single European Act, stained Thatcher's Euro-sceptic reputation with compromise. Though history suggests her instincts were right, her actions infuriated her loyalists without appeasing the pro-European left.

If Europe vexed many of the prime minister's colleagues it passed over the head of the party in the country. For that party trouble lay elsewhere. Local government spending under Thatcher had been relatively disciplined. Even on the threshold of the poll tax it was no higher in real terms than when the Tories came to power in 1979. Yet Thatcher seemed unable to accept that another source of democratic accountability could be more disciplined than her. She seemed determined to punish local government, Tory as well as Labour, if only for being right. Her venom against it was astonishing and deeply disconcerting to loyal Tory chairmen the length of the country. These front-line troops were the army on which the Conservative party had always depended for its electoral success.

Their volunteer zeal was the envy of Labour and the Liberals. The last thing any leader should do is upset or demoralize them. Thatcher now did just that.

On any basis it would have made sense in 1987 to leave the early curbs on local spending to bed down. The government had produced no fewer than fifty acts of parliament altering the basis of local finance and all had been disruptive and costly.[13] Penalties, plebiscites and fines had been reinforced by rate capping. Central government had denied electors the freedom to choose better local services by taxing themselves, as in every other country in Europe. If Thatcher had wanted to localize accountability, as she protested she did, she needed only to relax the central controls she had herself imposed and allow the local franchise to bite.

Thatcher was certainly reluctant to reopen the future of the rates. Since 1974 and her abortive review under Heath, she had detested the subject. Yet 'alternatives to the rates' remained a persistent Tory dream. Heseltine had examined the question in 1979. After the 1983 election the new environment secretary, Patrick Jenkin, did so again. Thatcher let him trot round the old track, assuming he would reach her own earlier conclusion that there was no sensible alternative. She was right. The rates were, said Jenkin's White Paper, 'well understood, cheap to collect and very difficult to evade'.[14] They should therefore remain 'for the foreseeable future'. Yet Jenkin could not let well alone. Desperate to appease his boss's presumed radicalism, he suggested yet another review that autumn. Thatcher remained sceptical, writing

There was a danger of raising expectations that we could not meet. After all, there had been previous reviews ... and only the most modest of mice had emerged. Unlike in October 1974 we must be absolutely clear that we had a workable alternative to put in place ... there must be no hint that we would go as far as abolishing the rates.[15]

Jenkin set up a study group led by his junior ministers, Baker and William Waldegrave, together with party officials, consultants and a friend of Waldegrave's, Lord Rothschild, formerly of the government's Central Policy Review Staff. They summoned evidence and papers. In March 1985 they briefed the relevant cabinet ministers on the evils of every sort of local tax, indicating their preference for a novel idea, a flat rate charge for local services. Like any 'charge' it would be levied on all residents, rich and poor.

Of those in the loop only Lawson was a persistent, indeed incredulous, sceptic. Such poll taxes, he said, were 'notorious through the ages'. They might give local decisions 'accountability bite' but they would seem unfair and become unworkable.

By the end of 1985 Baker was promoted to environment secretary in Jenkin's place, the fourth such secretary in three years. Each was more eager to conjure up a reform and more terrified of turning back. By the end of 1985 the group had prepared a fully worked-up plan for a fixed-rate 'community charge' or poll tax. An appalled Lawson was appeased by being promised that it would be capped, in return for which he would finance any transitional costs. Nobody seemed aware what this meant. Capping negated the central purpose of the charge, to make councils account to their electors for how much they spent on their behalf. It had been nobly intended to roll back the frontier of the state and re-establish the 'bite of the franchise'. Capping merely transferred accountability for fixing the rate to the capping authority, central government. Thatcher freely accepted that this undermined the tax, but she curiously felt 'our people' needed to be saved from its full force. She opined that, 'The world which years of socialism in our inner cities had created was far from ideal.'[16] This was hardly a good enough excuse.

The poll tax went to full cabinet in January 1986, where its approval was overshadowed by coinciding with Heseltine's sensational walkout over Westland. In the course of that year the tax as originally conceived by Jenkin's policy group was head-bashed by reality. Local treasurers, alert to the shifting sands of central funding, calculated that this was the time to increase their spending and blame it on poll tax transition. A sensitive central government dared not stop them. Surveys indicated that 80 per cent of voters, the least prosperous, would be those worst off under the tax. Plans were made to run old and new taxes side by side to hold down the level of the new one. Thatcher dared not risk having 'two taxes for one'. Baker now gave way to Ridley and Ridley to Patten at environment. As juniors Waldegrave gave way to Michael Howard and then Michael Portillo. It was like Argentina's 'dirty war', with the junta eager to tar all officers with its brush.

Ridley made a last bid to get Thatcher to reverse the Treasury's capping of the poll tax, aware that this would both nationalize the tax and nationalize blame for its size. But by now Thatcher's caution was directed merely at making the tax popular by keeping it low by any means. Parliamentary opposition was developing and the 1987 intake of Tory MPs, despite the tax being in their manifesto, brought the tally of potential poll tax rebels to 100.[17] Meanwhile a coincidental adjustment of rateable values in Scotland shifted the rates burden from businesses to residents. Because of a previous revaluation being postponed, Scottish residential rates soared. Thatcher was told that a similar horror was shortly to land on England. Desperate to avert this she decided on the earliest possible introduction of the new tax. She also decided it would start a year early north of the border, in 1989.

Connoisseurs of panic in modern government will find copious material in what happened next.[18] The Local Government Finance Act 1988 was a product of meticulous if cabalistic internal debate. Thatcher was right to reflect that 'few pieces of legislation have ever received such a thorough and scrupulous examination by ministers and officials in the relevant Cabinet committees.'[19] It is a sad comment on the state to which Thatcher had reduced internal party debate that this examination failed in what should have been its one purpose, to abandon the scheme. The poll tax was inept, encumbered with caps, dual runnings, rebates, transitional reliefs and safety nets. What was essentially a regressive tax had to be adjusted to limit the number of 'losers'. Money to relieve it began to haemorrhage from the Treasury, Lawson's punishment for failing to stop the tax in its tracks.

Chris Patten succeeded Ridley in July 1989 (he called his appointment a 'hospital pass') and demanded first £2.6 billion, then another £2 billion in transitional relief. Lawson was later caustic about Patten's pusillanimity in not forcing Thatcher to back down. 'What astonished me about Patten's behaviour,' he wrote, 'was that, while he was well aware that the poll tax was a political disaster, he made no effort whatsoever to abort it, even though he was in a strong position to do so.'[20] But Lawson had been in a much stronger position to stop it as chancellor and had allowed his eye to drift from the ball. Now in 1989 it was too late. The government was enmeshed in a policy that most ministers knew to be wrong. The poll tax bill had attracted 40 rebels on some clauses and 17 on second reading. This was a bigger revolt than Thatcher had yet experienced and was a portent of worse trouble to come.

Thatcher was unmoved. By early 1990 the tax was causing uproar in Scotland and was forecast to wipe out all Tory seats north of the border.

Conservative councillors resigned in Oxfordshire and Yorkshire rather than implement the tax. There were street protests in towns across England and, in March 1990, a violent riot in London. The press was universally hostile. The government lost a Staffordshire by-election on a 22 per cent adverse swing. Thatcher grabbed at every control and every subsidy to force down the level of the tax, supposedly a job for local electors. The first poll tax notices went out in the spring of 1990, with the Treasury having spent £2 billion on transitional relief already. Combined with the business rate, the eventual effect was to shift the financing of local services from 60 per cent dependence on local revenue to 40, 30 and then barely 20 per cent.[21] Local fiscal accountability, the whole point of the poll tax, had all but collapsed. The concept of devolving a charge for community services to local citizens may have been sound in theory. The politics of public expenditure was such that it could not be sustained by a regressive impost. Property taxes bore some relationship to wealth and thus ability to pay. The poll tax did not. It was seen as deeply unfair.

The poll tax was a curiosity in the Thatcherite canon. It was not a rushed or ill-considered reform but it saw no general debate, no committee of inquiry, not even a serious attempt to consult those to whom fiscal power was supposedly being devolved, local authorities. No lessons were learned from recent fiscal innovations abroad. The nearer the tax came to implementation the more it was adulterated. All of those involved, Jenkin, Baker, Waldegrave, Ridley, Howard, Patten, Portillo, later lost confidence in it. The tax was a political Dardenelles, a predictable disaster that had become unstoppable. Nor can one avoid the suspicion that some of those who agreed to it were hoping that it might indeed prove the lady's downfall. Here might be a trap from which she could not escape.

The trap had yet to be sprung. Thatcher was now spending increasing amounts of time on foreign affairs, understandably as the world at the time was reeling from the fall of the Berlin Wall and the collapse of the Soviet empire. In her buoyant party conference speech in October 1990 Thatcher dwelt at length on the victory over communism. She was high on Cold War triumphalism, anti-German vitriol and anti-Brussels hysteria. I remember listening to her and wondering whether she was on some drug. The audience responded with hysterical cries of 'Ten more years, ten more years'. Thatcher was little short of ecstatic. Then on 30 October Thatcher lambasted the European Union in a stunned House of Commons. Rejecting all monetary and federal union, she cried, 'No, no, no'. Her chancellor, Major, was shocked. He had recently persuaded her to join the ERM and here she was dismissing out of hand its logical next step, entry into the euro. He wrote that 'I nearly fell off my bench . . . I heard our colleagues cheer but knew there was trouble ahead.'[22]

Howe, supposedly still Thatcher's deputy and Commons' Leader, had not been informed that Thatcher had agreed with Major on entering the ERM until told in passing by the Queen.[23] Thatcher could by now scarcely bear to be in his company. She insulted him publicly, derided his docility at meetings and had Ingham dismiss his job of deputy prime minister as 'not real'. Then in the first week of November she went too far. She abused Howe in full cabinet over some bills for the Queen's Speech not being ready, a fault that was nothing to do with him. He had had enough and resigned on the spot.

In retrospect the fall of Thatcher was astonishingly sudden, yet at the time and with the denouement still unimaginable, it seemed to unfold in slow motion. On 13 November Howe made a devastating attack on the prime minister in the Commons, setting out their differences on Europe and protesting against her negotiating style. She had sent her team to the crease, he said, having secretly broken their bats in the dressing room. The attack was the more devastating for Howe's measured monotone. 'The knife went in early,' wrote Paddy Ashdown, the Liberal Democrat leader, in his diary, 'and never stopped turning.'[24] The following day, Heseltine announced his intention to stand as leader against the prime minister.

Thatcher casually asked the back-bench 1922 Committee for an early vote the following week, despite the fact that she would be abroad for much of the intervening time. She wanted this inconvenience over with as soon as possible. I interviewed her on the Saturday before the vote, 17 November. It was a stormy autumn afternoon in a dark and empty Chequers. Denis was out walking the dog. A handful of servicewomen, dressed like jailers, flitted about the gloomy corridors as waitresses. Thatcher was clearly depressed and kept referring to Heseltine as a socialist, stabbing at carefully marked passages in a book of his as she spoke. To her he represented the old guard, the Labour party, the 'three Cs' of consensus, compromise and corporatism. Saddam Hussein had just invaded Kuwait and America and Britain were preparing to fight him. 'A fine time to run a leadership election,' she said. 'And who will be cheering if he [Heseltine] wins? Who will be cheering most? Saddam!' She did not think she would lose but I could tell that doubts were beginning to invade her mind. She was preparing for an international summit in Paris to sign the post-Cold War treaty, a ceremonial event she would have done well to avoid in favour of pressing flesh among her back-benchers. Her last remark was ominous. As we exchanged small talk she suddenly blurted out, 'After three election victories it really would be the cruellest thing.' I drove away with thunder crashing round the Chilterns, convinced that Thatcher was not long for the world across which she had strutted so long.[25]

Back at Westminster the stage was being set for an execution. Thatcher's absence in Paris during the campaign unquestionably cost her votes that might have warded off Heseltine's first-round challenge. Like Heath in 1975 she misjudged her vulnerability. Having left her campaign in the inept hands of her parliamentary secretary, Peter Morrison, she heard the result in Paris: she had only 204 votes to Heseltine's 152. This was just short of the loaded majority needed to avert a second ballot. It was the same hurdle as had felled her predecessor, Heath. A second round would now take place, when new candidates, which might mean loyal colleagues, were entitled to enter the fray. She nobbled two of them, Hurd and Major, by asking if they would propose and second her. They did so with evident reluctance.

Thatcher flew straight back from Paris and sat up all night drinking with her personal assistant. By the following day London's political geology had already shifted. Plotters had gathered in clubs and private houses. Most owed their advancement to Thatcher and they were not necessarily eager to bring her down. But a change seemed unavoidable and their concern was not would she survive but who would succeed her. Thatcherites, which now meant most of the cabinet, had to concentrate their attention not on Thatcher but on Thatcherism's possible fate under Heseltine. He would not have reversed Thatcherism but he was obsessively pro-European and an overt interventionist in industry. Charismatic in the country, he was aloof and unpopular among his erstwhile colleagues. Since his Westland resignation four years earlier, they distrusted him and were disinclined to be led by him. (Only one cabinet minister, David Hunt, voted for him.) The question was therefore how to ward off a Heseltine victory on the second ballot, when other candidates might step forward, take votes from Thatcher and let Heseltine through. Hurd and Major had to be freed to stand and Thatcher had to be persuaded that her game was over. Who would bell the cat?

Thatcher then made a tactical error. She summoned cabinet members individually to her room in the Commons for advice. Freed of the tyranny of her dominance in a full cabinet meeting, they were emboldened to tell her what they really thought. For the first time in most of their careers, they said what she did not want to hear. It was like Caesar's assassins lining up one by one to drive in the knife. They said that the country was against her and the party was deeply concerned by the poll tax, which could lose them the next election. Nor did they think she could beat Heseltine. Where would that leave all she had done? One after another they said this, friend and foe alike. The cumulative effect was to collapse Thatcher's confidence of the night before. She could not stand it. Denis told her gently, 'Don't go on love.' She did not even wait to face her parliamentary party and resigned that morning. She remarked in her memoirs that 'I had lost the cabinet's support. I could not even muster a credible campaign team. It was the end.'[26] It was, she said on a number of occasions, 'treachery with a smile on its face'. Only Clarke and Tebbit are believed to have suggested she fight on.

Tory MPs had originally voted for Thatcher not out of any ideological enthusiasm but because she was not Heath and thus did not presage their dismissal at the polls. She had won three elections and was just two years from another, but this she seemed likely to lose. MPs clearly indicated on the first ballot that they were unhappy with her and that was signal enough. Thatcher accepted the black spot and went. On the second ballot, the conspirators' tactics worked. Heseltine was defeated and Major won the leadership. Lord Home's voting system had worked as he intended and ousted a leader who could not muster overwhelming support, independent of personal loyalty, in the parliamentary party.

Thatcher often protested that she never lost an election, but that was only because at the end her friends prevented her from doing so. She referred to the 'weasel words whereby they had transmuted their betrayal into frank advice and concern for my fate.'[27] But she had asked them a question, whether she was going to win on a second ballot. She thought she would have won if they had backed her and there is a measure of truth in that. But she would not have won an open contest, with Hurd and Major running, and all felt that she had been fatally wounded by Heseltine, a wound that would have led to her and their defeat.

The day after her resignation the prime minister decided to wind up a confidence debate in the Commons. It was a great parliamentary moment.

Thatcher was helped, as so often, by Labour's Neil Kinnock playing the fall guy in trying ineptly to attack her. She admitted in her memoirs that she could not have handled his sympathy or congratulation. She always needed something on which to bite and bite she did. She bellowed and boasted, slamming into questions and shouting at hecklers. 'I am rather enjoying this, Mr Speaker,' she said at one point. Her speechwriter, Ronald Millar, recorded that 'her domination of the House was so complete that her downfall seemed to some to have been a madness of the moment.'[28] A similar moment of madness had led to Thatcher's arrival. On both occasions there was method in it.

IO

Thank You and Goodbye

Many metaphors were produced for the downfall of Thatcher. Some observers saw a boyars' plot, others a Bohemian defenestration. Biffen's homely analogy was that all the routes on the illuminated Paris Metro map suddenly lit up to one destination, Thatcher's departure.[1] It was no repeat of Thatcher's peasants' revolt. The peasants never had a look-in. The cabinet club had acted to stem a possible popular uprising that might have led Heseltine to usurp it.

That said, Thatcher fell through sheer exhaustion. Her political cunning had deserted her. Every bone of her body was tired, and every bone of the body politic as well. Her final week found her in the wrong city, Paris, with the wrong team guarding her interest back home. Her cabinet was tired of a style and a bullying behaviour that had dominated their ministerial careers. Her parliamentary party was tired of the battles they were forced to fight on her behalf, not least over the poll tax. Even the nation was exhausted. It had taken Thatcher's medicine and needed convalescence. The toppling of Thatcher recalled Churchill's ejection from office in 1945. Sorry as many were to see her go, the nation breathed a collective sigh of relief.

The assumption in political circles was that, with Thatcher gone, Thatcherism had come to an end and Westminster would revert to the *status quo ante*. Conventional wisdom was that Thatcherism was a leadership style, a statecraft intrinsic to its author. Now it had gone something called post-Thatcherism would ensue, a wholly unknown quantity. For this wisdom there was no shortage of evidence. The state had not been rolled back other than in a handful of dying industries. A key indicator, taxation, actually rose as a percentage of the non-oil domestic product, from 35 per cent in 1979 to 37 per cent in 1990. There had been a severe recession, but if this was a structural 'supply-side' adjustment it was hardly productive. Over Thatcher's first eighteen months, industrial output fell by 14 per cent and unemployment rose by two-thirds, a squeeze unprecedented since the 1930s. National output per head rose by roughly 2 per cent a year over the Thatcher decade, lower than in the Wilson–Heath era. Monetarism as a tool of policy had been discredited by its vulnerability to inward and outward flows of money, specifically by Thatcher's ending of foreign exchange controls. Lawson's medium-term financial strategy had by 1990 fallen back on such traditional weapons as managed interest rates and regulated foreign exchanges. Thatcher began with one cyclical downturn and ended with another about to begin, that of the early 1990s.

The sceptics added that the welfare state under Thatcher expanded. She did not undermine the post-war welfare consensus. She retained such public-sector monoliths as the NHS, British Rail, the Post Office and the structure of social benefits. She let housing benefit soar and allowed the Treasury to botch the reform of hospitals. By the 1980s the British economy was moving out of extractive and manufacturing industry towards services, private and public. Health, education and social services were bound to be beneficiaries of this shift, yet they were activities in which the state still enjoyed a quasi-monopoly. One of Thatcher's colleagues and sternest critics, Ian Gilmour, refused Thatcherism all categorization. He viewed it as 'an ideology, style, mood, "I must have my own way", monarchism, 19th-century Liberalism, millenarian revivalism, right-wingery, a method of controversy, a set of moral values, statecraft, or a combination of all of them.'[2]

Thatcher never won anything approaching a popular majority. Most Britons simply did not like her, however necessary they may have felt her rule to be. Her eleven years of political supremacy depended on a divided Opposition, crucially on having the weak Michael Foot and Neil Kinnock as Labour leaders during her most critical years. Nor was there a majority in the opinion polls for her assault on the unions, for utilities' privatization or for cuts in top-rate taxes. In 1988 opinion was actually more favourably disposed to welfare socialism than when she came to power.[3] In 1976, Gallup had found a majority for the Thatcherite policy of curbing inflation over reducing unemployment, by 54 per cent to 36 per cent. By 1986 this had reversed to 13:81. There was a similar reversal of those wanting further tax cuts as against more welfare benefits. In these terms Thatcher left Britain more 'socialist' than she found it.

In other words we have yet more Thatcher paradoxes. She was a populist who never contrived to be popular. She was a supposed Conservative who despised the British Establishment. She believed in Victorian values, yet maintained an awesome welfare state and barely sought to shackle the 'permissive society'. Abortion was not banned or divorce made harder. Her 'Section 28' law preventing local councils from publicizing homosexual support was the nearest she came to legislating on sex. She claimed to be anti-planning, yet she demanded manpower targets in higher education and retained detailed town and country planning controls. She believed in free markets, yet controlled interest rates and joined the European Monetary System. An admirer of personal and community self-help, she persistently eroded local democracy. In day-to-day policy the author of Thatcherism found herself constantly restraining her more Thatcherite ministers.

In his extensive study of Conservative ideology, Richard Cockett remarked that 'whilst to her many detractors Mrs Thatcher always seemed a wild-eyed, hand-bagging revolutionary, to her advisers she was a cautious, insecure pragmatist, who eventually paid the price of not capitalising on her electoral success early or boldly enough.'[4] Small wonder the conservative economist Frank Hahn concluded in 1988 that,

Thatcherism as represented by Mrs Thatcher herself is intellectually without interest. It consists of homilies on the virtues of hard work and ambition and on providing the carrot and the stick to elicit those virtues. Her macro-economic views are so incoherent as to make them undiscussable . . . But her lack of intellectual power in these matters does not, of course, detract from her ability to inspire others to make an attempt to turn Mrs Thatcher into Thatcherism.[5]

To such a view, Thatcher was an unguided missile that just happened to come over the horizon at the right time and hit some useful targets. Her service to history was largely accidental. Peter Hennessy saw her as a conventional prime minister who had to struggle with her political base and ensure that she and her party kept power.[6] To him she was an opportunist, a victor then a victim of circumstance. She was blessed with luck and spliced on to it only such changes as the moment allowed. Compared with Blair she was a mild revolutionary. She respected the forms of cabinet government, circulated papers and conducted vigorous internal debate. Like many leaders she had favourites and, towards the end, retreated into a disastrously closed and sycophantic circle. But constitutionally she honoured the thesis that governors are always more prisoners of the past than they dare admit; they are 'heirs before they are choosers'.[7]

Thatcher did more than just build on the foundations of her inheritance. She certainly used history as a route map, but largely as a map of where not to go. The past was central to her political education, indeed without the failures of Heath, Wilson and Callaghan she would have been nothing like the Thatcher of Thatcherism. She learned the lesson that Britain's ills would not be cured by further manipulating the post-war consensus. The story of the early years, 1979–81, was that there was no point in repeating failure. Thatcher may have approached reform as a gradualist, testing the water and hesitating often, but she left her followers in no doubt of where she would like to go. Even if what was achieved in the short term was limited, there was no question that 1979 was a revolutionary moment. As the left-wing historian Andrew Gamble wrote, 'The Thatcherites were the first [political] group to grapple with the problem of turning their criticisms of post-war social democracy into practical programmes and policies.'[8] It was the start of a new British settlement.

This settlement at first seemed reactive and pragmatic. Yet even as Thatcher retreated before public-sector militancy and baulked at reforms to public services, she was cutting taxes, freeing labour markets and, as Howe put it, 'relocating' the economy. In the early 1980s Britain was truly the 'sick man of Europe'. In his first budget speech Howe had given a devastating account of the decline. In 1954, he said, France and Germany's combined share of world trade in manufactured goods was roughly the same as Britain's alone: 'It is now more than three times as large as ours. The French people produce half as much as we do. The Germans produce more than twice as much and they are moving ahead all the time.'[9]

Thatcher tore into this predicament. She was immune to what is now called 'political correctness'. As the rioters stormed through Toxteth and Brixton in 1981 her sympathies were entirely with 'those poor shopkeep-ers' whose premises were destroyed. Likewise the rhetoric of 'earning before spending' deepened the shock of the 1980–82 recession. Though Thatcher was often nervous at the impact of her policies on the poor, and was accordingly reluctant to attack the social security budget, her language could seem heartless and ruthless. It shattered the then widespread belief that government's job was to rescue industry and its employees from the stress of the market. Thatcher might have eschewed the language of lais-sez-faire, but she certainly applied its essence to the private sector. One of her most emphatic differences with Heseltine was his readiness to 'inter-vene morning, noon and night' to prop up British industries and protect British markets. She disagreed.

The first revolution, the assault on the size of the state and the advance of privatization and lower taxes, was one of self-reliance against the habit of dependency. It was the revolution of no free lunch. It came to Britain a decade before other European governments dared even to adumbrate it. A German diplomat bemoaned to me in 2005 that his country 'had no Margaret Thatcher' (before Angela Merkel came to power). Her rebuttal of 'bourgeois guilt' was real. In the 1980s 'rich lists' were greeted with unashamed glee, not least by those listed. The City of London was transformed from a place of aristocratic decorum to one of greed-is-good. From the repositioning of Essex as a place of tasteless wealth to the vulgarization of the Cotswold gentry, from the dramatic upturn in London cuisine to the boom in weekend breaks, Thatcher's Britain idealized money. She turned the working class from a repository of nostalgia and cultural romance into an aspirant bourgeoisie. Middle class was no longer automatically a derogatory term.

Most important, the first revolution was seen to work. By the 1990s Britain's economic image, if not yet its performance, had been transformed. Of the 22 counties in the OECD, Britain's ranking for 'economic freedom' and 'entrepreneurial welcome' rose from 15th in 1980 to top in 1999. This was an extraordinary turnround in economic confidence and received wide publicity abroad. The Reagan government in America drew inspiration from the bond between Thatcher and Reagan and from the apparent success Thatcher had in standing up to the trade unions after 1985. In Australia, John Howard as federal treasurer from 1977 to 1983 lauded Thatcher's anti-inflation strategy and commenced a programme of privatization that was to make a deep impression on Blair and Brown. New Zealand did likewise. A number of governments in Latin America, where Thatcher's femininity gave her the iconic status of another Eva Peron, also attempted privatization. In Brazil, Argentina, Chile and Peru state assets were sold, albeit often to friends of the regime. In the aspiring 'tiger economies' of south-east Asia, and even in India, the move was away from state control in the direction of open markets. The cry was taken up by the World Bank and the International Monetary Fund as conditions for loans. With the fall of the Iron Curtain, privatization became little short of a raging obsession in Russia and its former satellites.

Thatcher was a rarity in modern politics, a specific personality. She was not a Pangloss and, unlike Blair, never sought to be all things to all voters.

She embodied the partisan message that she wanted to convey. She did not resort to fudge or prevarication. The public sector did not need to wait for orders from Downing Street. As long as Thatcher was in office, people knew what was expected of them, whether they liked it or loathed it. She not only changed the public's expectation of government, she changed people's expectation of themselves as economic beings. Small wonder Peter Clarke, in his study of modern prime ministers, concluded that Thatcher's downfall 'unmistakably closed a heroic chapter in the history of political leadership'.[10]

All this came at a price. How was it that this champion of the first revolution, this warrior for liberty and a retreating state, could leave behind her the most potent and centralized government in the free world? Public services in Britain had some of their inputs privatized but schools, universities, hospitals, housing, welfare, law and public administration fell more, not less, under the thrall of central command and control, in particular that of the Treasury and Whitehall. Wherever Thatcher looked she strove to interfere. Nor was this confined to the public sector. Her political body language personified the nanny state. In a revealing passage in her memoirs, Thatcher wrote of family life that 'Only the most myopic libertarian would regard it as outside the purview of the state: for my part I felt that over the years the state had done so much harm that the opportunity to do some remedial work was not to be missed.'[11] It was the authentic voice of Thatcher's Victorian grandmother. Though she did little to carry this voice into legislation, it was hardly that of a libertarian.

This offers some clue as to how Thatcherism not only outlived Thatcher but was deepened and strengthened by her successors after she was gone. Her most potent legacy was potency itself. All revolutions crave power, indeed the greater the revolution the greater the accretion of power needed to achieve it. When the revolution's stated goal is to reduce power, it is vulnerable to self-contradiction. To succeed it must contain the seeds of its own destruction, or be charged with hypocrisy. That applies whether the synthesis of the dialectic is Marx's anti-state communism or Thatcher's anti-state individualism. Nor is this just playing with terms. History shows that a diminution of central power as a result of revolution seldom occurs. States do not implode except in response to some external force, as did Soviet communism after the Cold War.

While Hennessy confessed to finding Thatcher's sense of struggle in some degree 'Marxian',[12] it took a full Marxist, Eric Hobsbawm, to note the paradox of the two revolutions. In his obituary on Thatcher's time in office he noted that it was 'increasingly obvious that a government devoted to dismantling the state has inevitably strengthened it, since only the state can impose the utopia of *Daily Telegraph* editorials on recalcitrant reality.' The reason was that this reality, by 1979, 'largely consisted of people and institutions employed by, subsidised by, or otherwise dependent on, public funds'.[13] Hobsbawm continued,

Since the dream of an economy and people entirely independent on the Treasury is unreal ... the state must henceforth − in the interests of withering away − give ever more precise directions about how its funds should and should not be spent ... Central power and command are not diminishing but growing, since 'freedom' cannot be achieved except by bureaucratic decision.

In other words, Thatcher's second revolution was essential to the achievement of the first, and yet it was bound eventually to clash with it.

This goes some way to explaining the remorselessness of the second revolution after Thatcher's departure. Proclaimed enemy of the public sector, she had spent almost her entire career in it. It paid her salary and she met few people that were not its denizens. As the public sector had blessed her rise, so she in return enhanced its scope, its cost and its power. She might plead that she had to take more state power as a temporary measure to smash socialism (as over the universities), but what if there was no end to the smashing? Like the later war on terror, such goals can be a matter of definition. It can take as long as you like, and therefore you can demand as much power as you like. Thatcher's explanation of these paradoxes came close to self-parody. In her 1987 conference speech, after her third victory, she asked, 'Do we pitch our tents ... dig in ... stand where we are now?' Good heavens no, she said, there is always more to be done, and 'What's to stop us? Whose blood runs faster at the thought of five years of consolidation?' There would be no consolidation. The revolution would always be necessary because its enemies never died. As her close aide Lord Powell put it to the BBC, 'There was something Leninist about Mrs Thatcher which came through in her style of government, the belief that they're in a vanguard which is right which would go out and lay down the law and bully a bit.'[14]

This Manicheanism, of good and evil in perpetual contention, set

Thatcher apart not just from the liberal/conservative tradition of Butskellism and One Nation Toryism. It also required her to deny British politics its pluralism. A political as well as a cultural narrowness was Thatcher's greatest intellectual shortcoming. It led her to erect walls against new ideas or new people with whom she might disagree. It gave her tunnel vision. She rejected the 'tiered democracy' that conservative analysts from de Tocqueville to Hayek saw as essential if responsive government were not to degenerate to 'democratic atomism'. Thatcher might have left 60 per cent of the political economy to the wiles of the market, but the remaining 40 per cent was 'mine, all mine'. Thatcher was a revolutionary authoritarian, a true apostle of the dictatorship of the bourgeoisie.

Thatcher staged an aggrandizement of Whitehall power unprecedented since Attlee. She claimed to have read Hayek but she must have done so selectively. She clearly liked his attack on (small c) conservatives for their 'fear of change, a timid distrust of the new as such, while the liberal position is based on courage and confidence, on a preparedness to let change run its course even if we cannot predict where it will lead.'[5] But she ignored Hayek's central concept of managed anarchy, of the state as the light-touch regulator of a natural economic disorder. Thatcher wholly disregarded his warning of the 'deadly blight of centralisation' and his belief that democracy never works without 'a great measure of local self-government'. Critics such as Gamble were right to point out that her 'hegemonic' public sector was no less an operation of social engineering than was socialism.

The second Thatcher revolution was anything but Hayekian. It fell squarely into the elected dictatorship against which Lord Hailsham had warned in his Dimbleby lecture in 1976. He saw the office of prime minister checked between elections only by a fog of custom and practice, ministerial responsibility, a respect for parliament, an independent civil service and a 'treaty between equals' of central and local government. Thatcher respected some of these conventions. But the force of her personality was eventually too great. Like all revolutionaries, Thatcher was never a person at peace. She eventually showed the British constitution for what it was, the emperor's new clothes.

I first studied this process in 1995, towards the end of Major's term of office, and wondered how the second revolution might be handled by a new generation of politicians, not least on the left. Would Thatcher's 'nationalization of Britain' be denounced and reversed, or would it be seized with enthusiasm and even extended? Would future leaders tilt towards liberty or authority? The answer given by governments under both Major and Blair was unequivocal. They conceded Thatcher's first revolution as the right way to run a modern mixed economy, but they seized on her second as useful. It was the royal road to more power than the conventions of the constitution had ever permitted. It was the same power as had once been vested in the British monarchy, built on patronage and prerogative. Thatcher taught them that a constitution built on nothing more substantial that convention was a bluff waiting to be called.

PART FOUR

Deceptive Interlude

II

Thatcherism's Human Face

In November 1990 Conservative MPs needed a rest. After fifteen years of shrill and brittle leadership they duly sought respite in a shadow on Mount Olympus. Rarely has a shadow been better cast. Many prime ministers have been unspectacular but most have known where they were going and had thick skins in getting there. Neither was true of John Major. He was like a club Hon. Sec. pushed forward on the sudden death of the chairman. He owed his elevation to Thatcher's favour and his leadership was a farewell and rather guilty gift to her from her party.

No British prime minister, not even Ramsay MacDonald, has ever risen from such humble origins. Major's father was a circus artiste and salesman. He grew up in a bungalow in Merton in south-west London, then in a two-room flat (for a family of five) in Brixton with no bathroom and a lavatory shared with other tenants, who included three Irishmen and a burglar. When his mother died, he wrote only that 'lame ducks lost a saint'. The family could not afford holidays. For Major to get back to his secondary school in Merton required a 90-minute bus journey. He was bullied, not least because his parents added a family name of Major to his father's name of Ball. John Major-Ball sounded grander than John Ball but lent itself to instant ridicule. The early passages of Major's memoirs are often touchingly poignant: 'I cannot have been unpopular [at primary school] for I was elected captain of the football team. We won most of our games and were good enough to reach the final of a local schools' knockout competition, but lost 2–1 after I gave away a silly goal.'[1]

A tall, handsome and athletic young man, Major left school at sixteen and sought work as a bank clerk under his new name of John Major, spending six months unemployed looking after his widowed mother. He joined the District Bank and Brixton Young Conservatives and, at twenty, moved into the house of Jean Kierans, a widow and mother of two, twelve years his senior. The relationship survived even a year working for the Standard Bank in Nigeria, where Major was injured in a car crash and hospitalized home. To Anthony Seldon, the relationship with Kierans was a turning point. 'She made Major smarten his appearance, groomed him politically and made him more ambitious and worldly.'[2] In 1968 he was elected to Lambeth Borough Council and in 1974 stood in the safe Labour seat of St Pancras North.

Elected MP for Huntingdon in 1979, Major rose unnoticed through the Whips' Office, his job not to shine but to oil the machine of government. He later admitted that these were his happiest years in Westminster. Thatcher had never risked him as head of a big spending department and his brief stints as foreign secretary and chancellor of the Exchequer in 1989–90 were to fill breaches in the running crises that attended her downfall. Neither was a success. Yet it was his position at the Treasury, with support from the Whips' Office and with impeccable Thatcherite credentials, that clearly marked Major out as the candidate of safety and continuity after the turbulence that surrounded Thatcher's fall. His rivals for the succession, Heseltine and Hurd, were as unlike him as they were each other. One was a publishing tycoon whose political energy and glamour had won him the nickname Tarzan. The other was a patrician diplomat and novelist who had served in Heath's private office. Both were able and plausible candidates.

Thatcher reassured all doubters during the leadership election, 'John's pure gold'.[3] The truth appeared to be that the party wanted, above all, someone who was not Thatcher, not Heseltine and not Hurd. It was traumatized, sated on personality, and needed a period of calm and retrenchment. Major wore baggy sweaters, funny glasses and a nervous smile and professed an abiding love for cricket, of which he had an extensive knowledge. His wife, Norma, loathed politics and stayed in their Huntingdon home for most of his term of office. Yet Major cleaned the field. He won 185 votes to Heseltine's 131 and Hurd's 56. Somehow a quiet party insider of humble background had leapt forward and snatched the crown. I recall Kenneth Clarke remarking that he had longed for the day when going to Eton would be a disqualification for the Tory leadership, but not when the same applied to university. The Conservative party, in a post-Thatcher paroxysm, had done something quite extraordinary. Enoch Powell remarked of Major, 'I find myself asking, Does he really exist?'[4]

While every one of Thatcher's eleven years was crowded with incident, Major's seven seemed to vanish in a flash. The 1990s at Westminster were a time of political convalescence. Major entered Downing Street at forty-seven, the twentieth century's youngest prime minister, and remained there longer than Eden, Macmillan or Heath. Yet he was like a rabbit caught in the headlights of history. His friend, Chris Patten, emerged from his first cabinet meeting and compared it with the scene in *Fidelio* when the released prisoners sing of the joy of freedom. It was an ominous parallel. The prisoners were soon returned to their misery.

Major's election initially transformed the Tories' poll rating. Gallup showed it up from 34 per cent under Thatcher in September 1990 to 44 per cent in December. The new prime minister was given the immediate boon of a war, to free Kuwait from an invasion by Iraq. It was not 'his' war as was the Falklands for Thatcher. The Americans were in command, with Britain in the baggage train, and Major's visit to the troops in the desert was like that of a bank manager on holiday. But he exuded calm competence. Above all, he distanced himself from his patron by moving to abolish the poll tax. Michael Heseltine, long an opponent of the tax, was brought back into government and chosen to do the deed. Thatcher, still in the Commons, was furious both at the death of her controversial offspring and at the choice of murderer.

In December 1991 Major had to conduct his first serious European venture, the negotiation of the Maastricht treaty on further political union. This was the successor – in Thatcher's view a successor too far – of the Single European Act. Major's handling of the chaotic negotiation was masterful, winning plaudits from colleagues. He kept lines of consultation open to cabinet and sceptical MPs in London. Most of his European partners had been content to rubber-stamp whatever Brussels officials proposed and were furious as Britain sought to unpick, and eventually refuse to sign, the corporatist Social Chapter. Though the full impact of this opt-out was controversial, British labour costs over the next decade diverged markedly from the rest of Europe. For all the trouble it was later to cause him, Maastricht was Major's finest hour, strongly backed by his party. Like Thatcher at Fontainebleau he had shown Europe he was not a soft touch.

Reward came at the general election of 1992. For any party to win a fourth full term was unprecedented in the twentieth century. To do so after thirteen bitterly contentious years was the more so, not least when the polls expected the Tories to lose. The emollient refashioning of the Conservative image gave Major the biggest popular vote, 14 million, in electoral history, a fact many political observers found hard to believe at the time (and since).

It was two million more votes than Labour, more than Thatcher ever secured and half a million more than Blair received in 1997. Major's comment on it was correct, 'Above all, 1992 killed socialism in Britain . . . Our win meant that between 1992 and 1997 Labour had to change. No longer is Britain trapped in the old two-party tango, with one government neatly undoing everything its predecessor has created.'⁵ Yet such is the bias towards small urban constituencies in Britain's electoral arithmetic that Major's remarkable win was smothered by the smallness of his Commons majority. The Tories won 42 per cent of the poll to Labour's 34 per cent, but a parliamentary majority of just twenty-five. This potential for rebellion was to cause Major and his whips constant trouble and gave the parliamentary theatre of British government a brief resurgence. Major was never able to master his Commons support or rise above the slights it constantly visited on him.

The prime minister had a mandate of his own, yet no sooner was the election over than victory turned to wormwood. The Lawson boom was at an end and the economy was moving into recession, suggesting that 'boom-and-bust' had not ended with what Denis Healey had derided as 'sado-monetarism'. Inflation was climbing towards double figures and interest rates were at 14 per cent. The Treasury struggled to hold sterling inside the ERM at what seemed an overvaluation, albeit one chosen by Major himself as chancellor. On Black Wednesday, 16 September 1992, there was a classic run on sterling and the Treasury surrendered. The pound floated down, out of the ERM. Though this was a prelude to economic renaissance, Major never recovered his political composure. From 1993 to 1997 his government was wracked by intra-party strife. He won the Maastricht ratification vote but at a heavy price in personal authority. Divisions over Europe, magnified in the press, dogged his every step. When senior Tories found themselves in trouble – David Mellor, Jonathan Aitken, Jeffrey Archer, Alan Clark, Tim Yeo and others – their leader suffered. He lacked Thatcher's ability to ride a crisis and turn misfortune to advantage. At the party conference in 1993 he offered a clumsy lecture about family values and getting 'back to basics'. It was a hostage to every party mishap, not least to his own peace of mind.

Major kept up the business of government. He negotiated a brief ceasefire with the IRA. He conceded troops for Bosnian relief supplies and saw their mission 'creep' into a full deployment. He established more relaxed relations with the German chancellor, Helmut Kohl, and the American president, George Bush Snr. But his mind was haunted by domestic woes. In November 1994, with his poll rating down almost to 20 per cent, he wiped out a parliamentary majority already eroded at by-elections by withdrawing the whip from eight MPs rebelling on Europe. A year later he was goaded beyond endurance and resigned his party's leadership to secure a vote of confidence. He won the subsequent campaign only with Heseltine's support and with eighty-nine MPs voting for the stalking horse, John Redwood. The victory did nothing to stem the flight of confidence, which continued to slide until the eventual 1997 defeat.

Major's political troubles were seized on by historians to suggest that he represented a revision to the status quo before Thatcher. Peter Hennessy was one of many who wrote as if Thatcher had been a sort of blip. She only put traditional cabinet government on ice, he wrote, such that it could be restored 'in the few minutes it takes a new prime minister to travel from Buckingham Palace to Downing Street'.[6] Everything about Major's personality supported the thesis. He had a fixation with cabinet consensus. Decisions, he said, should be the outcome of discussion, not its precondition as with Thatcher. Major worked sitting in the cabinet room and gave interviews there. His political chemistry was the opposite of Thatcher's. What she had made subject to personal rule, Major tried to delegate and soften. He hoped to implement the St Francis quote which she had merely parroted, 'Where there is discord may we bring harmony.'

This view is that of the Westminster village, typified by Steve Bell's merciless cartoon image of Major as a bemused man with a weak chin and underpants worn over his suit. The satire *Spitting Image* depicted him entirely black-and-white on an otherwise coloured screen, what Pissarro once called 'the whole dazzling range of greys'. Worse, Major showed it hurt. He worried ceaselessly at the media's running commentary on his rule, acquiring a debilitating habit in a prime minister of reading newspaper first editions before going to bed. Journalists, ignored by Thatcher, scented blood and leapt to the chase. All Major could say was, 'Oh, there you go knocking me again.' I once ended an interview with him so exasperated by his paranoia that I pleaded with him not to read a newspaper ever again. His press secretary, Christopher Meyer, shrugged and said he was an addict.

Back in 1989 Major had told the Adam Smith Institute in a rare excursion into self-examination, 'I am not a moral philosopher, nor an economist, nor an intellectual.'[7] When asked for a political creed, he would reply with home-spun nostrums. His first policy unit deliberation, in January 1991, identified 'seven themes' as relevant to his programme. They were an opportunity society, equality of opportunity, quality of public services, enabling women, old people, wider ownership and voluntary action. Only motherhood was missing from the list. The real programme, Major told his colleagues, was 'Thatcherism with a human face', not a dilution but a consolidation — precisely the word Thatcher had rejected in her 1987 conference speech.

Initially Major was eager to be more Thatcherite than Thatcher herself, and even banned the use of the word, Majorism.[8] He wanted to be heir to Thatcherism, to dust himself with the gold of greatness, to render Thatcherism safe for perpetuity. After a while he felt the need to develop a political character of his own. Looking back, he professed scepticism towards 'the conventional view of the political right in the 1980s', that public service reform could be taken forward only by privatization. That way, he said, 'seemed to me to be too ideological, too lacking in vision or ambition.'[9]

In retrospect we can see that Thatcherism had at the start of the 1990s developed a momentum that would have required a concerted act of will to reverse. Its revolutions had come to permeate all tiers of government. The arrival of Major did not impede the first revolution's progress to privatization, indeed it released many of the brakes which Thatcher's caution had applied to it. Nor did it impede the second. Major may have demonstrated a weaker leadership style than Thatcher and was, of course, crippled by his small Commons majority, but the role of his office and that of the Treasury continued to grow. Whitehall had become dependent on central authority and its responses were conditioned by it. All Major's ministers were ardent centralists. The bathos of his period in office should not obscure the reality of the evolution of British government during his time.

As if to prove he was in earnest, Major immediately authorized three new privatizations which Thatcher had expressly forbidden, of the railways, coal and the Post Office. To Thatcher, British Rail was a manifestation of Britain's original sin, the coal mines were a national asset and the Royal Mail belonged to the Queen. Her political instinct was not even to discuss them. Major felt no such inhibition. He later downplayed his enthusiasm for privatization, typically as 'not the whole answer', but there was no half-way house. He had served in the Treasury and his close colleague, Norman Lamont, was running it. The privatizers were on a roll.

Thatcher's disposals extended only to industries that government did not need to own. Car making, shipbuilding and oil exploration were not natural monopolies. They could sink or swim on their own. Their successors in the queue, water, gas and electricity, could be run by private operators under public regulation, nor were they overly political. This did not apply to the industries which Major decided to tackle. Coal, mail and railways were regarded by the public as in some sense 'ours'. Their employees, miners, postmen and railwaymen, had their roots in the culture of working-class Britain. The latter two featured prominently in children's books and cartoons. They and their communities were engraved on Labour's soul and were likely to fight any change in their status.

Coal was ostensibly the simplest of the three. It was an extractive resource, like oil or gravel. Its chief market, electricity generation, had been privatized in 1990. With the threat of strike action gone, power generation was diversifying into gas and oil, and security of supply was less of a concern. In 1992 Major decided it was time to put coal into the market place. An extensive pre-privatization closure plan was prepared by British Coal, which involved shutting 31 pits and losing 30,000 jobs, half the mining workforce. Ten years earlier such a proposal would have provoked a general strike. The plan came to cabinet for approval in October 1992, immediately after Black Wednesday. Westminster was thus already traumatized and the economy in deep recession. The timing could not have been worse.

Thatcher would never have countenanced such a move, but Major ploughed ahead into what he referred to later as the worst time of his career so far, worse even than Black Wednesday itself. The closure programme went ahead and British Coal was privatized two years later, and successfully. The miners fought but in vain. The emotion had gone out of such battles. The final protest march on London, on 21 October 1994, was the last great demonstration by a heroic British industry and marked the passing of an age. Major had done what his mistress dared not do. But whereas she would have announced a triumph and demanded credit, he merely declared himself shattered.

Coal privatization required a bull to be taken by the horns. The Post Office was a different matter. Its sale had been on the cards since the telecommunications arm of the old General Post Office had been sold as British Telecom in 1984. Thatcher had baulked at going further, especially with a service named the 'royal mail'. Major ignored the issue at the 1992 election and saw privatization as needlessly unpopular in 1993. A year later Heseltine, by then President of the Board of Trade, prepared a White Paper on the subject. Major suspected him of trying to seize the Thatcherite mantle from Downing Street and felt the same of Heseltine's collaborator, the new chancellor, Kenneth Clarke. The latter was continuing Lawson's controls on the Post Office's investment such that even its boss, Bill Cockburn, was pleading for liberation from government ownership.

Whereas the miners had lost public support after the 1985 coal strike, the Post Office suffered no such negative image. It was symbolized by little red vans and cheery postmen at the gate. Where miners were a tribe, post-men were everyone's friends. Post offices were village meeting places and no one wanted any closed, least of all in Tory seats. One Conservative MP told Major that he regarded the prospect of 'Royal Mail plc' as he might his old regiment being privatized outside Buckingham Palace.[10] The cabinet failed to agree on Heseltine's 1994 proposal and a bruised Major was reluc-tant to push the issue, let alone risk a parliamentary defeat. Though Heseltine lobbied hard to proceed, the government backed down. What had been a tactical retreat in the face of public opinion was seen by the press as a 'humiliating defeat' for a man of straw. Both the coal and Post Office privatizations get no discussion at all in Major's memoirs, an extraor-dinary omission.

If selling coal was straightforward and selling the Post Office anything but, the railways were to be Major's highest profile contribution to the first revolution, and in the out-turn a case history of both Thatcher revolutions in one. It was doubly ironic that it was a privatization that Thatcher always refused to countenance. To her railways were too close to popular emotion, too sensitive and too complicated to succeed. To Major they were simply the next item on the list. If gas, electricity and telecommunications, why not rail? Battle was joined from the start of the new administration.

As a member of the British Rail board until 1990, I recall the plethora of consultancy reports and think-tank studies that went into preparing for the 'privatization that dared not breathe its name'. The railway had been nationalized after the war as a Morrisonian public corporation. The regional companies were grouped under a new British Transport Executive, set up in 1948 and supported by the Exchequer. Ownership was national but management was regional, able to rely on entrenched political, union and public support. Only when the Beeching reforms of the 1960s ended the age of steam and cut dozens of branch lines did the centre begin to exercise leverage, and only in the 1980s did the first Sir Bob Reid, as chairman, finally dismantle the regions and bring the railway under a fully 'nationalized' command. In 1990 BR's call on subsidy was £557 million. By the time of privatization in 1994 the operating loss was down to £267 million. BR was the cheapest and most cost-efficient rail network in Europe.[11] Had it been able to predict the rise in rail demand over the 1990s, planners would certainly have been forecasting a profitable network in the public sector.

As soon as privatization was mooted battle was joined on the various options. These embraced selling off BR as a whole, as with British Gas and BT; selling the subordinate business groups such as InterCity, London commuting and freight; or selling the old regional businesses and reverting to the *status quo ante* nationalization. Each had its champions and detractors. (I was strongly for the regional option as in Japan.) The chosen form of privatization wrecked that prospect. The Treasury had already disposed of the railway's subordinate assets – hotels, catering, ferries, docks, hovercraft, engineering works – mostly at a heavy discount to realize short-term cash. Full privatization now fell foul of Thatcherism's central paradox and the Treasury's dogma for a purchaser/provider split. A desire to de-monopolize an established industry was admirable in itself. But a rail network is not a fluid market. It is a myriad of non-competitive local monopolies which, the more they are fragmented, the more they require regulation.

The story of how the worst-case option came to be adopted has been well told by Christian Wolmar.[12] Both Major and Sarah Hogg, head of his policy unit, were in favour of breaking the railway into regions, the simplest of the break-up options. The Treasury resisted. It was strongly committed at the time to a purchaser/provider split and this involved a complex framework of internal contracts. It subsequently argued that European rules necessitated this (a necessity unknown to any other European rail network). Consultants were brought in to price everything: the value of a signal to a train, a platform to an operator or even (at Paddington) of a lavatory to its users. The Treasury negotiator, Steve Robson, bullied resistant transport officials into accepting a model that would deliver 'a reduced subsidy to a railway that was perceived as being in longterm decline.'[13] They capitulated.

The result was an extraordinary mistake. All reports on options for privatization had concluded that the one thing that should not happen was a break in management responsibility between infrastructure and those running the trains. Such 'vertical separation' would snap the line of command and lead to buck-passing and confused investment priorities. It would deprive train operators of control of their assets of track, signals and stations.[14] A railway was not a static bureaucracy with management matrices and legally enforceable internal contracts. It was more like an army in daily battle. Its generals must be accountable for every command in real time. A fragmented railway would lose that accountability and, through it, morale and public confidence.

The passage of the railways bill in 1993 was chaotic. John MacGregor, a transport secretary out of his depth, tried to claim that he was not privatizing the railway at all. He was merely bringing to it 'as much private-sector involvement, attitude, objectives and management as possible'. In honour of this the Treasury stipulated that any excess profit made on a line, the so-called 'franchise premium', would pass through the regulator to the Treasury. This meant that the Treasury would, from the start, be arbitrator of long-term rail investment. At first the infrastructure was to remain in public hands, but as the bill moved through parliament the Treasury, desperate for cash, undertook a U-turn and created what it had least wanted, a private monopoly, Railtrack plc. This would receive no subsidy but derive its highly regulated revenue from 'track access charges' levied on the private train operators. This concept was wholly unsustainable and could only have made sense in the most lofty of ivory towers. Within ten years of privatization Britain's railways were costing the Treasury five times what they had cost at denationalization in 1995.[15] Punctuality was down and so too was public satisfaction, though both did start to recover after 2004. From the passage of the act, rail reorganization was never off the government's agenda. What should have been energized by privatization was shattered by it.

The Treasury's treatment of the railway in the 1990s was probably the worst instance of Whitehall industrial mismanagement since the Second World War. It was worse than cars, ships, ports or mines because the railway was an expanding not a contracting business. It needed enterprise but not of the sort understood by Whitehall. The Victorian companies were based on integrated geographical markets mostly radiating from London. Those markets were to a remarkable extent the same in the 1990s. Yet from 1994 onwards an operator's profit relied not on generating more passengers but on the manipulation of government contracts. The fate of Railtrack depended on decisions of the Rail Regulator, and of train companies on decisions of a separate Franchise Director. Fares, schedules, track charges, safety standards, even industrial relations were all now vulnerable to ministerial interference.

The effect of privatization was to shift responsibility for the railway from the board of British Rail not to private entrepreneurs but on to ministers and regulators. Since transport ministers were soon being blamed for any shortcomings they assailed the Treasury for money. Reviewing the 1993 Act at the time, the transport economist Stephen Glaister predicted that 'previous privatizations were deliberately designed to place industries beyond the immediate reach of government. In the case of the railway, the industry may end up under more direct control than at present.'[16] Glaister pointed out that a framework which offered ministers scope for constant intervention would 'negate the achievements and improvements which privatisation was supposed to bring'. Glaister was right in every particular. In 1995 the outgoing chairman of BR, the second Sir Bob Reid, told the transport secretary, Brian Mawhinney, he might as well call himself chairman of British Rail whatever the act might say, since that is what he would become in the public's eye. The new structure came into being in 1996, in a flurry of bad publicity about the salaries and bonuses claimed by the new directors and managers. Within two years it began to collapse. Mawhinney attempted to control a Railtrack strike from Whitehall, and intervened in fare levels and scheduling decisions. The Major government did push the railway formally into the private sector, but command and control went in the opposite direction. Private companies became subcontractors to policy laid down in Whitehall.

Treasury officials argued in private that industries such as a railway cannot be half in and half out of the public sector. British Rail should either have been properly privatized, as were water, electricity and telecoms, with so-called light-touch regulation, or run as a government department. Yet the first was industrially naive and the second was achieved only in 2005 after twelve years of chaotic hybridity (see below). The Treasury gave birth to Railtrack and then rolled over and crushed it. Major's instinct, to reform the old regional companies, had been right but he did not have the grasp on policy which Thatcher showed over hospitals. As a former chancellor he was in awe of the Treasury and could not see the danger in what he was allowing to happen. The railway policy had been launched as an exhilarating adventure in privatization yet was ensnared in centralization.

Major's three attempted privatizations showed his commitment to Thatcher's legacy. Lesser ones continued as if on autopilot: the Stationery Office, the Crown Agents, defence suppliers and extensive 'sale-and-lease-back' of government property. The Treasury even privatized its own building on the corner of Parliament Square. The period also saw the extension of local government competitive tendering to white-collar administration. Bitterly fought by the Labour party under the Tories, public administration was to become one of the most lucrative areas of subcontracting under Blair. While internal transfer pricing within the public sector largely failed, private subcontracting rapidly became the default mode of British government.

The so-called 'disciplines of the private sector' did infuse the public sector as Lawson had intended. They honoured Ridley's dictum that the state need not own what it wished to control, provided only that it had the means and the staff to exercise that control. Major's term pushed forward the first revolution with determination, but the second revolution exacted a high price.

12

The Second Revolution Strikes Back

Major owed his accession to office principally to the poll tax. If Thatcher had to go because of the tax, so the tax had to go. If Major was to give Thatcherism a human face, he had to remove its ugliest blot. Ending the tax was thus 'the most vital policy issue facing me as prime minister.'¹ The question was whether in ending it the new government would restore accountability to local government, at least honouring the original intention of the tax. In 1990 the tax had been set at a nationwide average of £363, twice the original Whitehall estimate. As an average, and with many discounts, this was hardly crippling. Britain still had one of the lowest local tax regimes in Europe. But even this seemed unenforceable. Only 60 per cent of revenue was collected in the first year and local magistrates could not, or would not, handle the backlog of prosecutions. The National Audit Office reported that the cost of collection was twice that of the former rates. This was bound to raise the level of the tax in the second year, 1991, which it was now too late to cancel.

Two questions thus presented themselves to Major's cabinet: how to minimize the incidence of the tax before the forthcoming 1992 general election, and what might be offered to replace it. The matter was being discussed in Downing Street in February 1991 when an IRA rocket blasted the garden wall. Heseltine remarked laconically that poll tax was 'a more explosive issue than even I had thought.'² The cabinet pondered the familiar alternatives and all seemed equally horrible. One option, titled 'Big Bertha' by Sarah Hogg, involved lowering the cap and hurling money at local councils to force their revenue needs below it. The cost to the Exchequer could be as high as £8 billion. Another option, the 'salami slicer', involved ever more complex adjustments and reliefs to minimize losers.³ Both meant yet another shift in the burden of paying for local spending from localities to the centre. Nor did either option offer a replacement.

Major went for a modified version of Big Bertha. He demanded £4.5 billion from the Treasury to reduce the tax in the election year of 1992 to an average of £140 a head. A despairing chancellor, Norman Lamont, had to raise VAT by 2.5 per cent to an inconvenient 17.5 per cent to pay for it. This was a truly dreadful decision. By again reducing the poll tax Major ensured that any replacement would be extremely unpopular if it restored local taxes to near their original proportion of public spending. As a result local revenue fell yet further, from covering 60 per cent of the cost of local services in the mid-1980s to covering barely 20 per cent (and capped) under Major. At such a level local accountability was near meaningless. The decision was naked cowardice.

As for a replacement, Lawson's old plan to remove education from local control resurfaced. The Home Office likewise wanted to seize control of police forces and bring them under regional authorities appointed by itself. With much strategic planning and economic development also regionalized, this would have left only social services under some sort of local discretion, with county government wholly emasculated. Hogg remarked in her memoirs that British local democracy came close to abolition in the early months of the Major administration. 'It looked for a time as if local authorities might be cut right back to rubbish collection and street lights,' she wrote, 'the kind of services they might reasonably be expected to provide out of money they could raise themselves.'[4]

Heseltine, an intermittent enthusiast for local democracy, was now given an opportunity to recast British local government, and make his lasting mark on the constitution. A number of options offered themselves: a local income tax, as in many European countries, a French habitation or variable property tax, a local sales tax, taxes on business and/or enhanced charges for specific services, such as clinics, libraries and rubbish collection. Heseltine might have examined new constitutions, such as elected mayors or county governors. He could have done what Spain was doing and leave taxation to local authorities to determine, ending in a multiplicity of small charges. He did none of these things. He funked the issue and mooted another review of local government finance.

Nobody at Westminster was any longer interested. Raising a tax on income was anathema, but so was a tax unrelated to 'ability to pay'. Sales taxes were also out, unless imposed universally by central government as a purchase tax or VAT. Property taxes penalized old people with large houses, but any property tax unrelated to house size was no less unfair as 'falling equally on the duke and the dustman'. Eventually sheer exhaustion drove the debate back to where it had started, with a tax on the assessed value of property, a 'rate'. The oldest tax was still the best and easiest to collect, as Thatcher had concluded some twenty years earlier. It was the devil everyone knew. But could a government that had just abolished such a tax, at appalling political and exchequer cost, possibly reimpose it just two years later?

COUNCIL TAX

The answer was yes. A new levy on property was introduced, based on eight bands of value and called a council tax. Nobody could bear to call it a rate. Never was a British tax invented so fast or accepted with such relief. It passed into law in March 1991. At the bidding of the Treasury the new environment secretary, Michael Howard, promptly declared the council tax capped and asked for yet more money from the Exchequer to suppress the average level. The Treasury was ready to buy power at any price. The saga of the poll tax and its demise is told as a garish Whitehall horror story in *Failure in British Government* by David Butler et al. This portrays the poll tax as a mistake, later corrected. But the new council tax did not restore the constitutional *status quo ante*. Councils were not freed to fix their own taxes and decide their own service priorities. At a time when across Europe such devolution was being widely introduced (see Chapter 19) Britain, by contrast, merely advanced the ratchet of central control. Universal capping, whether explicit or implicit, implied a standard assessment of what local councils needed to spend and what resources were available to them. It was a mathematically complex mechanism of socialist equalization, to each according to his needs, from each according to his means. It was deeply un-Tory, denying communities the freedom to choose priorities for local services, however much they might still be equalized through central grants.

When introducing the poll tax Thatcher had almost casually decided to end local taxes on business property, or rather decided to fix and gather them centrally. These constituted more than half of all local revenue. She argued that since businesses did not vote (or pay poll tax) they should not be vulnerable to continued local taxation, which often discriminated against them. It was not an argument that worried central government in levying corporation tax. The bartering of business taxes are an accepted part of dynamic urban renewal worldwide. Yet without any leave or consultation

Thatcher in effect added the local business rates to corporation tax, collected them centrally and redistributed them to their relevant councils by a complex historical formula. The introduction of council tax offered an opportunity to restore business rates to local councils. Major declined to do so. Labour in Opposition pledged itself to reverse this decision, and then broke its pledge. The Treasury always ruled.

In 1994 the so-called uniform business rate yielded £12.3 billion, against £8.8 billion from the suppressed council tax, representing a huge transfer of fiscal control from local government to the centre. The centralizing of the business rate in 1990 was the biggest single act of true nationalization ever undertaken by a British government, yet it passed virtually unnoticed. By the end of the Major period, local treasurers reckoned that their discretion to vary their budgets in response to the local franchise had shrunk to near insignificance. Another curb on their freedom was central government intervention in public-sector pay negotiations, notably of education staff, and in overseeing their borrowing and investment. With local revenue now covering barely 20 per cent of expenditure, any discretionary rise in basic spending would cause a wholly disproportionate rise in council tax and risk running up against the capping regime.

The effect of these arcane shifts in policy was that, from then on, the quality of local services and level of local taxation in Britain came to be seen as ever more the responsibility of national rather than local politics. Butler and his co-authors concluded that after the poll tax, 'local government survived, but in so emaciated and withered a form that some doubt whether it deserves the name.'[5] High-spenders fought for extra ring-fenced grants over and above their cap. More economical ones had little reason not to spend 'up to the cap'. Local government spending, which had been held down in the early 1980s, rose faster after capping than before, and party politics required the Treasury to foot the bill. As with the NHS and the railway, the Treasury's quest for control proved counter-productive. What was near comical was that the council tax offered only temporary relief. A decade later, all parties at the 2005 general election plunged into the same mire, promising 'alternatives to council tax'. The Tories indeed promised simply to abolish it.

Major's cabinet left the theoretical debate over the future of local government unresolved, but not the practical one. There was now pressure across Whitehall to appropriate control of services that had, since time immemorial, been the responsibility of local communities. Politicians such as Major, Heseltine, Baker, John Patten, Virginia Bottomley, Chris Patten, William Waldegrave and Gillian Shephard claimed to believe in rolling back the frontier of the state. Shephard even wrote a book extolling local democracy. Yet ministers stood in the House of Commons to answer for what they called 'the nation's' schools, hospitals, police, roads, social services, housing and local development. They boasted of their achievements to the press and accepted blame for any failings. As if responding to some embedded DNA, they claimed to be decentralizing power. Yet they were in the grip of a force they could not resist, the force of the second revolution.

SCHOOLS

Nowhere did Major stick closer to Thatcher's legacy than in school reform. Local schools, both primary and secondary, had narrowly escaped nationalization under Lawson and did so again under Lamont in 1991. While primary schools remained more or less intact in Baker's 1988 Act, the campaign to induce secondaries to opt for grant-maintained status limped on into the 1990s. Thatcher had intended that most schools would opt out, though only some 4 per cent did so. The fall-back concept was that the secondary sector as a whole would thrive under 'competition' between central and local institutions. Good (central government) schools would expand, helped by extra money, and bad (local) ones would fail. The model was that of purchaser/provider split, with parents as purchasers and the market as provider. Though it was virtually irrelevant over most of the country it retained considerable first-revolution appeal to ministers.

Shortly before she was toppled Thatcher commissioned a paper from her policy unit on what she called 'unbundling' local education authorities.[6] Such authorities might act as advisory bodies and 'perhaps in the long term not even that', but the purpose of the reform, said Thatcher, was to 'ease the state still further out of education'.[7] This was a fantasy. Not only had opting-out failed, but the handful of institutions that had chosen this route found that they were not remotely independent of the state. Like trust hospitals and universities, the more their money depended on central disbursement from Whitehall the more they were controlled. Baker had claimed bizarrely that his act had been 'about devolution of authority and responsibility not about enhancing central control'. The standard legal text on the 1988 Act, by Bash and Coulby, remarked as follows: 'The proclaimed denationalisation of schools and colleges was actually a de-localisation and a centralisation – bluntly nationalization.'[8] The argument over British secondary education in the 1990s was not over the role of the state, merely over which state.

Major's first education secretary was an Oxford academic, John Patten, who outdid even Baker in his reformist zeal. He was determined to make opting-out work but, like Baker, soon found the Treasury sitting across his path. Its enthusiasm for virtual competition in the public sector was exceeded only by its aversion to manifest waste in public spending. The grant-maintained schools thought they would be free to select their pupils and use new Whitehall grants to expand capacity as they chose. But this could mean leaving neighbouring local schools with shrinking sixth forms, unused classrooms and unemployed teachers. To this the Treasury was implacably opposed. It was for total nationalization or total privatization or things as they were but not for hybridity. The result was that Patten's 1993 Education Act was more gargantuan even than Baker's in 1988. It had 308 clauses to Baker's 238 and a record 55 new clauses and 1,000 amendments tabled during its passage. These were to regulate what was still supposedly a local service.

The Patten act tore away the veil of autonomy round the 'opted-out' grant-maintained schools. They would answer to a new central Funding Agency for Schools (FAS), in effect a schools NHS. Patten would appoint its members and they would appoint and sack school governors and vet admissions and investment policies. At Treasury insistence the FAS could ban surrounding local authorities from setting up competing schools near one of its own. The clear intention was to make Whitehall schools superior, while controlling the environment in which they operated. The act envisaged that all secondary school investment would be vetted by the FAS, de facto nationalization. There would also be a 'common funding formula' whereby the Treasury would fix how much should be spent on every child nationwide.

This centralist egalitarianism clashed with Patten's desire to build into his system some incentive to performance and some reward to excellence. He adopted as government policy what had been a newspaper sales gimmick, the 'ranking' of schools nationwide into a league table by GCSE and

A-level results. In future, said Patten, the common funding formula and teacher bonuses might relate to league-table performance. This ostensibly objective quantification proved to be the death of extra-curricular activity in British schools. Sport and music instantly declined and there was a widespread selling of school playing fields. The number of playing fields in England fell from 78,000 to 44,000 over the next decade.[9] This was followed by a predictable meltdown in the common funding formula. In 1995 the Treasury, controlling teacher pay, conceded teachers a 2.7 per cent statutory pay rise but allowed schools, including FAS ones, only 1 per cent to meet it. The result was a mass sacking of teachers, justifiably blamed on central government. A desperate education secretary, Gillian Shephard, had to plead in cabinet either for more cash or for a lifting of the local authority cap on council tax so the staff could be paid. Appalled by the latter prospect, the Treasury conceded more cash.

The education service under Major continued in a state of suspended animation, the struggle between the centre and locality having been left unresolved by Thatcher and Baker. Shephard claimed that grant-maintained schools were 'completely independent of government'. Again we must turn to the lawyers to see through the spin. Longman's *Education and the Law 1994* set out the implications of Major's reform in stark terms: 'It would be wrong to view the funding agency as an independent body acting at arm's length from the central government. Rather it is the direct agent of the Secretary of State, amenable to centralised direction and control.'[10] Yet for all this effort the Treasury had failed to achieve a national school service. The government hoped to use salami tactics to induce schools to detach themselves voluntarily from council control and come under the FAS. Virtually none did so. Thatcher had funked Joseph's voucher scheme and Major funked nationalization. Secondary education was left with a messy, half-hearted version of both. The argument lived to fight another virtually identical day under Blair.

UNIVERSITIES

The contrast between the government's approach to secondary and higher education was total. Thatcher came to regret her treatment of universities and in 1990 demanded a plan to free them of a control that was 'not my kind of Thatcherism' in favour of 'a radical decentralisation of the whole system'. Major had not been to university and showed no sympathy for Thatcher's change of heart. Baker's nationalization of higher education now went into overdrive. Despite his initial attempt to express university grants as a 'contract' (parallel with Clarke's hospital contracts), higher education saw traces of the first revolution only in the requirement to seek private finance for capital development, a freedom they had enjoyed as charitable institutions before.

Universities remained a virtual market with students free to choose courses at will and government, in effect, giving them a voucher to cover most of the cost (over and above a means-tested fee of £1,200 a year). Only foreigners from outside the European Union paid the full cost. This offered universities a simple way of raising money, by selling themselves hard to overseas students. London's LSE became so 'international' that a majority of its students were foreign and it was soon deriving 80 per cent of its funding from non-government sources. What was new under Major was the determination to make all higher education 'comprehensive' not just in content but in policy. The replacing of the University Grants Committee by a Universities Funding Council had been paralleled by a separate Polytechnic Colleges Funding Council, still reflecting the binary character of higher education into academic and vocational. In 1992 John Patten abandoned this duality and combined all post-school education under a new Higher Education Funding Council, answerable directly to himself. It was soon virtually part of his department.

The reform was rich in irony. The intention was to honour a commitment that a third, eventually a half, of each age group would 'go on to university'. This was done by simply declaring dozens of former local authority colleges to be universities, roughly doubling 'university numbers' at a stroke. There was an immediate boom in cheaper humanities courses at former polytechnics as they expanded to benefit from government capitation allowances. This reduced diversity in that there was a cut in science and technology places, which were less cost-effective, while students could get highly classed degrees in arts subjects. All universities were now 'polyversities'. At the same time the Treasury ruthlessly cut the capitation grant by 25 per cent in real terms between 1990 and 1995 and by a half over the 1990s as a whole.

This led to one of the most bizarre manifestations of the second revolution. In 1994 the Higher Education Funding Council sought 'value for money' by closely monitoring what happened inside universities. The search soon developed out of hand. A Research Assessment Exercise attempted to audit scholarly output by quantifiable means as a basis for determining how many stars a particular university department should be awarded and thus enabling Whitehall to know whether to give it research funding. Thus 'quantity' crucially decided the future of a department and, through it, of its university. Inspectors tried counting books and articles written, then pages written. When this was criticized for taking no account of quality, Whitehall decided to count citations of research in indices of other publications. This spawned a burst of pseudo-research as universities set up 'income-generating units' and publishing subsidiaries. If grant went with output, output there would be.

The same principle was applied to teaching, with an exercise called Quality Assurance. This was more than just a lecturer's time-sheet and tried to associate teaching with examination results and student assessment of teachers. A new Higher Education Quality Council advertised for 'quality auditors', a vocation for which 'management experience in relation to education is preferred but not considered essential'. Academics would no longer be judged by their peers either within their university or within their subject sphere, as were doctors or lawyers, but by officials drawn from the world outside, mostly management consultancy. The imparting of scholarly wisdom, by its nature unquantifiable, had to be measured if money were to flow. The exercise was bitterly resented as an intrusion on professional freedom.

As so often in the second revolution a sound principle, a quest for accountability in public finance, was distorted by the means of its implementation, rightly derided by academics as crude 'bean counting'. In academia, probably more than anywhere else, the need was for an intermediate institution not dependent on political and Treasury patronage to replace the old UGC, a body sensitive to the autonomies of academic life. None was found. The result did nothing to increase Tory standing in this sector of public life.

HOSPITALS

If universities were autonomous but were treated as agencies, Britain's hospitals under the 1990 Act had been agencies but were now supposedly autonomous. Under Thatcher's hard-fought trusts they were supposedly free to sell their services under contract to doctors. They could manage their own money and raise their own funds. As we have seen, this did not happen because the Treasury retained control over the bulk of costs through the 'provider wing' of the NHS. Doctors' and nurses' pay was centrally determined, as was the cost of drugs. The Treasury refused the trusts freedom to borrow and thus controlled their investment. The national health service was still truly nationalized.

This centralization drove up the trusts' administrative overheads, which doubled within five years. Two administrators in Northampton General Hospital became seventeen. The *Spectator*'s medical correspondent counted twenty-six 'nursing administrators' in place of three at his hospital, and no more nurses. The process was overlaid by a new science of medical audit dedicated to keeping the centre supplied with statistics. The 1990 Act's bureaucratization was so great that when the NHS was asked in 1995 to cut costs it said it could offer 10,000 hospital managerial staff 'with no loss in efficiency'. A nervous health secretary, Virginia Bottomley, reacted to renewed criticism of the state of the NHS in the customary way. In 1993 she announced the fourth reorganization since 1979.

The 1994 Health Service Act abolished lay regional committees and replaced them with eight regional outposts of the health ministry, each with its own purchaser and provider wings in accordance with Treasury ideology. All plans, priorities and contracts would in future be set by the NHS Executive, with hospital trusts answering to NHS regional offices. Despite the fiction that trusts were still independent Bottomley declared that these offices would be in charge of 'performance management', development, education, training, research and public health. She declared, hilariously, that this change would 'continue the process of devolution' stimulated by past NHS reforms.[11] Like Baker and Shephard, Bottomley was in centralist denial. She signalled the final demise of whatever first revolution traces remained in the 1990 Act by telling the Commons that the new NHS would be 'not a market where the outcome is allowed to fall where it will . . . it is a managed public service.'[12]

There were now just 4,000 lay men and women (mostly Tories) on local health boards, a remnant of the tens of thousands of Britons who had for centuries overseen the charitable delivery of health and welfare. Under the new act they became no more than cheerleaders for local NHS institutions, with neither discretion nor responsibility. Managers answered direct to NHS headquarters in Leeds, from whom they received a myriad of 'targets' and bonus opportunities. Hence it was Bottomley, not a local health authority, who appeared in court in 1995 to explain the NHS's decision on how many beds should be allocated to individual emergency services. What had been a professional confederacy became an executive autocracy. A wave of closures of cottage hospitals followed, along with a drastic curtailment of local GP services.

Research published in 2005 indicated that fund-holding by GPs and tighter management within hospitals did bring down the key indicator of operation waiting times in the early 1990s, at a rate double that which followed in Labour's first six years.[13] But the cost was high. By the end of the Tories' time in office, Bevan's desire to hear the clatter of every bedpan in the corridors of Westminster had been realized. Every bedpan was not just heard but cleaned, counted and given a place on a Whitehall shelf. Defensive statistics matched aggressive reorganization. The NHS was micro-managed from the centre to meet the needs of short-term, media-led politics. The organization became highly politicized, consuming large amounts of money in return for never-ending reorganization. The NHS was indeed the Red Army of the second revolution.

POLICE

Under Thatcher the police had, like the armed forces, enjoyed immunity from revolution. Unlike teachers, lecturers and doctors police forces were assumed to know what they were about. The reason was Thatcher's gratitude for the Police Federation being the first trade union to campaign for the Tory party (in 1979). She duly raised its pay and left it alone. Under Major this changed dramatically. With recorded crime rising, it was assumed that the police (if not society) must be in need of reform.

Since the creation of a statutory constabulary under Queen Victoria, the police had long been subject to a tug-of-war between local and central government. To legal purists a national police force was a contradiction in terms. Its unique licence to coerce private citizens was based on consent. Local watch committees, formed of vestries, councillors and magistrates, gradually transformed Shakespeare's Constable Dogberry into Dixon of Dock Green. The British police were not a government gendarmerie or a paramilitary force. They were unarmed, visible on the streets and, at least outside big cities, usually known to those they guarded.

Robert Peel had sought a national force in 1828 and was refused by a fiercely 'localist' parliament. He was allowed to run only the Metropolitan Police in London while policing elsewhere was left to local watch committees. To the historian Robert Reiner, this devolved, community-based structure lay at the root of the worldwide popularity of the British police. It was not a symbol of state power but rather of 'rule-bound authority, enforcing democratically-enacted legislation on behalf of the broad mass of society, rather than any partisan interest'.[14] The police constable was an agent not of imposed control but of communal self-discipline.

This state of grace was tarnished in the 1960s by accusations of police corruption and incompetence in combating organized crime, notably in London, ironically the one force under direct ministerial control. The solution sought was not a reform of the profession of policeman but a (much easier) reorganization of the structure, invariably in a centralist direction. The 1964 Police Act reduced the 123 forces in England and Wales to 47, mostly by merging city and county units. The Home Office assumed inspection and vetting powers and told the police to put its faith in new technology. The televised constable was no longer on foot or on a bicycle but in a fast car. *Dixon* was replaced by *Z-Cars* and *The Bill*. Though a merging of city and county forces made logistical sense, the police in general began to lose their direct relationship with local representatives and answer more to their unions and the Home Office. As Reiner put it bluntly, the image of the police 'changed from plods to pigs'.

The force that came in for the widest criticism for waste and corruption, London's 'Met', remained under direct Home Office control. Its astute commissioner in the 1970s, Sir Robert Mark, commented that the failure of the Home Office to discharge its duty ... provided the weightiest ammunition for the reformers.'[15] Yet it was this same Home Office that now declared itself best qualified to engineer reform and act as the focus of police accountability nationwide. Thatcher's generosity led police pay to double in real terms between 1979 and 1994. Young police officers were soon earning more than teachers or junior doctors. As they saw the bonds tying them to their localities weaken, so they retreated into professional autonomy, fiercely defended by their union, the Police Federation, which regularly terrorized Home Office ministers. Their arrogance, especially towards ethnic minority groups, became a constant source of friction and controversy and drew police reform ever more into the political arena.

The police moved steadily out of the frying pan of local control into the fire of the Home Office fortress overlooking St James's Park. Already in 1988 the Home Office had taken powers to control police numbers, to vet investments over £1 million and to determine the purchase of police vehicles. In February 1994 the president of the Association of Chief Police Officers remarked that 'we are witnessing a move, perhaps unintended, for national control of the police by central government.'[16] He warned that public respect for the police had taken a blow from their being 'Maggie's boot boys' during the miners' strike. Police officers had sold their souls to Whitehall and the devil would demand its pound of flesh.

Major did not share Thatcher's indulgence of the police. The British Crime Survey (BCS) showed crime rising, and for him such figures had the same magnetism as hospital waiting lists and school league tables. They were the raw material for his daily shouting match with the media. Home secretaries soon considered it their job to fix the size of truncheons, the use of body armour and the response times to 999 calls. Kenneth Clarke as home secretary in 1992 was as dismissive of local police committees as he had been of local control of schools and hospitals. The 1993 local elections stripped the Tories of control of every one of the forty-one English police committees.

What happened next was a second revolution classic. Clarke staged a bid to become minister of police. A 1993 White Paper proposed that the forty-one forces should be amalgamated, to a number rumoured to be twenty-five or however many chief constables could be got round the Home Office conference table. In future their committees would be appointed by the home secretary from 'the business community' (code for Tory supporters). Clarke declared he had 'no faith in elected people' to run the police, which should be run 'independent of local councils'.[17] Yet even Clarke felt obliged to utter the mantra that his measure was intended to make the police more 'directly accountable to their local communities'. He was doing the precise opposite.

In the middle of the passage of the new legislation Clarke gave way to Michael Howard at the Home Office. Howard now had to face a hostile reaction to Clarke's plan in the House of Lords. One former home secretary after another stood up to protest. Lord Carr said, 'If I were still Home Secretary I would not accept the offer of powers of this kind. I would resign rather than accept them.' Lord Callaghan said there was no demand for the new powers, other than 'the desire of the Home Secretary to strengthen his influence'. He added eloquently that 'the strength of democracy comprises a web and complex of local institutions and local bodies made up of people serving in different ways.'[18] Not a single speaker on either side of the House was in favour of what was seen as a constitutional outrage. Howard diluted the structure and abandoned force amalgamation, but pressed ahead with control. The 1994 Police Act allowed the home secretary to set police objectives and publish results 'so the public knows what their force has delivered', albeit against his targets not theirs. The White Paper was explicit on this. Reform would 'refocus police priorities and direct them to those things which the government considers the police should be tackling as priority tasks across the country.'[19]

Political targetry became the bugbear of law and order. Anything that could be measured was measured, 999 calls, response times, staff on duty, clear-up rates and, above all, recorded crime. Ignored was anything that could not be measured, such as public reassurance through beat policing. Police recorded crime became an obsession, although it measured only what was reported to police stations and could thus be influenced by the opening or closing of stations or even the readiness to answer a phone. A minor change in insurance rules, a new definition of vandalism or the operation of a call centre all affected the recorded figure. So-called consensual crimes such as speeding, drugs and alcohol abuse rose or fell in response to enforcement. Crime figures were like quicksilver, yet they were the dominant raw material of control.

In a commentary on Howard's act the policeman-turned-academic Barry Loveday remarked that it gave Britain 'a new NHS', with chief constables as NHS executives. The 1994 Act meant that 'the police will cease to be a local service and will become effectively a state police.'[20] The result was predictable. The Treasury had argued for central control on the grounds that local forces had become wasteful and inefficient. A possible response might have been that practised in America, with one tier of police supplying specialized services on a federal and state basis but the generality of police under local authorities who paid their wages. Britain in the 1990s went in the opposite direction. It diminished local accountability and turned the police into what amounted to a government agency under the Home Office. Spending soared. Police costs doubled in real terms under Thatcher and rose by another quarter in Major's first four years. The more the Treasury pressed the Home Office to take control the more adverse was the impact on cost-effectiveness. Howard had no sooner passed the 1994 Act than he announced another 'fundamental review of police functions'. Whitehall could not keep still. Home Office targets encouraged reactive, high-tech policing. The public's experience of their constables was of officers in cars racing noisily through the streets, harassing their children and vulnerable minorities. Accidents involving police vehicles rose dramatically.[21]

One significant side effect of the 1994 Act was a boom in private security. Deprived of front-line and street police, the public's fear of crime rose and neighbourhoods turned to the private sector to supply night-time dog patrols. In London's Oxford Street in the late 1990s I counted four separate security agencies, the Metropolitan police, Westminster City's community support officers, the street association patrol and shop security guards. The Clarke/Howard reforms had detached Britain's police from their communities and sought to establish a national gendarmerie ruled by central targets. Not for another ten years did the public's cry for more 'police on the beat' reach the government's ears, and secure another bout of reform under Labour.

THE JUSTICE SYSTEM

One reason for the diversion of police effort from community reassurance and protection was the torrent of new laws laid on them by ministers. Every Tory manifesto professed a desire to shift power from the state to the individual, yet every Tory government shifted it in the other direction. There was never a White Paper on 'liberty', just dozens restricting every aspect of human and civic behaviour. A government lawyer told me that on his estimate Thatcher 'created' over 900 new offences in her term of office. They embraced drugs, litter, vandalism, terrorism, pollution, planning, matrimony, pets, noise, safety, assembly and minority rights, not to mention a mass of European Commission directives.

The tempo of legislation under eighteen years of Tory rule was unequalled in British history. Michael Howard's first speech as home secretary in 1993 promised twenty-seven new laws, on trespass, stop-and-search, antiterrorism, use of DNA, witnesses, bail and urine tests. Not one of these 'rolled back the frontier of the state'. All rolled it forward. Parliament passed just six criminal justice acts between 1925 and 1985. Thatcher and Major passed one every eighteen months. (Blair was to pass three a year.) This was legislation beyond the realistic drafting capacity of government and beyond the capacity of the police to enforce. The Home Office was like a signal box with its wires cut. It pulled levers that no longer responded and no longer delivered security. Rather than inspect and repair the wiring, it installed more levers.

Judicial independence was a core feature of the British constitution, but like all such features it was nowhere entrenched. It was 'embodied' by the status of the House of Lords as the supreme court and the presence of the Lord Chancellor in cabinet. Beyond this lay an archaic structure of criminal and civil courts with, at the bottom, a lay local magistracy handling 90 per cent of criminal cases. The more laws were passed, the more expensive this system became, not least because access to the law was meant to be 'means-blind', in other words free. Under Thatcher the cost of the legal system rose fourfold in real terms while legal aid rose even faster. Such open-ended spending could not be tolerated by the Treasury. The stage was set for an extension of control.

In 1985 the Thatcher government had replaced the system of local police solicitors with a new Crown Prosecution Service (CPS). This nationalized a previously private service. Such nationalization had been recommended by a Royal Commission in the 1970s but with an insistence that the service be kept accountable to local police committees. Anything else, the Commission warned, 'would involve a large bureaucracy and tend to lead to slow and remote decision-making'.[22] The warning was not heeded. Thatcher opted for nationalization but rejected the case against bureaucratization. She wanted a service not open to 'improper local interference' but was careless of the national variety. Local soliciting firms which had fitted police work into their normal business now had to become civil servants or withdraw from prosecution work altogether. Within eight years the CPS was being described in the *Criminal Law Review* as 'blatantly susceptible to the politically inspired policies ... of the latest Home Secretary'.[23]

Major did not return to the lost cause of reforming the Bar, which had defeated his predecessor, but if he could not reform the top of the judiciary he could at least attack the bottom. Magistrates had been key institutions of local autonomy since the Middle Ages. Selected by lord lieutenants through local appointments committees they were, like juries and parish councils, a familiar feature of British civic life. They were colourful and diverse, responding to local custom and practice. There was no public outcry calling for change, nor was it possible to claim that the magistracy did not work or was expensive.

The 1994 Police and Magistrates Court Act transferred all responsibility for magistrates from local jurisdiction to the Lord Chancellor's department in London. Howard, as home secretary, recited the customary chant, that this was not centralist but would improve the 'efficiency and effectiveness of the service ... and improve accountability both locally and to parliament.'[24] Accountability to parliament took the form of greater Treasury control. A total of 105 magistrates' committees was reduced to 50 or 60. Their composition would no longer be 'primarily representative', but based on 'business experience'. A new central inspectorate would be appointed, and a new computer bought. Magistrates lacked the clout of High Court judges and the reform stuck. Howard's improved local accountability was nowhere to be seen.

The government then advanced further into enemy territory. In 1995 a new Courts Services Agency (CSA) took over the running of all courts, magistrates, criminal, civic and High Court. The Lord Chancellor would in future appoint and employ all 10,000 staff nationwide. The CSA was another new Tory nationalized industry, alongside the Crown Prosecution Service, and it was shortly joined by a third. Legal aid was rising fast, fuelled by the flood of new legislation, from £180 million in 1979 to an astonishing £1.3 billion in 1995. Under Treasury pressure, Lord Mackay declared the legal aid budget 'cash limited', with private lawyers no longer free to invoice the state at will. Regional offices of a Legal Aid Board would subcontract work only to approved solicitors for whom legal aid would need to be 90 per cent of their work. This covered some 1,000 practices who were told they would have to subscribe to civil service terms and conditions for their staff. In its understandable bid to curb an exploding area of public spending, the government had created a Crown Defence Service in all but name.

The Crown Prosecution Service, the Courts Services Agency, the Legal Aid Board, the new magistracy and the centralized apparatus of ministerial sentencing all told in one direction. What had been a pluralist, localized and part-privatized judicial system was now a national industry. The Lord Chancellor's department became one of the largest in Whitehall, with what was to prove the most intractable budget and the most vocal lobby behind it, the legal profession. One consequence was to standardize sentencing, usually with more lenient parts of the country driven to conform to more draconian ones. The prison population rose persistently over this period, to which Thatcherism responded by inviting private companies to build and run new prisons. By the turn of the twenty-first century Britain had the highest proportion of its population in prison of any country in Europe.[25]

CHARITIES

That the British do not give readily to charity is a familiar complaint of those who rely on it. The traditional view used to be that the welfare state and the taxes that financed it, entrenched over half a century, had supplanted the 'giving culture' familiar in countries such as America. In Britain larger-scale charity had been nationalized and generosity subcontracted to the state. Giving to charity would therefore merely let the state off the hook.

By the late 1980s, British personal taxation was no longer high, indeed it was among the lowest in Europe. Yet the motivation to give by means of tax deduction remained weak. Government took the same view as had taxpayers, that if it was the lead player in the welfare business it should not forego taxes to encourage private citizens to do likewise. The Treasury refused, year after year, to concede personal tax relief for charitable giving. Charities could reclaim tax on covenants by givers, but there should be no charitable bias for philanthropists at the taxpayer's expense. As a result, in the 1980s Americans were giving roughly five times more per head than Britons.

Thatcher introduced a modest scheme of tax-free payroll giving run by companies for those on PAYE. It yielded so little that it did not even appear in the Treasury's published accounts. As soon as Major took office a proposal was circulated by an arts administrator, Denis Vaughan, for a state lottery to finance the arts. Lotteries had been used by the Georgians to end slavery, build Westminster Bridge and complete the Adelphi terraces, but the development of taxation rendered lottery finance both unreliable and undignified. Only when casino gambling came into favour in the 1970s did arts lobbyists begin to covet its revenues to pay for good causes.

No sooner was the proposal mooted in 1990 than the chief loser from any lottery, the football pools, rushed to defend their turf. With £13 billion in turnover and a large tax donation to the Treasury the pools found a ready ally in Major's first chancellor, Lamont. The outcome was a Sports and Arts Foundation financed from a surcharge on all gambling revenue, amounting to £60 million a year. Lamont proceeded to work on it. At the same time Baker, now at the Home Office, adopted a more ambitious project, for a monopoly national lottery run independent of existing gambling interests and generating far more revenue. It was what the Treasury most feared, a large but unpredictable flow of revenue detracting from the existing gambling tax and disrupting other public expenditure.

Baker won the support of Major and of the cabinet, thus scotching the Sports and Arts Foundation. A national lottery offered the prospect of pain-free money and the Treasury was forced to change its tune. It would support the lottery, provided it could control it. Baker recalls, 'It was typical of the Treasury that, having lost a particular battle, it now wanted to profit from it.'[26] He won an assurance that lottery donations would not replace existing public grants. This principle of 'additionality' was enshrined in nothing stronger than a Commons statement. The Treasury demanded 12 per cent of takings in tax and insisted that ministers should appoint the distribution quangos, retaining power to direct 'in the broadest terms how the money can be used'. As Baker commented, 'the Treasury officials needed a stake through their hearts before policies are safe from their clutches'.

The Treasury moved swiftly to protect its new revenue monopoly. Competitive lotteries were banned and no other form of public gaming could offer prizes of more than £25,000. The National Lottery was a new nationalized industry, subcontracted at a large profit to a private consortium named Camelot. Its directors became instant millionaires, to the fury of the entrepreneur Richard Branson, who had proposed a scheme run by a not-for-profit company. Camelot was a modern reincarnation of a medieval 'tax farmer'. In the Commons Labour and Tory MPs alike referred to Camelot as the 'unacceptable face of nationalization'. It diverted into its pockets a large share of Britain's gambling industry, initially estimated at £6 billion. Vernons Pools lost 15 per cent of its takings overnight. Camelot was a parastatal monopoly protected from market forces by government statute.

Any opening for a private lottery to raise money for specific causes, such as Covent Garden Opera, the British Museum or a sports stadium, was thus stifled. All applicants for money would have to go cap in hand to a central quango for largesse, whether for the arts, sport or philanthropic charities. As a member of one distributor body, the Millennium Commission, I was astonished at the triviality of projects coming forward for London approval and funding (quite apart from the staggering cost of others). It was clear that local sources of money were drying up in favour of national. Among the losers were not just the gambling interests but local charities which had depended on local giving. Tins for loose change in corner shops were replaced by Camelot's computer terminals. The raising and distributing of money for charity was overwhelmed by a hugely profitable private monopoly. The government had nationalized even the smallest and most intimate of civic acts, philanthropy.

As for the Treasury's pledge that lottery grants would be additional to normal public spending, this was soon broken. New projects for clinics, science centres, sport, the arts or conservation, once financed from taxation, were rejected on the grounds that the lottery could suffice. Ministers started referring to lottery projects as 'mine'. Like the National Insurance Fund and the Road Fund, what had been a tax hypothecated to a particular spending became just another tax and, in practice, a highly regressive one. Money from small-time gambling poured into such ventures as Covent Garden Opera, the British Museum and Tate Modern. In 2005 the lottery was ordered by its minister, Tessa Jowell, to finance the government's most treasured prestige project, the 2012 Olympic Games in East London. There was no nonsense about a special Olympics lottery. The distributing bodies found their allocations cut and their revenue diverted to building (mostly one off) facilities for the Olympics. The lottery had unleashed prestige expenditure reminiscent of the chauvinism of former eastern Europe.

13

The Treasury and the Cult of Audit

Major was not by nature an authoritarian leader. He was no establishment oligarch or elected dictator but rather a seeker after consensus. He was also rare among modern prime ministers in having served a respectable apprenticeship outside politics and in local government. He should have been well-disposed towards a dispersal of power rather than its concentration. That he should have taken so readily to the apparatus of control left him by Thatcher is puzzling.

The answer is that centralism was the only vehicle Major found in the Downing Street garage on arrival. He had no schooling in the conventions of the British constitution. Like his successor, Tony Blair, his parliamentary career had been spent watching Thatcher knock the stuffing out of such conventions. His rise owed little to his party nationally, and he had no professional loyalty to such autonomous estates of the realm as the law, academia, the City or the media. His only debt was to Thatcher's patronage and to his colleagues in the Whips' Office and the Treasury. Major's governmental experience was mostly confined within the walls of Nos 11 and 12 Downing Street, the offices of the chancellor and the chief whip.

The Treasury has featured prominently in this book because it is by far the dominant institution of British government, yet one persistently underrated by observers. Most of my working life has been employed in the private sector, but I have come into contact with the machinery of government through serving on the boards of various public institutions, a museum, two arts centres, two transport nationalized industries and three quangos in the fields of environment, charity and health. Over every one the Treasury's shadow has hovered, its generosity often considerable and its influence by no means always malign. But it has shadowed. It is far more than the nation's bank manager. It sets the rules of engagement for audit and accountability and, as a result, dictates the terms of success or failure for governors and staff. It is immensely powerful.

Yet the Treasury is one of the least reported, least studied and most secretive of British institutions. Westminster politicians and journalists treat it with a mystic reverence that puts it beyond comment or criticism. Ministers fear it, turning their faces at its approach as medieval abbots might avert the evil eye. Few Britons, even the politically alert, appreciate the full extent of the Treasury's power or how far it has conditioned the actions of successive governments and their servants. It is by far the most potent finance ministry in the free world, because it is subject to fewer checks or balances. The Treasury's leading personalities are little known outside the upper echelons of government, while their boss, the chancellor of the Exchequer, declares no parliamentary responsibility for public services, only for something vaguely termed economic management.

In any administration the Treasury's political power varies in inverse relationship to that of the prime minister. If the latter is weak, as was Major, the former is strong. The Treasury has an interest in every policy and a dog in every fight. Lawson, the most imperial chancellor of modern times, wrote that a ministry of finance should always be the fountainhead of government. It was 'in reality the Central Department, with a finger in pretty well every pie that the government bakes'.[1] By its control over public finance it holds in its hands the fate of ministers and their policies.

Treasury officials in the 1980s and 1990s were Britain's equivalent to France's administrative elite of *énarques*. Few had experience of the outside world, even of business, finance, academia or the media. Few had been consumers of Treasury decisions elsewhere in Whitehall or in the wider public sector. Their one constantly recalled trauma was the 1976 IMF humiliation described in Chapter 2. It led to an attitude of mind whereby all outsiders, ministers, civil servants, civic leaders and trade unionists could not be trusted. Everywhere was a potential ambush against sound finance. The Treasury duly approached any new government with deep scepticism, especially one laden with expensive election promises, as was Thatcher's in 1979.

At the time one of the Treasury's post-war giants, Sir Leo Pliatsky, was fashioning a new armoury of cash limits and planning totals specifically to prevent a repetition of 1976. To Pliatsky the Treasury was not just the nation's bank manager but its auditor, counsellor and guardian. He called it 'the Day of Judgment institutionalised'.[2] To such a man Thatcher, despite her spending pledges, offered hope. She had already pinned her colours to the mast of sound money. Departmental budgets should expect no automatic uplift for inflation, she had said. A cabinet 'star chamber' would curb extravagant ministers. When the new government proceeded with Howe's ferocious 1980 and 1981 Budgets, Thatcher's valiant defence of them persuaded the Treasury that here at last was a prime minister after its own heart.

A rare insight into the Treasury was produced by the BBC in 1983 in a series of radio interviews.[3] They revealed a department introverted and apart, a monastic order at the heart of government. One official, David Hancock, remarked that 'a system of financial control in any institution is essentially one of tension. The effect on those inside is essentially like people under siege: it develops a sort of fellow-feeling.' This detachment extended to the chancellor. The Treasury always sought to keep him above the political fray. He hardly ever appeared before parliament, whether at the dispatch box or before committees, yet he lived next door to the prime minister in Downing Street. The Treasury struggled to keep the chancellor both close to the seat of power yet not tarnished by its political rough and tumble. Blame for mistakes must never attach to him. When he won a spending battle, as he always must, it was for the defeated minister to defend the result in public.

Thatcher's chancellors were ideally suited to this job. Neither Howe nor Lawson was a charismatic figure. Neither attracted political lightning, nor were they plausible challengers for the top job. The same applied to Major's first chancellor, Norman Lamont, who even succeeded for a time in excusing himself from the Black Wednesday debacle. His successor, Kenneth Clarke, felt independent enough to oppose his boss over Europe but the partisanship later denied him his party's leadership. Not only are chancellors politicians apart, but that apartness blights their subsequent careers – witness Labour's Roy Jenkins and Denis Healey and the travails of Gordon Brown in succeeding Tony Blair.

Lawson long pondered how best to perfect Treasury control over the public sector. So obsessed did he become by this control that he and his successors were blind to how far it might vitiate the overriding objective of expenditure restraint. Lawson was right in seeing the public sector in a democracy as requiring constant and single-minded vigilance. He was wrong in believing that he would best achieve this ambition by centralizing control. He merely increased the pressure on ministers to spend. Lawson dismissed all other conduits of control, such as local democracy or autonomous agencies, wrongly believing them to be inherently more spendthrift than a central cabinet.

Thatcherism's greatest error was its belief that central government was the citadel of unvarying virtue in managing the public realm. At no point did a minister suggest that anywhere but Whitehall might be more effective in managing public services. The model hierarchy of public expenditure had Downing Street at its pinnacle, surrounded by a sea of indiscipline and extravagance. That this model was false can be seen in the figures, in the story of local government finance, in the cost of new schools or the management of the increasingly centralized health service. Tory governments in the 1980s and 1990s did not cut public spending. When Thatcher left office her claim on domestic taxation was little different from when she arrived.

The truth is that all ministers are politicians before they are Thatcherites. Their default mode is not to cut but to spend, because that is popular. The more a category of spending falls within their direct responsibility, the less inclined they are to cut it. Thatcher may have talked tough in general, but she rarely acted tough in particular. She indulged the budgets of defence, law and order and social security because they were hers. Every time she endorsed a shift from delegated to centralized power, she increased not just the political exposure of her ministers but the burden on the Exchequer. When ministers had to answer for the performance of schools, hospitals, railways or the police they fought ever harder for resources. No Thatcher programme (not even housing) became cheaper for being centralized. Public spending in the last quarter of the century did not just rise in real terms, it doubled.

The Treasury's campaign for greater mastery over the public sector took many forms. One concerned senior personnel. Before Thatcher, departmental permanent secretaries usually rose from within their ministries. In 1981 Thatcher allocated such appointments to the Treasury, and from then on permanent secretaryships went increasingly to Treasury alumni. A rare insight into this process was given by the Americans Hugh Heclo and Aaron Wildavsky. They traced how expenditure control after 1976 became the dominant ethos of Whitehall's elite, guided by 'a private political/administrative community of officials who knew each other and regularly exchanged jobs'.[4] Major was just the man to take forward this ethos. Though never a Treasury intellectual he was a member of its club. His campaign for prime minister was staged from the Treasury, led by his chief secretary, Norman Lamont. Sarah Hogg later recalled that 'Treasury officials liked, supported and encouraged him to stand. They relished his success . . . As they spread out across Whitehall on promotion to permanent secretary, he greeted them as long-lost friends.'[5] Not only did Major make Lamont his chancellor but he chose his cabinet secretary, private secretary, press secretary and home affairs secretary from the same department. Major's government was a Treasury coterie.

If the Treasury could not cash-limit welfare payments it could at least try to control the next biggest determinant of public expenditure, government 'pay and rations'. This included the number and remuneration of civil servants and other public employees such as teachers, doctors and nurses. It did so by insisting on a Treasury 'presence' at every public-sector pay negotiation and Treasury approval for all extra staff. The consequence was a contradiction. Whitehall would assure its new agencies and subcontractors of their executive autonomy within an agreed budget, but the Treasury would then meddle in every staffing decision. It would vet the pay of a British Rail board member, the number of nurses in a hospital or the need for a museum press officer. Nobody dared object. The control was instinctive and obsessive.

The Treasury fondly believed that it was a stern negotiator. It was not. Of the three groups of public-sector employers, local government, nationalized industries and the Treasury, the last was (and still is) the softest touch. Bringing labour of any sort under a monopoly purchaser allowed the unions to monopolize supply. They could inflate regional baselines to the price of labour in the tightest market, usually the south-east. The London-based Treasury seemed not to understand that pay varied widely across Britain and that employers were stronger in the north than the south. The result was swift public-sector wage inflation in the north. This in turn inflated private wages and thereby weakened the competitive advantage offered by cheaper labour in more deprived areas of Britain. A private employer in Sunderland had to compete for staff in a market determined by the price of teachers or nurses in Winchester. What should have been a virtue of Thatcherite decontrol of labour markets was vitiated by Treasury centralism.

As it struggled to control money, the Treasury delved ever deeper into policy. As we have seen, it secured 'Treasury clauses' in acts of parliament restructuring the public sector. Not an interdepartmental committee would sit without a Treasury official present. Not a paper was distributed for discussion without a 'view' from the Treasury. It even viewed with concern the partial decentralization of Whitehall into stand-alone agencies and quangos. By 1995 there were 51 such 'Next Steps' agencies and over 500 quangos, responsible for over half of central government activity. Other empires grew to regulate them. A wider role was sought by the Comptroller and Auditor General, the National Audit Office and the Audit Commission covering local government and health. These were supported by a booming industry of private consultants and accountants. Such groups were unlikely to confine their attention to balancing the books. They cast their net over efficiency, effectiveness and value-for-money. Audit could extend as far as a ball of string.

The Treasury under Thatcher had opposed Lord Rayner's Financial Management Initiatives, intended to measure departmental performance against targets. It also opposed Sir Robin Ibbs' Next Steps agencies and their delegated budgets. To the Treasury all such devices risked justifying higher spending. Lawson publicly warned Ibbs off his patch, telling him there could be no question of an innovation 'institutionalising present levels of expenditure and then trying to console ourselves that public-sector output has risen'. Value-for-money (VFM) was a Trojan horse, out of which would pour an army of lobbyists pleading for cash. Without the Treasury dominant, Lawson said, 'the alternative is no financial discipline at all'. He even cited the Treasury-less Soviet Union where 'the result is chaos'.[6] As for the National Audit Office, Lawson was infuriated by its ambition to bring departmental 'performance against policy objectives' into its remit. He saw this as so dangerous that he specifically vetoed any mention of it in the new National Audit Act of 1983.[7] He claimed the exclusive right to supervise 'the three E's of economy, efficiency and effectiveness'.

Government audit may seem as sensational as Oscar Wilde's History of the Rupee. Yet its evolution was integral to Thatcherism's second revolution. The fall of Lawson and the arrival of Major in Downing Street saw no let up in the struggle to quantify public service. Major's policy chief, Norman Blackwell, came from the consultants McKinsey, whose informal motto was that only the measurable is manageable. To pundits of expenditure control, VFM audit seemed at last to offer the philosopher's stone of modern government. By measuring 'inputs' against 'outputs' it offered feedback from the front-line to headquarters. The Treasury saw the nation as a firm, whose assets and liabilities only needed counting for an annual profit and loss to be declared. Whatever might be important, if it could not be measured it was trivial. It was as if the Utilitarian 'unit of welfare' had finally arrived at the heart of government. Now at last, it was thought, the aggregates of the public sector could be adequately controlled and Kant's crooked timber of mankind made straight. The only question was who should measure the timber. The answer, of course, was the Treasury.

The most public display of quantification was the craze for league tables. First adopted for school exam results by John Patten as education secretary, they swiftly spread from education to embrace university research, hospital waiting lists, infant mortality, heart disease, police performance, planning approvals, even fertility clinic success rates. League tables were taken up by the Audit Commission, charged with monitoring the performance of thousands of local councils and hospital boards across the country. The constitution might state that institutions such as schools, day centres, libraries, clinics and hospitals should be managed in accordance with the wishes of local people, but such local discretion collapsed before the onward march of performance monitoring.

In the 1990s the Audit Commission began issuing targets and league tables of ever greater complexity. Any divergence from the average was, by implication, an offence against national equity. These measuring tools were used not just to 'name and shame' backsliding councils and health districts but to allocate resources under what swiftly became a framework of top-down dirigisme. Executives 'managing the target' were constantly in the news. In hospitals fast operations took priority over slower ones. In schools, physical fitness, extra-curricular activities, music or after-work clubs fell by the wayside. The LSE's Michael Power referred to this period as one of 'audit explosion'.[8] Major preferred to call it 'the regulatory goad to raise customer standards'.[9] Most officials date its exponential growth from the early 1990s. Every police stop-and-search had to be written down. Every teacher had to answer in writing for every hour spent in school. Every medical treatment was recorded, usually in triplicate. Every risk was assessed and every journey logged. Health and safety became a by-word not for health and safety but for madcap rules, gold-plated and supercharged by European regulations, which Britain alone seemed to regard as holy writ.

Into this arcane world Major tossed his favourite contribution to public administration, the Citizen's Charter. This emerged from a common-sense analysis of Thatcherism's unfinished business. The public sector was, Major said, the forgotten rump left behind by privatization. It was run 'carelessly, wastefully, arrogantly and more for the convenience of the providers than the users'.[10] People were left complaining and public servants left without self-esteem. As a result, he said, Conservatives were regarded as uncaring custodians of services, grudging and embarrassed where they should have been confident and proud. Something must be done.

Major declined to go down the route then being pursued in Scandinavia and elsewhere on the Continent and take service delivery closer to the client. He launched a new centralist crusade. His Citizen's Charter would tackle the 'dark side of the coin' of public services, the broken telephone boxes, the rude receptionists, the delayed appointments, the anonymous call centres. New standards would be set by Whitehall to ensure quality, efficiency and VFM at a uniform level throughout the public sector. All these would need quantifiable outputs if the charter was to work.

The charter was Major's proudest boast, occupying twenty pages of his memoirs against barely three for privatization. Every domestic policy was to be shoe-horned into its framework. The charter spawned conferences, seminars and task forces. Consultants clustered round it, sensing money. Thatcher's carnivores were transformed into Major's herbivores. The charter evoked touchy-feely management, glass-box architecture and customer care awards. Everyone had to 'sign up' to it and then 'sign off'. Majorism was Thatcherism tamed and neutralized into a glorified Consumers Association.

Major was determined that the charter would have bite. One sure sign of this was the outbreak of a Whitehall turf war. Major's biographer, Anthony Seldon, remarked that 'not since 1964 had there been so much resistance and suspicion in Whitehall to a prime minister's wishes.'[11] The most scornful response came inevitably from the Treasury. The Citizen's Charter did not save money or promise privatization receipts, yet its mere existence seemed to threaten Treasury authority. As a former chancellor, Major understood this, commenting, 'The schizophrenia of the Treasury when presented with a scheme to improve public service was wonderful to behold.' It was happy to press on 'with privatization, contracting-out and competition policy', but fought against anything that might better the lot of the public sector. The real trouble, he said, was that the charter was 'not invented here'.[12]

The Citizen's Charter was in truth a classic of central micro-management. Its officials went about the country awarding 'charter marks' for altering the times of driving tests, improving the comfort of jury rooms and seeking compensation for passengers whose trains were late. It was vaguely reminiscent of Soviet commissars seeking popularity by overriding local officials with some benign gesture. It inevitably detracted from the accountability of subordinate government and attracted armies of inspectors and monitors from the centre. In short, it was a recipe for red tape. When Major departed in 1997 the charter withered away. But the zest to quantify did not die with it, enhanced each year by some new regime. The Treasury demanded that the entire public sector draw up a Domesday Book of assets and account for the value derived from them. Information was power, and the Treasury was voracious for it. Audit became dynamic and, for officials, accountants, consultants and lawyers, highly profitable. I sat on three public-sector audit committees in the 1990s and was astonished at the numbers round the table, notebooks poised, clocks ticking, taxpayers paying. They added no value commensurate with their numbers. They were defensive, risk-averse bureaucracy, the opposite of accountability. They bespoke officials covering their backs, ensuring that if anything went wrong they would not be to blame.

A subtle but significant change came over ministers at this time. They were no longer aloof 'policy-makers', responsible under statute to parliament. Policy slid upwards to Downing Street and its cabinet office policy units, either in conflict or in collusion with the Treasury. Spending ministers, so-called, became de facto chief executives, finance officers, publicists and fall guys. Not a day would pass without the media demanding 'something be done' about some front-page crisis. A child was denied a costly drug. Why? A prisoner escaped from prison. Why? A train crashed. Why? A factory was refused planning permission, a beach was soiled, a historic house demolished. Why? When all responsibility shot upwards it soon vanished into the clouds, leaving only public relations behind. A close observer of Thatcherism, Jim Bulpitt, quoted one Whitehall victim of this hyperactivity as complaining, 'It's like a Great War artillery bombardment. It goes on and on and destroys everything above ground.'[3] Talking to senior officials was like debriefing officers returned from the front. They described a never-ending trench warfare, caught between a Treasury barrage on one side and a media minefield on the other. The result was a frantic increase in the administration's version of 'defensive medicine', control.

Major's justification for the growth of central bureaucracy under his reign repeated Thatcher's. The accretion of power to the centre was temporary. 'Thereafter in time,' he recalled, 'I anticipated formal regulation withering away, as the effects of growing competition were felt.'[14] This concept of withering away runs as a leitmotif through the key texts of 'Marxism-Thatcherism', usually followed by a note of despair. By the time Major came to write his memoirs he admitted ruefully that 'We now appear to have the worst of all worlds.' Regulation had increased but the state had failed to wither as required. There were still poor services and 'intrusive and costly regulation'. Major deplored 'those who scoffed at the pettiness of the [charter] programme', but he agreed that it did not catch the public imagination. Perhaps, he mused, it would be 'on the agenda of the next Conservative government'.

Under Major, Thatcherism's second revolution reached a sort of stasis. The constitution was losing its informal checks on elected dictatorship. Although the Commons came to prominence in the mid-1990s through Major's small majority, it used this prominence to undermine the prime minister's position rather than increase scrutiny of the executive. There was no reinvigoration of local government. There was no enhancement of the civil service as a separate arm of government. The independence of the judiciary was infringed, especially during Michael Howard's time at the Home Office (1993–7). The constant reorganization of the NHS, schools, universities, the police and local government further curbed professional autonomy by injecting managers into positions traditionally held by senior professionals. While election turnouts declined, government increasingly saw the media as the conduit of public consent and a sounding board of policy.

The best the Tories might have hoped for at the 1997 election was marginal defeat and a swift return to power. Instead Major led them to humiliation, defeat by 165 seats to 419, their worst election result for a century. Nothing he achieved in office was as stunning as the manner of his leaving it. He departed a sad figure, a decent man who committed no grave error but was ill-cast for the task assigned him by history, to wind down eighteen years of Tory rule. Unlike Lord Home, who had performed a similar task with dignity in 1964, Major seemed perpetually hog-tied and miserable. Like the boy who had lost his football game 2-1, he was 'inconsolable'. The truth was as he recorded in his memoirs, 'It had all gone on too long.' Even the note he left for the Blairs in Downing Street was bathetic. Thatcher would have written, 'Don't you dare!' Major wrote, 'It's a great job – enjoy it.'[15]

Major rendered a sound service to Thatcherism, entrenching it over seven years when the lady herself would possibly have blown it by losing the 1992 election. He continued the first revolution with privatization, financial deregulation and subcontracting. With Clarke at the Treasury after Black Wednesday, he managed the economy into the most sustained period of growth seen since the Second World War. He semi-detached Britain from Europe at Maastricht and commenced the peace process in Northern Ireland. In retrospect, Major's achievement was not to have done worse in circumstances that constantly invited him to do so. More extraordinary was the effect that Major's seven years had on the Labour party. He held the ring while Blair and Brown brought their colleagues round to accept the Thatcherite settlement. If Major did not give Thatcherism a human face he contrived to anaesthetize the public's response to it. By postponing the day of Labour's return to office Major transformed that day from one of reactionary retrenchment to one of revolutionary advance. Over the next decade Blair's new Labour party was to deliver Thatcherism its most complete triumph.

PART FIVE

The Blair Project

14

A Cuckoo in the Nest

Tony Blair was twenty-one when Margaret Thatcher became leader of the Conservative party. Throughout his political education, she and her approach to politics defined his own. The British left in the 1980s was tormented, hurling at her all the frustration and abuse it could muster. Blair would never call himself a Thatcherite, yet he appears from the start to have instinctively respected something in Thatcher, notably her ability to speak to the nation in a language it understood, even if it disliked what it heard. She was clever and she was potent. She could use high office to command and control events round her. Blair would chant the litany against 'mindless Thatcherism', but just as she eventually came to see him as a worthy successor, so he regarded her endorsement as conferring on him a mantle he craved. As early as 1995 he was calling her 'a radical, not a Tory'.[1] By the time he took office their relationship was regarded by those round him as little short of a 'love affair'.[2] The mutual admiration of Thatcher and Blair was crucial to the maturing of Thatcherism through the 1990s and into the new century.

Blair was the most fundamentalist of the three Thatcherite prime ministers. From the moment he entered Downing Street he sought to govern in the manner of the forebear he most admired. He invited her to his new home two weeks after taking office and before any other former leader, Labour or Conservative, an act of honour and of deference.[3] While Thatcher came to Thatcherism by degrees, Blair seemed to have it buried in his political genes. Where she was hesitant, he was convinced. He took the first revolution into territory that she had regarded as unthinkable. He had no time for unions and believed strongly that government's role in the economy was primarily to promote business. Nor was Blair hesitant about the second revolution. He showed none of Thatcher's residual deference to the British constitution. Having revolutionized Labour's governance he went on to do the same for the nation's. Presidentialism came naturally to him. Thatcher's question, 'Is he one of us?' was never heard under Blair. Those who were not of the faith were nowhere to be seen.

The Labour party's conversion to Thatcherism's first revolution in the mid-1990s was the single dominant fact that ensured the survival of both. The Blair/Brown duumvirate seized it as a talisman of their ambition, first for Labour and then for themselves. Far from putting Thatcherism into reverse after taking office in 1997, as many Labour supporters had assumed, they supercharged it. Nor was there anything predictable or inevitable about this. The so-called 'Blair project' did not run with the grain of contemporary left-wing European politics. As we have seen, Thatcherism was not explicitly popular with the electorate. Labour's conversion was thus every bit as revolutionary as had been the transformation of the Tory party by Thatcher herself. Just as accepting Thatcher took the Tories into a period of conflict and self-doubt, the same was true of Blair and Labour.

The key in both cases was the personality of the respective leaders. Blair's swift rise to power was a product of Labour's predicament in the early 1990s, traumatized by Neil Kinnock's defeat in 1992 and the death two years later of his successor, John Smith. The party had seen four unsuccessful leaders in a row and its upper echelons had been shorn of talent by defections to the Social Democratic Party in 1981. Image, ideology and constitution appeared to have rendered it unelectable. A political party is remarkably anthropomorphic. When threatened with imminent death it will do anything to save its skin. Labour in the early 1990s yearned for someone to take it out of its misery into a promised land.

The appearance of a youthful, attractive and impetuous glad-hander was like that of Prince Charming in *Sleeping Beauty*. Blair's sheer difference from the run of Labour leaders was dramatic. Like Thatcher he was an intruder from outside the normal party cadre. Both were cuckoos in the nest, who would have been swiftly pushed out in better times. Blair's succession was reminiscent of Labour's choice of Ramsay MacDonald in the 1920s, its resort to a charmer likely to keep the left in check and reassure the middle classes. Yet Blair treated Labour as had none of his predecessors. He simply tore it apart. When the reconstruction was more or less complete in 1996 Labour was no longer a 'labour movement' but an electoral machine for the advancement of Blair himself, in effect his court. That machine was one of the most effective in modern politics, winning three election victories in a row. It did so by implementing what it had been sworn to oppose, Thatcherism.

Blair's parents were of Glasgow working-class upbringing. His father,

Leo, began life as a communist but changed to become a university law lecturer and aspiring Tory MP, even telling a contemporary that he intended to become prime minister.[4] This enabled Blair later to boast, 'I was not born into this party, I chose it.'[5] Leo's career was stalled by a stroke at the age of forty with Blair still in his teens. His mother, a warm and determined Ulsterwoman, saw Blair through public school at Fettes before herself dying of cancer when he was at Oxford. Blair was then on his own. If he inherited political ambition from his father and a stage presence from theatrical grandparents, he is said to have inherited his charm from his mother. Both parents clearly contributed to his political make-up.

Like Thatcher, Wilson and Heath before him, Blair was a beneficiary of the launch-pad of post-war meritocracy, Oxford University. He did not indulge in university politics, dabbling instead in show business, but Oxford gave him its greatest blessing, self-confidence and the expectation of success. It set him on the gilded path to the Bar, which Thatcher also followed. Both thus found stability after a socially fluid background in Establishment institutions, those of Oxford and the Temple, and both married fit to purpose. If Denis was 'a rock' to Thatcher so, in a different sense, was Cherie Booth to Blair. Child of domestic insecurity, she was as ambitious as her husband. They met as young lawyers in the legal chambers of Derry Irvine, later Blair's Lord Chancellor, and when they married at Tony's Oxford college, St John's, it was Irvine who gave Cherie away.

Cherie was more intensely political than her new husband.[6] Blair came to a career in politics under her influence and that of his waning affection for the law. He was in no sense an intellectual. He read little and had no grasp of history, culture or ideas, rather a breezy liking for anyone he met, a liking that often bordered on gullibility. What Blair acquired from the law was an easy mastery of speech, the art of persuasion and a fierce loyalty to what might be termed his clients. These qualities bound him tenaciously to aides and friends, whom he treated all alike, even such improbable soulmates as Bill Clinton and George W. Bush.

The Blairs first tangled with Labour politics when living in North London. No one who experienced Hackney socialism in the 1980s is likely to forget it. It was well cast to convince any newcomer that such a party, with its ideological feuds and late-night squabbles, would never win mass appeal. The Labour group on Hackney council was a running aversion therapy for old Labour and historians need look no further for an explanation of Blair's distaste for local government. He had experienced it at its worst. Indeed the Blairs might be thought natural defectors to the SDP in the early 1980s. That they did not do so has puzzled biographers, but it was a move Cherie was unlikely to countenance. Both she and Tony were by 1981 committed to a Labour career. Blair was only twenty-seven when the SDP was formed, and still politically insecure. The SDP was less a party than a 'set', based on a group of former ministers, Roy Jenkins, David Owen, Shirley Williams and Bill Rodgers, veterans of past wars. The academic Ralf Dahrendorf satirized them as wanting 'a better yesterday'. Their critique of Labour was identical to Blair's but hailed from a different generation. He was disinclined to exile himself from his adopted home. To Seldon, 'His personal attachment to Labour was strong: it gave him a sense of belonging which he never had before.'[7] Loyalty to Irvine, to Cherie and their milieu suggested caution.

As so often in his career, Blair put his stance differently. In a lecture in 1982 he roundly abused the SDP as failures, as 'middle-aged, middle-class erstwhile Labour members, who have grown too fat and affluent to feel comfortable with Labour and whose lingering social consciences prevent them from voting Tory.'[8] He added that their biggest mistake was 'to isolate themselves from organised labour'. In the authentic outlook of his adopted locale, the 'soft left', Blair chided them for distancing themselves from the root-stock of the Labour movement, the unions and the constituencies. As Rentoul remarked, his 'early forays into seat-hunting would have taught him how important factional networks were in making contacts and mobilising support in constituencies where he would otherwise arrive as a stranger.'[9] Blair joined both the anti-left Solidarity group and CND. He networked through the Bar as Thatcher never did. He was already writing papers for John Smith on privatization law, and dining with Smith and Irvine in the Commons. These were heady contacts which joining the SDP would have ruined.

Nothing in politics is so potent, or so little understood, as charm. Blair's curriculum vitae could hardly have been less promising to a new candidate. It was a public school, Fettes, then Oxford, the Bar and Islington. Yet his approachability and quick smile penetrated every barrier. He studied it in others, later most notably in Bill Clinton, and became addicted to 'winning over' people to his side, as if it were an exercise in itself. In 1982 he secured the by-election candidacy for the unwinnable seat of Beaconsfield. The election was held during the Falklands War, on which Blair took what would become a typically ambiguous position. He was for the task force yet also for a 'negotiated solution', and suggested a 'proportionality between lives lost and the cause at issue'. It was an unhelpful maxim in advance of a war and one which he never mentioned during Iraq. He also demanded withdrawal from the Common Market, 'but not as an article of socialist faith'. He supported CND and pledged himself 'to campaign against Trident and American cruise missiles on our soil'.[10] He declined an offer of support from Tony Benn.

A year later, and with a general election looming, Blair glided from Beaconsfield to the safe seat of Sedgefield in County Durham. Like Thatcher Blair was adept at reinventing his past. His application form was spattered with misspellings and mentioned only his litigation record defending trade unions, his membership of CND and his wife's family links with actors in *Coronation Street* (her father, Tony Booth, acted in *Till Death Us Do Part*). It did not refer to his education.[11] The CND affiliation he later denied but had to admit it when the application form was produced. Duly elected in 1983 he was in the House of Commons at the age of thirty. Cherie lost her bid for the Tory seat of Thanet and abandoned a political career. When Blair's name first appeared in *Hansard* as Mr Anthony Blair he rushed to the office to change it to Tony.

Michael Foot's election defeat that year was the beginning of what was to prove a long road back for Labour. It proved, if proof were needed, the crucial importance of a leader's image to a party's electability. Though the Liberal/SDP alliance had fallen back in the polls since its 1982 highpoint, it won 25.4 per cent of the popular vote, just two points and 700,000 votes behind Labour. Foot resigned and his successor, Neil Kinnock, knew drastic action was required, if not what sort of action. In 1985 Peter Mandelson arrived as head of communications and Philip Gould as pollster and 'political consultant'. Alastair Campbell, though continuing to work as a political journalist, offered advice on press relations and blatantly championed Labour in the columns of the *Daily Mirror* and *Today*. This group formed an early collaboration with two young MPs who had fortuitously been allocated the same Commons office, Blair and a new Scottish member two years his senior, Gordon Brown.

The son of a Presbyterian minister, Brown possessed few of the qualities normally found in a democratic politician. He had no career of substance before arriving at Westminster. He had been a student politician, wrote a book on the union leader James Maxton, and dabbled in television research. He had no noticeable public persona, and seemed unable to shed the dour factionalism of Scottish politics, a throwback to clan feuds and vendettas. An apparently jovial student had by adulthood become a thin-skinned politician, his facial appearance distorted by the loss of an eye in a football match. Brown was without artistic interests or tastes, a spectacularly unkempt bachelor who could neither drive nor handle money. Investigating the wreckage of a burglary at his Edinburgh flat a policeman remarked that he had 'never seen such mindless vandalism in thirty years in the force'. Brown professed to see nothing out of place.[12]

To Blair, Brown had the virtue of being rooted in Labour's northern soul. He respected Brown's knowledge of Labour history and lore and his grasp of detail. What appealed to Brown about Blair is more obscure. The Blairs were upwardly mobile, often embarrassingly so. Blair later said of his wife's love of luxury, 'Like lots of people who come from virtually nothing, I think that there's always a lurking anxiety it might all disappear one day.'[13] They were both susceptible to the blandishments of public life, to celebrity and to the often inappropriate generosity that came with their status. But if Blair's insecurity was that of an Islington *arriviste*, Brown's was visceral, that of a foreigner trading his wares among people he instinctively disliked, Londoners. Since it was here that his vocation called, the conclusion can only be that Blair offered Brown a sort of metropolitan anchor. The marriage was clearly of convenience, yet it was to prove astonishingly lasting.

Kinnock's reformism was to no avail. The party went on to fight the 1987 election on much the same tax-and-spend, pro-union platform that had proved disastrous in 1983, and the resulting defeat was total. *The Times* derided Kinnock's performance: 'Eight years of the most vilified prime minister of modern times, three million unemployed and a country apparently enraged by the condition of its health service, yet he could not win.'[14] Kinnock was shattered and his party demoralized. The pressure for change was correspondingly stronger. But across its path lay the formidable obstacle of Labour's constitution, the constitution that had delivered policies which the electorate did not like – nuclear disarmament, tax-and-spend and withdrawal from Europe – protected by the party's paymasters, the unions. The unions had been emasculated by Thatcher but not within the echelons of Labour.

While the Tory party is a monarchy, its hierarchy in the leader's gift and obedience (supposedly) its second nature, Labour's constitution in 1987 was federal. It still reflected historical ties to the national labour movement, a feature of which was an aversion to Scottish and Welsh devolution for fear that it might weaken union negotiating power. If Kinnock and his colleagues wanted to change any policy they had to go through a byzantine structure of committees and conferences. Previous leaders, such as Gaitskell in the 1950s and Wilson in the 1960s, had attempted to reform this structure but failed. When Kinnock launched a policy review at Labour's Brighton conference in 1987, the ambitious Blair defended it in the most unradical of terms, as a 'thorough and fundamental reaffirmation of existing policies ... no revision, no scrapping, no bonfire of commitments'.[15]

Blair's ability to dissemble developed early. He condemned Thatcher's government for allowing schools to opt out of local control, for leaving pensioners to take out private insurance and for stressing individual choice instead of social opportunity.[16] At the 1988 conference, he was asked if he favoured ending the party's constitutional Clause IV on public ownership and replied, 'It's not even a question of reinterpreting it. It's a question of giving effect to it.'[17] Blair had been an apparently convinced unilateral nuclear disarmer, yet when Kinnock dropped the policy in 1989, Blair supported him. Rentoul commented that 'none of Blair's positions in this period appears to have been sincere.'[18] To him policy was always to be the servant, not the master, of political power.

In 1987 Kinnock appointed Blair to one of his seven policy review groups, that on trade-union law. A year later he was elected to the shadow cabinet (then chosen by MPs), albeit down the list from Brown. He became energy spokesman and championed the party's attack on electricity privatization, telling the 1988 conference, 'We want it abandoned, here, now and for ever.' In 1989 he switched to employment, ostensibly to lead the fight against Thatcher's continuing union reforms. Five years earlier, in one of his first Commons speeches, he had declared it 'unacceptable in a democratic society' for government to interfere in the affairs of unions, including their closed shops.[19] Now Blair said the exact opposite. A shadow cabinet review under Michael Meacher accepted the Conservative government's view that trade unions had to be brought within the law and that traditional immunities had to end. Blair championed this change, praying in aid another remarkable volte-face, in favour of the EU and its 'Social Chapter' of employment restrictions then being formulated for the Maastricht treaty of 1991. Since the Social Chapter embraced a human right not to join a trade union, said Blair, Labour could no longer defend the closed shop. He set about what he did best, personally lobbying each union in favour of a U-turn, even winning over a leading member of the seamen's union, John Prescott.

Persuading Labour to accept Thatcher's employment law was Blair's first break from cover as a modernizer, undoubtedly aided by the broken-backed state of trade unionism in Britain in the 1980s. But where Brown at the time was agonizing as industry spokesman over whether to renationalize BT, Blair backed Thatcher's change with apparent energy and charm. He appeared often in party political broadcasts, telegenic, worrying over his suits and his hair, choosing the competent Anji Hunter, an old student friend, as his aide. Already Blair was regarded as 'papabile' and received 'future leader' mentions.

Kinnock's reform process was subject to constant stalling. The party could not escape its reputation for 'tax-and-spend', on which the Tories never ceased to play, while Kinnock kept losing focus and reverting to ethnic type, that of Celtic verbosity. He hailed from romantic Labour territory, South Wales, as did Brown from the Scottish lowlands, places that held politicians in the grip of history. Alastair Campbell warned Gould that 'there were an awful lot of things in the Labour party that were wrong, and [Kinnock] had a sentimental attachment to some of those things.'[20] No such historical or territorial romance held Blair in thrall, be it Scotland, Durham or Islington. He seemed to be from nowhere and everywhere. Again the parallel with Thatcher was uncanny.

Just when Thatcher's poll tax offered Kinnock what should have been a winning issue for a 1991 election, the Tories dumped her, abandoned the tax and postponed any election until 1992. With the arrival of Major the cup of hope was dashed and Labour's instinct for fratricide emerged in whispering about Kinnock's leadership. This was the prelude to yet another humiliating defeat in 1992, widely attributed to John Smith's pledge as shadow chancellor to raise the top rate of income tax to 50 per cent. Labour's failure was extraordinary, given thirteen years of often unpopular Tory government. The Conservatives won the largest popular vote in British history, with a lead of 7 per cent over Labour. Major was characteristically sorry for Kinnock, writing that he had changed his party 'when doing so was both

brave and difficult'.[21] The defeat persuaded Kinnock to resign, to be succeeded unopposed by Smith. Brown was the only front-runner who might
have offered him a challenge, but he declined to stand. It was a loss of nerve
that Blair noted with dismay, much as Thatcher had registered Keith Joseph's
reluctance to challenge Heath in 1975.

The imperative for reform now seemed overwhelming, but whereas
Kinnock had been a tentative believer Smith was more a traditionalist. Clare
Short recalled that he disliked 'Mandelson's divisive style of spinning the
tough qualities of the leader at the expense of the treasured values of the
party'.[22] But Smith had to recognize that continued inertia was no longer
an option. He agreed with Blair and the 'modernizers' that the Kinnock
changes had to be taken forward, even though all Labour's past attempts
at constitutional reform had meant bitter struggles within the party. The
difference now was that change was driven not by some ideological evolution but by a simple yearning on every side for electability. Party reform
might be arcane to the mass of Labour supporters but the objective was
not. As Blair and Brown moved to the forefront of the intra-party debate,
they were arguing not over a controversial matter of policy but over
mechanics – how could the party seem more up-to-date? The word
modernization was kept content-free. It was about image. Content would
be for later, much later.

Blair and Brown, acting as virtual Siamese twins, drew extensively from
the experience of centre-left parties overseas. Brown had attended the 1984
American Democratic National Convention. Blair had visited America in
1986 as part of a parliamentary tax delegation, travelling by Concorde and
combining the trip with a family holiday. (Such confusion of public and
private pleasure was to cause the Blairs frequent embarrassment in future
years.) In 1988 both men went together to the Democratic Convention,
and two years later they visited Australia, at Kinnock's suggestion, to study
Bob Hawke's Labour government and its success in applying Thatcherite
policies. After the 1992 election Philip Gould was asked by Bill Clinton's
campaign team to explain how Major had won (or Labour lost) against the
odds at the time. Gould formed a friendship both with James Carville,
Clinton's strategist, and with the British Embassy's point man on the campaign, Jonathan Powell (later to be Blair's chief of staff). On his return Gould
penned one of the founding documents of 'new Labour', a memorandum
telling the party to stop 'looking downwards and backwards'.[23] The 1992

election showed that securing the working-class vote was no longer enough to win Labour an election. It must rid itself altogether of its identification with trade unionism and high taxes and be ready to campaign aggressively for the middle ground. Above all, it had to signify that it had changed completely, and announce the fact in the most brutal terms.[24]

The ground was laid for yet another Brown/Blair visit to America in 1993, which Labour iconography puts on a par with that of the Frenchmen de Tocqueville and Beaumont in 1831. Blair was mesmerized by Clinton. He was intrigued in particular by his technique of personal projection, by his manipulation of the media and ability to bring a leader's personality into the homes of millions. Returning from one of Blair's later visits to America, an aide recalled that 'Tony is on a high and speaking of how wonderful it must be to run for president.'[25] Clinton's message was that modern politics was about charismatic leadership. The leader had to transcend interest groups and coalitionism. He must speak to 'the whole people', using television, radio and the press direct, without the mediation of journalists and editors. The media could transmit messages, but the leader must fashion the message to his own agenda. He must always hold the initiative over the messenger, something Major was conspicuously failing to achieve.

While Brown studied Clinton's economics, Blair was starry-eyed at the sheer glamour of American democracy, at buzzwords, focus groups, picture opportunities, media moments, planes and motorcades. Neither man had had much experience of the world, nor of their own or any other country. Their politics had little context, but they realized that a party of the left must, in Seldon's words, 'discard the old images of being obsessed with history and associated solely with the poor, the unions, minorities and special interests'. Instead it should 'forge a populism of the centre'.[26] This was Gould's relentless theme, that elections would in future be a battle for the centre ground. Blair said, 'We play the Tory game when we speak up for the underclass rather than for the broad majority of people in this country ... The aspirations that unite the majority of people in my constituency are infinitely more important than trying to divide people up into groups.'[27] What Labour traditionalists were to regard as class treachery was to Blair palpably obvious. Thatcherism's bourgeois ascendancy was electoral necessity.

The emergence of what came to be called 'the project', an electable Labour party, was thus liberated from past ideological content. Labour would be more like Australian and American parties of the left and wholly reform its approach to power. Everything that stood in the way of winning votes must be discarded. Blair complained significantly that modern socialism 'had no developed analysis of the limitations of public ownership through the state as a means of helping the individual'.[28] Socialists should move from a fixation with ownership towards a mixed economy. Blair camouflaged this shift to the right in a fog of abstraction, a fog that came to define Blairism. He declared that 'citizenship without community is empty rhetoric' and that 'system must not be a conspiracy against reason'. What he meant was that policy was pointless if you could not get people to vote for you. Machiavelli had finally found a home within British Labour.

From this emerged another lesson garnered from America. The new populism must not be over-concerned with economics. The most substantive charge Blair was able to level at Thatcherism was that it was the politics of materialism, indeed of greed. The mass of those actually voting – older and richer than the population average – might be chary of tax-and-spend but their wallets no longer dominated their lives. They were worried about security and what they called 'moral values' in the public domain. A modern party must speak to these worries. Blair's instinctive consensualism, his Christianity, his ideological detachment, thrilled to the so-called 'values' message. It became the icing on the cake of his oratory. In 1992 Blair accepted Smith's suggestion that he join the Christian Socialist Movement. He was soon talking about 'tough religion', about 'acknowledging right and wrong', good and bad. 'We know this, of course,' he wrote, 'but it has become fashionable to be uncomfortable about such language.'[29] The word 'fashionable' was already entering the right-wing lexicon as a term of abuse of the left, and Blair instinctively adopted it and continued using it into power. Suddenly half the shadow cabinet followed their leader. The small band of Christian Socialists found themselves overwhelmed not just by Smith but by Blair, Brown, Jack Straw and David Blunkett.

In the first shadow cabinet election of Smith's leadership in 1992, Brown and Blair came first and second. They were now a dominant partnership, and while Smith might be suspicious of their ambition he could not deny the primacy of their demand for modernization. Brown became shadow chancellor and Blair shadow home secretary. They were political greyhounds waiting for the off. Despite his more traditional Labour background, Brown was as committed as Blair to modernization. He was as adept at trimming sails and changing course, if not as relaxed about doing so. Back in 1988 he had been genuinely shocked when Lawson cut the top rate of tax to 40 per cent. He had wanted to pledge a higher rate even than 60 per cent and was relentless in opposing the spread of means testing.[30] To him, Labour's sacred duty was to punish the rich and raise up the poor.[31] It must also reverse privatization. All these positions Brown was to abandon as part of the 'electability agenda' in a series of revisions reminiscent of Joseph's in 1975. 'Brown was making an almost religious atonement for the sins of Labour's past', wrote his biographer, Robert Peston. 'He put on a hair shirt and insisted the rest of the party did so too.'[32]

In the early 1990s the best available hair shirt for a defeated Labour party was Thatcherism. Brown accepted Blair's U-turn on union reform and recognized that to make the party economically plausible ultra-respectability on the currency was essential. He was therefore unable to capitalize on the Tories' Black Wednesday woes in 1992 since he had publicly supported membership of the Exchange Rate Mechanism, against the support for devaluation of Robin Cook, Bryan Gould and even John Smith himself.[33] He did so because he was frantic that Labour should not seem weak on sterling, even ridiculing Lady Thatcher just a week before the collapse for having spoken out against the ERM.[34] As a result Black Wednesday was almost as much a humiliation for Brown as it was for Major and Lamont, though he was happily not in charge. Another biographer, Tom Bower, has him entering a mood of depression as his party enemies rounded on him. His future cabinet colleague, Peter Hain, co-authored a pamphlet in 1993 jeering, 'No wonder commentators allege there is little to distinguish Labour's macroeconomic policy from that of the Tories.'[35] Such senior colleagues as Prescott, Blunkett, Straw and the Tribune group regarded Brown as a not-so-crypto-monetarist.[36] Brown was unmoved. The project and electability were all.

Meanwhile Blair was growing into the Home Office brief. It perfectly suited his 'values agenda' and produced his most celebrated sound bite. Refusing to let law and order remain a natural Tory policy he chided the government for 'having given up on crime' and for seeking 'only a few headlines in the newspapers.' What the country needed, said Blair, was a national strategy that's 'both tough on crime and tough on the causes of crime.'[37] The empty phrase was in fact Brown's but Blair borrowed it, polished it, projected it and gave it a spurious sense of purpose. It typified what Rentoul called Blair's 'vacuo-Olympian style'. He told the Police

Federation, 'If we dare not speak the language of punishment then we deny the real world.'[38]

Although toughness is not an antonym for liberal, Blair liked to imply it was, especially if he could prefix liberal with fashionable. When asked about crime he would always begin, 'There is no excuse for it, none.' He saw no problem in jailing teenagers or increasing the prison population overall and in office was as good as his word. Strong families were necessary for a strong society, he said, completing the Blairism by adding that a strong society was also necessary for strong families. Labour's egalitarianism could thus be elided into a new equality 'of respect ... dignity ... responsibility', what Philip Gould called 'an equality of outcomes'. From this Blair moved on to the new communitarianism then being debated in America. Given any pressing social problem Blair could somehow launder it with an abstraction, some vague, alliterative phrase to which no one could take exception. His ability to strip words of meaning yet load them with impressionistic effect was extraordinary, and was to increase over time.

Blair never let any such vagueness distort his laser focus on the project. As he and Brown pressed Smith on the modernization agenda, they concentrated on the party's most vulnerable feature, its subservience to the unions. In 1982 Blair had jeered at the SDP because they had 'isolated themselves from organized labour'. Now he wanted Labour to do just that. He wrote in the *New Statesman*, already in leadership mode, that 'trade unions will have no special or privileged place within the Labour party', adding patronizingly that, 'It is in the unions' best interests not to be associated merely with one party.'[39] This was a high-risk game.

Labour's constitution shared power between unions, constituencies, socialist societies and the Westminster party, but with the unions dominant. Since union leaders could usually deliver the block votes registered in their name, great deference was paid them by the leadership. The party also relied on them for the bulk of its income. Union leaders were what the landed interest had once been to the Tories, and since they could not easily be confronted, Blair proceeded by salami tactics. In 1992 he championed a simple constitutional reform, the end of the union block vote in constituencies on candidate selection and in the choosing of the leader, to be replaced by OMOV, one member, one vote. This was the issue that he and Cherie had first confronted in 1980 as members of Hackney Labour party. He was adamant that the block vote should go and was startlingly explicit. On this he declared that there should be 'no compromise with the unions'.[40] This initially set him apart from Smith and Brown. Blair was attacking the very groups that would be needed to vote for the reform, the unions. The proposal for OMOV therefore seemed doomed, indeed reckless both for the party and for the ambition of anyone who advocated it. The unions had already conceded Kinnock a modest cut from 90 per cent to 70 per cent in their conference voting strength, and to two-fifths at constituency meetings. Smith was reluctant to go further, to universal OMOV. Smith was not a man for a fight nor, with the Major government in disarray just a year after the 1992 election, did he see any point. There was at last light ahead, so why rock the boat?

The ensuing struggle lasted for two years and, to the uninitiated, does not make for easy study. The distribution of power between members, trade unionists and MPs in the Labour party was central to the modernizing argument and thus to Smith's relations with Blair and Brown in the shadow cabinet. Smith himself was undecided, but he was impressed by one of Blair's smartest moves, to boost individual membership within his Sedgefield constituency party to over 2,000, making it one of the largest in the country. Its purpose was to imply that a mass membership independent of the unions was there for the asking. By July 1993 Blair had persuaded Smith at least to back OMOV for constituency candidate selection, with a complex three-way split for the election of the leader. Union members would vote as individuals, not by proxy through union blocks. OMOV became the modernizers' talisman.

Any change needed formal party endorsement and those with most to lose, the unions, were in a decisive position. At the 1993 Brighton conference the general mood was for modernization, but so radical a change was uncharted ground. Both Brown and Blair found themselves demoted in the shadow cabinet poll as a result of their outspokenness, but they had secured Smith's commitment to OMOV and regarded it as a test of his leadership. If the unions, especially the GMB's hard-line boss, John Edmonds, defeated him, Smith would have to make it a matter of confidence and might even have to resign. The reformers were aided by the support of conference favourite John Prescott, a support Blair would not forget.

Smith won his vote and the constitution was duly changed, but Blair immediately pressed Smith for a further change, this time to curb the block vote at the conference itself. This was a different matter, hitting not at candidate selection but at the unions' control over the central determination of policy. Indeed Blair demanded more than that, an end to the conference's sovereignty over the manifesto. He declared, 'If we can't actually trust ordinary Labour party members with decision-making within the Labour party how on earth are we going to go out and try and win support for the Labour party in the broader community?' In the twenty-first century, he said, Labour had 'to look like a party in touch with its local community because its local community is part of that party.'[41] Blair was demanding a remission of party policy from the conference and the union barons to members in the constituencies. The implication was to make policy subject to perpetual referendum, as in California's plebiscitary propositions. Blair was using radical populism to prise power away from conference. But as was to be seen later, this was merely a device, not to decentralize power from the party conference to the country but to centralize it from the conference to the party leadership.

Smith would tolerate no further constitutional battles. He had already risked his leadership and enough was enough. Blair had alienated himself from the traditionalists and from many of Labour's senior figures. Yet his confidence in his campaign seems never to have dimmed. He was smiling, intense, hyperactive, expressing open frustration with Smith to his associates. A paper from Gould early in 1994 suggested the rebranding of the party as 'New Labour'. Blair agreed, but was gloomily dismissive, 'Labour will only win when it is completely changed from top to bottom.'[42] As with his handling of the closed shop in 1989 so with OMOV, Blair's stance signalled him out as the most radical of the modernizers. He might wave with the wind on matters of policy. He might pursue a studied ideological vagueness, but on party structure he displayed the fanaticism, indeed the recklessness, of a revolutionary. Blair seemed at the time hardly a Labour party member at all, rather an alien political force employing the 'entryist' tactics once confined to the hard left.

While Smith was seeking calm waters, Blair was stirring up storms. He had led the campaign to force Labour to accept the Tory view that trade unions should no longer enjoy a privileged status in the economic and political life of the nation. Nor should they continue to enjoy their past privileges within the party. But he had not identified any new coalition of interests to take their place in the party's affections. Rather he had begun to shift Labour away from being any such coalition to being essentially a machine for winning elections. The effect on Blair's standing was emphatic. The struggles of 1993–4 enabled Blair to overtake Brown as a potential leader, not just as the darling of the focus groups but as an aggressive party manipulator. His image was no longer that of a gee-whizz youth but of a formidable politician. He had called the bluff of the union dinosaurs and had succeeded. Then, on 12 May 1994, John Smith had a massive heart attack and died.

15

Granita Rules

Tony Blair's election to the Labour leadership in May 1994 seems in retrospect to have been beyond doubt. It did not seem so at the time. The relationship between Blair and Brown has been the subject of documentaries, books, even a television play. They are depicted as conjoined opposites, sweet and sour, extrovert and introvert, jolly southerner and dour northerner. When they first met in the 1983 House of Commons, Brown was the senior partner in both age and political maturity and Blair the eager pupil. To those round them they were in perpetual if sometimes incongruous concord. They travelled together, plotted together, talked incessantly and co-authored the project to modernize Labour.

Central to this relationship were the pledges, spoken and unspoken, that marked its early course. Brown's champions have always claimed that Blair from the start ceded primacy to Brown and promised never to stand against him. Alternatively they claim that, if Brown gave way to Blair, Blair would serve a fixed term and then stand down. So firm are these claims that they are at least plausible. Yet they were the building blocks of the most celebrated grudge in modern politics, outranking even Heath's towards Thatcher. Whereas her leadership was initially dogged by her predecessor, Blair's was to be dogged by his successor. Brown's ambition to enter 10 Downing Street was the ill-concealed raw nerve in Blair's bland style of government.

After Smith's death Blair was in no doubt. His performance as a modernizer entitled him to the succession and nothing would prevent him from standing. He had dared on union reform when Brown had hesitated on privatization. He had put his head above the parapet on OMOV when Brown had dithered. Blair was a star in the media firmament where Brown was a cloud. Yet the day after Smith's death Brown assumed himself heir apparent. He gathered his close friends to discuss tactics for the leadership campaign and was given unpleasant news, that 'there was a bandwagon rolling for Blair in the media and parliament'. Blair would run and would almost certainly win. 'The shadow chancellor felt betrayed, devastated.'[1] Again Brown sulked and dithered. His venom against the apparent treachery of Mandelson, whom he thought was on his side but who had switched to Blair, was to be lasting.

The negotiating of Brown's subsequent decision not to stand against Blair is a vignette of British politics. The difference from their beloved America could not have been greater. What in America (and later in the Tory party) would have been a primary election in the glare of publicity was conducted by secret cabals in Islington kitchens, Scottish pubs and the houses of friends. Blair wanted the job and thought he deserved it, yet Brown was owed consideration. The question was how the oligarchs might smooth Brown's easily ruffled feathers, in a manner more eighteenth century than twentieth.

The result was a deal. The two men met in Scotland on 15 May 1994, an indecent three days after Smith's death. The understanding they reached was confirmed at a more celebrated meeting in Granita's restaurant in Islington on 31 May, after which Brown declared that he would not stand. The agreement had two strands. One concerned Blair's term as leader. It stipulated that Blair would have first crack at being prime minister, giving way to Brown after a due interval. The length of this interval was later hotly disputed, with both sides leaking versions of from seven years to 'two elections' or even ten years. The probable reason for confusion is that longevity did not seem important at the time. Winning was all. Also, such cosy power-sharing might seem presumptuous if made public. The general view is that Brown never demanded a pledge but that Blair offered it as consolation, in typically deniable terms.[2]

The second strand was Brown's quid pro quo and concerned their respective roles in government. Here Blair's concession was near sensational for a future prime minister. Brown knew his man well enough to suspect the depth of his left-wing commitment. He therefore wanted a pledge that a Labour government would stick to the entire 'social justice agenda' and that he, Brown, would be its guarantor as chancellor of the Exchequer. He would chair all relevant cabinet committees and be granted 'the power and freedom to establish his own political identity under Tony's leadership'. Indeed he wanted 'total autonomy over the [government's] social and economic agenda'. In other words, Brown wanted more than autonomy as chancellor. He wanted the new government to be a duumvirate, with primacy for himself in domestic affairs.[3]

Brown was so bruised by what he saw as Blair's 'terrible betrayal' that he went to the extraordinary length of insisting that this aspect of Granita be recorded. Blair duly conveyed its substance to Mandelson so a minute could be drafted, ostensibly for 'press briefing'. The minute had an unhappy birth. Blair's account stated that

Gordon has spelled out the fairness agenda ... which he believes should be the centrepiece of Labour's programme and Tony is in full agreement with this, and that the party's economic and social policies should be further developed on this basis.

When this wordy text was sent to Brown he disagreed with it. He rewrote the words, 'Tony is in full agreement' as, 'Tony has guaranteed that this will be pursued'. Blair did not accept this rewording. He claimed that no prime minister could be constrained in this emphatic way. It would be unconstitutional. Now it was Brown's turn to be adamant and insist on the word 'guaranteed'. Blair again demurred. He clearly did not trust his friend any more than Brown did him. According to Seldon, Blair told his team of his fear that 'Gordon would run everything domestically ... which he didn't like one bit because he didn't trust the Treasury and what Gordon might do from it.'[4] At this point the exchange lapsed and the minute was left in the air. But from Granita onwards Brown behaved as if 'guaranteed' were in print.

Blair's resistance to Brown's wording shows he was not unaware of the balance in British government. He had already conceded his friend both the Treasury and what amounted to day-to-day sovereignty over public-service reform. This offended the customary triangulation of power between the Treasury and spending departments, with the prime minister as adjudicator. To guarantee a chancellor supremacy in such appeals was for Blair too great a loss of prime ministerial face. Yet time and again in government Brown was to appeal to Granita in resolving disputes with other ministers and force Blair into varying degrees of submission. Granita thus appeared to formalize the Treasury aggrandizement that had been occurring for a decade under Lawson and Clarke. In theory it was a dangerous concession by Blair, taking forward this aggrandizement and threatening his position as prime minister. In practice however, he was little interested in economics or in the details of domestic policy, nor had he any wish to publicize what was clearly a concession on his part. Only when, in 2003, Blair seemed to have broken the alleged promise to stand down after a given period of time did Brown's friends ensure that the precise details of this constitutionally significant document became public.[5]

Even before then the Granita meeting was being satirized as the 'grim eater' and the 'last supper'. It resolved, albeit temporarily, the crisis in the Blair/Brown relationship that had been waiting to happen over the leadership. The outcome of the crisis was not in doubt. In 1994, Gallup put Blair at 47 per cent support among Labour members, with Brown at just 11 per cent. At the leadership election on 21 July, Blair secured 57 per cent of the vote, winning majorities in each section of the new electoral college, with MPs, constituency members and trade unionists voting individually. While union leaders had publicly backed Margaret Beckett or John Prescott (Blair's challengers), OMOV meant that this was of little account. Prescott became deputy leader, to be treated by Blair's circle as the 'token traditionalist'. Blair's campaign team transferred intact to the leader's office: Mandelson on presentation, Campbell on press, Gould on electoral strategy, Hunter as head of the private office and David Miliband on policy. The victory statement was vapid even by Blair's standard. It declared, 'We can change the course of history and build a new, confident land of opportunity in a new and changing world.' This was soon shortened to the motto, 'Traditional values in a changed world.'

Behind this screen the new leader turned at once to the unfinished business of modernization. During the leadership campaign he had resolutely denied that he wanted Labour to become an 'SDP Mark II'. There would be no further changes to the party's constitution, such as removing the conference block votes or rewriting the iconic Clause IV of the party constitution. This, said Blair, was 'not a priority that anyone wanted'.[6] It was all past history. Paddy Ashdown was later to call such Blair statements his 'Don Giovanni' pledges: 'He probably meant them at the time.'

Blair began by sacking Labour's general secretary, Larry Whitty, and selling the party headquarters in Walworth. He tried to sack the entire shadow cabinet, seemingly unaware that it was formally elected by MPs, and then disregarded it instead, preferring to treat his own circle as his 'cabinet'. He then returned remorselessly to his obsession, the Labour party constitution, despite having just promised to leave it alone. Modernization was a revolution that should never cease. Gould proposed that Blair ram home his victory with an 'electric shock', a 'defining moment'. The electorate had to be shown that the new Labour party was going to be truly different. Blair had personally to distance himself from its past image. He needed no persuading, telling Gould, 'I will never compromise . . . I would rather be beaten and leave politics than bend to the party. I am going to take the party on.'[7] He even told a group of businessmen that in government he would treat the unions in the same way that past Labour leaders had treated business. That this was dangerous did not escape his colleagues' notice. If Blair had a weakness, said Mandelson in an unguarded moment, it was to be 'good at taking the high ground and throwing himself off it'.[8]

The new leadership could hardly have selected a shock more electrifying than the rewriting of Clause IV. This committed the party to secure 'the common ownership of the means of production, distribution and exchange, and the best obtainable system of popular administration and control of each industry or service'. The clause had later been extended to ascribe to government 'the commanding heights of the economy'. Compared even with battles over the closed shop, OMOV and the expulsion of the Walworth establishment, Blair was invading sacred ground. In September 1994 he summoned his eight closest colleagues to a typically lavish venue, Chewton Glen Hotel in Hampshire, and laid his plans. He would do whatever it took to crush any remaining institutional or political constraints the Labour party might exert over him. He had to win now in order to gain freedom of authority in power.

By the time of his first party conference in the autumn of 1994 Blair felt strong enough at least to show his hand on Clause IV. Desperate attempts had been made to secure Prescott's support, since his standing among the party faithful would have made his opposition fatal. It was secured. Yet Blair dared not warn either his shadow cabinet or the party's ruling National Executive Committee (NEC) of what he intended to say. Nor did he demand the repeal of Clause IV as such, merely speaking of Labour's need for a new constitution that 'the Tories cannot misrepresent', one for 'the next century'. Even these words were omitted from the text distributed to conference members and the press. Blair just said them, and left his spin-doctors to brief the press that Clause IV was dead. It was smothered by the launch of 'New Labour', awash in red roses. The first party members knew of the loss of their once beloved clause was from a surprised and delighted press.

For all his tactical care, Blair lost the conference vote on revising Clause IV by a narrow margin. He was undaunted. The NEC, still a bastion of

Labour pluralism and packed with Blair's enemies, was bullied into agreeing a special conference in April 1995. Blair now put his charm on the line. He went on the road to sell New Labour and its new, largely empty constitution, barnstorming the country like an American presidential hopeful. Nobody had treated the party like this before. Members were addressed directly, not through the agency of committees, unions or smoke-filled rooms. They met their new and charismatic leader and found the attention paid them exciting. The tactic worked. At the special conference Blair removed the old Clause IV with 65 per cent of the vote.

This was Blair's third victory over old Labour and his most impressive. It gave him a hold over his party that he was to retain securely for over a decade. Seldon may not be correct in his view that had Blair lost the vote he would have resigned, but that he won was crucial. He addressed the media in gratuitously triumphal vein: already using the royal 'we' he declared that 'we are not going to be pushed around'. That autumn he casually cut the size of the union vote at party conferences from 70 per cent to 50 per cent. He also let it be known that he and not conference would be writing the manifesto. He later jeered at the embattled Major in the Commons, 'I lead my party, he follows his.'[9] For ten years Blair had been demolishing the Labour coalition. Now he was revelling in a freedom known to none of his predecessors. Before the 1997 election, he (or Campbell) boasted to the *Sun*, 'We will not be held to ransom by the unions. We will stand up to strikes. We will not cave in to unrealistic pay demands.'[10]

Some debate has surrounded the significance of Blair's party revolution. Meg Russell has contended that the change was more apparent than real. The same people still formed the bulk of constituency associations and attended party conferences, the same people canvassed constituencies and sat outside polling stations.[11] This was true, but what Blair had done was snap the chains that bound the leader to the party and plagued the lives of his predecessors in power. Labour's constitution had been unlike that of any other party, causing Kinnock, Callaghan, Wilson and Gaitskell constant anguish. Blair made it possible for a Labour prime minister to operate with the same flexibility as his Tory opposite number, or as a presidential candidate abroad. This was revolution enough for Blair's purpose. With his party under control, he could move to cover other flanks.

A minor one was intellectual. Blair's talent was to charm and its objective was power. But British politics requires ambition to be clothed, however thinly, in ideology. A leader is expected to maintain some contact with the party's history and tradition. If policies are to be overturned the political village likes to know why. For Blair this was akin to no more than a Catholic cardinal being required to speak Latin. But he did need to learn the language, one that would express his new values in traditional terms. From this emerged the *mélange* of third way phraseology that was to become known as 'Blairism'.

The thinnest chapter in Seldon's compendium, *The Blair Effect*, is by Raymond Plant on 'Blair and Ideology'. It opens with a clarion call from its subject: 'I have always believed that politics is first and foremost about ideas. Without a powerful commitment to goals and values, governments are rudderless and ineffective.'[12] The rest of the essay is a desperate, ultimately fruitless search for substance in these words. Plant is even reduced to citing Daniel Bell's 1950s welcome to 'the end of ideology'. Apart from a commitment to religion, wavering between Anglicanism and Catholicism, Blair seems to have believed deeply in nothing to which anyone could take exception. He read few books and admitted to Roy Jenkins that he regretted not studying history or English at university and as a result felt uneducated.[13] The Blairs were never seen at the theatre, concerts, the opera or art galleries. They did not (and do not) read books. Their cultural patronage rarely extended beyond rock musicians.

The new language was marked by a rhetorical device known as inversion, prefixing an imprecise positive with an emphatic negative to appear to give it substance.'Our ambition is not . . . our aim is not . . . we shall never allow a child to go poor to school . . . but must work together for a better society.' New Labour was not Toryism and not Liberalism, not old Labour, not the rampant free market and not old-style socialism. Blairism always relied heavily on qualifiers, as in 'I am not opposed in principle to joining the euro', or his 1983 classic that 'we should withdraw from Europe, but not as a matter of socialist faith'. He now wanted a trade unionism that 'never has to apologize to the Tories'. The apotheosis of this nonsense was the revisionists' emptiest phrase, the third way.

The idea of breaking out of the left-right dichotomy – the SDP being a banned word – had been articulated by Anthony Giddens in 1994 in a book, *Beyond Left and Right*. The term was taken up by Blair in a 1995 article in the *Daily Mail*, promising a health service that would be neither private nor centralized but 'locally-based, patient-led . . . a sensible third way'.[14] The third way came to be defined as definitely not a middle course, which steered too close to the Liberal Democrats, but as a 'principled pragmatism', a permanent revisionism, a reaffirmation of something called 'social-ism'. To Blair this social-ism, pronounced with a hiatus, was 'not about class, or trades unions, or capitalism versus socialism ... It is about a belief in working together to get things done.'[15] Giddens became archpurveyor of clichés to the Blair court, conjuring a locust swarm of abstract nouns, consuming all meaning in their path. Old-style socialism he condemned as 'fundamentalist', as was a 'harsh, uncaring Thatcherism' (unlike the other sort). Elevated in their place were community, responsibility, opportunity, inclusion and 'traditional values in a changed world'.

That words in politics may be content-free does not make them useless. Their associations can make audiences feel good or bad, angry or elated, stirred or calmed. They can fill time while the orator performs body-language on stage. They can also anaesthetize. Blair in 1994–7 needed anaesthetic by the syringe-full. He was effecting drastic surgery on a great political movement, destroying all that its supporters had been brought up to believe. They might crave victory, but Blair was going further than that. He was stripping them of all future power over their party, reducing them to mere voters, and he was going to make them support the programme of their most hated enemy, Thatcher. To change metaphors, Blair was Odysseus voyaging across the political ocean. He had heard Thatcher's siren call, but dared not let his crew hear it too.

Philip Gould was the man assigned to stuff their ears with wax. His task was to orchestrate obfuscation. His strategy was set out in a series of memorandums that would flood Blair's desk and would later form the basis of New Labour's bible, his *The Unfinished Revolution*. To Gould values were mood music. They were given a spurious specificity with policy-free targets such as 'better schools and hospitals by 2002' or 'halve world poverty by 2015'. Their essence was summed up by Gould's chapter heading, 'Reassurance, reassurance, reassurance'.[16] The apotheosis of this language was Blair's 1995 conference speech, when he stood at the lectern and purred banalities for over an hour. The audience were treated to a warm bath of change, renewal, partnership, opportunity, communities, families, 'our lads', with surface bubbles of 'faith based' commitment, conviction, belief, pledge, covenant and trust.

What was astonishing, given the talent available to Blair's team, was how little thought was being given at this time to actual policies that might be needed in government. Longevity in Opposition seemed to render Labour oblivious of the demands of office. The dominant question of the Major administration at the time was the reform of public services. Yet to this question Labour offered no coherent answers, no draft White Papers, only pledges to 'reverse' such items as opted-out schools and fund-holding doctors. Blair was in Downing Street for two years before his office produced an anodyne document on public-sector reform, 'Modernising Government'.[17] It is hard to avoid the conclusion that Blair's work in Opposition was dedicated only to acquiring power. As every military strategist knows, establishing a bridgehead on enemy territory is one thing, moving on from it is quite another.

This goes some way to resolving the conundrum of when and to what extent Blair was converted to the Thatcherism he so ardently espoused in office. Was it in the course of his and Brown's trips to Australia and America? Was it in the rough and tumble of opposing the Thatcher/Major reforms? Or was it a realization that in the crucial centre ground of politics, Thatcherism was already the only way forward – the one to which, as she had said in 1981, there was no alternative? Perhaps the most convincing answer was the simplest: something called Thatcherism had just won the Tories four elections. (When the new Tory leader, David Cameron, was asked in 2006 why he appeared to be aping Blair, he replied that 'he has won three elections, you know.'[18]) Politicians don't question success.

As far as Blair himself was concerned, he might reasonably point out that Thatcherism was domestic political economy and that was Brown's job, jealously guarded under Granita. Brown relied heavily on a young aide, Ed Balls, from whom he was inseparable. In William Keegan's account of Brown's Treasury apprenticeship in these years, Balls is referred to constantly as Brown's 'anchor' as he remained for eight years in office.[19] Brown and Balls were transfixed by Tory economic strategy, even to the extent of following it into the ERM and then out again. There must be no repeat of Smith's higher-tax gaffe in 1992. Whatever policy was being pursued by Major and Clarke at the Treasury, Labour would be committing suicide to imply its reversal. If Blair became a Thatcherite from ambition, Brown did so from fear. Granita was thus Thatcherism's Trojan Horse.

At the start of election year, 1997, Brown announced in a speech at the Queen Elizabeth II Centre in Westminster that Labour would not alter Tory upper or lower tax rates or vary Clarke's public spending totals for three years in office. Nor was there any expressed hostility to privatization. Brown welcomed Thatcherism with an inversion, declaring that public service 'does not mean government must act on its own, using public spending in every area'. The public interest could mean 'setting standards for the private sector or by the public sector working with the private sector to meet shared objectives.'[20] It was the essence of Thatcher's first revolution. The shared objective between public and private sectors was the saving or making of money.

The policies that might inform the first Blair government were never discussed by the shadow cabinet.[21] Brown had talked over his tax pledge with Blair, and phoned some senior colleagues with the gist of his speech the night before, but this hardly constituted a collective decision. This was Brown's first flexing of the Granita agreement and it held. He firmly shackled Labour to the fiscal and monetary path laid down by the outgoing Thatcherite regime, to a degree that amazed Treasury officials at the time. He was paying them, and their political masters, the greatest compliment. An electoral revolution might be in the offing, but there would be no corresponding fiscal one. In Brown's case there was to be no third way, no half-control of public spending. If Labour was to carry conviction with a sceptical public, it had to be *'plus royaliste que la reine'*. There was only one queen.

If Blair was happy thus to leave Brown with the conduct of the economy, to a degree unknown by any prime minister in modern times, he remained razor-sharp on election strategy. He approved Brown's approach because it guarded Labour's appeal to middle-ground voters, but he never took those voters for granted. Even as the Major government slid towards seemingly inevitable defeat he never allowed himself the comfort of security. Labour had seen too many false dawns. Blair had established what amounted to a new political party with a new name, fashioned after his own image. But he feared for the election and, above all, he feared a hung parliament. He needed to cover his flank with the Liberal Democrats.

This required negotiations of great delicacy. Hundreds of Labour candidates were about to fight an election with Liberal Democrats as the enemy. The SDP split had opened wounds that had not healed and any smell of a pre-election alliance with the defectors would be locally explosive. Yet Blair had become infatuated with the Liberal Democrat president,

Roy Jenkins. In his essay on their relationship, Seldon records meetings between them even before Blair became party leader. The Blairs visited the Jenkinses regularly at the latter's Oxfordshire retreat, leading to equally cordial relations with the Liberal Democrat leader, Paddy Ashdown. The latter's diaries list persistent overtures from Blair.[22] Ashdown and his colleague, Menzies Campbell, had coalitions and cabinet posts dangled before them, including even the foreign secretaryship.[23] Cherie and Mrs Ashdown briefly became bosom friends. The Blairs enjoyed no such intimacy with any Labour couple (certainly not with the Browns or the Prescotts). Jenkins settled happily into being a power broker of the centre-left and 'hugely enjoyed his role as mentor to Blair'.[24]

Such a promiscuous liaison with an electoral foe was reckless. Meetings were never discussed with the shadow cabinet and only vaguely with Blair's aides. Nor, as Jenkins and Ashdown later revealed, did Blair hide his ambition to do exactly what the SDP had failed to do, which was achieve a realignment of the left that excluded organized labour. A fusion with the Liberal Democrats was what Blair most dreamed of, a centre-left party unencumbered by sectional interests. As he told the *Observer* allusively in 1996, 'If we become the One Nation political party, if we can attract support from the centre as well as the centre-left, then we will be able to benefit significantly.'[25] The possibility of such a realignment was even accorded the dignity of the word 'project', or so Ashdown thought. It was one of many uses of the word in New Labour's lexicon.

Buying an insurance policy against a hung parliament was one thing, sleeping with the enemy was another. Yet Blair now toyed with the ark of the Liberal covenant, proportional representation. After discussion with Jenkins and Ashdown, a commission 'on electoral reform' was promised in the 1997 Labour manifesto, which Blair said he would ask Jenkins to chair. As election-day approached and a landslide beckoned, Blair's promise and his general dalliance with the Lib Dems cooled, but a Joint Consultative Committee between the Lib Dems and a new Labour government was pledged and even met, briefly. The entire flirtation was opportunistic.

Blair heaped scorn on Major's Conservative government and its deeds, but for one Tory he had nothing but respect. As far back as 1995 he told an Australian audience that 'Mrs Thatcher was a radical, not a Tory.' It was an accolade he was never to retract.[26] He later told the *New York Times* that Labour would be 'unelectable' if it pledged to dismantle Thatcherism. The lady herself, by now contemptuous of Major, loved Blair's compliments. Her former aide Charles Powell was brother of Blair's chief of staff, Jonathan, and was able to keep open a conduit between them. She returned the favour in fulsome terms, even when her old party was fighting for its life at the 1997 election. In January that year she told the Tory Carlton Club that 'Tony Blair is a man who won't let Britain down'.[27] He happily referred to this blessing in the *Sun*, pointing out that there were things that 'the 1980s got right'.[28] He was no Johnny-come-lately Thatcherite, and by election-day he did not care who knew it.

As Blair's machine rolled towards victory, his authority was complete. He had meticulously achieved the goal that Philip Gould had set out. 'Labour must replace competing existing structures with a single chain of command, leading directly to the leader of the party. This is the only way that Labour can become a political organisation capable of matching the Conservatives.'[29] Blair went so far as to tell the *Observer* that as of now those who disagreed with him 'need their heads examined'. Indeed they 'require not leadership but therapy'.[30] The days of Labour-party pluralism were over. As Blair told the Newspaper Society in March 1997, 'People have to know that we will run from the centre and forever from the centre.'[31] The British people were ready for a change, and Blair's unitary command structure was ready for them. The climax of the two revolutions was at hand.

PART SIX

Blatcherism Ascendant

16

Something of Napoleon

Tony Blair had changed the British Labour party beyond recognition. On 2 May 1997, he set out to 'change Britain'. His objective was not to achieve any great policy upheaval. He had shown no interest in reversing the first Thatcher revolution and in power he respected it. Just as the post-war 'welfare settlement' had held sway through governments of both parties for thirty years, so now the Thatcherite settlement assumed an equal bipartisanship. Debate was concerned with how to make it work. But Thatcher's second revolution, the revolution of control, Blair was to make his own. He declared his intention to invert the 1945 Labour slogan, 'We are the masters now' to 'We are not the masters now, the people are the masters'. But there was no question which people he meant – his people.

When Tony and Cherie Blair strode euphorically into Downing Street just three years after Blair had become Labour leader, he was forty-two years old. He had no experience of executive office and little of the workings of the British constitution. His 419 MPs had crushed one of the great electoral machines in modern politics, the British Conservative party. Tories were suddenly an extinct species in Scotland, Wales and across almost the entire canvas of urban England. New Labour was more than an innovation, it was a sensation. The purpose of Blair's project had come to fruition. He had achieved power and had done so largely through the endeavours of himself and a small group of associates. At the moment of victory that May morning, the Labour party as such was not in evidence. The coronation was Blair's.

The new prime minister immediately stamped his personality on the mechanism of power. As he planned, the methods that had bent Labour to his will were extended to the machinery of government. An attempt by the cabinet secretary, Sir Robin Butler, to get him to adhere to constitutional convention in staffing his office with civil servants was brushed aside. Blair would run his office his way, not what he saw as Butler's way. In a significant remark before the 1997 election, Jonathan Powell told a gathering of civil servants that under Blair there would be 'a change from a feudal system of barons to a more Napoleonic system'.[1] Blair was as good as Powell's word, though his knowledge of Magna Carta feudalism always seemed tenuous. Absolute power would be concentrated not just in Downing Street but on the prime minister's personal office.[2]

What might have seemed a handicap in forming a new cabinet – not one minister having senior ministerial experience – Blair turned to advantage. He was not naturally 'collegial' except within his close circle, treating ministers not constitutionally, as sovereign over their departments under statute, but as might a president. But he did honour Granita. Ministers answered to Brown at the Treasury for any policy with financial implications and to Blair for the timing and presentation of announcements. A result was that the latter became increasingly obsessive. Anything that was done or said in the name of government, including all interviews and press conferences, had to be cleared with Downing Street. The phrase 'being on message' became a running joke for ministers and Labour MPs alike.

Blair was not the first prime minister to conduct business 'bilaterally', but he treated his cabinet in a more cavalier way than any peacetime predecessor. Even Thatcher had felt the need to clear her policies through cabinet, circulating papers and agendas. Blair's cabinet was no longer the forum in which business was discussed and was properly used only when, as over Iraq, Blair needed to claim support for what he had decided. Meetings tended to be short and were mostly to brief ministers on what the prime minister was doing or had already done. One of Blair's cabinet secretaries, Sir Andrew Turnbull, recorded the change over his career. In 1975 the British cabinet met 56 times and received 146 papers. In 2002 it met 38 times (and briefly) and received just 4 papers.[3] Turnbull's predecessor, Butler, excused this trend endearingly as a reversion to the eighteenth-century practice of the cabinet as 'a conversation of equals'.[4] That was not how participants regarded it. For the first time the prime minister's political advisers were present, including a press officer, Alastair Campbell, known to be keeping a diary for publication and blessed with a licence to leak. This was no conversation of equals.

The unitary command principle required that those closest to Blair should be able to exercise power in his name. He duly told Butler that he expected members of his personal team to give orders to the government machine rather than go through the civil-service secretariat. As a result a separation of roles once considered crucial to the integrity of Whitehall was ended. This was wholly new. Thatcher, Wilson, even Churchill, had their kitchen cabinets, and much trouble it usually caused them. But the distinction between temporary and permanent staff had always been maintained and the conduits with the civil service kept clear. Like Thatcher, Blair had watched *Yes, Minister*, but saw it as a comedy from a lost age. Blair's preferred model was the pacy, events-driven Washington series *The West Wing*. No. 10 staff were addicted to it.

Blair's Opposition team moved intact into Downing Street. Campbell was for ever at his master's side, Rasputin to his Tsar. By deciding what should be Blair's daily face to the world he set the running agenda of government. Meanwhile the chief of staff, Powell, had a prefectorial power over the government machine greater than any formal private secretary. David Miliband continued as head of the No. 10 policy unit, which doubled in size. Mandelson, until he became a cabinet minister with a department of his own, moved quietly between these figures and his own media contacts, plotting and fixing. It was as tight a team as No. 10 had ever seen. The number of political appointees in No. 10 rose swiftly from eight to twenty-four.

Only Gordon Brown had a licence to penetrate this group. He enjoyed unbridled access to the throne, drifting in and out of Blair's room for talks at which no officials would be present. Neither Blair nor Brown liked to have their (or any bilateral) meetings minuted. Of seventeen meetings in No. 10 in one day, only three were recorded, so Jonathan Powell told the Hutton Inquiry.[5] This lack of minutes left officials floundering, but Butler told his protesting officials there was nothing he could do, 'blood was thicker than water'. It was an open secret that he deplored the collapse of the politician/civil servant dichotomy. He took his revenge on the 'democracy' of Blair's sofa government in the 2003 Butler Report on the preliminaries to the Iraq War. The revenge passed unnoticed.

Parliament was to fare little better than the cabinet under the new regime. The prime minister disliked attending the Commons, let alone listening to its debates. Though he was a masterful performer he reduced prime minister's question time from two to one session a week, albeit for longer. Otherwise he turned up only when a colleague under pressure needed visible support. His voting record was worse than any twentieth-century prime minister since Churchill.[6] Back-benchers were told explicitly that their job was not 'to tell us what to do', but to act as 'ambassadors for the government'.[7]

Blair did not see parliamentary committees as independent or significant, and (like Thatcher) expected the whips to keep them in order.

Parliamentary discipline held remarkably for the first term, though not beyond 2001. The number of back-bench rebellions then rose to the highest as a percentage of all votes of any since the Second World War. Those on hunting, foundation hospitals and student fees were handled without seriously undermining Downing Street's political authority. Labour MPs even voted for the Iraq War, which they overwhelmingly opposed in private. Only when Blair's standing began to wane after 2005 and his authoritarianism became more overt were Labour back-benchers bolder. Revolts over terrorism and schools legislation saw the parliamentary party, privately supported by many ministers, lose patience and give Blair serious reverses, which he found it increasingly hard to disregard.

A truism of the British constitution is that the chief check on the executive is informal, the respect of its participants for procedure. A prime minister agrees the conventional constraints of cabinet and parliamentary government, irrespective of the size of his or her majority, because experience suggests that business is more efficiently conducted that way. Where a prime minister proclaims a radical agenda, as did both Thatcher and Blair, the conventions of the constitution can seem an obstacle. And since they are mere conventions, they are a bluff that is easily called.

Called it was. The veteran MP Tam Dalyell said, with only a hint of exaggeration, that to understand Blair's government the modern historian should read not a politics textbook but Saint-Simon's memoirs of the reign of Louis XIV. Public affairs were driven not by any constitutional form but by a miasma of intrigue and vanity. To Dalyell (and others) Blair's Downing Street was not a premiership nor even a presidency – known political entities – but a court, the expression of the personality and whim of a monarch 'whose flickering eye follows the comings and goings of those who wish him well, and those who don't'.[8] An Australian political scientist, the late J.H. Grainger, wrote an entire book describing Blair's use of power in terms of Weber's 'ideal leadership type' (described in the Introduction).[9] Such leaders, spellbound by their own charm, put themselves above party or constitution. They fashion themselves on the basis of a popular vote as the political expression of the nation as a whole. Their policies are never specific but are expressed as 'values', couched in quasi-religious terms such as covenants, pledges, contracts and trust.

To Grainger, Blair was in the tradition of the charismatic heroes of German romanticism. 'He springs neither from an established nor a dissenting church ... but from the accidents of life and education within a liberal society.'[10] No sustaining tradition claims him. Such a leader is a chameleon, an outsider with neither hinterland nor destination. Blair's family background was that of a communist turned Tory, lower-middle class turned upper-middle class, Scots, Irish and north-eastern, yet somehow metropolitan. He seemed socially rootless, his accent and taste impossible to define. In this he was extraordinarily like Margaret Thatcher. When Roy Jenkins told Blair he preferred a 'first-class politician with a second-class mind' to the converse, Blair quoted it in mild self-admiration.[11] Hence the ease with which he could claim to be not socialist, not centrist, not Thatcherite, not neo-conservative yet somehow all these things. He artlessly told the *Sun* shortly after his election, 'Sometimes I forget I'm prime minister. To me I'm just Tony Blair.'[12] There was something in Blair of the Cheshire cat.

To students of political history, such leadership is prima facie dangerous. It asks democracy to legitimize not a programme or a set of interests but a person. In a Fabian pamphlet on Blair's leadership, Colin Crouch goes so far as to call Blair a 'post-democratic' leader seeking authority in the vaguest of terms: 'We have a covenant ... Give me your faith ... I give you my word ... Trust me.'[13] Such language has always been alien to British politics, at least since the House of Stuart, not just because it lacks the specific content by which an electorate can hold politicians to account but because it suggests feet starting to lift off the ground. It implies absolutism. The British people relied heavily on satire to keep their image of Blair in proportion. Harry Enfield, Rory Bremner, *Dead Ringers* and *Private Eye* all caricatured Blair as versions of a naive and sanctimonious vicar.

The presidentialism of Downing Street under Blair has become a cliché but that does not make it inaccurate. Some Westminster observers, such as Peter Hennessy and Peter Riddell, see Blair as doing no more than honouring Asquith's much-quoted dictum that the job of a prime minister is whatever a prime minister chooses it to be. They point out that much of Blair's innovation recognized what had become common practice under his predecessors. Even as it trebled in size, the No. 10 establishment was small compared with presidencies abroad. As for the divide between political aides and civil servants, the apologists argue that it was increasingly meaningless. Cabinet and parliament had been paper tigers for years. Blair might indeed be calling the constitution's bluff, but so what?

While there is force in each of these points individually, the sum of Blair's executive reforms lessened the checks and balances on Downing Street and concentrated power to a new degree.[14] Properly democratic presidents are subject to constitutional restraint. They usually face a separately elected and legitimized assembly and a supreme court. They serve fixed terms and must barter power with subsidiary government, regional, civic and local. Blair's presidency recognized none of this. He never achieved a popular majority in any poll or any election, never even beating Major's record of 14 million votes in 1992. Riddell accepts that Blair had 'surprisingly little instinctive feel for constitutional issues. Questions about the mechanisms of power are much less important for him than how power is used.'[15] The truth is that Blair behaved as if his authority was absolute. He did whatever he chose.

The chief check on Blair was his craving for approval, from associates and from the wider political and public community. All power needs a mirror of which it can ask, 'Who is fairest of them all?' If the constitution's formal mirrors are tarnished or broken, something else must suffice. Blair's dependence on Campbell and Mandelson lay in their status as mirrors, in their being direct not with the public but with him. Bremner's satire of the relationship of Blair and Campbell, as of puppet and puppeteer, was said to be so close to the mark that the Blairs could not watch it. Campbell was portrayed as constantly drawing the prime minister's attention to the Murdoch press and chiding him for his wetness. When Blair protested that he had his in-house critics he was right, but they were critics as court jesters. They too needed mirrors to assess their performance and that of the government. That mirror was the media.

No government in history had spent so much time and effort on its media image. It was a check on his performance to which Blair was constantly alert, because it was the one he did not own. Blair's team granted the 'fourth estate' unprecedented access and constitutional significance. If accountability were to be sought between elections, it would not be through parliament but through a daily 'conversation with the nation'. Government announcements would dominate each day's agenda. Scrutiny and cross-examination would take place on radio and television. Carefully managed, this process enabled the prime minister to 'write the narrative' of the government through a perpetual '24/7' media operation directed at keeping Blair in the public eye. He would address the nation not as a faction leader in the House of Commons but as a secular pope, '*urbi et orbi*', whether from sofa or podium. Campbell took over the old chief whip's house at No. 12 Downing Street for his expanded empire, thus symbolizing the changing geology of Blair's regime. The media was taking the place of parliament as the forum of British government accountability.

In most countries the media comprises two or three powerful groups which, with state-regulated broadcasting, can usually be manipulated by those in power. Britain's broadcast media might operate under layers of state regulation and, in the case of the BBC, depend on government for its revenue, but it remains determinedly autonomous and politically independent. As for the press, Britain is unusual in having nine raucous and competitive national dailies, with no less competitive Sunday siblings. These papers revel in their contempt for office and are inherently unbiddable. This very fact made their opinions an obsession of Downing Street.

Campbell and Mandelson had colluded with the press in opposing the Major government, but they mistook collusion for compliance. Campbell, a journalist and party publicist, had gleefully turned his blowtorch on the hypersensitive Major, but when the same blowtorch was turned on him he disliked it. Like most holders of his office he ended up railing against the mendacity and bias of the press. He had Blair write platitudinous 'guest columns' for the *Sun* and had him stand alongside Thatcher to give a eulogy on the death of the right-wing press magnate Lord Rothermere. Blair in turn seemed startlingly naive. He would use his family to court publicity, yet resent it when publicity led to criticism. With his closest aide doubling as his spin-doctor, media reaction became his daily overnight review. Ministers eager to gain Blair's ear found the quickest means was through the columns of the *Daily Mail* or the *Sun*.

Press influence on policy became enormous, from taxation and crime to drugs policy, health, immigration and, above all, war. Journalists had grown used to Major's sensitivity to their criticism. Now they found a government inviting them to write each day's political agenda. Editors are not natural governors. Their motivation is as much commercial as political and their time frame seldom longer than a week. Journalism's instinct to draw blood needed no further encouragement. Any vulnerability in Blair's court was attacked with a ferocity that left Downing Street stunned. Blair's favours to friends and donors were widely publicized, such as his indulgence of the Formula One boss Bernie Ecclestone, the financier Geoffrey Robinson, and the wealthy Hinduja brothers. Blatantly money-raising honours lists were ridiculed. Ministers had only to trip and the press would pounce, as the hapless deputy prime minister John Prescott found to his cost. Criticism of the government's Iraq War policy drove Campbell into a bunker mentality that cost Blair a disproportionate row with the BBC.

Campbell was accused of using the power of government to corrupt the media. This was faulty analysis. He used the power of the media to corrupt government. Each day saw a hyperactive, media-led blast of initiatives registered on Campbell's daily grid of Whitehall activity. Policy was whatever Downing Street needed to prove that 'something is being done'. Short-termism swept aside any concept of a sustained programme. Whitehall had to view the accidents of public administration entirely through Campbell's prism. Blair told his colleagues that their job was to deliver good publicity for the government, to find 'eye-catching initiatives' with which he could be associated.

Such conduct of power was instinctive rather than systematic. In Opposition Blair's ambition was to win office and once in office to keep it. This was not cynicism but rather the absence of any other ambition to hand. Blair was not a policy enthusiast and had no great message, no visionary legacy, to bequeath the nation (except possibly the results of his foreign adventures). Just as Major's effectiveness as prime minister was blighted by a poor image, so Blair's came to be blighted by the opposite, a good image substituting for substance. The word 'spin' came to have the same connotation for Blair as sleaze had for Major. As Seldon put it, 'Blair lacked the intellectual equipment to devise a coherent agenda of his own' and allowed the media to suffice.[16]

These factors offer an insight into Blair's highly successful 'occasionalism' discussed in the Introduction. Most prime ministers deplore the 'tyranny of events' as distracting them from the higher calling of office. They see the short term as bad and the long term as good. Blair was the opposite. With no particular destination, events were his spur to action, his friend and ally, his call on stage. The death of Princess Diana, 9/11, foot-and-mouth, the tsunami, the Olympic bid, the London bombs were like scripts delivered to his door by the casting director of history. How would 'the people's Tony' turn them to account? Each offered a chance to master ceremony, to express pain, joy, action or repose. Blair was brilliant at exploiting them, especially those that called him to an international stage.

Most prime ministers come to foreign relations relatively late in office. Blair was bitten from the start by the glamour of abroad, finding in foreign affairs a natural outlet for the simplicity of 'command and control'. Whereas he had to defer to Brown in matters of domestic policy, he felt no such deference to his foreign secretaries, Robin Cook, Jack Straw and Margaret Beckett. He led from the start. Foreign policy, by its nature usually reactive, responded to the occasionalist in Blair. As a result his period as prime minister was more dominated by overseas events and pressures than any leader's since the war. Any judgement of his contribution to Thatcherism must start from this base.

Blair determined early on to demonstrate his can-do authority by picking up Major's ever-stalled Northern Ireland 'peace process'. The IRA and hard-line Loyalists were, to Blair, no different from the trade unions of his past. Their intransigence would melt before his negotiating talent and charm. Northern Ireland also offered an avenue to the wider stage of foreign affairs. Blair exploited the bond formed in Opposition with Bill Clinton, whom he asked to mobilize the American end of the Irish republican lobby in favour of peace. A supposedly British problem would thus be 'triangulated' with Washington.

In the event, Blair fell victim to the charm of others, notably the IRA's Gerry Adams. He would immerse himself in the details of an issue but would soon get bored, back off and set deadlines amid a media frenzy. The road to the 1998 Good Friday agreement was a classic of Blair hyperactivity, awash in such phrases as, 'It's not a day for sound bites really . . . I feel the hand of history on our shoulder.'[17] The agreement itself was surrounded by a cloud of Irish mist. It nudged forward what had already been begun by Major, but its most immediate outcome was to concede the IRA its most coveted goal, immediate prisoner release. Ulster's prisons were emptied of some of the most dangerous people in the land, so enraging the Unionists as to destabilize the ostensible purpose of the agreement, to restore devolved local government to the province. The result stabilized Major's ceasefire but it led to the downfall of Ulster's most plausible statesman, David Trimble, and his replacement by the rabble-rouser Unionist Ian Paisley. Eight years later provincial devolution was as far from realization as ever.

The Northern Ireland agreement, lauded by Clinton at a glittering Belfast ceremony, was a brilliantly spun opening to the Blair era. The new freshness and confidence were uplifting after Thatcher, the hectoring nanny and Major, the insecure apologist. Blair oozed dynamism. He rode to a euro-summit on a bicycle, instigated referendums on devolution for Scotland and Wales and mooted reform of the House of Lords. A commission on elec-toral reform was set up as promised to his friend, Lord Jenkins (but soon forgotten). Celebrities enjoyed easy access to the Blairs' drawing room in a series of dazzling 'Cool Britannia' receptions. The death of Diana three months into Blair's office was the supreme occasionalist moment, offering an opportunity to perform as the voice and emotion of the nation. It was undeniably well done and stimulated much talk of Kennedy and Camelot.

In May 1998 Blair and Cherie were invited by the Clintons to the grandest dinner Washington had seen in decades. To the British ambassa-dor, Sir Christopher Meyer, Blair's arrival with a large retinue (some thirty compared with Thatcher's usual ten)

had about it more than a whiff of imperial progress. The whole No. 10 team from the PM downwards pulsed with ill-suppressed excitement. Washington. Bill Clinton. Third Way. World Stage. This was the Big One.

Two hundred and forty guests from Congress and show-business caroused to the strains of Barbra Streisand, Elton John and Stevie Wonder. When Wonder sang 'My Cherie Amour', recalled Meyer, 'Cherie herself looked star-struck, almost overwhelmed by the glamour of the occasion.'[18]

Blair was depicted by the American commentator Joe Klein as 'Clinton's kid brother'. If he was discomfited by his new friend's womanizing, he was overawed by Clinton's ability to convey confidence in public.[19] Blair's bizarre return gift was a conference on 'the third way', conducted in New York and with Clinton in attendance. It was recalled by Meyer as of mind-bending emptiness, all 'windy generalisation ... less a coherent philosophy of government more a tactic for election-winning'.[20] On the Blairs' return the press was filled with rumours that they wanted a 'Blairforce One', rather than having to make use of the Queen's Flight. They were said to want a larger personal staff and even a move from No. 10 to a 'proper' mansion, possibly Dover House round the corner in Whitehall. Blair was immune to accusations of extravagance. When flying to his first G7 summit in Denver in 1997 he chartered Concorde, at a cost to the taxpayer of £250,000.

The new prime minister loved the paraphernalia of military command, telling his surprised party conference in 1997 about the boxes, switches and nuclear codes with which he was surrounded. Before the Iraq War he had to be restrained from demanding a sand box in his office with troop deployments and flags marked on it. An early bond was formed with the extrovert chief of the defence staff, Charles Guthrie, a bond that protected the defence budget from Treasury cost-cutting. Blair often contrasted military efficiency with the 'amateurism' of the politicians round him.[21] He did not enjoy war but, like Thatcher, he found it a satisfying theatre of power, where orders were obeyed and things happened. He committed British troops to overseas combat five times in his first six years in office, more than any prime minister in half a century.

Thatcher had advised Blair from the start to keep at Washington's shoulder lest it 'go wobbly'.[22] He needed no encouragement. Military operations with America somewhere in the world were a backdrop to Blair's entire office. Britain was alone with America in Operation Desert Fox, a bombing campaign against Baghdad in 1998 that was claimed to have 'successfully eliminated' Saddam Hussein's weapons of mass destruction. The entire operation seemed, in retrospect, more an attempt by Clinton to distract attention from possible impeachment over his relations with Monica Lewinsky, as Blair came embarrassingly to realize.[23]

A year later, in Kosovo, it was Blair who took the lead role, inducing a reluctant Clinton to fight Serbia to protect the Kosovan Albanians from ethnic cleansing. It was, Blair said, 'the first of a new generation of liberal, humanitarian wars' to which Britain was now committed as part of the new world order. In Chicago in April 1999 Blair adumbrated a highly interventionist doctrine whereby national security and self-interest should no longer limit British military operations abroad. Foreign policy should become an altruistic crusade in pursuit of humanitarian 'just wars'. The *Financial Times* concluded that Britain was now 'Nato's most hawkish country'.[24] The speech, largely written by the London academic Lawrence Freedman, was dismissed by Henry Kissinger as 'irresponsible', and Washington even protested that the British leader was 'sprinkling too much adrenalin on his corn flakes'.[25] When in 2001 an overtly isolationist George W. Bush arrived at the White House, Blair told his team, 'We've got to turn these people into internationalists.'[26] Blair was the new Palmerston.

The al-Qaeda attack on America on 11 September 2001 pre-empted that role. It ousted Blair from the interventionist driving seat and replaced him after all by the American president. Suddenly roles seemed to have been reversed. The rest of the world expected Blair to use his 'special relationship' with a belligerent president to exert a restraining hand. The 'new world order' that had so attracted Blair to his humanitarian crusade was taking a more alarming turn. America, the most powerful state on earth, was transformed overnight into a condition close to paranoid hysteria by dint of one, admittedly awful, terrorist incident. Every past tenet of American foreign policy fell by the wayside.

Blair's first instinct on hearing of 9/11 was characteristic. According to Seldon, 'he was not interested in what the government machine was doing. His mind was already on the world stage.'[27] Events presented him with a challenge and another opportunity to perform, which he exploited with panache. He embarked on a frenetic exercise in shuttle diplomacy to build a Muslim consensus to suppress al-Qaeda, capture Osama bin Laden and thus avert American military action. This had some success among Muslim leaders but did nothing to restrain Washington, which thought Blair was on a fool's errand. In his party conference speech a month later Blair asserted, to a bemused audience, 'This is a moment to seize. The kaleidoscope has been shaken. The pieces are in flux. Soon they will settle again. Before they do, let us reorder the world around us.'[28]

Britain was duly dragged into a sequence of 9/11 postures under America's wing, which were to continue in one theatre or another throughout Blair's administration. From the moment bombs started falling on Kabul on 7 October 2001, Blair seemed more like a man wrestling to keep up with his more powerful friend than one exercising restraint. His decision taking Britain to war against Afghanistan was never discussed in full cabinet. He was riding a tiger of American rage and retribution, yet was constantly seeking to elevate his action to a moral crusade. Blair pleaded for British planes to be used in the first strike on Kabul.[29] 'Even when al-Qaeda is dealt with,' he told MPs, 'the job is not over. The network of international terrorism is not confined to it.'

Britain's two wars against Afghanistan and Iraq met no plausible criterion of British interest. The Anglo-American special relationship was never absolute, having always been treated by both parties as à la carte. America rejected British pleas for alliance during Suez and the Falklands. Britain refused to help in Vietnam and protested over Grenada. Yet Blair felt trapped by his eagerly sought bond with the White House and by the wider commitment to intervention of his Chicago speech. In both Afghanistan and Iraq he claimed variously that America should never be left acting alone, that British interests were identical to America's and that Britain was a restraining hand. Thatcher had told him to stay close to America and Clinton had told him to stay close to Bush.[30] He honoured the advice to the letter.

The curiosity of Blair's foreign policy was that, for all his frenetic activity, he was never its master. He did not know how to handle an ally as basic and bruised as was America after 9/11. He merely asserted over and again that 9/11 'changed the rules of the game' without articulating what this meant.[31] Since his nature when trapped was to make the best of a bad job, he did so by converting a problem into an abstraction. Like a good lawyer with a poor brief he could only tell the jury, 'Trust me.' Blair startled even his own staff by his inability to influence unfolding events in Washington. The evidence was overwhelming that Bush had decided on regime change in Iraq by the time of his meeting with Blair in April 2002 at his ranch in Crawford. Blair knew he would have to be part of such an operation but, sensing that his cabinet and party would be sceptical, he found himself sucked into a morass of deception which slowly poisoned his credibility as a leader. As accounts by early participants began to emerge in the course of 2005, he was portrayed as a 'patsy' towards the White House.[32] The charge was fiercely repeated during the Israel–Lebanon conflict in the summer of 2006.

In the event, nothing caused Blair more anguish or did more to undermine trust in his leadership than did Iraq. He made occasional attempts to wrestle from it some sort of policy gain, for instance a revamped Middle East peace process or a role for the United Nations, but they came to nothing. Instead Blair's attention was concentrated on somehow proving to the British people that their security required the imminent overthrow of Saddam Hussein and the elimination of the threat of his weapons of mass destruction. It was a threat which, whatever Blair may or may not have been told at the time, he must have known was grossly exaggerated.

The result was one of the saddest episodes in modern British government, a display of what historians call cognitive dissonance, the craving to believe the unbelievable.[33] Material was disseminated by Downing Street claiming Saddam posed an 'imminent threat' to Britain, even a 45-minute threat. This not only denied the much-trumpeted efficacy of the 1998

Operation Desert Fox. It also led to suspect evidence being exaggerated and broadcast with all the powers that Downing Street's spin-doctors could muster. For whatever reason the public was massively deceived and no amount of subsequent explanation could conceal the fact.

The most revealing documents on Blair's style of government were not the kiss-and-tell memoirs of dissident staff but the leaden prose of the Hutton and Butler inquiries of 2004 and 2005. One was into the suicide of a defence analyst, David Kelly, after disclosing Downing Street manipulation of intelligence on Iraq. The other was into whether Downing Street deliberately distorted that intelligence. Both formally cleared the government but in terms that only deepened suspicion that something improper had indeed occurred. Both revealed the extraordinary power of Alastair Campbell's media machine over Whitehall. Butler concluded that the head of the Joint Intelligence Committee, John Scarlett, had 'not been demonstrably beyond influence' by Campbell.[34] No less devastating was the revelation that the attorney general's legal advice on the war had been altered to conform to the exigencies of Blair's policy. The image left by Hutton and Butler was of a regime that had cast form, decorum and constitutional convention to the winds.

The impact of the Iraq War on Blair's leadership was similar to that of the Falklands on Thatcher. Indeed the two conflicts stand as bookends on the Thatcherite narrative. But for Thatcher the Falklands was positive, for Blair negative. The reason was that Blair in Iraq, unlike Thatcher, was never in control of events. He had involved British troops in a shooting war whose course, conduct and outcome were in the hands of the Americans. No British interest was at stake in Afghanistan or Iraq. The wars killed over a hundred British troops and were increasingly unpopular in the country at large. They appeared to make Britain more, not less, vulnerable to terrorism.

The nation suffered only one successful attack from Muslim extremists, in July 2005, compared with dozens from the IRA in the 1970s and 1980s. Yet security came to preoccupy Blair's agenda more than that of any prime minister since the Second World War. It seemed to obsess him, affecting every corner of the political system. It dominated the work of his Foreign Office, Home Office and defence ministry. It changed policy on asylum and immigration, civil rights, free speech, crime and punishment and relations between the executive and the judiciary. Public buildings, including the Palace of Westminster, were turned into ugly fortresses. Security was rarely off the front page, affecting all that Blair did at home and abroad. In the run-up to the 2005 general election he seemed dimly aware that he had deceived the public in going to war, but he hoped that in appealing to trust and invoking the threat of terrorism he could transcend this.

One effect of Iraq was to compromise Blair's long-standing ambition to leadership in Europe. The man who had promised as a young candidate in 1982 that 'only a Labour government' would have the courage to take Britain out of the EU now wanted to be 'at its heart'. Immediately on coming to power the government signed up to the Maastricht Social Chapter, from which Major had laboriously 'opted out'. This made remarkably little difference in practice since the government failed to implement what it had now agreed, and fought every attempt to extend European competence into employment and social affairs.[35] Blair soon joined Thatcher and Major in finding the reality of European diplomacy a far cry from his ideal. European summits were every six months or more. For Blair, as for his predecessors, they were mind-numbingly dull yet contrived to lob one grenade after another into the domestic pond.

French intransigence on every matter from beef imports to military co-operation brought Blair nothing but anguish. His charm failed to soften France's president, Jacques Chirac. Anglo-French relations were worse than at any time since de Gaulle. Despite all this Blair, influenced by Roy Jenkins, persuaded himself that British membership of the euro zone, together with a rewritten EU constitution, were vital, indeed achievements that might lead him to a second career as a European leader. In 2001 he asserted that success in Europe and delivering public services were to be cornerstones of the new parliament. Yet by 2005 Europe was rivalling Iraq as the topic that seemed most to plague Blair's sleep.

The euro proved the most vexing of the many bones of contention between Blair and Brown. It was the cause of histrionic shouting matches which Brown seemed always to win.[36] Brown had drawn up five tests for euro entry, some would say insuperable ones. They included the convergence of British economic cycles with Europe's and a requirement that Europe 'demonstrate sufficient flexibility in labour and product markets'. As Philip Stevens pointed out, Brown was here extending Granita to give himself a veto over a crucial area of Blair's foreign policy. 'Blair could not advocate a referendum on the [euro] unless and until his chancellor decreed that the economic conditions were right.'[37]

The fate of the euro was soon subsumed in that of Europe generally. The cause was a new constitution, written by the former French president Valéry Giscard d'Estaing but with Blair in enthusiastic support. As it emerged over the course of 2004, clothed in near incomprehensible jargon, Blair secured an agreement with Chirac that they would both submit it to referendum. While few leaders are so reckless as to treat a referendum as a vote of confidence, Blair virtually did so. He said during the 2005 election campaign that the constitution would 'build a new and constructive relationship with Europe. This is my covenant with the British people. Judge me on it.' Yet he shrewdly waited for Chirac to go first into the lists. The result was disaster. In June 2005 the French people rejected the new constitution, followed by the Dutch the same week.

Such an event would have thrown most leaders into turmoil. Heath would have sulked and Thatcher gone into ecstasies of glee. Blair showed himself the supreme occasionalist. To French fury he immediately declared the constitution dead and his past support for it nugatory. Suddenly relieved of controversy over both the euro and the new constitution, Blair seemed delighted. With deft opportunism he seized on the French vote as a chance to push France aside and 'create a new Europe' during Britain's EU presidency in the second half of 2005. He added that the 2002 Common Agricultural Policy reform, still heavily biased towards France but which he had help negotiate, should be considered dead.

Blair was acting wholly in character, able to discard as irrelevant what Attlee called 'the mess of centuries' when it suited him. For Blair the French vote was significant only in adjusting the realpolitik of Europe. But it offered a chance to complete one of the last pieces in the map of Thatcherite foreign policy. He would not only champion the Anglo-American bond but lead a neo-capitalist Europe, its markets free to embrace the countries of eastern Europe. It was the same vision Thatcher briefly entertained after the Single European Act in 1986. This was not the Europe of the French and Dutch referendum majorities, which had rejected the new constitution as being overly free-market. It was a Europe ready to meet the challenge of globalization, truly a creation of a son of Thatcher.

Again Blair misjudged his environs. His EU presidency proved a miserable experience as Chirac took his revenge at what he regarded as British perfidy over the constitution. France demanded that Britain surrender the budgetary rebate that Thatcher had won in 1984. Blair adamantly refused. He put forward a plan for a new European budget, freezing spending, redirecting funds from farm support to East European infrastructure and equalizing national payments into EU funds. He offered to cut Britain's rebate but only if France abandoned the 2002 CAP reform. France pointed out that Blair had personally signed this reform at the time, to last to 2013, in return for France agreeing reluctantly not to veto EU enlargement. Britain could hardly go back on the agreement so soon. In December 2005, with Christmas pressing, Blair was forced into a humiliating concession of a 20 per cent cut in the rebate and an increased budget overall, with no French concession on agricultural reform. Brown refused publicly to applaud a bargain which he clearly thought inept. It was a repeat of the Thatcher/Lawson split over Europe, but without its catastrophic outcome.

The prime minister emerged from his third election victory in 2005 chastened by the lowest percentage vote of any government since 1832, though the constituency bias to Labour gave him a safe majority of sixty-six seats. Within two months of victory he seemed to have laid the ghost of his European constitution defeat. He scored a personal triumph in winning the 2012 Olympics for London and a sort of vindication of his counter-terrorism emphasis in the London bombs of July 2005. But some of the Blair magic had gone. He had declared before the election that it would be his last, and though he also said he would serve 'a full term', the remark both weakened his authority and infuriated Brown, who had expected him to go earlier. Blair acquired the characteristic of long-term leaders, of being accident prone. His reforms to public services came to seem ever more wayward (see chapter 18) and his parliamentary party rebelled with increasing regularity, on schools, health and terrorism legislation. His manipulation of the honours system recalled the worst days of Lloyd George and even provoked a police inquiry in 2006. Every incident or chance remark reopened the dominant question: when would Blair go?

In December 2005 the Tories elected a youthful and attractive new leader in David Cameron. The wars of the Thatcherite succession within the Tory party appeared to be over. Cameron instantly paid Blair a similar compliment to that which Blair had paid Thatcher. He stole his clothes. Cameron's team studiously read the works of Philip Gould. Tory speeches resounded to the same 'caring and compassionate' agenda, the same 'continuity and change' phraseology, that Blair had long made his own. The personality of the leader was projected over against that of the party rather than in harmony with it. The Blair rulebook was followed to the letter. At the first prime minister's questions after his election, in December 2005, Cameron unnerved Blair with the gibe, 'You were the future once', yet a smile of recognition crossed the older man's face.[38] This was surely his doppelgänger. A Thatcher grandson was born. Addressing Rupert Murdoch and his Newscorp executives in California on July 30, 2006, Blair declared the death of left and right as political terms. 'On policy cross-dressing is rampant,' he said, 'the era of tribal political leadership is over.'

17

Gordon Brown, Thatcherite

'No pair of politicians in our modern history has wielded so much power together.' So concluded James Naughtie in his study of the Blair/Brown relationship, *The Rivals*.[1] A fairer title might have been The Partners. For all Blair's unified command structure described in the last chapter, its foundation lay in the bargain struck in the Granita restaurant in 1994 acknowledging Brown's Treasury as a no-go area for No. 10 and his primacy in domestic policy. That the agreement led to rivalry was hardly surprising. The Treasury and Downing Street have long contended for power in British government. What was extraordinary, given the personalities involved, was that it retained its equilibrium for over a decade.

The reason was simple. While Blair may not have honoured his alleged pledge on Brown's succession, he honoured the rest of Granita. He granted Brown more power than any chancellor in history. This was not a constitutional check on Blair's presidentialism, as the delegation was always within his discretion. It was rather a bipolarity within the court. Explosive material was contained within the walls of Downing Street. Whenever it seemed to go critical John Prescott raced to defuse it. When relations came close to breakdown before the 2005 election, some primitive survival instinct drew the two men back together and had them campaign as Siamese twins. The conclusion of political opinion was always the same, that Brown's behaviour was both understandable and appalling. The two judgements somehow cancelled each other out.

On coming to office Brown seemed the answer to the Treasury's dreams. His monastic asceticism appeared immune to high spending and thus proof against the failings of Labour chancellors down the ages. He had not served in a spending department or shown any sign of susceptibility to lobbying. On the other hand his career had seldom been exposed to the raw winds of politics and he had never stormed the hustings in defence of some unpopular policy. Before the 1997 election, he committed Labour to Kenneth Clarke's three-year spending targets and made great play of his mistress being called prudence. Public finances would adhere to a 'golden rule' whereby revenue and spending would balance over the course of an economic cycle. All this was an unprecedented compliment by a government to its predecessor. The Tories had in 1979 brought with them an expensive basket of election pledges. Brown had brought none, apart from a vague commitment to spend more on education ('from the reserves').

If the Treasury was ready to welcome Brown to its bosom, Brown did not reciprocate. This was not a matter of any policy difference: it was personal. Brown had never been a minister or chief executive of anything. He had barely chaired a committee let alone handled a complex hierarchy of clever and cultured people. Like Blair he had always worked informally with a small group of loyal friends, people who preferred soccer to symphonies and profanities to the formal locution of Whitehall. Shy in the company of strangers, especially English ones, Brown was inexperienced in the group dynamics of somewhere like the Treasury and was certainly unwilling to learn. Like Blair in Downing Street he brought to the Treasury a cabal of aides and shut the door on anyone else.

The long-serving Ed Balls was to Brown what the Campbell/Mandelson ménage was to Blair. The dependence was total. They were so inseparable that Brown's most sympathetic biographers, William Keegan and Robert Peston, often refer to them as virtually a single entity, Brown/Balls. In Opposition the duo formed a quartet with a raucous press officer, Charlie Whelan, and a courtier/millionaire, Geoffrey Robinson. They would meet, chat and watch football over champagne at the latter's Grosvenor House suite. This so-called Hotel Group, plus a policy adviser, Ed Miliband, continued to meet behind closed doors in office, to the mystification of Treasury officials. The permanent secretary, Sir Terry Burns, was ostracized from Brown's confidence, soon resigned and became a virulent if private critic of the chancellor.

Brown's entourage paralleled Blair's, instigating a partisan feud that reached Plantagenet proportions. Brown's executive style was everything Blair's was not. He could not perform the pleasantries, the backslapping, lunching and casual corridor recognition of daily Whitehall business. He was a publicist's nightmare, refusing to smile for photographers and replying to rare interviews with a statistical babble. His moods were awesome. When in office Blair made a conference speech which Brown saw as a coded attack, he refused to applaud in full view of the cameras. That a man apparently warm and humorous among close friends could be so cold in public made his seeking a career in politics seem perverse. Opposition spokesmen, with whom parliamentary relations are customarily cordial, found him aggressive and distant.

This did not mean that Brown was unsusceptible to the blandishments of power, but the blandishments were different. Blair was dazzled by the glamour of high office but found economics and finance tedious. Brown was bored by occasion and diplomacy, but loved the presence of money. He did not crave it for himself, and snubbed such City traditions as 'dressing' for dinner, but he admired people who were rich and he spent unprecedented sums on bankers and consultants. The former Blair aide, Geoff Mulgan, remarked on the government's strange affection for 'the super rich, big business and the City'.[2] Brown slid easily into the jargon of Thatcherism. 'Greater competition at home,' said Brown, 'is the key to greater competitiveness abroad.'[3] He spattered his speeches with buzzwords such as turbo-capitalism, tiger economy, cyber-revolution, globalization and e-government.

Granita had been regarded as a concession by Blair and a consolation for Brown. Blair said that he 'did not trust the Treasury and what Gordon might do from it'.[4] The preposition 'from' was significant. In the event Granita reflected the different métiers of the two men. It freed Blair from aspects of government that simply bored him. When Brown left him ignorant of his first Budget strategy until two days beforehand, Blair's staff were furious. Blair let it ride, never keen to force an issue with his colleague.[5] As he spent more time on foreign affairs, fighting with the Treasury was unnecessary and Brown became literally the 'prime minister'. Nor need Blair worry that Brown would interpret Granita as a Trojan horse for old Labour socialism. If Brown was wheeling any horse into fortress Labour it was the same as he had wheeled in during the immediate pre-election period, that of Thatcherism. Westminster lore has Brown sidelining the Treasury and its mandarins from his decisions. Yet that did not render him immune from the department's acquired ideology.

Throughout the 1980s and 1990s the Treasury had been the institutional temple of Thatcherism. The spirits of Howe and Lawson hovered over it like Marx and Engels over a Soviet ministry. Anyone who thought that Blair's sympathy to the creed had been merely an electability device was soon disabused. If Thatcherism in Opposition was a means of acquiring power, by the same token it was the means of keeping it. Besides, as the 1997 manifesto made clear, the new government had no other place to go. Blair had conceded in Opposition that there was 'much good about the 1980s'. The Treasury's job was to ensure that Thatcherism was now 'owned' by New Labour. The task was to prove easy.

Distant though they were from each other, the Treasury and Brown shared many characteristics. Both revelled in secret power, shunning publicity and denying responsibility or blame for any mishaps in government policy. Both craved control. Under Brown power continued to radiate from the Treasury building overlooking Parliament Square, but it was power untrammelled by public sensitivity. Brown was politically inexperienced and, unlike Downing Street, had no feel for handling the media. As for the Treasury, it had long grown accustomed to letting others take responsibility for its mistakes, of which there were to be many.

Not even Brown's predecessor, Kenneth Clarke, expected him to keep to the Tory spending targets for 1998–2001, but Brown did so.[6] The first Labour spending round made the first Thatcher one in 1979 look spendthrift. Manifesto pledges on poverty, schooling, health and crime had been left deliberately vague. In power Brown ensured that any new Blair initiative was cheap, ring-fenced and of short duration. If not, like those on education, they were covered either from the contingency reserve or by new and regressive 'stealth' taxes. A windfall utilities tax (raising a one-off £5 billion) supposedly paid for the New Deal employment initiative. Further revenue came from the ending of pensions tax credits and advance corporation tax (totalling £7 billion).[7] Brown even cut what was left of the Tories' mortgage interest tax relief, a subsidy no Tory chancellor had dared withdraw.

Brown's early days at the Treasury were dominated by a *coup de théâtre*, his handing over to the Bank of England the monthly task of fixing interest rates, subject to his decision on what the inflation rate should be. He balanced this by removing financial regulation from the Bank, to its fury. The change was essentially technical, delegating to an out-of-house committee what had been decided between Bank and Treasury (the 'Ken and Eddie show' after Clarke and the Bank's governor, Eddie George). Riddell has argued that this was no more than a formalization of the low-inflation policies pursued by Lamont and Clarke since 1993, 'a process rather than a sharp dividing line'. The outcome was no manifest change in monetary policy, indeed Riddell suggested that an economist from Mars 'would conclude that the same government had been in charge throughout the second half of the 1990s'.[8]

Whether the reform justified the hyperbole of Brown's apologists must be moot. William Keegan first described it as Labour 'taking leave of its senses', before later regarding it as 'a major constitutional reform'.[9] Whenever anyone complained of Brown being a Treasury 'control freak' the Bank decision was always presented as a sign that he was not. Yet it was the only such decision he made and – like Scottish and Welsh devolution – it was made before the centralist juices had begun coursing through his veins. It was also a delegation to the one community for which Brown had an inordinate respect, banking.

What was unprecedented was Brown's freedom to discipline cabinet spending without appeal to the prime minister. There was no Thatcher 'star chamber' to resolve disputes since Granita had predetermined such appeals in the Treasury's favour. The triangular balance of power in cabinet government between departments, the Treasury and the prime minister was at an end. Only defence staged successful flanking actions to protect its budget via No. 10, playing on Blair's enthusiasm for war. This internalization of the cut and thrust of the spending round was not without risk. As Derek Scott put it,

Transparent and open were not the words that always sprung to the lips of cabinet colleagues as they caught Brown settling matters affecting their departments behind their backs, but he was only able to do this because the prime minister had allowed his own authority to be diluted.[10]

Without cabinet committees and colleagues preparing the political ground, the government was vulnerable to the Treasury's lack of political touch. In 1997 Brown decided to honour a Tory 'pro-family' cut in single parent benefit and in 2000 came a notorious 75p rise in the annual pension. On both issues the government was forced to back down after a public outcry. Neither Brown nor Blair made any concessions to Labour's old allies, the unions. A minimum wage was introduced, but at so low a level as to be almost invisible. A new Employment Relations Act recognized the European Social Chapter but, as Geoffrey Owen noted, 'It was not expected to have a major impact on the character of British labour relations', since Brown, strongly guided by the Confederation of British Industry, fought any extension of the chapter in practice.[11] He had no interest in reviving ghosts helpfully laid to rest by Thatcher. Blair, in his first speech on union reform after taking office, declared with typical inversion, 'Let us make it impossible to dismiss trade unions as old-fashioned, defensive, anti-progress.'[12] He boasted in the 1998 employment White Paper 'Fairness at Work' that Britain had 'the most lightly regulated labour market of any leading economy in the world'.

Brown's greatest early achievement was negative. He was the first Labour chancellor not to present his colleagues with an economic crisis within months of taking office. Credit for this must go largely to the Tories and the 'electability' agenda. Adherence to Kenneth Clarke's three-year spending limits was firm, but it evaporated as soon as the three years were up. Between 1997 and 2000, public spending declined as a percentage of GDP from 40.6 per cent to 37 per cent.[13] But as soon as this self-restraint was over, in time for the 2001 election, Brown put his foot on the accelerator. He took public-spending growth from zero to 4 per cent in real terms over the next six years, with health in the lead. As a result forecast spending soared to 42 per cent of GDP in 2005, and headed for an estimated 45.7 per cent in 2007. This was by far the fastest rate of growth in Europe and broke the EU discipline on which Brown had been so insistent before.

There is no reason to suppose that when Brown came to office he abandoned what he saw as his political ambition, the pursuit of 'social justice'. What was almost eerie was his employment of the tools of Thatcherism to achieve it. If he differed from the Thatcherites it was that they hoped they were shrinking the public sector while he was proud of extending it. By mid-2005 a fifth of total UK employment was of public employees, and that was excluding some half a million decanted into private-sector subcontracting.[14] Yet Brown never gave up on what can only be termed the unfinished business of Thatcher's first revolution, the disposal of public assets, the privatization of public services and the reform of social security in the direction of means-testing and workfare. His attachment to all these policies bordered on the messianic.

The same forces as had impelled the Treasury towards privatization under Howe and Lawson reasserted themselves under Brown. Thatcherism meant privatization, privatization meant money and money balanced books. If Brown intended to spend and not tax sufficiently to cover it then other means had to be found to bridge the gap. That meant selling and borrowing. Since the government was running out of assets to sell and had limited itself on public borrowing, it had to resort to two devices. One was the selling of forward contracts with the private sector to supply public services, such as running hospitals, schools, roads, prisons, pensions and traffic control. The other was shifting investment in public institutions 'off balance sheet' into risk-bearing capital. Both would save money in the short run but be expensive in the long. In a nutshell, the government would mortgage both its current and its capital account to balance its annual books.

In Opposition, Labour had excoriated all forms of privatization. Brown and Blair had both won their spurs opposing it. They had seen the Treasury's Private Finance Initiative (PFI) as corrupting the public-service ethos and had damned Tory proposals for the City funding of public institutions as 'creeping privatization'. Blair was especially scathing of Tory rail policy dismissing it as 'replacing a comprehensive coordinated railway network with a hotchpotch of private companies linked together by a gigantic bureaucratic paperchase of contracts, overseen by a clutch of quangos.'[15] When Labour took office there was an instant U-turn. Partnership with private enterprise was now eulogized at every opportunity. Blair put his conversion in typically allusive terms. Introducing his 1999 White Paper on 'Modernising Government' he wrote of public-service reform, 'Privatisation should have a role to play not out of dogmatism but out of pragmatism.'[16] The Treasury did not care what it was 'out of'. Since Lawson, its cast of mind towards public service had been simple. Since financial incentive must be more conducive to efficiency than any 'public-service ethos', shifting a service into the private sector must be value for money. Few Treasury staff had ever provided a front-line service and showed considerable contempt (in private) for those who did, whereas daily contact with consultants and bankers made them naturally more conversant with the profit motive. When I mentioned to one official how dedicated I had found British Rail executives to the public-sector ethos he snorted, 'You can't seriously believe that rubbish' (and went off to work in a bank).

Brown tore up all he had said in Opposition and hurled himself into a frenzy of privatization, scouring the cupboard for things to sell. He faced down union opposition by seeking to dispose of air traffic control, the Royal Mint, the Commonwealth Development Corporation and Tote on-course betting. The privatization of the Post Office, banned by Thatcher and dropped by Major, was halted in 1998 only because its departmental sponsor was Brown's sworn enemy, Mandelson. It was tentatively revived in

2006. Property proved particularly fruitful. What was euphemistically called affordable (that is cheap) public housing was subcontracted to housing associations, as had been the case under Thatcher, but Brown expected councils to dispose of their housing also to private developers. Hard-to-let and hard-to-sell council blocks soon found eager takers. In 2004 I visited a two-day-old queue of young people seeking flats in two Liverpool towers, about to be transformed by private ownership. Privatization spread even to Whitehall. The Inland Revenue sold its entire estate to a private developer, John Ritblat, who transferred it, quite legally, to an offshore tax haven. Officials trying to curb tax havens were benefiting from one themselves. The Treasury even sold and then leased back its own headquarters in Parliament Square.

By far the biggest Brown privatization was of public borrowing. The Tories' PFI, sometimes sanitized by Brown as Public-Private Partnership (PPP), had been introduced by Norman Lamont as a vehicle to get the private sector to bear risk and increase the efficiency of public investment. The assumption was that such a gain would more than compensate for the considerably higher cost of private loan finance. In 1992 Brown was scathing, calling such an argument 'a cynical distortion of the public accounts'.[17] In office he turned turtle. He needed to increase public investment without wrecking the government's annual budget. It would have to borrow in such a way as not to appear on the public accounts. By July 2003 Brown was boasting the completion of 450 PFI projects, including 34 hospitals, 239 schools, 34 fire and police stations, 12 prisons and 12 waste projects.[18] The NHS had by 2005 borrowed some £6 billion for PFI schemes, with a further £11 billion in the pipeline. By the mid-2000s virtually all health investment was being financed by the private sector. A new bureaucracy sprang into being to guide this work. It included the Private Finance Panel, the Treasury Taskforce, the Office of Government Commerce, Partnerships UK, the Private Finance Unit and the Public Private Partnerships Programme.

Assessing the degree of risk in each of these projects became an art rather than a science. Brown and his aides had to fight running battles with government accountants over which borrowing was and was not risk-bearing and thus could be hidden from the public borrowing total. Some 43 per cent of PFIs by value were classified as off balance sheet in 2004.[19] A different figure of 60 per cent was given by the Office of National Statistics in 2005.[20] The public sector's accumulated liability was difficult to calculate given the variety of guarantees and definitions that surrounded the various debts. The first official estimate of the gross debt, buried in a Treasury Commons answer, put the figure at £110 billion in 2003, including projects both on and off balance sheet, but it excluded debt beyond twenty-five years' duration.[21] Separate research by Philippa Roe and Alistair Craig put accumulated off-balance sheet debt at some £100 billion, including £21 billion for the railways.[22]

This was extraordinary. Thatcher had approached each privatization ad hoc, judging a proposal for its financial and political risk. None of this concerned Brown, to whom buy-now-pay-later became holy writ even for core public institutions such as hospitals and schools. Departments and agencies were told that project finance had to be 'partnership based' in whole or part. Jeremy Coleman of the National Audit Office (NAO) said they should be 'under no illusion that PFI was the only game in town'.[23] Desperate to keep this semi-concealed, Brown was, in effect, selling project-linked bonds covered by varying degrees of government guarantee and only limited project control. He was spending now and expecting future generations to pay. His ally, Alistair Darling, had warned against this sort of spending (albeit when in Opposition): 'apparent savings now could be countered by the formidable commitment on revenue expenditure in years to come'.[24]

Since the objective was to get things built without using current expenditure, value for money became an afterthought. Half-hearted attempts were made by the National Audit Office and others to assess the value of these various forms of privatization. Those involving major construction work were on the whole rated a success. One comparison showed 88 per cent of projects completed on time and budget compared with 70 per cent of public-sector projects being late and over budget. But comparing like with like was difficult. The NAO revealed huge windfall profits on a number of hospital contracts, including £73 million at the Norfolk and Norwich Hospital. When a project failed, as in a £1.1 billion Paddington hospital scheme, the cost of £14 million in fees was spectacular.[25] In December 2005 another £1 billion scheme, to rebuild the Royal London and Bart's hospitals, appeared close to collapse with building work already happening on site. It was rescued only after a public campaign, clearly against the better judgement of the Treasury. As much as 20 per cent of such hospital budgets would in future be going on loan service (against none before). It was near inconceivable that efficiency gains would be sufficient to merit such high financing costs. The NHS was being overwhelmed by private obligations. If anything went wrong, either the state would have to pay enormous compensation or the entrepreneurs would seize the assets and the NHS really would become private.

The most controversial PFI was for the London Tube. Advised by an aide imported from bankers UBS/Warburg, Shriti Vadera, Brown split the track between two consortia on thirty-year franchises. The contracts ran to 2,800 pages and 7,000 targets, yet they bore no appreciable risk and eventually cost £500 million in fees to negotiate. Not a penny of this money went to the Tube, nor was it subjected to value-for-money audit. When in 2001 the relevant minister, John Prescott, together with Blair himself sided with the Tube's American boss, Bob Kiley, in preferring a public-sector trust for the Tube, Brown simply overruled them.

The surface railway fared no better. As described in Chapter 11, the Tories' vertical disintegration of railway management between Railtrack and the operating companies had been a disaster. Blair's failure to reverse it could be explained only in terms of cost and the image it might convey of old Labour nationalization. Despite pledges made in Opposition Brown refused to buy out the infrastructure company, Railtrack, but instead regulated it meticulously. Ever greater interference from Whitehall over investment confused responsibility and deteriorated efficiency. When a serious crash occurred at Hatfield in October 2000 the entire network seized up. Ministers were crawling over every corner of the industry and a railway which, in BR's day, would have returned to normal working within two weeks was still crippled after two years.

The heavy losses caused by the aftermath of Hatfield drove Railtrack towards bankruptcy. The government refused to allow the rail regulator to bail it out and forced it instead into administration, transferring its assets to a public not-for-profit trust. The mechanism was orchestrated by Vadera and the transport secretary, Stephen Byers, avoiding the government paying shareholders compensation, a device that led to a High Court trial. (This exonerated the government but revealed much of the inner workings of Brown's Treasury.) Railtrack was replaced by Network Rail, whose guaranteed borrowings of £21 billion and immunity from bankruptcy Brown somehow declared 'off balance sheet'.[18] This was exactly the model which he had fiercely rejected for the London Tube. The boundary between public and private finance was becoming little short of whimsical.

Five transport ministers came and went under Blair, until by 2005 the railway was costing the taxpayer five times what it had cost as a single nationalized industry. Subsidy rose from £1.35 billion (at 2005 prices) to £6.5 billion.[27] By 2004 Brown was again reorganizing the railway. This time the Strategic Rail Authority was abolished and brought under direct Treasury control through a central Railway Directorate. Train operators were now awarded virtually risk-free management contracts. Trains were subject to creeping renationalization but with none of the executive clarity that came from the old arm's-length principle. Virgin contracted to receive a guaranteed subsidy of £400 million over two years on the West Coast Mainline alone. It had been profitable under BR. Not until 2006 was Network Rail approaching something like stability, and then only by bringing its maintenance division back 'in house' from subcontractors. The chairman, John Armitt, declared that this move, de facto renationalizing rail maintenance and doubling Network Rail's staff to 30,000 employees, 'reduced our costs and did a great deal to reinforce people's self-confidence in the organisation'.[28]

The truth was that the railway was a privatization too far even for Brown. As under Major, the second revolution, driven by political as well as financial imperatives, had overwhelmed the first. The transport economist Stephen Glaister concluded briskly that 'railway policy under Blair has proved to be indecisive, ineffective and very expensive ... delegated to Prescott and hijacked by the Treasury.'[29] When the transport secretary Alistair Darling went on BBC radio to explain his policy for railways for 2006, any listener would have assumed that he was the chairman of its board.[30] The difference was that he took credit for everything and blame for nothing (including his own missed targets). He pledged only an ever higher burden of public spending in response to rising passenger numbers, unaware that under privatization rising demand for a utility should mean lower subsidy.

The impact of Brown's PFI borrowing on Britain's public infrastructure was undeniably spectacular. It was hard to visit a school or hospital site in Britain in the early 2000s that was not shrouded in scaffolding. Labour honoured its commitment to rebuild public institutions especially in education and health and PFI certainly freed the Treasury from its previous public investment logjam. But it did so by mortgaging future public spending to an extraordinary − and undisclosed − extent.

Meanwhile privatization extended its reach to day-to-day public administration. The euphemisms for this grew ever more exotic. Marketizing, franchising, outsourcing, contesting and partnering were applied to education authorities, hospital managers, prisons, personnel units, pension funds, debt-collection and even local finance departments. Subcontracting was forecast to cover 20 per cent of current public expenditure by 2007 (or some £68 billion). Within three years the private sector's role in health and education was planned to double and in defence triple.[31] In response there sprang into being a new industry of private contractors of public services. Most had backgrounds in the construction industry and recruited freely from the civil service. Firms such as Skanska, Carillion, Serco, Capita, Jarvis and Balfour Beatty expanded rapidly from their former bases, usually as construction companies.[32] Capita alone had a turnover of £112 million when Labour came to power in 1997 and £1.4 billion in 2005. It won contracts to run Individual Learning Accounts, the Criminal Records Bureau, teachers' pensions, miners' compensation, the London congestion charge and the BBC licence fee. When Capita's boss, Rod Aldridge, was found to be a major donor to Labour Party funds he was forced to resign from the company's chairmanship in March 2006.

These new companies adopted the language of 'ethos' even as they fought for profit. Serco, manager of prisons, defence stores and speed cameras, declared that 'our culture is infused with the spirit of public service'. Robert Cole in *The Times* commented on the lip service paid by contractors 'to cuddly sentiments that make a vaguely left-leaning government more comfortable about privatising activities that were previously state-run'.[33] The Cabinet Office minister, John Hutton, added reassuringly that 'profit can be compatible with public service'. But when Stoke-on-Trent was advised by Whitehall to subcontract the running of its 125 school buildings to Balfour Beatty, it had to let the company close up to 30 of them without penalty should they prove unprofitable. Within two years sixteen were closed, to the rage of local parents.[34] The privatization of school buildings was to prove as costly as that of hospitals (see next chapter).

Assessing what became a radically changed structure of public administration in Britain was hard. Some privatizations seemed to work. The entire administration of Westminster City Council was subcontracted to a private company, and though citizens found it odd to telephone their council and be answered by a call centre in Lancashire, efficiency was reportedly maintained. On the other hand, contractors lacked the commitment of a public servant. A scheme for running home repairs in Camden had to be abandoned after outraged complaints from tenants, as did a costly £1 billion project to privatize military training. When WS Atkins walked out of a contract to run Southwark's education service, it was able to give as the reason the loss of bonus income due to its own poor performance. Schools were left in turmoil. A prominent PFI company, Carillion (formerly Tarmac), treated its contracts like any other asset. It sold to another contractor the job of running a Kent hospital and maintaining the M40 motorway.[35] Such an approach to public management yielded neither continuity nor loyalty. By 2006, the Public Accounts Committee recorded that a full 40 per cent of PFI deals had seen a change in investor.[36]

Most controversial was a decision in 2004 to privatize the entire British parole service. This was described by the home secretary, Charles Clarke, as a 'vision of expanding contestability in the delivery of offender services' aimed at creating 'a viable market in offender management'.[37] Private companies and voluntary organizations would be able to bid to supervise some 200,000 offenders on parole. Having just reorganized the entire parole service three years earlier, this was both reckless and bizarre. There seemed no area of the public sector that was sacrosanct. In early 2006 the parole project collapsed, at a cost of millions of pounds in consultancy and executive reorganization fees. Nobody explained why or took responsibility.

Brown's one concession to the increasingly punch-drunk public-service unions was to concede that workers should not lose money or security when transferred to the private sector. This was a serious concession. It preserved in the private sector the inflationary negotiating frameworks introduced by the Treasury under the Tories. It sweetened the unions' path to privatization because it enabled them to pursue comparability claims between public and private employers safe in the knowledge that the state would pick up any enhanced bill. As the health budget soared after a 2004 NHS settlement that awarded some doctors a rise of 20 per cent over two years, the Treasury attempted to rescind the concession for privatized health workers. A threatened strike led to Brown backing down. The cost was to cripple NHS finances by 2006.

One clear beneficiary of Brown's first-revolution enthusiasm was the financial sector. He off-loaded on to City law and accountancy firms much that had previously been done by civil servants. To get any project up and running, departments soon learned to hire whatever consultant was currently in favour with the Treasury, the more celebrated (and expensive) the more persuasive. In 1995 the British government spent £300 million on management consultants. By 2003 the Office of Government Commerce put the figure at £1.7 billion. A year later it was found to be £2.5 billion, equivalent to a penny on income tax. PricewaterhouseCoopers were, in 2005, recorded as consultant on an astonishing 174 government projects, with a capital value of £31.4 billion. Labour's spending on consultants between 1997 and 2006 was estimated at £70 billion by two analysts, David Craig and Richard Brooks.[38] The industry itself estimated that some 40 per cent of its output was in the public sector.[39]

Brown extended his circle of advisers to embrace not just political aides but private bankers and consultants, such as Vadera and James Sassoon from UBS/Warburg, Chris Wales from Arthur Andersen and Richard Abadie from PricewaterhouseCoopers. Given the dominance of the Treasury many of these newcomers became 'virtual' spending ministers. When preparing his pension and tax credit reforms Brown hardly bothered to discuss them with the Department for Work and Pensions. He had an aversion to consulting cabinet colleagues on almost anything and insisted they deal direct with Balls, Vadera and others.[40]

After 2001 Brown turned his attention to ground on which even Tory angels had feared to tread. Where Kenneth Clarke had been a tentative 'workfare' enthusiast, Brown was unashamed. He wanted 'to turn Britain into a nation of victors over adversity rather than victims trapped on benefit'.[41] Thatcher would have called them workers not shirkers. The goal had defeated every Conservative chancellor, largely because every reform evoked an eruption of fury from the Labour party. Brown would brook no opposition. He sent emissaries to study workfare in Wisconsin. He appointed outsiders to oversee 'work incentives policies' within the Treasury. A deaf ear was turned to all objections, however constructive. Brown had no interest in what Blair or his social services ministers, Harriet Harman and Frank Field, had to say.

The Treasury was exhilarated to find a Labour chancellor specifically proposing a declining budget for social security, comprising as it did almost half of current public expenditure. Since pensions could not be cut, this implied big falls in unemployment, housing, family and disability benefits. Brown introduced a plethora of initiatives, rarely thought through in advance, built round the slogan, 'Work is the best Welfare'. The sums involved were gargantuan. The New Deal to force the workshy into jobs cost £4 billion. Almost half those 'found jobs' returned to the dole within six months and most of the rest were assessed as likely to have found jobs unaided.[42] The NAO reported in 2002 that only 3 per cent of participants were genuinely helped into work, at a cost of £8,000 a job. Administering such schemes became a multi-billion pound industry, with tens of thousands employed in counselling, training and mentoring.

Brown did not achieve a cut in social security. The budget rose from £97 billion in 1997 to £127 billion in 2004 even at a time of declining unemployment. Nor did the Treasury achieve one of its goals, an end to fraud. An estimated £21 billion in fraudulent payments rose to over £30 billion, while income tax evasion was costing a further £25 billion.[43] Yet Brown seemed impervious to criticism. He also gave himself unlimited amounts of money for his own initiatives, cutting across other departments and ministers. Grants to adults to spend on further education, so-called Individual Learning Accounts, were subcontracted to the ever-favoured Capita, who gave money for education courses to virtually anyone. When the police were finally summoned, some £100 million from a budget of £273 million was considered stolen. Another Brown venture was a computer-based 'University for Industry', which collapsed with estimated losses of over £200 million. An e-university blew £50 million recruiting just 900 students before it was closed. Its chief executive was given £225,000 for a year's work.[44] The strangest scheme was sold to Brown by a business-man on holiday in New England, sinking £68 million in an Anglo-American science partnership between Cambridge and MIT. The chief beneficiary was MIT, which walked away with £13 million from the British taxpayer.[45] For none of this money did Brown render any public account.

There were even bigger fish to fry. Brown sought to tackle head-on another challenge that had defeated every previous chancellor, the disincentive to poor people to seek work for fear of losing benefit, the so-called poverty trap. The clawing back of means-tested benefit taxed anyone on welfare their entire benefit if they returned to work. It was a de facto 100 per cent income tax on the poor. Labour's traditional answer, to which Brown had long subscribed, was to end means-testing and hand out benefits to all within certain categories of claimant, whether or not they worked. (Thus every family qualified for child allowance.) This could only be afforded if the benefits were kept low. If they were raised to lift pensioners and others above the poverty line, there was no alternative to means-testing. To avoid the poverty trap this has to carefully taper upwards to retain an incentive to work.

Brown duly forgot his lifelong opposition to means-testing and became its most ardent advocate. He applied it first to pensions, with a restless series of reforms intended to lift the poorest pensioners above the poverty line. This could only be achieved by topping up a low basic pension with means-tested supplements. Eventually Brown's pension credit was means-tested for some 65 per cent of all pensioners.[46] Lord Turner's report in 2006 regarded the extent of such means-testing as undignified and excessive, precisely Brown's (former) criticism of it. Yet Brown soldiered on, eventually reaching a compromise with Turner (and Blair) to raise pensions to link with earnings in 2012.

The pensions benefit was at least simple to understand. More troublesome was Brown's effort to conquer the poverty trap for those receiving family and income support. As long ago as 1964, Geoffrey Howe had devoted his maiden Commons speech to the subject, proposing a 'Receive as You Earn' negative income tax.[47] The intention was to give all those returning to work a tax credit that tapered as they earned more income. Two problems had always stood in its way. One was to avoid the government merely subsidizing employers of low-paid staff. The other was to stop the impact on beneficiaries who continued to receive credits after their income had risen beyond the next threshold, credits that would then have to be recouped after probably being spent.

Brown's working families tax credit (WFTC) finally emerged in 2003 after four years of trial and considerable error. It merged the tax and social benefits regime under the Inland Revenue, leaving the latter's computer to deal with the problem of recouping overpayments. This meant that beneficiaries who had returned to work found that they were being 'taxed' for excessive benefits received since their previous assessment. These excesses could be as much as they were now earning, plunging millions not into a poverty trap but worse, into rolling debt, precisely the hurdle that Howe and others had been unable to surmount. Brown was simply deaf to every attempt to modify or improve his scheme.

By 2005 almost half of all WFTC beneficiaries were in debt to the government because their incomes had risen over some taper threshold.

Money was being demanded by a computer print-out sent through the post. Far from helping the poor into work, the scheme was impoverishing the recently incentivized. At the height of the WFTC chaos an estimated 3,600 civil servants were devoted to handling complaints. The scheme was costing over £400 million just to administer, three times as much per head as income tax.[48] In July 2005 the government had to climb down and disregard some £2 billion of past overpayments. A year later, the problem had not been solved with a further £2 billion overpaid. It was an extraordinary and costly exercise in maladministration. If another agency or local council had been guilty of this, the Treasury would have sent in commissioners and demanded heads roll. As it was Brown refused even to admit responsibility. He made a junior minister, Dawn Primarolo, defend the scheme in public and it was Blair who finally stood up in the Commons and apologized for the mistakes, while Brown sat silent behind him. This reluctance to accept blame was the chief charge against Brown by those opposing his succession to the party leadership.

Tax credits, assuming they could settle down, were undoubtedly a radical innovation in public finance, lifting poorer families from total reliance on the state into a regime that made it worth their while earning money. Despite their embarrassing expense, they were probably Brown's most signal policy success as chancellor. When I asked Geoffrey Howe what he thought of Brown finally achieving the 'negative income tax' which he, Howe, had once proposed, he spat fury at their being so ineptly handled.[49] But handled they were. Nor were they the limit of Brown's Thatcherism. He finally turned his attention to another social security reform at which the Tories had baulked, sickness and incapacity benefit, notoriously vulnerable to fraud. The Treasury intended, from 2008, to cut the number on such benefit from 2.7 million to 1 million, by ending what amounted to long-standing maladministration. The mere announcement of more stringent rules secured a sudden drop of 80,000 claimants. Future beneficiaries would require interviews, tests and time-limited periods of sickness, rather than the lax doctor's certificate. In 2006 similar tightening was announced of benefits for the 150,000 lone parents of teenagers. In July that year the work and pensions secretary, John Hutton, forecast £7 billion of savings from these reforms.

Such 'tough love' targeting of social security on the deserving poor was either Thatcherism or more equitable public administration, according to taste. Any social benefit regime tends to suffer 'drift' over time away from those most in need towards those most adept at working the system, and Brown deserves the credit he claims for seeking to correct this drift. Under his regime the elderly were better off, albeit at the price of means-testing. Some specific programmes such as tax credits, New Deal and Sure Start benefited those of the poor whom they were able to reach, but at a high cost in administration. That said, any modern welfare state would expect to see reductions in poverty from rising levels of public spending. The attack on child poverty, to which Brown directed hundreds of millions of pounds, delivered measurable improvement, though it raised Britain above only Italy, Spain and Portugal in the European league.

More worrying for Labour was the conclusion of the Institute of Fiscal Studies in 2005, that the gap between the very rich and very poor had actually widened since 1997. The report concluded that 'income inequality in Britain is still higher than at any time in the previous 18 years of Conservative rule and probably for at least 20 years before that.'[50] The March 2005 issue of *Social Trends*[51] showed the gap between the 'generally rich' and the generally poor widening over the period 1991 to 2003. Poor working families were better off through tax credits, but 7 per cent of the working population, many of them recent immigrants, was still estimated to be untouched by social security and existing in the grey economy.

Brown's era at the Treasury will intrigue historians. His youthful aversion to Thatcherism was intense and tribal. His conversion to it over the course of the 1990s was at first tactical, then institutional. He emerged from the first nine years of the Blair government as a Treasury radical in the Lawson mould. He had kept the British economy on an even keel and his conduct of macro-economic policy was a success, in itself no mean achievement for a Labour chancellor. He adhered to Lawson's maxim, privatize what you can and centralize what you cannot. However, he was inefficient in his policy-making and remarkably shambolic even when doing the right thing, as on family credits. Part of the reason must have been his hostility to the civil service and his resulting reliance on inexperienced aides and private consultants. His concept of so-called 'enabling' government held that the Treasury, in partnership with firms such as UBS/Warburg and Capita, could run a better welfare state than its traditional custodians, the civil service and local government. He put his faith in capitalism as a tool of social redistribution, where his socialist forebears put theirs in public service. Like

Lawson, he saw private-sector disciplines as a-priori virtues in pursuit of public-sector goals.

What this had to do with any aspect of the Labour movement is obscure. It is doubtful if even the most ardent Thatcherite could dispense altogether with a dedicated public service, especially one growing in numbers as it was under Brown. A 1999 survey for the Public Management Foundation found that few civil servants were motivated by hope of a bonus. They declared a professional commitment 'to improve public service' and felt most valued when 'trusted to show discretion in achieving performance'.[52] As a result, 'recognition for good performance was more important than financial reward.' When civil servants saw their work subcontracted to the private sector, they were bemused not only at the motives of ministers but at how they should work differently themselves. If they were not trusted to use their professional judgement in disbursing public funds what were they trusted to do? A 2005 Cabinet Office survey of civil service morale, released under freedom of information, revealed an extraordinary level of dissatisfaction across Whitehall. At the work and pensions department just one in ten had 'confidence' in senior management, while at transport half the staff were 'seriously considering' finding alternative work.[53]

This was reflected in an intriguing metaphor for the changing welfare state conceived by the LSE academic Julian le Grand. He saw public servants as no longer paternal 'knights' distributing philanthropy to 'pawns', as users of the NHS or social services were termed. Nowadays 'knaves' were serving 'queens'. In other words public servants, often highly unionized, were essentially in it for the money, while recipients were becoming choosey and free to move their 'custom' into or out of the public sector at will.[54] Such a caricatured account of the public's view of the welfare state might be accepted by Thatcherite neo-liberals. That le Grand's metaphor should have been espoused by a Labour government and used as the philosophical underpinning of its entire public service reform was remarkable.

The Labour historian Kenneth Morgan saw Brown as conforming to the party's traditional pragmatism, one of constant 'change and renewal'.[55] A reaction against Keynesianism in favour of Thatcherism was to be expected from any new Labour government, given the failure of the Wilson/ Callaghan period. To Morgan, if such pragmatism involved a number of policy U-turns, that was hardly surprising. If Labour supporters regarded them as a betrayal of what they thought their party represented, that too was hardly novel. To others, including many voters in the much-favoured middle ground, Brown's adherence to so much of the Tories' domestic agenda seemed a good reason for continuing to support Labour at the polls. To this extent Brown was sustaining the Blair project, reassuring the middle classes that the British economy was safe in Labour's hands, with a spicy admixture of raw Thatcherism into the bargain. This was as much in Brown's interest as in Blair's – the more so as he was expecting to fight the next election in 2009/10. A Granita deal intended to ensure Blair's conformity to Labour's 'social agenda' had ironically enabled Brown to advance Thatcherism further and faster than anyone before him.

Nobody gazing on Britain in the middle of the first decade of the new century could regard it as ruled by a government of the left, least of all in comparison with Labour governments past or left-wing governments abroad. This simple observation was a monument to Thatcher's greatest achievement, to have won over not her allies but her enemies. Of these none had been more implacable than Brown. He was Thatcherism's most coveted St Paul, a convert and soldier of the faith. He had yet to reach his Rome.

18

Tony Blair and the Commanding Heights

Brown's aversion to Thatcherism in the 1980s and early 1990s was visceral. Blair's was rather the warpaint of his adopted tribe, easily washed off. A young man of middle-class background, tastes and social aspirations, his turning away from his Labour past seems to have been easy and painless. He rejected Labour's trade unionism explicitly, as he did its faith in local councils, comprehensive schools and nationalized industries. As home affairs spokesman he had no problem with 'tough on crime'. His admiration for Roy Jenkins and then for Thatcher herself was ill-concealed even before his arrival in Downing Street. He was no laissez-faire libertarian and abroad he showed himself an ardent neo-conservative, eventually preferring the Republican George Bush to the Democrat Bill Clinton. In all his responses, values and body language, Blair was what an ordinary citizen would call right wing. He was a natural Tory.

Hence Blair's contentment with what he perceived as Brown's policy at the Treasury. It was not his business and as long as the commentators thought a good job was being done he was relaxed. Blair was concerned with presentation. Only when results and presentation ceased to mesh did he become frustrated. He respected Brown's supremacy over domestic policy but this respect depended on delivery and delivery, or at least its public manifestation, became the running obsession of Blair's time in office. As early as 1999 he was showing signs of impatience. This was to be, he had told his 1998 party conference, his 'Year of Delivery', but it did not come to pass. Blair complained of 'forces of conservatism' holding him back and later told a conference of businessmen, 'You try getting change in the public sector and public services: I bear the scars on my back after two years in government.'[1] Two years soon became eight. Memoirs of the period are filled with complaints of the failure of the Whitehall machine to respond – or of Blair's failure to respond to that failure. Seldon's interviewees remarked variously, 'The strong centre was meant to drive the agenda forward but in fact it held everything up', or 'ideas were there but there wasn't the follow-through.'[2] Accounts of 'sofa government' in the Hutton and Butler reports arc reminiscent of a car full of back-seat drivers, none of whom knows how to turn on the engine. As at the Treasury, the failure to engage the normally smooth-running civil service machine was apparent. Blair lived in constant fear that the reform process, or 'agenda' as he called it, was slipping beyond his grasp. By the 2005 election, delivery had become a fixation. Like Thatcher at the same stage in her term of office (1987), Blair was exasperated that services on which he had expended huge sums of money were offering no political gratitude in return.

Those who wish to change the world need tools. At the Treasury Brown at least had some tools, but at Downing Street Blair had none. A prime minister traditionally used his cabinet to effect business. It was a formal command structure, nudged or goaded by a stream of memorandums from private secretaries. Under Blair cabinet government no longer worked as such. Sofa government brought decisions in-house but, in doing so, distanced them from existing systems of delivery. Notes would go out to departments from political advisers in the Cabinet Office, but departments were unsure how to respond. Had the decision been cleared with the Treasury or other cabinet ministers? Had interested parties been consulted? Lines of command were confused and fractured.

Blair turned in despair to the habits of the second revolution. He enhanced four streams of power inherited in embryo from Thatcher and Major. He expanded the political directorate; like Brown, he drastically increased the use of outside consultants; he advanced so-called e-government; and he employed an unprecedented battery of targets. All supplemented rather than replaced the existing processes of Whitehall. They were the most potent armoury a peacetime government had brought to bear on the public sector, but they never conquered the inherent confusion.

From the moment he entered office Blair disregarded permanent officials even more than had Thatcher. She considered civil servants at least worthy of armed combat. Blair had an aversion to any corps of sophisticates bred to 'speak truth to power'. They used a different language from the tabloid jargon of Campbell and Mandelson and made Blair uncomfortable. As we have seen, he declined Butler's request that he make use of the formal civil service structure to execute his commands. His expanded private office shielded him from independent advice and induced sycophancy in those round him. The pliability to Campbell of the head of the Joint Intelligence Committee, John Scarlett, revealed in the Hutton Report, astonished past holders of the office, as did Scarlett's reward in being promoted to head MI6.

The erosion of the institutional divide between politician and civil servant worried successive Whitehall cabinet secretaries (titular heads of the civil service), Butler, Sir Richard Wilson and Sir Andrew Turnbull. All suffered exclusion from the inner cabal of sofa government and this communicated itself to the service generally. The exclusion was not entirely new; all prime ministers had favourites. But Blair developed No. 10 into a department of personal appointees over 100-strong. He regarded civil servants as 'deliverers', not partners in the process of government. Having never served in government he had no idea how to mobilize its strengths, only a conviction of its weaknesses.

Butler and Wilson proceeded to plead for statutory protection for civil servants, to preserve their independence of political pressure. They feared their profession was going the way of American diplomats, as bag-carriers to political appointees thronging the upper reaches of Whitehall. Turnbull felt less strongly, distinguishing a permanent civil service from permanent civil servants, and accepted that ministers would want favourites round them and that officials would come and go over time.[3] But all three men agreed that if civil servants lost not just their status in government but also their access to top jobs, public administration would be the poorer.

Blair could hardly have cared less. He pointed out that independent advice aplenty came from the press and think tanks and he needed loyalty close to hand. It was the skills of Campbell or Mandelson in political strategy and presentation that he needed, not argument from smart officials. Even when these two aides departed, Blair still felt most comfortable with young political appointees, eerily alike in dark suits and red ties, thronging the corridors of Downing Street. To them government was a stream of buzzwords, abstractions and headline-grabbing initiatives: spot fines for hooligans, Britishness tests for imams, a parenting college, a respect 'tsar' and 'a dozen ways to combat terrorism'. These were seldom related to Whitehall and rarely followed through. Their purpose was to 'score' media attention or neutralize some other bad news story. Blair's staff not only lacked experience of public administration, they lacked that crucial resource in any policy machine, a memory.

The government soon suffered the normal hazard of sofa rule – disaffection by those not on the sofa. Whitehall officials traditionally served their masters and retired to dignified silence, loyal not to ministers but to a professional ethos. When political advisers left Blair's Downing Street they went in search of an agent. The first burst of kiss-and-tell memoirs emerged from short-stay aides such as Derek Draper, Peter Hyman, Lance Price and Blair's economic adviser, Derek Scott. The last offered a devastating revelation of arguments over Europe between Blair and Brown.[4] The list of authors soon extended to public officials, to Lord Stevens, Sir Christopher Meyer and Sir Jeremy Greenstock, though the last was curbed by civil service rules. Eventually the head of the diplomatic service, Sir Michael Jay, told his staff to regard anything they wrote down as in the public domain.[5]

Public administration did not interest Blair. Whenever the subject of management arose he acquired 'the Blair garden look'. This involved him gazing out of the Downing Street window into the middle distance, as if dreaming of a new foreign adventure. In an outburst in 2001 the cabinet secretary, Wilson, told Blair and Brown together, 'Your problem is that neither you nor anyone in Number 10 has ever managed anything.' A surprised Blair retorted that he had managed the Labour party. Wilson replied, 'You never managed them, you merely led them.'[6] The distinction seemed beyond the prime minister's comprehension.

Under such pressure Blair fell under the spell not just of his cabal but of the outer ring of courtiers that gathers wherever power is personalized and informal. Friends, lobbyists and hangers-on were coming and going through all the doors in Downing Street. Blair and Brown seemed to believe that anyone earning a large salary was blessed with special virtue. The day of consultancy government was at hand, at Downing Street as at the Treasury. Just as Brown was recruiting aides from UBS/Warburg so Downing Street came under the influence of the 'McKinsey mafia'. At various times, five senior advisers had links with or were paid by the firm, Lord Turner, Sir Michael Barber, David Bennett, Nick Lovegrove and the 'blue-skies thinker', Lord Birt. McKinsey was a propagandist for ever more complex systems, for 'matrix management' and big is beautiful.[7] It was earning millions in Whitehall contracts, from the NHS to the defence ministry, which access to Downing Street could only promote. Though McKinsey staff protested that they never openly advocated bigger government, the government overhead ballooned during their ascendancy.

Under Blair the focus of this activity was the Cabinet Office, a prime minister's department in all but name. A policy and performance unit was set up 'to complement the Treasury's role in monitoring departments'. In 2001 this was enhanced by the delivery unit under Sir Michael Barber, a former academic who had served at the education department (and went on to McKinsey). The unit later moved to the Treasury. A revolving door of 'friends of friends' was established with think tanks and lobbyists. Career civil servants could only look on in envy. With consultants came computers, so-called e-government. Just as quantification was the way to measure the output of government, so computers, matrices and feed-back mechanisms were the way to ensure delivery. Whitehall in the late 1990s went computer mad. By 2000 an astonishing £14 billion a year (more than on school or hospital building) was being spent on machines which line managers rarely claimed to need. It was hard to cite a single Whitehall computer project that worked to time, budget or specification, or improved service or saved money. Computer failures hit the Criminal Records Bureau, the magistrates' database, the Passports Agency, air traffic control, the abortive 'e-university' and an extraordinary and little-publicized £4 billion scheme to 'link every desk in real-time capability' in the Ministry of Defence.

In 2000 an £880 million contract with ICL for a Post Office computer to pay social security benefits had to be abandoned. The Child Support Agency (CSA) was sold a £500 million machine to replace the old card index system of court orders for child maintenance. Before the switch to computers, seven out of ten orders were met. Afterwards the proportion fell to three out of ten. One billion pounds had to be written off in uncollected maintenance, twice the cost of a machine intended to save money. Two giant projects took on a life of their own. One was for a politically controversial Home Office ID card, whose cost soared from £8 billion to £12 billion and, on some predictions, to £30 billion. Since the card would not be compulsory and would thus be of scant use against terrorism, ministers defended it as a way to stop credit card fraud. It would, some commented, have been cheaper to stick with the fraud. Another giant machine was planned for the NHS, part of it known as 'choose and book'. This put every hospital and, in theory, every patient on one database, so that hospital places could be found by GPs anywhere in the country. By 2006 the machine was two and a half years overdue and the cost rising past £6 billion towards estimates of £25 billion.[8] It was hard to find a doctor or a patient who wanted a choice of hospitals anywhere in the country. Most wanted an available bed at their local hospital, dozens of which were by definition being closed to pay for the computer. The National Audit Office found 61 per cent of doctors did not want it at all, and a year later a Medix Poll declared that only 6 per cent of doctors with access to the machine used it regularly.[9] When charged with the low usage of the scheme, the project manager remarked to *Computer Weekly* that 'low usage is not something I can do anything about'.[10]

Whitehall lacked any competence in judging value for money in 'e-government'. A project known as Gateway was designed to vet all projects for value. The Commons Public Accounts Committee reported that it was circumvented by a third of 250 cases referred to it. Only fifty-seven of all the projects were given green lights. The vetting reports were considered so embarrassing as not to be publishable.[11] Central competence in this area of procurement was deeply awry. A survey published in September 2005 ranked Whitehall worst of seven major governments for computer procurement, measured in 'scrap rate' (failed projects), weakness in contract negotiation and unbalanced supplier market.[12] Most extraordinary was that not only did Whitehall officials learn nothing from each failure but that the same firms were awarded new contracts with remarkably little oversight. American computer salesmen through the 1990s and into the 2000s regarded London as a honeypot. Many of the schemes were contracted to the Texas firm EDS, which emerged unscathed from both the CSA and tax credit fiascos.[13] By 2006 this one firm had amassed over a third of the UK government computer market. The contractors bitterly protested their innocence and blamed incompetent civil servants and ministers for the failures. The one successful public-sector computer project was Transport for London's congestion charge. But this had been commissioned and operated not by Whitehall, which ridiculed it, but by local government in London.

Nothing married politics, consultants and computers more readily than the fourth weapon in Thatcherism's second-revolution armoury, the target. The target was quantification with teeth. It was a concept born of old-fashioned socialism, of the utilitarianism of Bentham, Mill and the Webbs. It revived the Victorians' payment by results, inputs balanced by outputs, satirized by Dickens in *Hard Times* as the 'age of the commissioners ... when every inch of the existence of mankind from birth to death was to be a bargain across a counter.' Such an approach to government reached its zenith under Lenin's Gosplan, though he wisely confined his confining to measurable units of manufacture.

Targets were the reduction of Thatcherism to absurdity. While conceptually sensible and presented as a sort of 'public school discipline', in reality they were micro-managerial offspring of the Whitehall planning culture, stretching back to the Second World War. Fixing a target for road building or medical education or housing starts or water supply required some pre-determination of supply and demand. Otherwise the targets would be mere whimsy. They were duly calculated and fixed between the Treasury and spending departments, monitored by the Audit Commission and the Cabinet Office delivery unit. Each year the process became more detailed and its impact more intrusive. Blair would hold periodic press conferences at which Barber would be called upon to flash up powerpoint graphs, meticulously charting the progress of targets across the 'commanding heights' of the new public sector. It was reminiscent of generals reporting success in war through enemy 'kills'.

The targets ranged from the ruthless to the comical. For health they covered not just waiting lists but numbers of emergency treatments, surgery appointment times, in-house infections and peri-natal mortality rates. Schools had targets not just for exam results but for truancy, reading ages and time taken filling in social service forms. A London comprehensive in Tottenham balanced its high truancy rate against the better GCSE percentages that came with it. A police force had to balance more police car crashes against improved 999-call answering times. Museums had targets for ethnic minority visits. Kew Gardens had a target to 'receive 30,000 herbarium specimens a year'. The Atomic Energy Authority was told to 'increase the proportion of favourable media coverage by 43.9 per cent'. The Foreign Office had a target for 'global peace and stability'. The agriculture ministry was told to eradicate BSE 'in two years', despite the incubation period being four.[14] There was no absurdity to which the official mind could not descend when quantification ran wild and accountability was only to the centre.

At his 1999 party conference Blair boasted that he had '500 clear, demanding targets' for the entire public sector. This number varied. The Commons Public Administration Committee counted 366.[15] A year later the deputy prime minister, John Prescott, was claiming 2,500 targets imposed on local government and transport alone. These varied between the banal and the mad. Some had nothing to do with him, such as a specified target for the (private sector) London Underground infrastructure companies to 'cut journey times by increasing capacity and reducing delays'.[16]

Section 14 of the 1999 Local Government Act gave Prescott draconian powers to intervene where local councils failed to meet targets. Within two years there had been forty-two such interventions in education and social services alone.

By Blair's second term, the target culture was near maniacal. The Audit Commission league tables scored councils by how many 'library items were issued per head of the population'. They recorded how many 'nights of respite care were supplied per 1,000 of the adult population'. They recorded what 'percentage of statements on special needs children were prepared per six months'. Lest anyone query the answers, private auditors from KPMG were hired to audit the audit. Quangos recruited internal and external auditors to mark the Treasury's public auditors. Turnbull, then head of the civil service, was a defender of targets, deriding old-guard public administrators as 'knightly professionals left to their own devices'. He felt that doctors, teachers, police chiefs and housing officers had for too long been content with a 'comfort zone' level of service. Targets, said Turnbull, had made public servants 'focus their efforts, requiring them to work more closely with others in the delivery chain'.[17] Yet even he admitted that targets had sometimes proved 'too top-down, demeaning professional standards, encouraging gaming, undermining trust, distorting priorities.

One facet of targetry that operated well was its central co-ordination. The potential for conflict between the two poles of Downing Street power, Downing Street and the Treasury, was considerable but liaison was close. Targetry was, by its nature, objective and gave both teams a clear sight of such old enemies as spending departments, agencies and local authorities. In 2004 Barber's delivery unit moved to the Treasury building, not so much a Treasury victory as an acceptance that the core thrust of the second revolution was shared between its two principal agencies of implementation.

The object of this framework was the control of a public sector consuming over 40 per cent of Britain's domestic output. Its sophistication was meant to rebut any suggestion that political delegation beyond the remit of Whitehall might serve any purpose. What could be more efficient than a computerized target, fixed by those who knew best and measurable across the entire public service? Indeed fundamentalists in the Treasury and Downing Street came to regard even most of the central civil service as superfluous, what they called 'heat loss through executive friction'. Spending depart ments, quangos and regional offices impeded the flow of resources to the front line. So did counties, towns, districts and lay boards and committees. Intermediate tiers of government were once understood to represent local priorities and respond to changing needs. In a bizarre set of metaphors the Treasury now wanted money 'passported direct to the point of delivery' down 'policy silos'. Downing Street needed constant information on performance to obtain 'political traction'. The ideal public-sector pound would go straight from the Exchequer to the patient, teacher, care home, policeman or pensioner in direct proportion to their pre-assessed requirements. It was the perfection of the Marxist maxim, from each according to his means, to each according to his needs. Everything in between was waste.

There was no denying the radicalism of such public-service reform. Turnbull's argument that every public servant was at last on his and her mettle was, in a sense, true. Public money was at stake. But just as the first revolution was vulnerable to commercialism, so the second fell foul of risk aversion, defensive administration and red tape. It was procrustean, chopping, hacking and sawing the public sector to fit it into a preordained shape. Throughout this period I would ask various Britons the Thatcherite question: was the state 'rolling back its frontiers' in their field of activity? Did government rules and regulations impact more or less on their lives? Did their state wither or did it grow?

The answer was invariably the same. There were cases where privatization had released enterprise and energy, and had improved some services such as refuse collection and telephones. For most people, however, state intrusion had increased on every side. I put the question to shopkeepers, publicans, farmers, hoteliers, architects, bus operators, social workers, vicars, small businessmen. Each reeled off a list of inspectors, risk assessors, health and safety officials and traffic wardens. They brandished tendering rules, employment codes, licences and permits. The cause might be well-meant, a safer swimming pool, a cleaner loaf, a less dangerous playground, a more accessible castle. The result was usually daft. Police chiefs had to 'risk-assess' a crack house before raiding it. Children canoeing on my local river were accompanied by a motor boat with safety equipment. The pub kitchen was visited by officials with clipboards sticking thermometers into dishes and demanding 'rare steak customer indemnity forms'. A local bonfire night was cancelled on the advice of a safety consultant who 'could not be sure' that someone might not fall over on the hill in the rain. The publicity attached to any accident or divergence from a national norm was enough to drive any official into paroxysms of risk aversion.

Thatcherism promised less bureaucracy yet delivered more. Red tape tsars came and went, from Lord Rayner and Lord Haskins to Better Regulation Taskforces galore. Form-filling only increased. This may seem the small change of Thatcher's second revolution, but for most Britons it was their one experience of government. To them it meant bad administration, defensive, expensive and over-restrictive. Whitehall, which often agreed with these criticisms and usually blamed them on 'Brussels', seemed trapped. One service after another fell into a frenzy of monitoring and consequent reorganization, its frustration vented on staff and customers alike.

I sat at the time on a regulatory quango, the Human Fertilization and Embryology Authority. It had been set up in 1990 to regulate the growing private market in assisted conception (in vitro fertilization) and to advise the government on embryo research. By 2000, IVF clinics were in practice no different from other private clinics. They needed no special regulator, except possibly for policing the ethical frontier of treatment and research, and for that there was a Human Genetics Commission. During my time on the authority its staff tripled. It surrounded itself with consultants, seminars, conferences, publicity and training, for which additional money always seemed forthcoming. Clinic inspection became ever more meticulous. Files were opened and dust noted on shelves, staff were counted, temperature controls checked and fire brigade rules monitored. Clinics were required to ask patients questions about home and family backgrounds. The authority's risk aversion bordered on paranoia. It banned payment for donated eggs or sperm and banned donor anonymity, drastically cutting supply. My colleagues were fixated by a desire to control every corner of the industry, fearful of the tabloid press and how ministers might react to it. This was the regulation of what was supposedly a private industry enforced by government. Yet there was no money to spend for fertility treatment on the NHS, as was available in many other countries in Europe.

SCHOOLS

David Blunkett arrived at the education department in 1997 committed to delivering Blair's triple pledge, to make his priority education, education and education. He was overseeing a local service which had survived a series of centralist takeover bids under Thatcher and Major. His approach to the job was that of a former leader of Sheffield council writ large, not that of a strategist but of a micro-manager, emitting catchy, spur-of-the-moment initiatives. Within two years he had issued 387 new regulations, 315 consultation papers and 437 notes of guidance.[18] He had required every local education authority in England and Wales to complete seventeen separate plans, including plans for development, literacy, numeracy, communication, organization, class size, lifelong learning, asset management, admissions, behaviour support, action zones and even a 'plan for plans'. By 2001, *Hansard* reported that in a single year English schools received 3,840 pages of instructions (including one guidance note called a 'bureaucracy-cutting toolkit').[19]

With this regulation came a plethora of new funding streams under Blunkett's direct control and deliberately independent of local education budgets. Heads could tap into twenty-six grants tied to 'ring-fenced' initiatives such as a Numeracy Strategy, Home/School Agreements, Desirable Learning Outcomes, Social Inclusion, National Grid for Learning and Behaviour Improvement. There were £100 fines for parents of truants, an initiative opposed by almost all teachers. Blunkett laid down targets for homework and even prescribed bedtime stories (20 minutes). He had no experience of central government and his hyperactivity seemed to many of his officials one stop short of madness.

In 1997 Blunkett met his manifesto commitment to abolish the Tories' opted-out grant-maintained schools, albeit allowing them to continue as locally financed 'foundation' schools. In 2003 Blair U-turned and allowed his education adviser, Andrew Adonis, to make the third bid in a generation to bring all schools under central control (again under the guise of them becoming 'independent' of local councils). The bid was beaten off by the new education secretary, Charles Clarke, but at the price of conceding to the Treasury what amounted to a central five-year plan for school building, planning and development, subject to new buildings being based on PFI money. Undaunted, Adonis returned to the fray. He persuaded Blair to revive precisely the institutions he had just abolished, the grant-maintained schools. Blair ennobled him and sent him as junior minister under Ruth Kelly to the education department to push through Blair's most extraordinary and controversial volte-face, the 2004 schools White Paper.

The original Blair/Adonis plan was virtually indistinguishable from

Thatcher's 1987 proposal (updated by John Patten in 1993). The Tories saw opted-out schools as coming under a central funding agency. Blair was more radical in hoping that faith organizations, charities and private businesses would take them over with a central capitation grant. To him all schools would be independent trusts, with freedom to raise money and select their own staff and pupils. They would receive a proportion of their capital and their running expenses from the state. Popular schools would expand and wipe out unpopular ones, a sort of institutional Darwinism. Local authority schools would not be allowed to expand anywhere near opted-out schools. The concept was market-tested by Adonis's 'city academies', in fact facsimiles of the Tories' grant-maintained and city technology colleges, which Labour had fiercely opposed.

These were among the oddest of Blair's innovations, freelance public enterprises under Downing Street sponsorship. Companies, churches or tycoons were induced to give £2 million each to set up twenty-seven centrally funded academies, which government would top up with an average of £25 million a school (though one in Bexley was reported to have cost £50 million in public funds alone[20]). For this sum, donors would have de facto control of a school, including of its curriculum. The academies were gold-plated institutions, three to five times what a normal school cost.[21] Blair was little short of frantic to see these places established, even hoping one day to see 200 of them. An astonishing burst of activity in 2005 saw his new education secretary, Ruth Kelly, pleading with accountancy firms, the City of London, liveried companies, the Church of England and the Roman Catholic Church to take over or found new academies. Knighthoods and peerages were mooted as an inducement, leading to an extraordinary 'schools for honours' scandal in 2006.

Blair's fixation on what was bound to be a tiny group of schools exactly paralleled Thatcher's on opting out. He was desperate for 'his' schools to be seen as better than local council ones, boasting of how much better they did (where this was the case) in league tables. Private schools were even approached to take over 'failing' state schools, with the American operator, Edison, invited for discussions at the education department. The pressure on teachers was duly intense. Two academies in Middlesbrough expelled sixty-one poorly performing pupils in two years, against fifteen in all other schools in the borough.[22] A Bristol school set aside £37,000 for incentives to pupils to meet GCSE targets, with £10 for each predicted grade and £5 for each grade surpassing it. Seventeen A-level pupils who won university places received £500 each.[23]

Adonis's desire to extend the 'academy' principle to all English secondary schools was problematic in that it relied, as had Baker's and Patten's schemes, on schools volunteering for trust status. This led to the same argument as under the Tories over who should 'own the decision', teachers or parents or local electors. Matters were further complicated by the government's encouragement of the use of PFI finance and management subcontracts to all schools. Blair hoped that trust schools would be popular in offering parents 'choice'. This was fanciful since by definition parents would want the most popular local school, which would immediately be oversubscribed. Few schools were keen to expand because it would alter their ethos and because a broader intake might damage their league ranking.

The supposed autonomy of trust schools meant they could in theory become selective grammar schools, reintroducing eleven-plus discrimination between schools. This was anathema to the Labour party and in 2005 led to the most determined parliamentary revolt of Blair's career. Adonis was forced to concede that all schools would continue to have a comprehensive intake overseen by a Whitehall Office of the School Adjudicator, who was given power to vet admissions policies. The prospective bureaucracy, with every parent entitled to appeal against a rejection, beggared imagination. By May 2006, a series of concessions to backbenchers had rendered the academies and prospective trust schools little different from their local council neighbours, at least in intake.

The Treasury was familiarly unenthusiastic about open competition between local and trust schools, since expansion in one school meant empty places and wasted resources elsewhere, sabotaging the Treasury's five-year plans for school investment. It therefore insisted on local councils being able, in effect, to plan investment in local buildings coherently, contradicting Adonis's desire for a free market in school places. It was a repeat of the stand-off that followed Patten's attempt to develop a rival, central school network. In March 2006 a survey suggested that barely 5 per cent of local authority schools would opt for trust status anyway. The extraordinary political furore which the innovation had caused appeared to have been a storm in a teacup.[24]

After almost two decades of Thatcherism, schools were remarkable chiefly for the degree to which they had resisted a sustained government campaign to nationalize them. They had remained loyal to local councils, given the poor quality of administration the latter had often supplied in the past. But remaining local did not free them from ever-greater intrusion by Whitehall. All schools shared a rising tide of central monitoring. In 2004 one local council school recorded 350 policy targets and 175 efficiency targets. A head teacher placed one term's worth of Whitehall paperwork in a wheelbarrow and found she could not move it. The then schools minister, David Miliband, demanded of his officials 'a 25 per cent reduction in inspection, a 30 per cent cut in red tape and a 40 per cent cut in data submission', plus a 'simplified funding' initiative.[25] Nothing further was heard of this initiative. The cynicism of these presentational gimmicks was total.

By Blair's third term the amount spent in real terms on education had doubled and almost every school had seen some capital investment. The priority he had placed on education had been honoured in that the money was spent, mostly through ring-fenced initiatives. The Association of School and College Leaders reported in March 2006 that £700 million was being 'sprayed' at schools through such plans as Excellence in Cities, Leadership Incentive Grants, Fresh Start and fifteen other headline projects. What was impossible was to tell whether this had led to any parallel increase in value for money. A leaked inspectors' review in December 2005 concluded that fully a third of primary school children were still passing to secondary schools 'not competent in the three Rs' and that any progress since 1997 had 'largely stalled'.[26] The view was that league tables had led teachers to concentrate on brighter pupils. The emphasis on English and maths exams meant other subjects (notably sports) were 'rarely a priority'.

The apotheosis of the target was the school examination. Its value had been discredited by the teaching profession at the start of the twentieth century after what Dickens attacked as the crudity of Victorian payment-by-results. It was restored by Patten and his successors in the early 1990s as a control tool, since results were easily classifiable and less tangible forms of education were not. Exam oversight was centralized under a Qualifications and Curriculum Authority sitting above a National Assessment Agency. The administrative cost of this had by 2003 risen over the previous ten years from less than £10 million to £610 million.[27] In 2005 the head of the league table's 'top' primary school angrily attributed her success to 'ignoring the government's literacy and numeracy strategies'. She pleaded with ministers to stop telling schools how to teach.

They could not stop. They knew no other way of governing. Successive Ofsted reports recorded a teaching profession demoralized and confused by external interference. The government had sought to break the link not just between school and community but between children and the professional esteem of those teaching them. In March 2006 the head of the Qualifications and Curriculum Authority, Ken Boston, admitted that British pupils were examined more often and more intensely than any in the world. 'The assessment load is huge,' he said. 'It is far greater than in other countries and not necessary for the purpose.'[28] Boston, like all his predecessors, suggested that such over-regulation should cease. The message was that throwing money and regulation at a public service was unlikely in itself to deliver steadily rising benefits. The message fell on deaf ears.

HOSPITALS

Hospitals are the most reorganized institutions in Britain. When Labour took power in 1997 the NHS was battered and bruised but Britons were receiving reasonably cost-effective health care. Thatcher's fund-holding GP scheme had been a minor success by delegating health rationing to the front line. At 5.7 per cent of GDP in 1998, the NHS offered the cheapest comprehensive health care in the developed world. The EU average was 8.4 per cent and France and Germany were spending near to 10 per cent each.[29]

This economy caused Blair not pride but pain. In 1997 he abolished the Tories' fund-holding system in favour of local primary care trusts, and he abolished the related internal hospital market. Then, in a pledge on the *Frost Programme* in January 2000, he undertook to bring NHS finance up to the European average in five years. Gordon Brown was angry at what appeared to be Blair usurping Granita, but with health pre-eminent on the political agenda he could hardly complain, and the two men duly rivalled each other as high spenders on health. Blair was advised by a McKinsey émigré, Adair Turner, Brown by a banker, Sir Derek Wanless. The outcome was that real spending on health in Britain rose from an average of 3 per cent a year in the decade before 1997 to 4.8 in Blair's first term and 7.4

in his second. This was an astonishing rate of increase, the fastest in Europe. Some doubted if the NHS could efficiently absorb such resources.

All attention turned on one target, hospital waiting times. These fell dramatically and by 2005 Blair was able to boast a cut from 18 months to 18 weeks, the best figure since 1988 (this was contested by the Tories). To achieve this, hospital managers were subject to draconian disciplines. In 1997 Labour's manifesto had promised 'no return to top-down management' and the 'rooting out of unnecessary administrative costs'. The government proceeded in the opposite direction. Within two years, 40 new health service agencies had been set up, sending GPs and hospitals over 400 targets. In 2001 came a ten-year plan, likened by one Plymouth surgeon 'to being in Russia under Stalin'. He found his budget being charged £1,500 for a shelf which he previously would have bought for £100 at his local store.

In 2002 a new NHS Act gave the health secretary, John Reid, fifty-eight new powers over health delivery. A dozen 'tsars' were appointed to supplement a miasma of quangos with names such as the Commission for Health Improvement, the NHS Modernisation Agency and the Patients Access Team. The Institute of Health Care Managers listed 1,700 separate job categories in 1995. By 2002 this had grown to 5,529. The degree of detail demanded of the service at every level was phenomenal. At the 2005 general election the prime minister was told that a patient had been unable to get an appointment from her GP for two days ahead when the health minister had said that 99.89 per cent of patients could do so. It turned out that GPs had been given a bonus if all appointments were made for under 48 hours. Most understandably told their receptionists never to make an appointment for a longer period.

More serious was health's failure to win public acclaim as an improving public service. Blair imitated Thatcher in 1987 and decided on his second fundamental restructuring of the NHS. Like all observers he concluded that the system was over-centralized and hospitals should enjoy more autonomy. He duly proposed facsimiles of Thatcher's trust hospitals, called foundations. (Blair renamed Thatcher's foundation schools trusts and her trust hospitals foundations.) Whitehall responded by allowing only hospitals with adequate league table scores to have 'earned autonomy' status. This was awarded to just twenty, creating a far more obvious 'two-tier' service than had Thatcher.

The foundations, soon referred to as trusts, would have boards of their own. They were promised elected members, freedom from NHS bureaucracy and scope to raise investment in the money market. The elections to the trusts' boards were farcical. Hospitals were awarded 'constituencies' virtually at random over their catchment areas. Millions were spent on publicizing the elections, but electoral registers were chaotic and only tiny numbers, mostly medical staff, ever voted. Few Britons were aware of this parallel local democracy being created in their midst.

The Treasury reacted to Blair's foundation hospitals as it had to Thatcher's trusts. It tried to kill them. Since they were not private and were unlikely to be allowed to go bankrupt, they could not be given true autonomy. A furious battle ensued in the summer of 2003 between Brown at the Treasury and the health secretary, Alan Milburn. Brown adamantly refused to exempt the foundations from Treasury control, though he encouraged them to subcontract all they could to the burgeoning private health sector. By the time Milburn had won hospitals foundation 'status', Brown had ensured it was largely meaningless and Milburn resigned. In August 2004 *The Times* reported that few of the proclaimed freedoms had materialized. Nor could the *British Medical Journal* find any sign of an 'improved quality of care, satisfaction or health outcomes' following the change.[30]

Blair had supported Milburn against Brown but was still mystified as to where the extra money pouring into the service was going, as was the public. The tabloids were splashing multi-billion pound headlines and demanding, 'where has it all gone?' A service costing £65 billion in 2003 was heading towards £105 billion by 2007 and Blair announced yet another reorganization, his third. Consultants were brought in to suggest a 'Change Programme' under which fourteen NHS Directorates would be reorganized into three business groups to assist in the 'central command of the NHS chief executive'. A new contract for GPs was proposed, which eventually increased GPs' salaries by 20 per cent to an average of £100,000. For the first time in history the requirement that a local doctor offer patients round-the-clock care was ended. The new contract was later described by the King's Fund think tank as having delivered huge gains to doctors but few noticeable improvements to patients. It was a scathing comment on central government mismanagement.[31]

By 2005 the NHS was £800 million in debt. This was not crippling on an annual budget of £72 billion but in a centralized system one loss-making hospital was, for ministers, one headline too many. In addition, any shift of resources from a successful to a loss-making trust infringed the lingering principles of trust autonomy and budgetary independence. The bulk of the new money had gone on what was outside trusts' control. Roughly half had gone on the new 2004 pay settlement agreed by the health department and the Treasury. A further 20 per cent had gone on 'reorganization' and central services. Over £6.2 billion had been allocated to a new national health computer (see the previous chapter), an estimate soon to rise to £20 billion.[32] A survey by Sir Tony Atkinson of Nuffield College, Oxford, suggested that less than 30 per cent of Blair's increased spending had gone on actual health care. Sixty per cent more support and administrative staff had been hired since 1998.[33]

This was taking place against a background of Blair's reintroduction of a central Thatcherite concept, that of an internal market. The 2004 Act not only introduced trust hospitals but required that they rival each other in surgical costs. 'We only got big falls in waiting times,' Blair told his 2004 party conference, 'after introducing competition for routine surgery.' Nor was the competition only between primary care trusts and hospitals. By 2006 doctors were once again fund-holders, or rather 'commissioners', able to buy operations from hospitals at will. The recently created 330 local primary care trusts were to be reorganized yet again into roughly 100. Patients were to be offered a choice of four hospitals for every procedure. Hospitals were charging for operations and payment-by-results was applied to 80 per cent of hospital procedures. The NHS was reported to be entering into talks with a private firm, BMI Healthcare, to take over the running of failing hospitals.[34] The prime minister said that 40 per cent of all operations could be performed in the private sector by his new NHS Partners network (composed of eleven companies). Thatcher would not have dared go so far. The situation seemed to both the health industry and the public little short of chaotic.

The return to the open market led to precisely the weakness of Thatcher's original scheme. Under payment-by-results hospital managers could not predict their patient numbers and thus their cash flow, let alone plan investment. The arrival of independent and specialist hospitals threatened to remove much bread-and-butter surgery from general hospitals, which in turn led general hospitals towards specialism, then survival depending on whether they could compete. One hospital, just three years old, the

£14 million Ravenscourt Park in West London, faced closure when it found it had attracted only half as many operations as it was expensively equipped to perform. The pressure to specialism encouraged hospital trusts to close some eighty cottage or 'community' hospitals within their areas (roughly a third of the total). When this evoked furious public and parliamentary opposition the government backed down, reversed the policy and declared itself in favour of more community hospitals.[35] This in turn meant overturning trust autonomy and further distorted the trusts' financial planning. Britain was getting the worst of privatization, waste, with the worst of a nationalized industry, a politicized bureaucracy with no concomitant advantages in resource planning.

More alarming, the PFI schemes (described in the last chapter) were starting to draw down large sums in rent, interest and contract payments. Virtually all hospital investment under Brown was privatized. This meant that over £6 billion of debt had to be serviced on seventy-nine health projects since the 1980s, with double that in the pipeline. Hospitals were setting aside large reserves that would previously have gone on health care. The debt on the Queen Elizabeth Hospital Trust in Woolwich was estimated to rise to £100 million by 2008, while that on the revived Royal London and Bart's scheme was £120 million. Such figures threatened bankruptcy at some time in the future. Chris Hams of Birmingham University, a long-time critic of NHS privatization, warned that this was 'an early signal of all that is going to happen to big PFI schemes in due course'.[36]

The sheer ferocity of the NHS central command under political pressure from Blair and his new health secretary, Patricia Hewitt, was becoming relentless. In October 2004 something called the Healthcare Commission listed 102 inspection regimes to which hospitals were now subject, defying all talk of 'trust autonomy'. The East Sussex Hospitals NHS Trust recorded seventy inspection visits in one year.[37] Each year ministers promised less regulation and delivered more. All the new foundation trusts declared themselves more bound up in red tape than before 'autonomy'.[38] When in 2004 the Treasury asked how much health could contribute to a general cut in Whitehall administration costs, the department casually offered £500 million 'with no loss of efficiency'. In 2006 the NHS said it could again offer 6,000 administrative job cuts and £250 million savings.[39]

As with schools, so with hospitals. Blair's enthusiasm for the first Thatcher revolution ran up against his own and the Treasury's commitment to the second, to command a public service and control its delivery. There seemed no way in which this could be resolved. The World Health Organization put Britain seventeenth in its league table of 'responsiveness to the needs of patients'. An unequivocal *Which?* opinion poll in August 2005 found that 90 per cent of people did not want choice of health care, the central purpose of Blair's policy of competition and computerization. They wanted a good general hospital within easy reach of their home.

The NHS was by the mid-2000s no longer the wonder of the world. It seemed oversized and stumbling under the weight of its own overheads, dazed by constant change. Britain was not alone in suffering a crisis of over-demand for health care and was still not spending as much as America or most of Europe on it, though it was fast catching up with the latter. What was unusual was the degree of public dissatisfaction with the service nationally and in the extent to which it tried to run all its doctors and hospitals as a civil service, centrally from its capital city. With each institutional bid to decentralize came a political craving to centralize. No one was any longer coming to Britain to learn how to do it.

THE POLICE

The police had been a backwater of Thatcherism under Thatcher and moved into the mainstream only with Major. Under Blair the mainstream became a torrent. He seized on his Opposition catchphrase, 'tough on crime, tough on the causes of crime' but found the first had more appeal than the second. He introduced forty-three crime bills in his first eight years in office, an unprecedented total. In Opposition, Blair had strongly opposed Howard's 1994 Police Act, calling it the deed of 'a government that resents local freedom with an aversion bordering on paranoia'. In power he introduced what Howard had failed to introduce. The 2002 Police Reform Act took centralization a step further. It empowered the home secretary to fix police budgets and direct local police authorities more or less at will. This included the power to sack police chiefs over the heads of local police authorities. In the hands of Blunkett and Charles Clarke it ushered in a greatly enhanced regime of targetry. Sir John Stevens, head of London's Metropolitan Police, was supposedly responsible to the new Greater London Authority but claimed that he was also accountable to 14 separate central bodies and 154 Home Office crime-busting initiatives. These covered topics as diverse as shopping-centre crime, mobile-phone theft, credit-card fraud, football hooliganism, Internet child abuse, anti-social behaviour, curfews and crack houses.

Blunkett at the Home Office was as hyperactive as at education. A perusal of his annual report showed agencies and task forces operating almost everywhere as 'virtual' police forces. An example of his technique was a 2002 plan, Safer Streets, to combat London street crime. For this he secured £67 million from the Treasury, almost all of it spent on police overtime. There was a temporary downturn in mugging at an estimated cost of £14,000 for each crime 'prevented'. The figure later returned to what it had been before. His successor, Charles Clarke, proved no less susceptible to the cries of the tabloid press and of Home Office officials eager to set up a national police force. Securing a supportive report from Her Majesty's Inspector of Police, Denis O'Connor, Clarke revived the Home Office's old plan to merge the forty-three local police authorities into as few regional forces as possible, under the managerial authority of the home secretary. This was the policy that had evoked Blair's most ferocious opposition as Labour home affairs spokesman in April 1994, opposition as 'a matter of constitutional principle'.

The Tories had suggested twenty-five forces. O'Connor now proposed to reduce the number to twelve, described as 'fit for purpose in the twenty-first century'. Only such a size, said O'Connor, could handle the new world of global terrorism, drug trafficking, paedophilia and computer crime. This was despite the Home Office having in 2006 set up its own fully staffed Serious and Organized Crime Agency (SOCA) for just such purposes. It had also requested £60 million from the Treasury for 2,000 officers to set up a Counter Terrorist Command, and deputed the Met to be the lead force in counter-terrorist intelligence. In launching SOCA in March 2006, Blair even let slip that it should liaise with the new 'regional' forces, a word that Clarke had scrupulously denied.

Top-down policy now required as much amalgamation as the home secretary of the day could engineer. This was despite continuing evidence that large forces were not more efficient. In addition, a 2002 poll by ICM found that 68 per cent of the population regarded the police as detached from their localities in matters of service priorities. It found that the best-performing forces were traditional county-based ones, while large amalgamated forces performed no better than small ones.[40] Millions of pounds were now offered to forces to co-operate in their own demise. Why combinations of Kent, Sussex and Surrey or Cornwall, Devon and Gloucestershire would be better able to police their regions than, say, six even bigger forces was never explained. Nor was any thought given to a two-tier police force, as in most other countries, with organized, computer and terrorist crime (under 2 per cent of the total) handled by a national force while the overwhelming majority of police work remained locally accountable. A later survey by Loveday and Reid recorded that such options as forces remaining distinct but co-operating on specialized crime were 'expressly left out of the final draft and the report's general tenor strongly suggests that its conclusions were preordained.'[41] The Home Office in its new proposals had adopted 'a clear presumption against the options of collaboration or federation' irrespective of evidence.

The chief concern within the Home Office was standardization. It disliked differences in crime rates and was criticized in the media whenever different areas diverged in their treatment even of something as minor as speeding, parking or alcohol offences. The junior police minister, Hazel Blears, declared in October 2005 that 'reducing variations in performance between forces is a cornerstone of the government's reform agenda'. Centralism could hardly have been more explicit. The British constabulary, once the envy of the world, was thus to be removed from rendering any account to its community. Forty-three forces were few enough, but the proposed regionalism was de facto nationalization. It was a drift which had over the years seen beat policing collapse and violent and street crime rise. In May 2006 a new home secretary, John Reid, announced that he might go slow on the force mergers after all. Nothing was coherent, everything uncertain.

The events of 9/11 in America in 2001 and the London bombs of 2005 fuelled Blair's inclination to push the second revolution into areas that had been no-go to liberals for decades. He discarded the Labour party's traditional attachment to civil liberties and became overtly authoritarian. After 2001 counter-terrorism statutes were being presented to parliament at least once a year. Many, such as the provision for control orders and 90-day detention, had to be amended and diluted under back-bench and media pressure. Much argument surrounded a twelve-point plan, put forward by Blair in July 2005, to suppress 'glorification' of terror, facilitate deportation, close mosques and bookshops and restrict asylum. The measures were not discussed with the Home Office and almost all had to be weakened in debate.

The image of the police under Blair was of a heavily armed and ubiquitous force whose energies were tilted towards an agenda topped by fighting terrorism, combating violent crime in the capital and protecting VIPs and government property. One afternoon in 2004 I counted fifty uniformed police in and round Whitehall and not one in the central West End. To ordinary members of the public, law and order was a matter of wailing car sirens and minibuses full of policemen waiting in side streets. In their own neighbourhoods, they perceived a government pursuing 'zero tolerance' of any offences to do with cars and traffic, yet an extraordinary acceptance of petty crime, even after the introduction of new 'anti-social behaviour orders' (Asbos). Ministers protested at references to Britain becoming a police state. But under Blair measures taken against terrorism went beyond anything introduced to counter the far more immediate IRA threat to Thatcher's government. His use of detention without trial and curbs on freedom of speech and assembly were wholly new.

The criticism directed at ministers over their counter-terrorism legislation needs to be balanced against some undoubted advances of civil liberty under Blair. The entrenching of European human rights' law into United Kingdom statute under the Human Rights Act 1998 opened the way to controversial litigation on the family, planning control and employment rights, but was widely welcomed as a step towards 'rights-based' law. The much-abused increase in health and safety regulation did have benefits, for instance in curbing the scale of industrial injuries and traffic accidents. The government's freedom of information law, despite much early backtracking, opened up areas of government to public scrutiny. The public was able to discover how many times Blair had used the Queen's plane and how many times the CIA had used British airports for 'extraordinary rendition' flights. A growth in the number of ombudsmen offered greater public redress. The social disciplines imposed by government must always respond to changing circumstances, whether they concern international terrorism or teenage misbehaviour on the streets.

What was distinctive about these responses under Thatcherism is that they invariably drew power away from communities and towards the agencies of the centre. Street police intelligence, widely regarded as a key to uncovering home-based terrorist cells, was diluted in favour of national terrorism task forces. The sort of neighbourhood leadership that helped discipline youths in an Italian or Spanish town was in Britain disempowered and replaced by magisterial 'Asbos' and a rush to the courts. To each and every ill that afflicted a British community, the cry that 'something must be done' was increasingly interpreted as something by central government.

PLANNING

Labour's most concerted centralization was curiously in one area where finance was hardly an issue. John Prescott's appointment as Blair's planning, local government and environment minister from 1997 to 2006 was rooted not in his expertise at the job but in party politics. Prescott never found a language in which to marry the demands of conservationists and 'nimbies' with those of the property and development interests crowding his door, nor did he make any secret of his bias towards the latter. On one matter he was implacable. He shared Blair's belief that local democracy should have no part in planning land use. He was determined to remove that power from city and county authorities and vest it in his own office.

The result was the 2004 Planning and Compulsory Purchase Act, one of those laws, barely noticed in parliament, that shape not just the British constitution but the appearance of Britain itself. Since time out of mind, cities and counties had exercised general oversight of local planning. They had determined suburban expansion and negotiated the sites of new development. They decided where countryside should be preserved. The new act stripped them of this power. In future, regional and national officers of Prescott's own department would decide where and in what form development should occur. Insofar as they consulted at all it was with a new quiverful of regional development quangos, whom they themselves appointed. Britain became the only free country in the world where the planning of the use of land was removed from local democratic determination.

Much in the 2004 Act was sensible, including measures to reduce delays in the development process. But its essence was to nationalize planning. Prescott would in future decide where tower blocks might go, where green-belt might be sacrificed to warehouse estates, where phone masts and wind turbines could be erected. Communities were allowed to write local development frameworks, but these were vetted by Prescott's office to ensure conformity with central policy. Rowland Parker's village of Foxton in Cambridgeshire, subject of his classic history, *The Common Stream*, had experienced three traumas over the two millennia of its recorded time, the Saxon invasion, the Black Death and the arrival of combine harvesting, decimating its labour force. Now it was to experience a fourth and final one, disappearance beneath the suburbanization of Whitehall's new low-density Cambridgeshire linear city.

Prescott was under pressure from the Treasury to increase the supply of land for development and new housing, and under the same pressure from the construction industry, whose lobbyists had Downing Street's ear. There was no comparable defence of the countryside. The 2004 Act was variously likened in impact to the Luftwaffe (by the *Spectator*), Soviet social engineering (by *The Times*) and the death of rural England (by the Green Party). Prescott was unmoved. To show his cast of mind he overturned the local council and his own inspector to permit an astonishing fifty-storey block of luxury flats opposite Westminster at Vauxhall. It was dubbed Prescott Towers and would stand as totem to his rule.

Within weeks of the 2004 Act being passed fields in the Cotswolds were being sold as building plots. Speculators gambled on the government over-riding previous zoning controls and forcing development on local councils. Farms near towns in the south-east soared in value from tens of thousands to millions of pounds. As the Victorian ditty ran, 'The finest crop that a field can grow/ Is hundreds of houses all in a row.' Despite occasional references to the importance of green belts, the lack of any concept of valued countryside or other means of defining the bounds of urbanization left rural Britain vulnerable as never before to the decline in farm incomes.

In the same year Prescott announced the revival of comprehensive house clearances. Some 150,000 homes, many of them restorable terrace properties, in Lancashire, Yorkshire and the Midlands were scheduled for mass demolition and replacement. This was after the consultants who would be involved in the work were paid an astonishing £130 million to recommend it.[42] This required compulsory purchase powers to be used on so wide a scale for the first time since the 1970s. The code for the plan was Pathfinder, also the name for the bombing campaign against German cities in the Second World War. Destruction was returning to British town planning after three decades in abeyance, fuelled by public money and the eagerness of architects and builders for fees. This time the agent was not local government but the centre.

REFORM, REFORM, REFORM

What constitutes good government has vexed political philosophers for centuries. The American republican John Adams reflected that of all arts the only one not to have improved since ancient Athens was that of politics. Citizens and their leaders blunder into folly, knowing it as folly yet somehow unable to escape. Barbara Tuchman considered this the inevitable product of collective government, since such government negates the genius of leadership. It forms itself into lines of least resistance so that individuals can avoid blame and curry favour with electorates.[43] This occupational disease of democracy is one to which, if it loses immunity, dictatorship has an easy answer.

In a powerful diatribe against the Blair government, the veteran Whitehall observer Sir Christopher Foster remarked that 'in the past 25 years we have had two peace-time attempts at presidential government (Thatcher's and Blair's) and both have failed.' The reason, for Foster, was that no part of the constitution was performing as the textbooks required, 'not parliament, not cabinet, not ministers, not the civil service, not local authorities ... the clothes are much the same but the bodies inside are not.'[44]

I am better disposed towards radicalism than Foster and am therefore more inclined to ask, if Thatcherism in power is not working as hoped, why that might be. We have witnessed two revolutions in contention. The first revolution was meant to liberate both individuals and organizations from the rigidities of the past, notably those imposed by an archaic state machine. If that involved doing some damage to the constitution, it would be in a good cause. Blair and Brown honoured this revolution, as had Thatcher and Lawson, by privatizing anything that could be sold or mortgaged, and controlling anything that could not. The problem, which both Tory and Labour Thatcherites soon discovered, was that the new privatized public sector proved to be every bit as expensive as the old nationalized one, while the nationalized one reacted to control by becoming stubborn and bureaucratic. To neither predicament did the second revolution have a satisfactory answer. The test of competence in modern government, short of a government's ejection at election time, is some running tally of public satisfaction, however expressed. No government under Thatcherism ever won a clear popular majority at an election, nor was privatization ever popular in opinion polls. Between the late 1970s and the mid-2000s the number of Britons believing that 'the quality of government needs improving' doubled.[45] A YouGov poll in 2003 showed a majority declaring 'public services have deteriorated under Labour'. Whatever spin is put on these figures they suggested that the new management of the public sector had yet to win public support. Blair's fortress services, health and education, were under what seemed perpetual siege, with professionals on the inside and politicians without.

Blair in his third term had no response to this. Brown's Treasury was still plodding on with the sale of the Post Office and British Nuclear Fuels, privatizing the parole service and the Jobcentre workforce (10 per cent of all civil servants).[46] Private companies such as Capita and EDS were walking in and out of Whitehall with expensive contracts reminiscent of arms manufacturers of old. Despite some twenty years of supposed privatization and decentralization, the government had contrived to recruit an extra half million public servants and expand the public payroll to one fifth of total employment. Blair revealed in 2005 that government running costs had risen 13 per cent in real terms, or three times the rate of inflation, in just three years, and by 7 per cent in the past year alone.[47]

When Blair addressed his post-election party conference at Brighton in 2005, he let out what amounted to a wail of frustration. Where was the return on his initiatives, white papers and statutes, where were his ceaseless calls for change and reform, his pleas against the forces of conservatism and the scars on his back? What had gone wrong? All he could offer was yet more of the same: 'Reform, reform, reform'. Deaf to cries of 'no more reorganization' from across the public sector, Blair protested that he had been timid for too long. Every time he surveyed a past reform, 'I wished in retrospect I had gone further.'[48] Even as his leadership came under serious challenge from the Brownites in spring 2006, Blair's response was to list all the public-service reforms that he had still to do.[49]

A sanguine comment came from one of his early associates, Peter Hyman, who had left Downing Street to work in an Islington secondary school. He wrote in 2005 that Blair's obsession with surface presentation was impeding service delivery and infuriating front-line professionals. 'What they require [from a prime minister] is a policy framework and goals, not hundreds of micro-announcements.'[50] Blair could not see that every act of central intervention was not a call to arms but a catalyst to bureaucratic growth. Every reactive policy instigated a regulatory deluge. It might be greeted by the media as showing that 'something was being done', but those who demanded intervention in the short-term tended to deplore it in the long. The media cried for action, yet attacked the red tape that action created. It was the worst guide to policy.

This is another way of saying that the Thatcher revolutions had by the middle of the new decade reached exhaustion. Centralization and targetry had not delivered value for money and conventional political wisdom had no alternative to offer. Blair was radiating the same irritation as had Thatcher after her final conference, 'There is so much more to be done.'[51] He and Brown had created in Downing Street the most potent machine for administering a modern state anywhere in the world. Yet the story told in this and the preceding chapters is that it was riven with inefficiency, waste and misdirected effort. It was not working. Something had gone wrong.

19

The New Localism

In January 2006 the Spanish defence minister, José Bono, ordered the house arrest of the head of his land forces, General José Mena Aguado. The latter's offence was to summon his fellow officers to defend the nation's integrity against a change in the Spanish constitution granting extensive autonomy to Catalonia. The law offered the province a programme of legislative independence and the retention of half the national income tax paid by Catalans. The incident illustrated the tension in all European countries between central governments and their regions and localities. Localism is never peaceful yet for the past quarter century its ramifications have swept Europe.

Europe's history is that of tribes. Only the smallest countries are ethnically and culturally homogeneous. Even as Europe's leaders struggled to establish another pan-European imperium under the EU at the start of the twenty-first century, nation states found provincialism and subsidiary democracy still assertive and inconvenient. Constitutions are not just about the legitimacy of a central power but also about its relations with its subordinate communities. Nor is a constitution fixed for all time. It is the servant, not the master, of its citizens. The constitution of western Europe has been in negotiation for half a century. Just as power tends to be centripetal so democracy tends to be centrifugal. Politics has always been the art of resolving these forces.

The end of the Second World War saw a reaction against the centralism of the Axis powers, a revulsion against dictatorship and a craving after ethnic identity and small statehood. To this the victorious Allies assented. They broke up the German and Italian regimes in such a way as to curb any return to centralized power. In West Germany sixteen *länder* governments were established and the capital moved from grand Berlin to modest Bonn. Under the 1949 constitution the *länder* were given autonomies akin to the old pre-Bismarck principalities, whose names they also took. The federal government was saddled with a constitution of checks and balances to prevent the re-emergence of the *Führerprinzip*. Localism was a democratic virtue.

While peace was seen as demanding decentralization among the vanquished, it was not so seen among the victors. The British felt no need to dismantle the domestic mechanisms established to propagate the war, but converted them to meet the demands of the modern welfare state. Military command over planning, transportation, housing, health and welfare was adapted to civilian command. Administrative swords became ploughshares. As the ideals of democratic socialism took root across Europe so did the concept of a welfare state and a minimum standard of public services. These reinforced national security as powerful incentives to centralism.

Centralism was everywhere contentious, not because it was socialist or redistributive but because it removed power from localities. France saw separatist opposition in Corsica and Brittany. In Italy antagonism between north and south destabilized successive governments in Rome. Belgium suffered violence between Flemings and Walloons. The collapse of the Franco regime in Spain meant Madrid conceding autonomy to Basques, Catalans and Galicians. In the United Kingdom the Northern Irish were in regular argument with London, sometimes violently so.

By the 1980s centre/local relations were a running theme of European reform, heightened by the breakdown of the Soviet empire. Belief in centralism as guarantor of security was dissolving after half a century of peace. With the end of the Cold War, eastern Europe fragmented into its Baltic, Slavic, Caucasian and Balkan components. The attempt to hold Czechoslovakia together failed, likewise Yugoslavia. In one state after another, devolution and possible separatism was seen as an accompaniment of democracy. The Council of Europe's 1988 European Charter for Local Self-Government ordained that public administration be kept as close to citizens as possible. It stipulated local tax discretion and, under Article 4, local democracy 'not undermined or limited by a national or regional authority'. European governments tended to respect such devolution largely because their constitutions made them answerable to electorates with strong provincial loyalties.

This was not true of France. The dirigisme of French government had long been the butt of British smugness, illustrated by the chauvinism of a Paris clock dictating activity in every school and every courthouse in France. But despite the celebrated power of the *départements* and their *préfets*, a tradition of commune leadership survived and flourished. The French mayor was always a significant civic figure and a local base was considered vital for high political office. It was from this base that, in 1982, a minor revolution seized French politics. A coalition of socialist mayors and local elites resentful of prefectorial power persuaded the Mitterrand government to introduce the *loi Deferre*. This stripped the *préfets* of much of their power and devolved public administration to elected regional and subordinate councils, including health, education, local policing and planning. It is said that when some *préfets* heard of the passage of the 1982 Act they broke down and wept, fearing it spelled the end of the state.[1]

The 37,000 communes are the underpinning of French democracy. Some are as large as Paris, but 80 per cent have fewer than 1,000 inhabitants. Their mayors are powerful, owning state property and responsible for planning, environment, elementary school buildings and civic ceremony. They can raise local taxes to pay for them. Mayoral elections are often bitterly fought and turnouts high. The result is a civic pride visible in every French municipality. As many British visitors to France know, such administration can be bureaucratic, dilatory and expensive (unless you are French), but communal democracy in France has a vitality often lacking at the national tier. The French would never surrender it.

A similar revolution occurred in Italy. After the fall of Mussolini power was devolved by the Allies to provinces based on ancient dukedoms and kingdoms, to break the back of Fascism. This produced weak government in Rome but the emergence of strong politics in cities and provinces. Autonomous status was granted to Sardinia, Sicily and Val d'Aosta in the north.[2] In his study of modern European democracy, Robert Putnam described how the new Italian state 'found itself strengthened not weakened when it faced a vigorous civic society'.[3] The motor of Italian economic revival was the quasi-independence of cities such as Milan, Turin and Bologna. In the early 1990s drastic constitutional reform swept aside many of Italy's postwar structures and empowered both provinces and regions. The former took over from central government control of health and education, the latter took planning and economic development. Corruption remains endemic in Italian administration but reformers saw its cure not in greater central control but in the opposite, decentralization. In 1993 the percentage of regional spending covered by local taxes rose from virtually nothing to 47 per cent, and of municipal spending from 15 to 45 per cent.[4]

Scandinavia is regarded by localists as a paradigm. Sweden, Norway and Denmark long enjoyed a similar pattern of local government to that in

England, based on counties and municipalities. Where politics was left-wing, such government was often expensive. In Sweden both counties and municipalities could raise income taxes to finance health, education, housing and other social services. Sweden had by the 1980s become one of the highest-taxed states in Europe, but in 1991 this ended. Conservative reform relieved all but the top 15 per cent of taxpayers of central income tax, but left a local income tax in place, structured so as to ensure redistribution from rich to poor districts.

This had a number of intriguing consequences noted by a study commissioned by the Blair government in 2004, the Balance of Funding review. One was a marked though not wide divergence in service levels between areas in response to local elections.[5] Despite this a 2004 Swedish parliamentary commission recommended no change in the local income tax regime 'since it has clearly encouraged a high degree of interest and participation in local politics by the Swedish electorate'. The British review discerned in Swedish local government 'at least five different policy models, from traditional social democracy to Thatcherite neo-liberalism'. This gave the lie to the thesis that modern social democracy could not tolerate local diversity of service standards.

More radical was Sweden's institution in 1984 of the 'free commune' concept. This stipulated that towns could opt to supply certain services on their own if they were prepared to finance them. David Marquand wrote that 'this followed growing evidence during the 1970s of public disillusionment with the public sector, which was seen as unresponsive and over-bureaucratic. Service was not close to the public and failed to involve the public as citizens.'[6] Initially nine municipalities and three counties were awarded almost total autonomy to run, variously, schools, primary health care, welfare and housing, subject only to audit and grant redistribution. Within five years, 284 'freedoms' had been delegated, a quarter for education and the rest for local inspection, housing, planning and primary health care. Many of these powers were demanded by communes not from central government but from superior counties.

The free commune idea swept Scandinavia, being adopted by Denmark in 1985 and Norway in 1986. In Denmark this followed a comprehensive restructuring of the state in 1970. Public services were devolved to 14 counties, roughly the size of England's, and 275 municipalities. Half the latter were of no more than 10,000 people, often no bigger than British parishes. Counties ran hospitals and secondary schools, municipalities ran primary schools, care of the elderly, roads, culture and the administration of state benefits. The county hospitals have only 5 per cent of patients choosing (as they are free to do) out-of-county care and are considered among the most cost-efficient in Europe, consuming just 6 per cent of the national income. They also register a high level of satisfaction and performance.[7] Two-thirds of all public spending in Denmark is local, financed 70 per cent by a local income tax, 22 per cent by central grant and the rest from a local property tax. Localism gives Danish municipalities a sense of ownership. Their disbursing of state benefits has avoided much of the fraud prevalent in Britain.

In each of these countries the bugbear of all local government reform has been deciding on the appropriate pattern of financial redistribution, how to marry a desire for national standards to an acceptance that local choice may lead to inequality. No state resolves this paradox in the same way, or without conflict. In France and Italy each decade has seen a battle between localities and the centre. In Sweden and Norway attempts have been made to cap local income tax and ring-fence central grants. In Germany localism is regarded as an impediment to economic reform. Power shifts back and forth and argument does not cease. Localism is the stuff of politics.

This debate has been fiercest in Spain. The death of Franco and the new 1978 constitution posed the same questions as faced the Allies in post-war Germany and Italy — how to appease regional sensibilities previously checked by dictatorship. The result was a 'state of autonomies' in which each province enjoyed a variable devolution from Madrid. A 1992 constitutional reform offered partial autonomy to all provinces, similar to that previously granted to Catalonia, Galicia and the Basque country. Delegated functions embraced health, education, police and even lawmaking. Big cities are now largely independent of their provinces. The mayor of Barcelona travels the world as head of a virtual city state. In 2006 Catalonia voted itself even more autonomy.

In Spain an extraordinary range of taxes can be levied locally, including property and business taxes and imposts on wealth, gambling, construction, vehicles and a negotiated portion of national income tax. The Madrid government must fight each rich province to withhold enough money to redistribute to poor ones, yet accepts that these autonomies are crucial to maintaining the integrity of the state. As in Germany and Italy, a respect for the dignity of Spanish cities has been the key to their renascent morale.

Only in the United Kingdom has the political establishment remained largely immune from this devolutionist movement. After the Second World War the nation came to see itself as a unitary welfare state, politically monolithic and administratively homogeneous. Britain realized Henry James's claim that 'all England is a suburb of London.' Its dominant institutions were concentrated in the capital, home to MPs, civil servants, journalists, commentators, finance and commerce. Any complaint of maladministration was sent to London. Anyone who sought a lottery grant sought it from London. Each morning those administering the state tuned in to the BBC in London or opened a London-edited newspaper. Public debate on hospitals or schools almost invariably referred to those located in the capital, because that is where those conducting the debate lived. In December 2005 I watched a BBC interviewer, Jeremy Paxman, lash out at a junior minister for the inadequate supply of foam to meet a fire in Hertfordshire. No one had died and the fire was eventually put out. Yet it did not occur to either interviewer or interviewee to point out that putting out fires had nothing to do with London ministers. They were a local responsibility. If a story was important enough for national television then responsibility had to be national, as if it was beneath the BBC's dignity to interview someone from local government.

Those inhabiting the metropolis felt little need of contact with provincial Britain. The nation beyond the capital was that of a university town or weekend cottage. Proudly familiar with Paris, Rome, Barcelona or New York, London's establishment of politicians and journalists would be lost in Manchester, Birmingham or Leeds. English words used of the provinces were contemptuous: parochial, tin-pot, petty, parish pump, bog standard, the word provincial itself. National stories about local government, in general or particular, tended to be derogatory if not derisory. This approach to localism was reflected in statistics, usually in the form of lists. These became a national obsession. To the 'ten best' and 'hundred best' were added league tables, pie charts and bar charts galore. Pages of newspapers were filled with best and worst schools, hospitals and police forces, with comparative waiting lists, mugging figures, speeding fines and cannabis penalties. The most potent political cliché of the age was the post code lottery. It suggested that any variation in a public service was not democracy working but a sin against the constitution. That a waiting list should be longer in Doncaster than Dorchester, a driving fine higher in Cumbria than in Kent or a school library bigger in York than in Yeovil was 'scandalous'. There was never mention of post-code choice.

The principle behind league tables, like that of government targets, was not ignoble. It was that of social equity, a relic of welfare equality in a unitary state. But it was dangerously potent. The media was encouraged to hunt down 'worst performers' and castigate them. Any citizen in receipt of a lower quality of public service than any other had a grievance not against his or her council but against central government. The failure to prescribe the same drug, offer the same school place or impose the same punishment was not a local choice but an offence against the nation. The instinctive response was that it must be stopped, and by a minister.

British centralism in the 1980s was the new opium of the people. Worn out by decades of bad news, Britons simply wanted recourse to nanny. They wanted to be able to hide behind her skirts and burst into tears when anything went wrong. When the media howled, government reacted with soothing platitude and subsidy. Society conformed to de Tocqueville's description of the social atomism of post-Revolutionary France:

Every man is a stranger to the destiny of others. His children and personal friends form for him the entire human race. As for the remainder of his fellow citizens, he is beside them but he does not see them ... while above them rises an immense and tutelary power, that of the state.

This state, in the 1830s as in the 2000s, 'enforces without difficulty an admirable regularity to the routine of business, provides skilfully for the details of social control ... and perpetuates a drowsy regularity in the conduct of affairs.'

The consequence has been a remarkable collapse of British public life. A citizen of a typical American suburb or small town might expect to devote a night a week to some civic activity. French, Germans, Swiss or Scandinavians are commonly embroiled in the affairs of their commune, not just because it rules part of their lives but out of a sense of democratic obligation. Eighty per cent of Germans can name their local mayor. Few Britons can name any elected politician below the level of cabinet. Fewer Britons are actively involved in elected office than in any other democracy. Each of 22,000 elected British councillors answers to an average constituency of

2,600 voters. The equivalent collective is 667 in Sweden, 250 in Germany and 116 in France.[8] In most democracies people expect to know those who represent them. As a result local election turnout is 80 per cent in Sweden and 70 per cent in Germany. In Britain it is 35 per cent and in cities drops below 30 per cent. Local politics is inert.

I do not believe that Britons are inherently less democratic than others. They practise other forms of lay participation, serving on public bodies such as school governing boards or non-elected quangos. Alongside 22,000 elected councillors are ranged some 60,000 appointed local equivalents, nearly three times as many. This so-called 'new magistracy' rules Britain under the patronage not of direct democracy but of ministers of the Crown. Even under the newly elected Greater London Authority, roughly ten times as many Londoners involved in governing the capital are appointed as are elected. The pattern is repeated everywhere in a proliferation of health authorities, police authorities, development agencies and training councils. These people serve on one condition, that they need not submit themselves to election. The condition reflects what Bernard Crick has called Britain's 'fear of politics', an aversion to democratic answerability. Some might call it a hangover of monarchical deference. People will volunteer to be consulted ad hoc. They will rise and fight a threatened housing estate, wind farm or hunting ban. They will do 'just-in-time' politics. But regular participation is beyond their comfort zone.

The British have grown used to delegating upwards, to leaving to national government the job of supplying public services on demand – and to complaining bitterly when they are not delivered. Yet behind this apparent acquiescence with centralism is a growing disaffection, reflected in a mismatch between what people claim to want from their services – usually locality, convenience and efficiency – and what Thatcherite ministers claim to offer – competition, privatization and choice. That a solution might lie not in accreting further power to the centre but in devolving it has long been present in political debate, but tentatively and in Opposition rather than in government.

The young Tony Blair claimed to be alert to all this. He had been drawn to John Macmurray's Christian socialism, to the ideal of citizens owing a duty to society alongside that owed by society to them.[9] This was rekindled by his acquaintance with the American sociologist Amitai Etzioni, who held that Thatcher's individualism had been at the expense of 'communitarianism'. Etzioni was even lauded as 'the father of Tony Blair's big idea'.[10] An enthusiasm for some vague appreciation of community empowerment was the nearest Blair came in Opposition to an ideological reformulation of new Labour socialism. When in 1995 I and others produced the report of the Commission on Local Democracy, Blair went to the trouble of noting it and summoning us to talk about it. From a creative conversation emerged his commitment to elected mayors. These found their way into the 1997 manifesto, alongside devolution for Scotland and Wales and a pledge of 'a ten-year programme of reform to revitalise local democracy'. I was impressed by Labour's localist programme and was duly ridiculed by the Tory centralist David Willetts as one of 'Blair's communitarian gurus'.[11] In retrospect, it was probably another of Blair's Don Giovanni moments – something he meant at the time.

The new Labour government did honour its manifesto in signing the ten-year-old European Charter of Local Self-Government but it did not honour the honouring. The charter required extensive local autonomy, including that 'public responsibilities shall generally be exercised . . . by those authorities which are closest to the citizen.' Powers given to local authorities 'should normally be full and exclusive'. Central grants should not be ring-fenced. Localities should be left with 'discretion in adapting their exercise of powers to local conditions'.[12] None of this was implemented, indeed under Brown the charter was disregarded lock, stock and barrel. Despite clear manifesto commitments there was no end to rate capping and no return of business rates to council control.

The one project on which the new government did embark was Scottish and Welsh devolution, pledges so specific there was no escape. Bills were presented for a parliament in Scotland and an assembly in Wales, with another to install an elected mayor and assembly in London. Other cities were empowered to choose mayors, though in such a way that few did. Scotland won most. It acquired a First Minister and cabinet, could levy a 2p income tax and run its own health and transport services, in addition to its existing education and legal autonomy. The new powers were little more than Scottish local government had lost since the 1970s, but allying them to an accountable parliament in Edinburgh made the devolution seem new. The Scots were to complain about their parliament, not least the cost of its fine building, but there was never any question of reverting to direct rule from London.

The same applied to a lesser extent in Wales. Unlike in Scotland, the assembly was given no legislative status or fund-raising powers, indeed the Cardiff executive enjoyed less autonomy than a Welsh county council before Thatcher. Yet the fusion of devolved administration with a political entity, the assembly, enabled even Welsh devolution to take root under the leadership of Rhodri Morgan. When a revision of assembly responsibilities was suggested by Lord Richard in 2005 the only question was how many more might be granted. A measure of de facto legislative devolution was granted in 2006. Living part of the year in Wales I have no doubt that political and executive devolution has been real.

Devolved government, however, is not local government. A condition of Scottish and Welsh devolution was an insistence by Whitehall on 'unitary authorities' beneath them. These bore no reference to communities on the ground, which found themselves stripped of true self-government and subject to officers resident many miles away. Towns and villages in rural Wales and Scotland were not empowered by devolution but disempowered. The mid-Welsh seaside village of Aberdovey found itself administered from Caernarvon in North Wales, unreachable by train and almost two hours away by car. The nearby market town of Machynlleth used to have a council, a leader, a town hall and ownership of its local institutions, as would any other European municipality. It was now ruled by the unitary authority of Powys. Its local politics were reduced to constant protests against distant authority. What is devolution seen from above is the opposite when viewed from below.

In the case of devolution to London, Blair refused to surrender power remotely commensurate with its size and status. The Greater London Authority Act was so full of ministerial discretion, the so-called 'Henry VIII clauses', that it was the longest ever passed by parliament. Though the Metropolitan Police was supposedly devolved to a new police authority, the Home Office continued to treat it as its own. Roads, housing policy, commuter railways, the restructuring of the Tube were all retained by ministers. Whitehall's Government Office for London was, by 2005, actually larger than it had been before the Greater London Authority existed.

Elected mayors elsewhere were strongly opposed by local Labour parties dominant in the big cities. Only twelve had appeared by 2001 but where they did break the mould of party control they proved popular, experiencing three times the recognition rate of previous council leaders. Ten were re-elected for second terms in 2005.[13] Other councils opted for cabinets to replace open committees, if anything entrenching the party control that mayors were intended to break. Elected mayors were a ghostly presence in later reform proposals, but as long as local party leaders were free to reject them they had little chance of revival.

Earlier chapters have shown how devolution ran against the grain of Westminster and Whitehall. A senior official suggested to me that had Blair not been so committed by the manifesto, the Treasury and Downing Street together would have stopped the Scottish Parliament and Welsh Assembly in their tracks. Blair himself was angry when the Welsh rejected the man he had chosen as First Minister, Alun Michael. Likewise in London he tried to deposit his health secretary, Frank Dobson, into the new mayoralty as Labour candidate and was humiliated by the success of the independent, Ken Livingstone. When both Scotland and Wales adopted different policies from England on hospital care and student fees, Blair was furious. He admitted to Paddy Ashdown that had he known what devolution meant he would not have gone ahead: 'You can't have Scotland doing something different from the rest of Britain ... I am beginning to see the defects in all this devolution stuff.'[14]

The minister charged with pushing through English devolution was John Prescott, who did at least have a framework in mind. If Scotland and Wales were to enjoy a measure of autonomy, he said, why not the regions of England? In 1994 the Tories had set up eight regional offices of Whitehall to relocate staff away from the capital. These had already developed empires of their own as chief recipients of power progressively removed from elected county councils and districts. Labour in Opposition had protested that they should be more accountable and Prescott decided to honour that commitment by making them subject to elected assemblies, a dream set out in his 2002 White Paper, 'Your Region, Your Choice'.

The attempt was a fiasco. Prescott's eight regions were intended one day to be distinct governments on a par with Scotland and Wales. But the regions proposed were mostly meaningless geographical entities named by compass points. More serious, they came with Prescott's threat to wind up subordinate counties altogether. He initially proposed referendums on the most plausible regions, Yorkshire, the North-West and the North-East. The first of these, for a North-East assembly, was held in November 2004 and resoundingly rejected, by 78 per cent to 22 per cent on a considerable turnout of 48 per cent. The North-East vote was clearly a rejection of a new tier of government that would deprive people of Durham and Northumberland of their counties and remove civic power from Newcastle, Gateshead and Sunderland. Prescott's reaction was extraordinary. What was clearly a democratic rejection of regional government as such, he treated as a rejection only of giving such an entity a democratic base. He duly proceeded to set up a fully staffed regional office at an administrative cost of £2.2 million a year. Wary of any more referendums he repeated this undemocratic structure on his own initiative across the seven other English regions.[15] As an exercise in devolution it was cynical.

Regional Development Agencies, quangos already launched in 1999, now blossomed into complete government entities untrammelled by any local accountability. Instead of elected assemblies Prescott appointed consultative boards enjoying resources and powers direct from him. The Eastern board even established 'embassies' in Paris, Chicago and Tokyo.[16] From 2004 the regions enjoyed a 'cross-departmental single pot' of £1.8 billion, though with little control over its spending. Suspicious of quangos, the Treasury ordained that 'decisions on switching funding between policy areas would be made as part of the spending review process within the national context.' This would be determined 'by the relevant secretary of state'.[17] This was not English devolution in any form.

The reason for the failure of elected regional government in England was not hard to see. Regions are top-down constructs. Britons, like most Europeans, identify with tiers of loyalty, with their neighbourhood or parish and with a superior city or county. Such entities as Brittany or Sicily or Catalonia derive from ancient kingdoms or principalities. They have cohering histories, geographies and dialects, constituting what social geographers call communities of sentiment. Loyalty to them is often as fierce as to an overarching nation. They are a political fact recognized by the European Union in its 'committee of the regions'.

In the United Kingdom such loyalty certainly attaches to the Irish, Scots and Welsh, now reflected in varying degrees of devolution. England is seen from Whitehall as politically homogeneous, its subdivisions essentially a matter of administrative convenience to be redrawn at will. Yet it too has its subsidiary loyalties, reflected in counties. These embrace the separatism of Cornishmen, the chauvinism of Lancastrians and Yorkshiremen and the milder local pride of Cumbrians, East Anglians and men of Kent. (Among cities, only Bristol has never formally been part of a county.) Prescott's regionalism ignored this geography, regarding county loyalty as a sporting foible and music hall joke. He viewed national administration as a seamless web while his officials saw counties as too small and disparate for their convenience. Far from acting as the building blocks of a new devolution, like Wales and Scotland, counties were a threat both to sound government and to national standards.

The desire of central elites to break the ties of localism has a long tradition. America's founding fathers struggled, with only partial success, to suppress states' rights. The French Revolution disempowered feudal provinces by creating *départements* which cut across their boundaries. Historic place names were replaced by those of natural features, such as Var, Seine and Lot-et-Garonne. When in the 1970s Whitehall reorganized metropolitan government, its instinct was that of the *directoire*. It abolished Bristol, Hull and Liverpool and replaced them with Avon, Humberside and Merseyside. It imitated Orwell's *1984* with anonymous names such as West Midlands and the extraordinary 'South-East-Lancashire-North-East-Cheshire' or 'Selnec'. When amalgamating police authorities the Home Office revived a Hobbit-land of forgotten kingdoms such as Mercia, Wessex and Powys. Nor could Whitehall ever agree on what was a 'standard region', let alone one that might be recognized as such by electors or citizens. Cornwall was forced into the same region as Gloucestershire, Buckinghamshire as Kent and Cheshire as Cumberland. A MORI poll in 2005 reported that fewer respondents had heard of a quango called the South-East England Regional Assembly than recognized the entirely fictional 'South East Environmental Group', inserted by the pollsters as a control.[18] In his 1996 survey of regionalism in England, Brian Hogwood discovered no fewer than 100 different ways of subdividing the country variously in use in Whitehall.

Having established his administrative regions, Prescott did everything to draw power up to them from subordinate authorities, chiefly from counties and cities. Below the level of region he wanted all local government to be 'unitary', based on cities, small counties such as Worcestershire or Berkshire, or giant districts (as in Wales). Thus the once-proud town of Cirencester in Gloucestershire was to become Cotswold District in the South-West Region. The town of Totnes was to become South Hams District and Devon was to be forgotten. The chief responsibilities of English counties in land-use planning, economic development and education were to be removed from them and given to regional officials. To Prescott counties were about cricket teams and lord lieutenants.

The size of Prescott's unitary authorities became a source of constant confusion. Outside big cities the lowest tier of administration in England is the borough or county district, of which there are 472 with an average population of 118,400. During discussions over a regional body for the north-east, Prescott proposed sub-regional districts with populations of some 300,000. Similar lowest-tier authorities were formed in Wales, few of which corresponded to any area of local identity. These are units of local government beyond all comparison in size or intimacy with administrations abroad. In France democratically accountable communes have an average population of 1,600. The German average is 5,000, the Italian 7,000.[19] Government at such a distance from its electorate is not local at all.

Not a year passed under Labour without a new plan involving the de facto abolition of English counties. All White Paper references to devolving Whitehall powers referred to regions or 'communities'. Local government ministers such as David Miliband and Yvette Cooper lauded the virtues of localism yet without regard to its democratic underpinning. The occasional mooting of elected school governors, district police authorities and hospital trust boards scrupulously avoided reference to county, city or even parish councils. It was as if ministers found local politics an aberration, a ghost of Labour's past. Outside London they were like T.S. Eliot's magi, who found 'the cities hostile and the towns unfriendly and the villages dirty.'

The difficulty for ministers was that a beleaguered local democracy continued to exist through all this hostility. It still administered roughly a quarter of all public services, struggling with the most complex framework of central control anywhere in Europe. In 1999 I sat in the offices of York city council, a medium-sized unitary authority. Until Thatcher's rate-capping, its councillors and officers had decided for themselves how to take forward the affairs of York. They were not irresponsible. They fixed local priorities and if citizens did not like what was offered, they could say so at council meetings or in the press. If necessary they could vote the council out of office, which they periodically did. Councils were regularly toppled. In London in the 1970s a majority of London boroughs changed hands at least once. It was just not true, as ministers of both parties kept saying, that 'local government is not working'.

Yet by 1999 democracy had become a pathetic wraith flitting through

York's majestic Mansion House. On the chief executive's computer were listed some 600 Whitehall performance indicators covering every aspect of his work. The targets related not to any locally determined policy or priority. They related to the ambitions of ministers, as decided between spending departments and the Treasury. Dotted lines on graphs led all over the place, to agencies and quangos with different pots of money attached to them. There were sixty-seven such agencies listed. The chief executive pointed out that his diary was entirely filled with visiting inspectors, many angry that he did not have time to see them all. Had he done so he would have done no other work.

The pages of the *Local Government Chronicle*, *Municipal Journal* and *Public Finance* listed each week's batch of targets with mounting incredulity. On to Public Service Agreements were spliced best-value indicators, supplementing the Audit Commission's 1992 performance indicators, which soon rose to fifty-four. For a while councils had two sets of targets for the same service, quite apart from local ones. A conscientious council struggling to fix rubbish collection schedules or ambulance response times would find it had no sooner done so than a new target was on its screen. An army of accountants and inspectors came into being to try to order this chaos.

For local councils targetry was further complicated by the ring-fencing of central grant. This required the Treasury to follow every pound of public money through the system. Grant was first cohered into a functional 'silo', say for education or roads, and then 'passported' direct to the relevant local department. Other money was parcelled between central task forces and agencies, to be distributed ad hoc and with its own targets attached. If a council wished to get extra money for a project it might have to choose from fifteen central agencies relevant to that cause, each brandishing a mission statement and performance regime. Money might also be subject to competitive bidding within a cash-limited pot.

When the London Borough of Hammersmith refashioned its youth programme it had no scope to finance it locally. Such spending would drive it up against its rate cap. Instead it had to go to Whitehall, where it faced sixteen possible programme sponsors in a variety of Whitehall ministries. Apart from those dealing directly with children and young people these included Building Safer Communities, Domestic Violence Coordination, Drugs Strategy Capacity Fund and Criminal Justice Intervention. Each had offices, staff and consultants to be fed before any cash reached the front line. Hammersmith's perceived need for its youth services would eventually bear little relation to what it might secure from the centre.

By the time of the 2001 election the failure of centralism to deliver public satisfaction in the conduct of public services led some observers of modern British government to question its central premise. Might the trouble be not a lack of sufficient command and control at the centre but an excess of it? Might Thatcherism's solution not be the problem? Under Blair's second administration the 'new localism' became the subject of steadily widening debate. Think tanks devoted to the subject sprang up on the left and right, such as the New Local Government Network (NLGN), Policy Exchange and Localis. The NLGN had produced a pamphlet entitled 'Towards a New Localism' in 2000, harking back, somewhat unfortunately, to Thatcherism's ill-conceived concept of a contractual relationship between arms of the public sector, in this case the centre and locality.

The Tories produced a series of documents supposedly recanting their own centralism in government. The Conservative Political Centre attacked the 'vicious circle of escalating control', with a bizarre claim that this began only with the Labour government in 1997.[20] In 2004 Michael Howard as Tory leader decided that elected mayors were not a bad idea after all and even proposed directly elected police chiefs. In 2005 the new Tory leader, David Cameron, told his MPs to eschew national policies and become local personalities. The message was to adopt 'extreme localism' in their constituencies.[21] He did not say what this meant, but the word had acquired the status of a political icon.

Even the government was infected. Gordon Brown found himself making a speech in January 2001 in which he claimed that the country was 'moving from the old Britain of subjects, where people had to look upwards to a Whitehall bureaucracy for their solutions, to a Britain of citizens where, region by region, we are in charge.' The 'we' was not intended to be royal. Four years later he was in the same mode, with the extraordinary declaration (for the Treasury) that

Our long held commitment to liberty demands also that we break up any centralized institutions that are too remote and insensitive, devolving and decentralizing power, encouraging structures and initiatives so that the power so devolved brings real self-government to communities.[22]

He added that his own view was that 'the new politics cannot be a reality

unless we make local accountability work by reinvigorating the democratically elected mechanisms of local areas – local government.' Singing from
the same hymn-sheet was Brown's aide, Ed Balls. Having recently fought to
centralize the schools and prevent hospital autonomy, Balls announced that
state centralization 'saps morale . . . destroys innovation and experimenta-
tion . . . and fails to allow that different policy areas must in fact be
interconnected at the local level.'[23] It was hard to tell if he was serious.

Prescott's office soon had a department devoted to writing speeches and
White Papers (more green than white) with such titles as 'Strong Local
Leadership – Quality Public Services'. They called for a rebirth of 'civic pride'
and trumpeted the 'magnificent municipal achievements of the nineteenth
century'. A Home Office minister, Hazel Blears, declared that 'if new
localism is to be anything more than the latest political buzz-phrase it must
mean passing real power to local communities.'[24] The health secretary, John
Reid, after appointing twelve 'tsars' claimed that the NHS was 'moving
beyond managerialism into genuine local ownership'.[25] Meanwhile Sir
Andrew Turnbull, for the civil service, announced in 2003 that 'decentralisation hasn't gone far enough' and that Whitehall's role in local government
should be only to ensure that it 'meet certain minimum standards'.[26] In his
valedictory lecture Turnbull, a supporter of targets, admitted they had led
to 'a wholly nationalised public sector with an intolerable burden of responsibility falling on ministers and central officials.'

This burst of interest in localism was best summed up by the outgoing
head of Blair's strategy unit, Geoff Mulgan. 'After several decades of centralisation,' he wrote in 2002, 'the pendulum is now decisively swinging in
the opposite direction. Politicians and civil servants have recognised the limits of central command, particularly over services which are inherently local
. . . The emphasis now is on devolution, fewer targets and more local accountability.' Mulgan was at least aware of a potential clash between such
emphasis and calls from the Westminster community for standardization and
equity. Across the localist path, he wrote, lay 'the uneven capacity and legitimacy of local government . . . and the fact that public demands for
guaranteed minimum standards are, if anything, becoming more intense.'[27]

These demands confronted the new localism with another Thatcherite
paradox. The economist John Kay pointed to an open conflict 'between
legitimacy conferred from the top down through the blessing of elected
politicians . . . and a market-based economy in which legitimacy in economic

matters is carned from the bottom up in meeting consumers' needs.'[28] Some Thatcherites had posited the new local democracy as that of consumerism, the choice being not of the ballot box but of the market place. Labour appeared to be reverting to the Tory localist ideal of choice-based health and education. Might that be localism enough?

To the left-wing commentator David Walker, this was precisely the danger in the whole debate. Local elected autonomy (especially if it were Tory) was no more egalitarian than Kay's local market. If it meant diversity on any basis it was unacceptable, since diversity implied unfairness.[29] To Walker equality of treatment in a modern social democracy could only be delivered through central discipline, whether or not this meant the superstructure of the classical welfare state. Walker could not explain why social democracies throughout Europe contrived to resolve the localist paradox.

To those working in local government all this was little more than a Westminster conversation. More real by far were the increasing signs that centralization was approaching Whitehall parody. A body called the Better Regulation Task Force declared in 2002 that there were now so many regulators that it could no longer list them.[30] In the same year a review of 'devolved decision-making' called for the number of Public Service Agreements to be slashed from over 600 to 130. Sensing the new mood the Audit Commission pledged a 'target cull' and the Treasury a 'quango cull'. The latter even set a target for reducing 'arm's length bodies' by half, their staff by a third and their expenditure by a quarter. Gordon Brown ordered Sir Peter Gershon to see how this could be done. Gershon concluded that 80,000 posts, many only recently filled, were surplus to requirements, with £9 billion available for savings. Nobody asked who had authorized such extraordinary waste in the first place. These cuts targets proved to be mostly fantasy. Though some reductions took place in 2003–4, they were usually jobs shifted or redefined. The Treasury felt obliged to repeat similar pledges annually. By 2005 the amount supposedly available for cuts had risen to £21 billion within three years.

The Treasury body charged with implementing this, Gershon's own Office of Government Commerce, grew exponentially. It was revealed in 2006 to have spent £43 million itself on 'cutting bureaucracy' while in one year alone its budget for external consultants had risen from £5.8 million to £9.2 million.[31] In autumn 2005 the Local Government Association bitterly pointed out that the only branch of the public sector that had met

Gershon's efficiency targets that year was local government. In February 2006 researchers for BBC *Newsnight* found that while 19,000 civil service jobs had indeed been 'cut' more than that had been hired, yielding a net increase of 300 jobs. The Office of National Statistics was less forgiving. It revealed in July 2006 that public sector staff numbers rose by 79,000 in 2004 and 24,000 in 2005.

A more successful attempt was made to reduce targetry in local government. In 2001 Performance Indicators, Best Value targets and the Beacon Council scheme were merged into Local Public Service Agreements, no longer imposed top-down but supposedly negotiated with local councils. A year later these were swept up in yet another initiative, Comprehensive Performance Assessment. This was based on a five-division league table of councils, with twenty-two 'excellent' (formerly beacon) ones in the premier division. This group was termed an Innovation Forum under which winners selected by Whitehall were allowed various financial benefits and autonomies. They were even invited to Buckingham Palace garden parties. As for bad performers they would be subject not to the judgement of their electors but to 'a comprehensive programme of inspection to monitor progress'. Lest anyone think this meant decentralized policy, priorities or tax-raising, the Treasury announced in 2004 that full rate-capping, so far observed only in the breach, was to be reintroduced for 2005.

In a development that came close to farce, Whitehall then decided that localism required yet another adjustment to the oversight of local government. The recent Comprehensive Performance Assessment was not enough and had to be supplemented with Local Area Agreements (LAAs), cohered into Local Strategic Partnerships. These were to embrace councils, health and police authorities, businesses and the voluntary sector. They sought to compress some seventy revenue streams from seventeen Whitehall sources into three 'themed pots' within which councils could enjoy a measure of discretion over allocations. The themes were typically Blairite: 'safer and stronger communities', 'healthier communities and old people' and 'children' not including education. Schools and police would remain in ring-fenced silos. Local Area Agreements were described by Whitehall as 'experiments in delegation' (they were in truth a return to aspects of old local government). In a wide-ranging analysis of these attempts at decentralization, Tony Travers of the LSE concluded that 'by 2005 new localism had not demonstrably improved either the quality of public services or the strength of local democracy in the way its proponents had hoped.'[32]

Oddest of all was the government's concept of lowest-tier local government. David Miliband and others gave speech after speech on what he called 'double devolution', in which neither tier was defined. To John Prescott, before his replacement by Ruth Kelly in 2006, it appeared to mean regions and unitary authorities but to Miliband it sometimes meant city regions and districts, sometimes counties and 'communities'. Miliband said merely that 'devolution should not stop at the town hall'[33] and that rather than give more power to town halls, there should be 'opportunities for all communities to have more control over their own neighbourhoods'.[34] A White Paper on 'Why Neighbourhoods Matter' (2005) preached 'a more adaptive state' and demanded choice, responsiveness, creativity and reliability. Whatever this meant, the most obvious candidates for double devolution were England's 8,500 parishes and town and neighbourhood councils, albeit serving only 30 per cent of electors, mostly in rural areas. Though their powers were minimal – in most cases just a few thousand pounds a year for street decoration and community centres – they were elected and in place, and the closest Britain came to communal representation on a European model. Yet ministers seemed averse even to them. They wanted 'good localists', defined as unelected single-issue bodies such as foundation hospital trusts, school governors and social housing boards. They did not want bad localists, associated with political elections. The Labour government's bias against democracy was near pathological.

Ministers lauded a new stage army of so-called stakeholders, partners, conveners, voluntary organizations and 'social entrepreneurs'. The word stakeholder was intriguing, redolent of those with some privileged position or access, as opposed to ordinary citizens. They seemed to replace citizens as meriting consultation or concern, reminiscent of Burke's men of property, the yeomen and copyholders of the restricted franchise whose chief characteristic, as Burke said, was precisely 'to be unequal'.[35] Blair's stakeholders carried banners blazoned with such words as sustainable, participation, inclusion, diversity, contestability and choice. Equal in the eyes of government they were not.

In one area the pressure for change moved from fantasy to practicality. Each year the stuff of localism, the council tax, had to be fixed. The banding system for valuing property had proved particularly severe on old people. Each year yielded a handful of pensioners demonstrating in Whitehall and even going to jail. Blair found himself falling under the same spell as had afflicted Major, Thatcher and Heath. In 2003 he repeated the pledge to review Britain's local tax system in favour of some 'more acceptable' alternative. He seemed blind to the bloodstained walls and stalking ghosts of Downing Street, and announced a 'balance of funding review' under his local government minister, Nick Raynsford. Its purpose was, yet again, to find some new way of financing local services other than the existing one.

Raynsford's 2004 report was remarkably thorough. It investigated local taxes across Europe and offered a series of options for ministers to consider 'on their merits'. It warned that Britain's local revenues were among the lowest in Europe, covering just 4 per cent of public-sector income and falling lightly on richer tax-payers. The top valuation threshold of £350,000 was clearly too low and should be increased (as it was with the recently introduced I-band in Wales). Witnesses suggested other taxes, including on businesses, incomes and possibly tourism. Ministers facing the 2005 general election panicked and shelved Raynsford's report. Instead a Downing Street appointee, Sir Michael Lyons, was asked to review the review, but not until after the election. This was the seventh substantive inquiry into local finance since 1979, and Blair's third.

Ministers were as terrified as was Thatcher of any change in property valuation. Blair refused to allow the revaluation scheduled for 2006 to proceed, fearing that rich home owners would find their property jumping a band (even if poorer ones by definition dropped one).[36] With the Tories recklessly promising to 'abolish the council tax' and the Liberal Democrats offering a shift to local income tax, the outlook for reform was grim. After the 2005 election, the Lyons review was further postponed by being asked to embrace the whole function of local government. Such a constitutional reform would once have involved a bipartisan Royal Commission, as with Redcliffe-Maud in 1969. Now it was put in the hands of one man and a small office, rendering his advice the more easy to reject.

If radicals were hoping that the new localism might have led British government towards a synthesis of the first and second Thatcher revolutions they were disappointed. There was little doubt that the political establishment craved a new approach to public service reform and even sensed where it might lie – witness speeches and writings advocating decentralization by almost all the players in British politics in the new decade. In an article in February 2006 Blair himself acknowledged that his centralism had become unsustainable, pleading that 'I have given away more prime ministerial power than any predecessor for more than 100 years'.[37] The reality was that for all this talk, a constitutional movement that had swept Europe in the last quarter of the twentieth century avoided the United Kingdom. This was not for any lack of revolutionary zeal. It was because Thatcher, Major and Blair seemed unable to stand back and analyse British government at each stage in their revolution. They never dared ask if the resistance they encountered to reform in the public sector might have arisen from accreting too much power to their office rather than too little. They each ended up with a revolution, indeed two revolutions, but with nowhere to take them.

PART SEVEN

The Third Revolution

20

The Third Revolution

I once met a man walking his dog in a small seaside township in Connecticut, New England. He was a Wall Street lawyer, a second-homer in the town
and the elected comptroller of its council. Though not a long-standing local
he held the job with pride and took it seriously. One reason was that the
local taxes on his simple clapboard house were $20,000 a year. He told
me he was about to face a town meeting at which he had to persuade his
fellow citizens to pay for a new fire station. They would be furious at the
expense and it was his job to find a fair way of imposing the burden. The
decision would be on a show of hands, a tradition of local democracy that
stretched back to the English vestry, imported at the time of the Pilgrim
Fathers.

The town meeting was a controversial feature of New England democracy. To some it was self-government at its most pure, to others it was mob
rule in microcosm. But any idea of abolishing it would have sparked a second American revolution. The elementary school, the fire station, the library,
the park, the quayside, the character of the neighbourhood, belonged to
the town's citizens, as did revenue from the quay and the car park. They
expected to be involved in the life of their communities, even at a considerable cost in time and money. It was their right and their obligation, handed
down from those who once called themselves 'free-born Englishmen'.

Self-government is not and never can be an idea distinct from its practical purpose as a means of organizing a social collective. To work properly
requires citizens to have sufficient information about the doings of a community and some acquaintance with those governing it. That is why the
town meeting remains the ideal against which all forms of government
should be tested. It marries information and acquaintance to consent. Political theory acknowledges this. It reiterates that democracy relegated to the
atomized accountability of a periodic national ballot is barely worth the
name. It requires the habit and practice of association, which for most
people can have meaning only in the context of their locality. As the American maxim puts it, all politics is local. In ordering a modern state the only

question is how local is local and how is that locality to be related to the state. In other words democracy is essentially a matter of tiers, or as another maxim puts it, 'blood, sweat and tiers'.

Even the United Kingdom is locally pluralist. Ask someone where he or she is from and you receive answers reflecting different levels of loyalty and identity. Someone from London, Manchester or Newcastle will say just that, unless pressed to specify Islington or Trafford or Jesmond. Smaller communities evince more complex answers, such as 'Cromer in Norfolk' or 'Howden in Yorkshire'. Into the Celtic fringe the tiers become threefold: Scotland, Oban in Argyll or Wales, Newtown in Montgomeryshire. Such names are not just historic hangovers. They have socio-geographical references, concentric circles that people expect to see reflected in how they are known and how they are governed. Government is always about tiers of identity, not just administrative convenience.

A localist programme for England, Wales, Scotland and Northern Ireland must in some degree respect the counties, cities, boroughs and parishes to which British people claim allegiance, as they never do to 'districts' or regional designations. The attempt of recent governments to eliminate traditional nomenclature is not just anti-democratic but, as was seen with Avon and Humberside, doomed to fail. Tradition has kept the institutions of government of these places in being, even as their powers have been stripped away. Counties and cities still retain statutory responsibility variously for schools, roads, social services, care homes, fire, police and ambulance services, albeit often in collaboration with neighbours. Only health and the administration of justice fall wholly outside their scope.

My third revolution would formally, fiercely and emphatically take powers from the centre and restore them to British counties and cities and subordinate communities in precisely the way that other European states have done with success and to general public satisfaction. The powers would be those that have been usurped over the past half century. There would be remarkably little difficulty in doing this. The centralization of recent decades has been effected largely through discretionary or 'Henry VIII' clauses in statutes, allowing ministers to make orders at will. Powers removed by executive order can be restored that way. Whitehall can withdraw its assumed control over education, planning and economic development merely by saying so and dismantling the regional offices through which things are ruled. The policy initiatives, ring-fenced budgets and 'policy silos' can be abolished and replaced with the clean-cut block grants as before. Exactly this process was enacted in Sweden in the 1990s.

Local government would revert to local democracy, as expressed through local elections, from the great corporations of Birmingham, Bristol and Leeds to the smallest village parish. The cities, like the pre-1970s county boroughs of over 150,000 people, would be unitary authorities. Outside the cities the counties would resume their old functions, forming alliances where appropriate with adjacent cities (as with police and ambulances)[1] or with other counties. The one additional function that should be delegated to local councils is health care. Public health devolved to local government is, throughout Europe, more efficient and delivers greater satisfaction than does the increasingly crippled NHS. Primary care and hospital trusts should revert to the local government administration that existed before the Second World War, with which many are already coterminous. The present government's crude attempt to make NHS trusts locally elected has failed. If local accountability is craved, as clearly it is, use the democracy already in place.

I set out such a programme in detail in *Big Bang Localism*.[2] It is designed to involve no great redrawing of boundaries or reallocating of functions, no widespread hiring or firing of staff (except within Whitehall). Yet it would abolish two complete tiers of existing public administration. The two to go would be the regions and most existing rural districts. The first is not radical. Regions are new and both Opposition parties called for their abolition at the 2005 election. They are dispersed replicas of Whitehall, multiplying by eight what was previously done in London and extraordinarily expensive, chief cause of the extra civil servants hired since 1997. The abolition of district councils would be more controversial, but they have been an unstable, often anonymous, form of local administration, too distant from their communities yet not distant enough to have been given any real discretion by counties or government. Below the level of counties local government should be truly local, devolved to what are currently town, community and parish councils, the 'communities and communes' of new localist lore.

The latter would become the building blocks of local democracy. Such communes are familiar to every known democratic system. In France they are as large as a city or as small as a hamlet. They are noble or corrupt, rich or poor, but they belong to their citizens. Any trawl across the Continent, to Switzerland, France, Sweden or Germany, finds such local communities delivering services which in Britain have long departed to higher authority. Management theorists from Schumacher to Drucker have pleaded that economies of scale are illusory, except in armies and manufacturing industries. Most organizations are more effective in small units, especially those delivering personal services. They are more open to innovation and respond better to leadership. Any study of the United Nations will attest that tiny states can enjoy full sovereignty without loss of efficiency, indeed the smaller they are the more contented they tend to be. Europe's smallest political entities, Luxembourg, Slovenia, Denmark, Iceland, are most successful deliverers of public services. Economies of scale do not exist in public administration, least of all in the age of privatization and subcontracting. Size is not an issue. The issue is who decides, who gives out the contract, who votes and who is responsible to the voters.

Taking British local administration closer to the grass roots would reinvigorate what is in fact a 'sleeping tier' of democracy, the 10,000 mostly rural parishes (in England and Wales). Some are relatively active, administering small budgets on environmental and leisure services. My own in Wales has an annual budget of £4,000, spent chiefly on potted plants. Most are purely consultative. Yet they are elected, meet and consult with local people and know local circumstances. Roughly 100,000 councillors nationwide already constitute by far the largest pool of active democratic participation, yet it is one that is almost completely unused. Not just counties but cities should be required to formulate a framework of community (or 'neighbourhood') government, much as is being tried in Birmingham. The Labour government committed itself to introducing 'urban parishes' in 1997 but declined to implement them.

Under full county devolution, district councils would be abolished, their staff and councillors redistributed to subordinate towns and parishes. The Continental tradition of the local town hall, the 'vestry houses' of old, would be the one-stop shop for such administration. These councils would not only administer local by-laws, licensing and possibly the administration of social benefits (as in Scandinavia). They would have charge of local public buildings, including sports halls, markets, pavilions, churches, clinics and possibly primary schools. One of the saddest features of British civic life is the lack of pride taken by local people in their immediate environment. The reason is that they do not own or control it. It 'belongs' to some distant authority in a town other than theirs. They are in every sense disempowered.

This is no great or radical reform. It restores rights and autonomies to civic life enjoyed in the eighteenth, nineteenth and twentieth centuries and removed only recently. Two-tier local democracy – perhaps a genuine version of Miliband's ersatz 'double devolution' – would be universal. To make any new pattern of local democracy bite it has to have access not just to power but to money of its own. For twenty years the Treasury has been tilting the balance of funding from local to central government, reducing the burden on local ratepayers and increasing it on national taxes. In the past five years this process has been reversed and local taxes have risen by more than double the rate of inflation, much to the fury of those on fixed incomes, who regard such taxes as national ones, locally imposed. Britain's local taxes are still among the lowest in the world, raising just 4 per cent of total public-sector revenue. That proportion is 50 per cent in Sweden, 18 per cent in Germany and 13 per cent in France.

For the new devolution to have meaning, local taxes must increase their contribution to spending. The British were once said to pay their income taxes in sorrow and their rates in anger. The reason is that central taxes are usually deducted at source, whereas local ones require the signing of a cheque. But this is why local taxes are politically responsive. They have democratic bite. Thatcher defended her poll tax for precisely that reason: it would engage citizens in the efficient delivery of services and drive them to the polls. 'The principle of accountability underlay the whole reform', Thatcher wrote. She then negated it by introducing 'more extensive capping than was ever envisaged under the rates'.[3] A true Thatcherite should at least recognize the good amid the bad.

The way to bring both greater fairness and more democratic accountability to local government would be to spread the fiscal load. All local taxes in Britain are on property, which has always seemed unfair to poorer people, especially the old still living in big houses. It is unfair also to those living alone or on fixed incomes when local taxes are rising faster than inflation. Property taxes, though they are efficient and a reasonable impost on living space, are associated with unfairness. The obvious solution is to mix them with other forms of taxation, as apply universally in other countries, usually reflecting some ability to pay. Income taxes now comprise a third of local and provincial revenue in most of Scandinavia and 100 per cent in Denmark. The allocation to local councils in Britain of up to a 2 per cent income tax would hardly breach any constitutional principle, as it is already allowed in Scotland. A fiscal mix might thus include a reduced property tax topped up by a small tax on businesses and incomes and a wider range of service charges, as in America's business improvement districts. Such a proposal is hardly radical. It was set out in the Local Government Association's evidence to the balance of funding review in 2004. A similar plan was discussed by Tony Travers and Lorena Esposito in *Nothing to Lose but Your Chains*.[4] Douglas Carswell put forward a vigorous case for a local sales tax in *Paying for Localism*.[5] There is no shortage of ideas on the table for paying for local government, only the courage to implement them.

The Labour government's objection to all such fiscal reform was summed up by two Labour ministers, Nick Raynsford and Yvette Cooper, in a pamphlet in 2004. Local tax-raising would lead, said Cooper, to 'the worst kind of nimbyism, divisive inequalities and deep conservatism'[6]. She did not explain how the rest of left-wing Europe lived with just such a system. Any framework of local taxation must grapple with the issue of equity. But that is what every framework does already – including Britain's. It must embrace redistribution from rich to poor, both within and between territorial jurisdictions. A model is offered by McLean and McMillan in their proposed 'coarse' scheme, avoiding the obscure mathematical formulae beloved of Whitehall.[7]

Any move from Britain's centralism to a dynamic localism would be traumatic for some. The cry would go up that local politicians are no good, that local institutions cannot take the strain, that all reform is expensive and that the system is not so broken as to need mending. Highly publicized failures would encourage people to plead for a return to the comfort zone of centralism. Two assumptions lie behind such objections. One is that central officials and politicians in Britain are inherently more competent, better qualified and less corrupt than local ones. There is not a shred of evidence for such prejudice, asserted though it is daily in the press and by (national) politicians. On any measure of efficiency, such as sticking to budgets, cutting bureaucracy or toughness in pay negotiation, local government now outperforms central government. Local councils are not allowed to go into the red, as the NHS does, or borrow beyond their own limits, as does the Treasury. The great fiascos of public finance of recent years, notably in computer procurement, have come from Whitehall. The supremacy of British central administration over local is simply a myth.[8]

The other assumption is that the quality of people available for local government would not be up to the extra duties imposed on them. The obvious answer is that good people will not do work that is not worth doing. There is no doubt that the decline in trust and responsibility allowed councillors by the centre had led many to retire to private life or to less stressful quango appointments. Yet research conducted for the Commission on Local Democracy (CLD) found it hard to justify a claim that councillors were appreciably less qualified or that turnover was higher than used to be the case.[9] The chief handicap to service most often cited was not time but the dominance of local parties over the opportunity for advancement. There can be little doubt that party politics has dogged the reputation of local government service and prevented new blood from coming forward for positions of leadership. The most marked difference between cities in Britain and elsewhere in Europe is the absence in Britain of charismatic and ambitious leaders using local politics as a springboard for national office. Yet deploring the role of political parties in local government is naive. Parties are the cornerstone of responsible government, the key to accountability and a defence against both mob rule and elected dictatorship. They are a component of democracy and, given the widespread decline (not confined to Britain) in party membership, their future is a matter of concern.

Modern parties reflect the changing environment in which they operate, especially where they are in power for long periods of time and come to be identified with government itself. The rise of the Liberal Democrats locally is a sign of a reaction against this longevity, and shows that local democracy is still in working order. In more open democracies parties are more the servants of aspiring leaders than their masters. They are conduits, not dams, to participation. It was this above all that motivated the CLD to press for direct mayoral election in local government – and this that motivated local parties fiercely to oppose it. The opening up of politics in cities that did opt for direct election, such as London, Middlesbrough, Hartlepool and Stoke, has proved the point. If British citizens are less active in running their communities than foreigners it is because local party machines form so hostile an environment.

The devolution of power from the centre to localities lies at the heart of my third revolution. Restoring local autonomy within the United Kingdom involves no leap in the dark but a return to a constitutional dispensation familiar both from Britain's past and from the rest of Europe's present. The drift of power to the centre has eroded but not ended the tradition of local participation. It has diluted the will to engage in civic affairs and dimmed the obligation to community service. Thatcher, Major and Blair have been enemies of civic pride. Yet nobody could say that Britons are inherently more selfish and less democratic than Germans, French, Danes or Americans. This must be an absurd claim.

Any revolution aimed at diminishing the power of central government must probably originate in Opposition. Parties out of power are more likely to promise to divest government of power than parties in it. It was a policy developed in Opposition that led Labour's momentum to devolution in 1997–9, and even then the forces of centralism fought back. That is why I believe such innovation requires both a strong manifesto commitment and an emphatic programme such as a democracy 'Big Bang', similar to the overnight deregulation of the City of London in 1986. This would involve a highly publicized movement to involve people afresh in community government, followed by an overnight transfer of power to local institutions, a 'bonfire of controls' like that with which the Tories returned to office in 1951.

The bonfire should be a literal one, with teachers, doctors, police officers and council officials wheeling cartloads of circulars and central documents to a prominent local site and burning them. The moment would be like the passage of France's *loi Deferre*, a transfer not of ownership but of responsibility, of obligation. Like all revolutions, such a Big Bang would need national political initiation. The functions remaining to central government would need specifying, including mechanisms for auditing minimum standards and fixing the basis of grant redistribution. Such audit should be under statutory rather than ministerial control, under a local government commission independent of Whitehall. This commission would have two functions. The first would be to oversee Britain's honouring of the European Charter of Local Government, as yet in abeyance. It would formally vet each county and city proposal for second-tier devolution, to ensure that functions are properly allocated to subsidiary neighbourhoods, municipalities and parishes. The second function would be to oversee fiscal redistribution, both between central government and the counties/cities and within those entities, between communities. As McLean and McMillan point out, 'the new localism requires robust non-political grant commissions, independent of central government, to determine needs both at the level of the regions and at the level of the individual local authority.'¹⁰ None of this is problematic for the simple reason that everyone else is doing it already. Models exist abroad and were listed in the government's own 2004 balance of funding review.

Some such devolutionary framework is essential if this third revolution is to guard the legacy of the best of the Thatcher era and dispense with the worst. It means a willingness on the part of the London political community to devolve to subsidiary democracy the sort of power it has already learned to shed to Scotland and Wales. This means also shedding the universalist assumptions that have underlain that power, the aversion to local option and the obsession with post-code lottery. It means a shift from less visible to more visible taxation and, in most parts of the country, a shift in the tax burden from poorer to richer citizens. Nor should such devolution be confined to geography. It should restore professional autonomy to groups which have endured constant upheaval over the past two decades both in and on the fringes of the public sector, doctors, teachers, academics, lawyers, policemen, civil servants. Such upheavals may have been necessary for a while but are now starkly demoralizing. Reform should be aimed at reducing the inclination whenever anything goes wrong to expect the government to act, and in doing so relieve professionals of responsibility. It should pluralize not just government but responsibility, trust, risk and blame.

Few people in the free world are lucky enough to live in communities run on similar lines to that of my Connecticut banker. He is rich and able to conduct his self-government within the courtesies of a stable and comfortable community. But most people round the world, rich and poor, enjoy a local empowerment that has become unknown in Britain. From the shanty-towns of Latin America to an Indian village or a Swiss canton citizens expect to be involved in decisions affecting their immediate surroundings. They know by name those who purport to be in charge of them, be they honest or corrupt. They acknowledge that welfare requires public administration to be firm and equitable. But they also expect to choose local priorities and pay for them. The concept of individual and family choice so beloved of Thatcherites should extend to their neighbourhoods and their communities. Self-government cannot define itself as government by others.

Conclusion

Thirty years after its genesis, Thatcherism was still regarded by most Britons with bemusement. What was this word, this ideology, this policy, this woman, who dominated the lives of so many yet with which few seemed to have sympathy? To its acolytes there was no argument because there was no alternative. To both left and right the conservative tradition in British politics was as good as dead. Revolution, reform, change was all. Thatcher said so and Blair agreed. His continued quest for competition and choice in state health and education left his party angry and the country baffled. Nor was his chancellor, Gordon Brown, far behind, as he struggled to privatize ever more of the health service, the Post Office, law and order and even job centres. There was no evidence of public support for any of these measures, indeed quite the reverse. One survey found only 19 per cent of the public eager for choice in public services and 43 per cent who wanted 'an end to continuing reforms'.[1] Yet the Blair government seemed on a Thatcherite autopilot. It could not stop.

Young Britons viewed the Thatcher era much as older ones had viewed Attlee's welfare state. They took it for granted. They had forgotten, or never knew, what it was to live in Seventies Britain, in a nation defeatist and at war with itself, sliding towards the bottom of the European league. They accepted the essentials of the first Thatcher revolution: state institutions privatized or put out to tender, taxes diverted from income to expenditure, markets deregulated and social background no longer crucial to wealth or influence. Immigration was widely tolerated as part of an open economy, if not an open community. Britain in the new century was a lean, tough, enterprising place, ready to fight its corner in the world.

Those who maintain that this revolution was merely a swing of the political pendulum must acknowledge that a transformation occurred in Britain after 1979 that was not seen elsewhere. The bitterly fought reforms of the 1980s were not replicated in the rest of Europe, and are being so only now. By the turn of the century governments round the world were recognizing that a more prosperous Britain had found at least one answer to the resistance to change that afflicts modern social democracies. Domestic competition and privatization inspired both Reaganomics in America and the market economics that swept East Europe after the fall of the Iron Curtain. Even those most acerbic anti-Thatcherites, the corporatist states of Continental western Europe, came grudgingly to admit that the lady had something right. She had an answer to the stresses that globalization imposed on a national political economy, an answer summed up in the word leadership.

Blair and Brown can take credit for recognizing this in the mid-1990s, when left-wing parties on the Continent were in the relative Dark Ages. They, like Thatcher, had watched 'socialism tested to destruction' under successive Labour and Conservative governments. They accepted her cry that 'there is no alternative', if only because they conspicuously had none of their own. Their zeal to change became a zeal to sustain the revolution. In education, health and transport they undid Thatcher's reforms but, within five years, were re-enacting them. The public sector was soon awash in 'para-government', in public/private partnerships and social entrepreneurs. Public investment in hospitals and schools all but ceased in favour of private. National and local services were handed over to private firms while consultants supplanted career civil servants at the heart of Whitehall. The ethos of Blair's government could not have been further from Labour's political roots. Its leaders openly consorted with business tycoons and showered honours on the very rich. At the 2005 election all three major party manifestos subscribed to the Thatcherite consensus. Nothing suggested a reversion to the *status quo ante* 1979.

Yet we are left with the demoralized and turbulent condition of much of British public administration in the middle of the new decade, and the discontent of the public and the political community with the state of public services. Only when viewed as a whole does the recent incompetence of modern British government come into focus: the poll tax, rail privatization, the on-off saga of hospital autonomy, computer procurement, child maintenance, farm support and tax credits. The litany seems endless. These are fiascos that have cost taxpayers untold billions of pounds. Twenty-five years into the revolution, there is no sense of a job well done, of a new regime in place and working. There is only a cry from government for more reform, more reorganization, more change and a supporting chorus for more to be done, for more power to be grasped and deployed, for more of the second revolution.

The localist must accept that this revolution is not something that the British people instinctively resist. Unlike Thatcher's first revolution, the second has not overly alarmed the electorate. As long as the new 'elected dictators' submit themselves to a periodic franchise, Britons seem content with what Michael Oakeshott called a 'warm, compensated servitude', slavery mitigated by the welfare state.[2] They might moan about regulation, red tape, the nanny state and 'control freaks' in government, but the concept of an overbearing central power does not upset them as it does most Continental Europeans. Britons might deplore bureaucratic aggrandizement in Brussels, but they take in their stride a similar aggrandizement in Westminster. They have been taught, some might say indoctrinated, by Whiggish historians that parliament offers an institutional safeguard against dictatorship.

A partial explanation for this complacency is relief after the horrors of the 1970s. Thatcherism in whatever form is given credit for rescuing Britain from the politics of the past. Government is no longer associated in the public mind with crisis, decline and scandal. Ministries no longer stand or fall on recessions and currency collapses. Domestic politics does not mean strikes and riots but concerns itself with such mundane matters as a bankrupt hospital, an undermanned police force or a dodgy peerage. If centralism is the price to pay for this comparative triviality, so be it, goes the argument.

As a result matters that would barely merit a national headline in most countries are laid at the door of central government. It agrees to take responsibility for every aspect of public service because politicians like an opportunity for gaining credit even at the cost of accepting blame. Such centralism relies on public complacency and also fuels it. It is bread and circuses, with bread as ever more egalitarian welfare and circuses as the regular evisceration of a politician at the hands of the national media. As we saw in Chapter 17, the performance of British public administration is not wholly negative. A curiosity of regular MORI polls was that satisfaction with the local delivery of a service tended to be far higher than the reputation of that service nationally.[3] There were marked improvements over the 1980s and 1990s in primary schools, child poverty, property crime, hospital waiting lists and the welfare of old people. Whether the improvement was commensurate with the greatly increased sums of money spent was hard to determine. Less happy was performance in mental health, penal policy and aspects of public transport. Yet none of this impacted on the central fact, that those who were consuming and paying for these services professed themselves unhappy with them.

Government's response was more of the same. Centralists, like Marxists, are adept at suggesting that their revolution would work better if only they had imposed it with more conviction, and perhaps 'got their message over better'. Those pondering the future of the British constitution in the age of public-sector turmoil spill over with ways of updating and selling it. There are numberless London think tanks devoted to such arcane topics as House of Lords reform, changes in voting systems, a better civil service, e-democracy or an independent supreme court.[4] Their fascination with buzzwords knows no bounds. But every suggestion is a version of the same, how better to manage an ever more centralized state. Thus the 'steered centralism' adumbrated by Miliband and others, like earned autonomy and trust status, is Blair's old communitarianism repackaged for the new hands-on patronage state. It is not so much a corrective to the second revolution as its holy confessional.

Blair's response was classical Thatcherism. In 2005–6 he appeared desperate to fashion a legacy based on re-establishing the internal market in the NHS and its equivalent in secondary education, and in privatizing the delivery of a range of public services. Brown's 2006 Budget showed no let-up in the zest for private risk capital to underpin his targets for public investment. Yet these reforms were besieged on two fronts, from angry Labour MPs and from the delivery system itself, engulfed in reorganization and bureaucracy. As fast as civil servants were laid off they were rehired as inspectors and auditors. As fast as regulations were repealed, new ones were passed. The growth in central regulation under Thatcherism was attributed to many causes, to the European Union, negligence law, league tables and rising public expectations, but whatever the cause the effect was more red tape. In 2006 well-established services such as emergency GPs, legal aid, child support, immigration control and farm subsidies were close to collapse. The failure of the deportation system for released foreign prisoners brought the dismissal of the home secretary, Charles Clarke. It was hard to claim that Britain in the 2000s was being well governed.

When Sir Andrew Turnbull defended the target culture as concentrating the civil service mind on value for money, he entered a caveat as to the cost in diminished professional respect, leadership and trust. These are not tangential concerns. Management theorists have long pointed out that self-aggrandizement is the natural law of bureaucracy. As government distances itself from direct contact with the public, impersonal regulation replaces local discretion. Individuals and groups, no longer empowered to judge priorities for themselves, trust others only insofar as they are scrupulously and manifestly fair. The media punishes any deviation from the national norm as a 'post-code lottery'. The effect is to remove personal discretion from a citizen and bestow it on an agent of the state.

In her 2004 Reith Lectures the philosopher Onora O'Neill sounded a note of warning about this. When individuals and the professionals on whom they customarily rely are denied responsibility for risk, said O'Neill, a part of their humanity is diminished. The individual is socialized. You may increase openness and transparency in government, as Thatcher and Blair pledged to do, but this does not increase trust. Indeed if anything trust had receded as transparency advanced. 'Perhaps we should not be surprised,' said O'Neill, 'that the technologies that spread information so easily are just as good at spreading misinformation and disinformation.'[5] Trust in self-government depends on trust in confidences, even secrets, bred of personal acquaintance and professional respect. People long to trust others but if they have bred in them a 'culture of suspicion' they will not do so. This problem echoed that described by le Grand (in Chapter 17) where the knightly professionals of state philanthropy are transformed into the knavish subcontractors of Thatcherism. It is a conundrum to which neither of Thatcherism's revolutions had an answer, except to bring in the lawyers and accountants.

The political scientist Kieron O'Hara offered small-c conservatives at least one answer to this. The duty of reform, he wrote in *After Blair*, is to re-establish bonds of trust between leaders and led. 'Older forms of social interaction have been rendered irrelevant or irrecoverable by changes ... brought in under the freedom facilitated by market liberalism.'[6] Conservatism to O'Hara properly relies on continuity of institutions and processes. It has little future in a world 'with a dramatically decreasing local element, as globalisation continues to promote cultural homogeneity'. Hence the conservative mind has both to grasp the necessity of the Thatcher revolution and yet tame it and return it to the institutional cohesion that another Tory thinker, John Gray, said it had destroyed. To such observers Thatcherism has very little to do with conservatism and everything to do with its antithesis, radical liberalism. As Gray put it, 'By imposing on people a regime of incessant change and permanent revolution, unencumbered market institutions deplete the stock of historical memory on which cultural identity depends.'[7]

Such neo-conservative responses to Thatcherism and the Blairite 'change agenda' have been suggested for too many years to count. Both the debate and events have passed them by. The revolution has proved too powerful. The consequence has been the remorseless march not of big government as such but of big, intrusive and incompetent government. That is why I prefer to seek the trust of which O'Neill, Gray and O'Hara speak, with justified concern, in a political tradition lost in Britain but alive abroad. That tradition is of self-government properly so-called, lying at the intermediate tier above family and neighbourhood but well below that of the nation state. Democracy can only be based on tiers of autonomy, on people trusting people who trust other people, on a hierarchy of trusts. Only thus will we allow others to exercise judgements and accept risk on our behalf. Otherwise public service degenerates into a miasma of league tables and statistics.

The icon of Thatcherism's public-sector ideology is the contract, the idea that a legal bargain can somehow be struck between the state and a subcontractor in favour of a third party, a private citizen or community of citizens, between the producers and consumers of personal services. The contract principle met its nadir in railway privatization, in NHS purchasers/providers and in deals between local councils and firms such as Capita and Serco. They came to supersede the quasi-philanthropic relationships on which public service used to be based, where loyalty and continuity, a concern for others, even acquaintance, formed the basis of social responsibility.

Because I doubt whether the contract principle can ever forge a compromise between the first and second Thatcher revolutions, I have searched for a third. Modern government, whatever its purpose, becomes more inefficient the more distant it is from its patron, the voter and taxpayer, and its consumer, those same people. Such distance wastes huge sums of money. It subcontracts delivery in the belief that this will be more effective, and merely finds it less effective. It employs ever more staff to check on ever more staff because it does not trust people to act alone. As we have seen throughout this book, it ends by promising the opposite of what it does, centralizing when it claims to decentralize. As David Runciman has pointed out in *The Politics of Good Intentions*, intentions are rarely in touch with the politics of reality. Dictators say the same as democrats, that they meant well and perhaps history will be a fairer judge than the present.[8] When they fail to deliver they claim that it is not their fault but is somehow 'systemic', to use a favourite Blair word.

I regard centralism as Thatcher did socialism, as inherent in the nature of the modern state. It is a consequence of power. The tendency of states unconstrained by constitutions to self-empowerment is instinctive and ineluctable. This was crudely apparent after 2001 when Blair exploited the politics of fear in insisting on Britain's vulnerability to 'global terror'. He declared, 'I feel passionately that we are in mortal danger of mistaking the nature of the new world in which we live.' A novel risk properly exploited is, as Ulrich Beck has written, always an elixir to an ailing leader.[9] Saddam Hussein and a London bomb were enough for Blair to put the state on constant alert and demand an ever greater concentration of power on Downing Street. It fed the appetite of the second revolution and its most avaricious champion, the Home Office. Terrorism bills were being passed every year, seeking temporary powers but making them permanent. Americans were appalled when the president tapped phones, against the rules of the constitution. In Britain there was no such outcry because there was no constitutional tradition of such civic rights. When no limit is set to state power, it is indeed unlimited. The wall round Downing Street always rises and the prime minister's entourage always needs another armoured car and another phone-tapping directive.

Such statism has no answer to the classic paradox of Leviathan, how to prevent the beast from savaging its master, how to prevent the state from devouring the freedoms it was created to uphold. That is why the third revolution to which I have pinned my colours confronts state power head on. It seeks to fill what William Waldegrave, in *The Binding of Leviathan*, called 'the vacuum between the state and the individual', by reviving communities in which the individual participates, against which he appeals the state ... but which [do] not look to the state for their origin or substance.'[10] It challenges the state from outside, from other sources of democratic legitimacy and political participation, those of locality in the form of the subsidiary provinces, counties, cities and parishes of the United Kingdom. It makes rolling back the frontier of the state not a utopian ideal but a practical reality, achieved through specific changes in the practice of White-hall. It is not the whole answer to constitutional reform, but without it I am confident there will be none.

Politics never delivers endings. Its conflicts are regulated by ideologies which are themselves creatures of time and place. The philosopher R. G. Collingwood pointed out that all constitutions are by their nature relativist.[11] Their custodians are therefore under a duty not just to keep their charges in good repair but to read history and be guided by it. At the time of the millennium the Norwegian government commissioned a group of scholars to survey the state of their democracy and predict where it might be in a century's time. The work, some fifty volumes long, inquired into every aspect of Norway's political life.[12] Its conclusion was not optimistic. Norway was sliding away from the participatory self-government it had enjoyed for a hundred years. The conduits of public consent were becoming choked. Material comfort had led to a diminution in voluntary participation in public life, reducing it to 'just-in-time' activism. Parties, unions and other quasi-political groups had withered and thereby ceded power to an Oslo elite of politicians, technocrats, bankers, lawyers and journalists. Many Britons might find the analysis familiar at home. The scholars suggested that democracy as traditionally conceived might even prove a passing phase in Norway's history, to be replaced by a meritocratic oligarchy, an updated version of Aristotle's aristocracy.

Every student of political thought knows that an atomized, centralized democracy is not democracy but a pastiche. It offers the individual a vote followed by a temptation to relax, to escape from the obligations of family and community in favour of some more generalized top-down welfare. It is a macrocosm of the parent who cannot be bothered to discipline the child and leaves the teacher, policeman or magistrate to do it instead – and then complains when it is not done. Such an attitude to public life may be comfortable for the time being. Such a democracy may exchange elites, though under Norway's proportional representation it does so rarely. But individuals come to lose what they most crave, control over the circumstances of their environs, self-government. They are politically lobotomized.

It was never part of either the liberal or the conservative prospectus, of radicalism or of continuity, to sacrifice individualism on the altar of egalitarianism. Democracy is a bargain struck between personal and group autonomy and the authority of the state. But it is a bargain not a subjugation. The history of twentieth-century Europe is evidence enough of the importance of that distinction. The Norwegian prescription is similar to mine. Self-government must be an active concept. Working democracy, participatory democracy, must be tiered according to sub-national loyalties and identities. Individuals, families and neighbourhoods must be empowered as they are in the vigorously democratic settlements of North America. Europeans may point up the flaws in American democracy, but it has absorbed the most sustained human migration in modern times while continuing to nurture human freedom and sustain prosperity. As Jonathan Freedland remarked in his spirited essay on the virtues of American constitutionalism, the basis for this achievement was a political tradition exported to America by European Puritans – and now much in need of repatriation.[13]

The history of democracy in Britain began as local, baronial consent granted upwards to the monarch. Over the course of the nineteenth century it became a form of government granted downwards by the centre to localities and then withdrawn, at least in respect of local administration, in the latter half of the twentieth century. I believe it to be as a result of this withdrawal that the British people are exceptional not in the poor quality of their public services but in their restless dissatisfaction with them. They endure a constitutional fatalism, an acceptance of centralist drift, as part of their belief in a quiet life. Yet centralism cannot deliver. While power by its nature seeks the centre, so a dynamic constitution must disperse it to the periphery, to find citizens ready to keep it in good repair. The localist route to democratic revival is plausible. It has been operating across Europe for two decades as the one movement likely to stem the rise in the power and scope of the modern state. It is thus the true synthesis of the two revolutions which Thatcher initiated in 1979 and which have formed the character of British politics ever since.

Select Bibliography

Abse, Leo, *Margaret, Daughter of Beatrice*, Jonathan Cape, 1989

Allen, Graham, *The Last Prime Minister*, Politico's, 2003

Ashdown, Paddy, *Diaries, 1988–1997*, Penguin, 2001

Baker, Kenneth, *The Turbulent Years*, Faber and Faber, 1993

Batley, Richard and Gerry Stoker, *Local Government in Europe*, Macmillan, 1991

Beer, Sam, *Britain Against Itself*, Faber and Faber, 1982

Beetham, David, Iain Byrne, Pauline Ngan and Stuart Weir, *Democracy under Blair*, Politico's, 2002

Blick, Andrew, *People Who Live in the Dark*, Politico's, 2004

Bower, Tom, *Gordon Brown*, HarperCollins, 2004

Butler, David, Andrew Adonis and Tony Travers, *Failure in British Government*, Oxford University Press, 1994

Campbell, John, *Edward Heath*, Random House, 1993

—, *Margaret Thatcher*, 2 vols., HarperCollins, 1993, 1995

Carrington, Peter, *Reflect on Things Past*, HarperCollins, 1988

Clark, Alan, *Diaries*, Weidenfeld and Nicolson, 1993

Clarke, Peter, *A Question of Leadership*, Penguin, 1991

Cockett, Richard, *Thinking the Unthinkable*, HarperCollins, 1994

Commission for Local Democracy, 'Taking Charge', *Municipal Journal*, 1995

Craig, David and Richard Brooks, *Plundering the Public Sector*, Constable, 2006

Crouch, Colin and David Marquand, *The New Centralism*, Blackwell, 1989

Foster, Christopher, *British Government in Crisis*, Oxford University Press, 2005

Freedland, Jonathan, *Bring Home the Revolution*, Fourth Estate, 1998

Freedman, Lawrence, *History of the Falklands War*, Routledge, 2005

Gamble, Andrew, *The Free Economy and the Strong State*, Macmillan, 1994

Giddens, Anthony, *The Third Way*, Polity Press, 1998

Gilmour, Ian, *Dancing with Dogma: Britain under Thatcherism*, Simon and Schuster, 1992

Gould, Philip, *The Unfinished Revolution*, Abacus, 1999

Grainger, J.H., *Tony Blair and the Ideal Type*, Societas, 2005

Hastings, Max and Simon Jenkins, *The Battle for the Falklands*, Michael Joseph, 1983

Hennessy, Peter, *The Prime Minister*, Penguin, 2001

Hogg, Sarah and Jonathan Hill, *Too Close to Call*, Little, Brown, 1995

Hood, Christopher, et al., *Regulation Inside Government*, Oxford University Press, 1999

Hoskyns, John, *Just in Time*, Aurum, 2000

Howe, Geoffrey, *Conflict of Loyalty*, Macmillan, 1994

Howell, David, *The Edge of Now*, Macmillan, 2000

Hurd, Douglas, *End to Promises*, Collins, 1979

——, *Memoirs*, Macmillan, 2003

Hyman, Peter, *One out of Ten*, Vintage, 2005

Jenkins, Simon, *Accountable to None: The Tory Nationalisation of Britain*, Penguin, 1996

——, *Big Bang Localism*, Policy Exchange, 2005

Jones, Nicholas, *Soundbites and Spin Doctors*, Cassell, 1995

Jowell, Jeffrey and Dawn Oliver, *The Changing Constitution*, Clarendon Press, 2004

Kampfner, John, *Blair's Wars*, Free Press, 2003

Keegan, William, *The Prudence of Mr Gordon Brown*, Wiley, 2003

Lawson, Nigel, *The View from No 11*, Bantam, 1992

Letwin, Shirley, *The Anatomy of Thatcherism*, Fontana, 1992

Macintyre, Donald, *Mandelson*, HarperCollins, 1999

Maddox, Brenda, *Maggie*, Coronet, 2003

Major, John, *The Autobiography*, HarperCollins, 1999

Mandelson, Peter and Roger Liddle, *The Blair Revolution*, Politico's, 2003

Marquand, David, *The Decline of the Public*, Polity Press, 2004

Marr, Andrew, *Ruling Britannia*, Michael Joseph, 1995

Meyer, Christopher, *DC Confidential*, Weidenfeld and Nicolson, 2005

Mount, Ferdinand, *The British Constitution*, Heinemann, 1992

Naughtie, James, *The Rivals*, Fourth Estate, 2001

Oborne, Peter, *The Rise of Political Lying*, Free Press, 2005

Oborne, Peter and Simon Walters, *Alastair Campbell*, Aurum, 1999

O'Hara, Keiron, *After Blair*, Icon Books, 2005

O'Neill, Onora, *A Question of Trust*, Cambridge University Press, 2002

Peston, Robert, *Brown's Britain*, Short Books, 2005

Pliatsky, Leo, *The Treasury Under Mrs Thatcher*, Blackwell, 1989

Prior, James, *Balance of Power*, Hamish Hamilton, 1986

Pugliese, Stanislao and Iain Dale, eds., *The Political Legacy of Margaret Thatcher*, Politico's, 2003

Randle, Anna, *Mayors Mid-term*, New Local Government Network, 2004

Rawnsley, Andrew, *Servants of the People*, Penguin, 2001

Rentoul, John, *Tony Blair*, Little, Brown, 2001

Richards, Paul, ed., *Tony Blair in His Own Words*, Politico's, 2004

Riddell, Peter, *The Thatcher Era*, Blackwell, 1991

—, *Hug Them Close*, Politico's, 2003

—, *The Unfulfilled Prime Minister*, Politico's, 2005

Ridley, Nicholas, *My Style of Government*, Hutchinson, 1991

Roe, Philippa and Alistair Craig, *Reforming the PFI*, CPS, 2004

Routledge, Paul, *Gordon Brown*, Simon and Schuster, 1998

Runciman, David, *The Politics of Good Intentions*, Princeton University Press, 2006

Russell, Meg, *Building New Labour: The Politics of Party Organisation*, Palgrave Macmillan, 2005

Scott, Derek, *Off Whitehall*, Tauris, 2004

Seldon, Anthony, *Major: A Political Life*, Weidenfeld and Nicolson, 1997

—, *Blair*, Free Press, 2004

Seldon, Anthony, ed., *The Blair Effect 1997–2001*, Little, Brown, 2001

Seldon, Anthony and Dennis Kavanagh, eds., *The Blair Effect 2001–5*, Cambridge University Press, 2005

Sherman, Alfred, *The Paradoxes of Power: Reflections on the Thatcher Interlude*, Imprint Academic, 2005

Skidelsky, Robert, ed., *Thatcherism*, Chatto and Windus, 1988

Stephens, Philip, *Blair: The Price of Leadership*, Politico's, 2004

Stoker, Gerry, *Why Politics Matters*, Palgrave Macmillan, 2006

Stothard, Peter, *30 Days, A Month at the Heart of Blair's War*, HarperCollins, 2003

Sutherland, Keith, *The Party's Over*, Imprint Academic, 2004

Sutherland, Keith, ed., *The Rape of the Constitution?* Imprint Academic, 2002

Thatcher, Carol, *Below the Parapet*, HarperCollins, 1996

Thatcher, Margaret, *The Downing Street Years*, HarperCollins, 1993

—, *The Path to Power*, HarperCollins, 1995

Toynbee, Polly and David Walker, *Better or Worse: Has Labour Delivered?* Bloomsbury, 2005

Travers, Tony et al., *The Government of London*, Joseph Rowntree Foundation, 1991

Urban, George, *Diplomacy and Disillusion and the Court of Margaret Thatcher*, Tauris, 1996

Waldegrave, William, *The Binding of Leviathan*, Hamish Hamilton, 1978

Wheatcroft, Geoffrey, *The Strange Death of Tory England*, Penguin, 2005

Wolmar, Christian, *On the Wrong Line*, Aurum, 2005

Worcester, Robert, Roger Mortimer and Paul Baines, *Explaining Labour's Landslip*, Politico's, 2005

Young, Hugo, *One of Us,* Macmillan, 1989

Young, Hugo and Anne Sloman, *'But Chancellor'*, BBC Books, 1984

Notes

Introduction

1. Private information.
2. Robert Skidelsky, ed., *Thatcherism*, Chatto and Windus, 1988, p. 18.
3. See Ivor Crewe in Skidelsky, ed., *Thatcherism*.
4. Brenda Maddox, *Maggie*, Coronet, 2003.
5. Described in Richard Cockett, *Thinking the Unthinkable*, HarperCollins, 1994.
6. See Alfred Sherman, *The Paradoxes of Power: Reflections on the Thatcher Interlude*, Imprint Academic, 2005.
7. See J.H. Grainger on Weber and Blair in *Tony Blair and the Ideal Type*, Societas, 2005.
8. Isaiah Berlin, *Karl Marx*, Fontana, 1995, p. 41.
9. Ibid., p. 112.
10. Ibid., p. 16.
11. Eric Hobsbawm, *Politics for a Rational Left*, Verso, 1989, p. 90.
12. Margaret Thatcher, *The Path to Power*, HarperCollins, 1995, p. 277.
13. David Marquand, *Ramsay MacDonald*, Jonathan Cape, 1977, p. 791.

1 Climbing the Ladder

1. John Campbell, *Margaret Thatcher*, 2 vols., HarperCollins, 1993, 1995. Vol. I, p. 2.
2. Alan Clark, *Diaries*, Weidenfeld and Nicolson, 1993, p. 384.
3. But see Thatcher, *Path to Power*, p. 107.
4. Leo Abse, *Margaret, Daughter of Beatrice*, Jonathan Cape, 1989.
5. Charles Dellheim, in Stanislao Pugliese and Iain Dale, eds., *The Political Legacy of Margaret Thatcher*, Politico's, 2003.
6. Thatcher, *Path to Power*, p. 106.

7. Campbell, *Margaret Thatcher*, I, p. 33.

8. Ibid., p. 49.

9. Ibid., p. 50.

10. Thatcher, *Path to Power*, p. 48.

11. Ibid.

12. Campbell, *Margaret Thatcher*, I, p. 64.

13. Ibid., p. 85.

14. Carol Thatcher, *Below the Parapet*, HarperCollins, 1996, p. 63.

15. Brenda Maddox, *Maggie*, p. 63.

16. *Finchley Press*, quoted by Campbell in *Margaret Thatcher*, I, p. 139.

17. Maddox, *Maggie*, p. 80.

18. Thatcher, *Path to Power*, p. 119.

19. Campbell, *Margaret Thatcher*, I, p. 145.

20. Thatcher, *Path to Power*, p. 119.

21. Carol Thatcher, *Below the Parapet*, p. 91.

22. Thatcher, *Path to Power*, p. 135.

23. House of Commons, 6 July 1965.

24. Thatcher, *Path to Power*, p. 136.

25. Campbell, *Margaret Thatcher*, I, p. 191.

26. *The Times*, 6 May 1966.

27. House of Commons, 27 June 1966.

28. Thatcher, *Path to Power*, p. 142.

29. *Sunday Mirror*, 28 December 1969.

30. Campbell, *Margaret Thatcher*, I, p. 178.

31. Thatcher, *Path to Power*, p. 149.

32. *Financial Times*, 22 October 1969.

33. Campbell, *Margaret Thatcher*, I, p. 198.

2   The Sorry Seventies

1. David Howell, *A New Style of Government*, Conservative Political Centre, 1970.

2. Richard Cockett, *Thinking the Unthinkable*, p. 203.

3. John Campbell, *Edward Heath*, Random House, 1993, p. 311.

4. *Spectator*, 12 March 2005.

5. Campbell, *Edward Heath*, p. 576.

6. Campbell, *Margaret Thatcher*, I, p. 227.

7. Thatcher, *Path to Power*, p. 166.

8. Campbell, *Margaret Thatcher*, I, p. 218.

9. Thatcher, *Path to Power*, p. 178.

10. Cockett, *Thinking the Unthinkable*, p. 291.

11. *Guardian*, 14 January 1974.

12. Thatcher, *Path to Power*, p. 191.

13. Campbell, *Margaret Thatcher*, I, p. 251.

14. Thatcher, *Path to Power*, p. 221.

15. Ibid., p. 197.

16. Douglas Hurd, *End to Promises*, Collins, 1979, p. 152.

17. Peter Hennessy, *The Prime Minister*, Penguin, 2001, p. 365.

18. James Callaghan, *Time and Chance*, HarperCollins, 1987.

19. Hugo Young and Anne Sloman, '*But Chancellor*', BBC Books, 1984.

20. See Peter Jay in *The Times*, 1 July 1974.

21. Quoted by Joel Barnett, *Inside the Treasury*, Deutsch, 1982, p. 175.

22. Sam Beer, *Britain Against Itself*, Faber and Faber, 1982.

23. See Nick Tiratsoo, ed., *From Blitz to Blair*, Weidenfeld and Nicolson, 1997.

24. Denis Healey, *The Time of My Life*, Penguin, 1990, p. 430.

25. Milton Friedman, 'Inflation and Unemployment', Institute of Economic Affairs Paper No. 51, 1977.

26. Bernard Donoghue, *Downing Street Diary*, Jonathan Cape, 2005, p. 190.

27. Margaret Thatcher, *The Downing Street Years*, HarperCollins, 1993, p. 7.

3 A Constitutional Coup

1. Richard Cockett, *Thinking the Unthinkable*, p. 232.

2. Cockett lists, among others, Hugh Thomas, John Vaizey, Robert Conquest, Paul Johnson and Caroline Cox.

3. Published in *Reversing the Trend*, Centre for Policy Studies, 1975.

4. Thatcher, *Path to Power*, p. 253.

5. Ibid., p. 251.

6. Ibid., p. 149.

7. Stockton Speech, published in *Reversing the Trend*.

8. House of Commons, 27 July 1974.

9. Thatcher, *Path to Power*, p. 266.

10. Campbell, *Margaret Thatcher*, I, p. 284.

11. Thatcher, *Path to Power*, p. 257.

12. Alistair McAlpine, *Once a Jolly Bagman*, Weidenfeld and Nicolson, 1997, p. 191.

13. Campbell, *Margaret Thatcher*, I, p. 291.

14. Campbell, *Edward Heath*, p. 672.

15. Geoffrey Howe, *Conflict of Loyalty*, Macmillan, 1994, p. 94.

16. Campbell, *Margaret Thatcher*, I, p. 310.

17. Thatcher, *Path to Power*, p. 277.
18. Campbell, *Margaret Thatcher*, I, p. 294.
19. Ibid., p. 366.
20. Ibid., p. 354.
21. Thatcher, *Path to Power*, p. 320.
22. House of Commons, 22 May 1975.
23. *The Times*, 15 September 1977.
24. Quoted in Hugo Young, *One of Us*, Macmillan, 1989, p. 223.
25. Campbell, *Margaret Thatcher*, II, p. 677.
26. Campbell, *Margaret Thatcher*, I, p. 385.
27. Ibid., p. 393.
28. Thatcher, *Path to Power*, p. 421.
29. Ibid., p. 422.
30. *The Times*, 10 October 1978.
31. Campbell, *Margaret Thatcher*, II, p. 4.

4 Civil War

1. Campbell, *Margaret Thatcher*, II, p. 22.
2. Thatcher, *Path to Power*, p. 467.
3. Thatcher, *Downing Street Years*, p. 28.
4. Alan Clark, *Diaries*, p. 139.
5. Personal interview, 1981.
6. Thatcher, *Downing Street Years*, p. 18.
7. Campbell, *Margaret Thatcher*, II, p. 474.
8. Ibid., p. 472.
9. Clark, *Diaries*, p. 147.
10. Douglas Hurd, *Memoirs*, Macmillan, 2003, p. 242.
11. John Hoskyns, *Just in Time*, Aurum, 2000, p. 86.
12. Private information.
13. Campbell, *Margaret Thatcher*, II, p. 130.
14. Geoffrey Howe, *Conflict of Loyalty*, p. 130.
15. Ibid., p. 142.
16. Thatcher, *Downing Street Years*, p. 44.
17. Quoted in Campbell, *Margaret Thatcher*, II, p. 105.
18. Thatcher, *Downing Street Years*, p. 132.
19. Clark, *Diaries*, p. 205.
20. Howe, *Conflict of Loyalty*, p. 195.
21. Campbell, *Margaret Thatcher*, II, p. 55.
22. Howe, *Conflict of Loyalty*, p. 202; see also Hoskyns, *Just in Time*.

23. *The Times*, 30 March 1981.

24. *Guardian* lecture, quoted in Campbell, *Margaret Thatcher*, II, p. 109.

25. Thatcher, *Downing Street Years*, p. 149.

26. *The Times*, 3 August 1981.

27. Thatcher, *Downing Street Years*, p. 154.

28. Thatcher, *Path to Power*, p. 155.

29. Thatcher, *Downing Street Years*, p. 153.

30. John Junor, *Listening for a Midnight Train*, Chapman, 1990.

31. Thatcher, *Path to Power*, p. 149.

5 Epiphany at Port Stanley

1. Personal interview, 1982.

2. See Max Hastings and Simon Jenkins, *The Battle for the Falklands*, Michael Joseph, 1983, for information on these events.

3. Hastings and Jenkins, *Falklands*, p. 38.

4. Campbell, *Margaret Thatcher*, II, p. 15.

5. Hastings and Jenkins, *Falklands*, p. 36.

6. *The Times*, 2 April 2002.

7. See Hastings and Jenkins, *Falklands*, ch. 3; Lawrence Freedman, *History of the Falklands War*, Routledge, 2005.

8. Personal interview.

9. Hastings and Jenkins, *Falklands*, p. 80.

10. Campbell, *Margaret Thatcher*, II, p. 139.

11. Hastings and Jenkins, *Falklands*, p. 141.

12. Thatcher, *Downing Street Years*, p. 177.

13. Private information.

14. Campbell, *Margaret Thatcher*, II, p. 156.

15. Alan Clark, *Diaries*, p. 331.

6 Marking Time

1. Campbell, *Margaret Thatcher*, II, p. 160.

2. David Butler, Andrew Adonis and Tony Travers, *Failure in British Government*, Oxford University Press, 1994, p. 35.

3. House of Commons, 5 November 1981.

4. In *Political Quarterly*, No. 55, 1984.

5. Thatcher, *Downing Street Years*, p. 274.

6. Campbell, *Margaret Thatcher*, II, p. 643.

7. Simon Jenkins, *Accountable to None: the Tory Nationalisation of Britain*, Penguin, 1996, p. 44.

8. Nigel Lawson, *The View From No 11*, Bantam, 1992, pp. 565–6.

9. Campbell, *Margaret Thatcher*, I, p. 14.

10. *The Times*, 4 April 1982, quoted in Campbell, *Margaret Thatcher*, II, p. 179.

11. Thatcher, *Downing Street Years*, pp. 284–5.

12. Lawson, *View From No 11*, p. 245.

7 The Revolution Takes Shape

1. Adam Zamoyski, *Holy Madness*, Weidenfeld and Nicolson, 1999.

2. Shirley Letwin, *The Anatomy of Thatcherism*, Fontana, 1992, p. 54.

3. Thatcher, *Downing Street Years*, p. 306.

4. Nicholas Ridley, *My Style of Government*, Hutchinson, 1991, p. 86.

5. Letwin, *Thatcherism*, p. 33.

6. Thatcher, *Downing Street Years*, p. 306.

7. Ibid., p. 308.

8. Campbell, *Margaret Thatcher*, II, p. 240.

9. David Marsh, in *Public Administration*, Vol. 69, 1991, p. 465.

10. *Daily Telegraph*, 31 July 1987.

11. Quoted in Simon Jenkins, *Accountable to None*, p. 39.

12. Tony Prosser, in *Public Law*, January, 1986.

13. Campbell, *Margaret Thatcher*, II, p. 363.

14. Thatcher, *Downing Street Years*, p. 686.

15. John Rentoul, *Tony Blair*, Little, Brown, 2001.

16. *Hansard*, 22 November 1983.

17. Campbell, *Margaret Thatcher*, II, p. 94.

18. Woodrow Wyatt, *Journals*, Macmillan, 1998, p. 579.

19. Ian Gilmour, *Dancing with Dogma: Britain Under Thatcherism*, Simon and Schuster, 1992, p. 100.

20. Peter Carrington, *Reflect on Things Past*, HarperCollins, 1988, p. 319.

21. George Urban, *Diplomacy and Disillusion at the Court of Margaret Thatcher*, Tauris, 1996, p. 79.

22. Campbell, *Margaret Thatcher*, II, p. 311.

23. Thatcher, *Downing Street Years*, p. 556.

24. James Prior, *Balance of Power*, Hamish Hamilton, 1986, p. 197.

25. Carol Thatcher, *Below the Parapet*, p. 219.

26. Campbell, *Margaret Thatcher*, II, p. 494.

27. Ibid., p. 388.

28. Letwin, *Thatcherism*, p. 23.

29. BBC interview, quoted in Campbell, *Margaret Thatcher*, II, p. 352.

30. Thatcher, *Downing Street Years*, p. 435.

31. *Spectator*, 6 November 1993.

8 Enter the Second Revolution

1. *The Economist*, 11 March 1995.

2. Thatcher, *Downing Street Years*, p. 625.

3. Ibid., p. 607.

4. Personal interview, November 1990.

5. Thatcher, *Path to Power*, p. 48.

6. Campbell, *Margaret Thatcher*, II, p. 38.

7. Simon Jenkins, *Big Bang Localism*, Policy Exchange, 2005, p. 53.

8. Campbell, *Margaret Thatcher*, II, p. 464.

9. House of Commons Health Committee, 15 July 1950.

10. Thatcher, *Downing Street Years*, p. 606.

11. 'Patients First', Department of Health and Social Security, 1979.

12. Rudolph Klein, in P. Jackson, ed., *Implementing Government Policy Initiatives*, Gower, 1985.

13. Roy Griffiths, 'NHS Management', Department of Health and Social Security, 1983.

14. See Patricia Day and Rudolph Klein, *Accountabilities*, Tavistock, 1987, p. 87.

15. Thatcher, *Downing Street Years*, p. 607.

16. Ibid., p. 571.

17. Ibid., p. 609.

18. Nigel Lawson, *View From No 11*, p. 613.

19. 'Working for Patients', Department of Health and Social Security, 1989.

20. Malcolm Balen, *Kenneth Clarke*, Fourth Estate, 1994, ch. 10.

21. House of Commons, 17 January 1990.

22. David Hughes, in *Journal of Social Welfare Law*, 1990, p. 303.

23. Kenneth Baker, *The Turbulent Years*, Faber and Faber, 1993, p. 161.

24. Robert Morris, *The Central and Local Control of Education*, Longman, 1990.

25. Thatcher, *Downing Street Years*, pp. 591–2.

26. Julian Haviland, *Take Care Mr Baker*, Institute of Economic Affairs, 1988.

27. Thatcher, *Downing Street Years*, p. 594.

28. Paul Meredith, in *Modern Law Review*, Vol. 52, 1989, p. 216.

29. Maurice Kogan, in *Political Quarterly*, April, 1991, p. 229.

30. Thatcher, *Downing Street Years*, p. 595.

31. Lawson, *View From No 11*, p. 609.

32. Nicholas Timmins, 'No Such Thing as Society', p. 445.

33. Baker, *Turbulent Years*, p. 220.

34. Thatcher, *Path to Power*, p. 174.

35. *Sunday Times*, 8 May 1988.

36. Campbell, *Margaret Thatcher*, II, p. 399.

37. Ibid., p. 395.

38. Michael Shattock, *The University Grants Committee*, Open University, 1994, p. 95.

39. Quoted by John Griffith in *Political Quarterly*, January, 1989, p. 51.

40. Campbell, *Margaret Thatcher*, II, p. 400.

41. 'Meeting the Challenge', Department of Education and Science, 1987.

42. Griffith, in *Political Quarterly*, 1989.

43. Quoted in Campbell, *Margaret Thatcher*, II, p. 399.

44. Thatcher, *Downing Street Years*, p. 599.

45. For a full account of Lawson's bid to nationalize the education service see Lawson, *View From No 11*, pp. 607–10.

46. Thatcher, *Downing Street Years*, p. 599.

47. Ray Forrest and Alan Murie, *Selling the Welfare State*, Routledge and Kegan Paul, 1988.

48. Geoffrey Howe, *Conflict of Loyalty*, p. 280.

49. Thatcher, *Downing Street Years*, p. 671.

50. Private interview.

51. Quoted in Forrest and Murie, *Selling the Welfare State*, p. 213.

52. Quoted in Peter Malpass and Alan Murie, *Housing Policy and Practice*, Macmillan, 1990.

53. Details in Simon Jenkins, *Accountable to None*, p. 179.

54. Government's Expenditure Plans, Cmnd 9702, 1986.

55. Tristram Hunt, *Building Jerusalem*, Weidenfeld and Nicolson, 2004, p. 344.

56. Evidence to House of Lords Select Committee on the Environment, 1981.

57. Tony Travers et al., *The Government of London*, Joseph Rowntree Foundation, 1991.

58. House of Commons, 3 December 1984.

59. Lawson, *View From No 11*, p. 565.

9 All Politics is Local

1. Thatcher, *Downing Street Years*, p. 588.

2. *The Times*, 9 October 1987.

3. Thatcher, *Downing Street Years*, p. 589.

4. Campbell, *Margaret Thatcher*, II, p. 529.

5. Andrew Marr, *Ruling Britannia*, Michael Joseph, 1995, p. 85.

6. Campbell, *Margaret Thatcher*, II, p. 299.

7. Thatcher, *Downing Street Years*, p. 628.

8. 'Work and Organisation of the Legal Profession', Home Office, 1989.

9. In *International Lawyer*, American Bar Association, 1990.

10. Private interview.

11. Nigel Lawson, *View From No 11*, p. 824.

12. Campbell, *Margaret Thatcher*, II, p. 588.

13. Lawson, *View From No 11*, p. 564.

14. 'Rates', Department of the Environment, 1983.

15. Thatcher, *Downing Street Years*, p. 646.

16. Ibid., p. 649.

17. Ibid., p. 652.

18. See David Butler et al., *Failure in British Government*.

19. Thatcher, *Downing Street Years*, p. 667.

20. Lawson, *View From No 11*, p. 581.

21. Butler et al., *Failure in British Government*, p. 180.

22. John Major, *The Autobiography*, HarperCollins, 1999.

23. Campbell, *Margaret Thatcher*, II, p. 710.

24. Paddy Ashdown, *Diaries, 1988–1997*, Penguin, 2001, p. 96.

25. *The Times*, 19 November 1990.

26. Thatcher, *Downing Street Years*, p. 855.

27. Ibid.

28. Ronald Millar, *A View from the Wings*, Weidenfeld and Nicolson, 1993, p. 356.

10 Thank You and Goodbye

1. Campbell, *Margaret Thatcher*, II, p. 710.

2. Ian Gilmour, *Dancing with Dogma*, p. 8.

3. See Ivor Crewe and Anthony King in Robert Skidelsky, ed., *Thatcherism*.

4. Richard Cockett, *Thinking the Unthinkable*, p. 323.

5. In Skidelsky, *Thatcherism*, p. 123.

6. Peter Hennessy, *Prime Minister*, p. 435.

7. See Richard Rose and Phillip Davies, *Inheritance in Public Policy*, Yale, 1994.

8. Andrew Gamble, *The Free Economy and the Strong State*, Macmillan, 1994, p. 209.

9. Geoffrey Howe, *Conflict of Loyalty*, p. 135.

10. Peter Clarke, *A Question of Leadership*, Penguin, 1991, p. 325.

11. Thatcher, *Downing Street Years*, p. 632.

12. Hennessy, *Prime Minister*, p. 402.

13. Eric Hobsbawm, *Politics for a Rational Left*, p. 46.

14. *How to Be Prime Minister*, BBC2, 1996.

15. Friedrich von Hayek, *The Constitution of Liberty*, Chicago, 1960, p. 400.

11 Thatcherism's Human Face

1. John Major, *Autobiography*, p. 11.

2. Anthony Seldon, *Major: A Political Life*, Weidenfeld and Nicolson, 1997, p. 21.

3. Personal conversation.

4. In Geoffrey Wheatcroft, *The Strange Death of Tory England*, Allen Lane, 2005, p. 185.

5. Major, *Autobiography*, p. 311.

6. Peter Hennessy, *Prime Minister*, p. 436.

7. Seldon, *Major*, p. 133.

8. *The Times*, 21 January 1991.

9. Major, *Autobiography*, p. 247.

10. Seldon, *Major*, p. 503.

11. See Terry Gourvish, *British Rail 1974–97*, Oxford University Press, 2002, p. 292.

12. Christian Wolmar, *On the Wrong Line*, Aurum, 2005.

13. Ibid., p. 52.

14. Simon Jenkins, *Accountable to None*, p. 206.

15. Wolmar, *Wrong Line*, p. 333.

16. Stephen Glaister and Tony Travers, *New Directions for British Railways*, Institute of Economic Affairs, 1993.

12 The Second Revolution Strikes Back

1. Major, *Autobiography*, p. 215.

2. Ibid., p. 217.

3. Sarah Hogg and Jonathan Hill, *Too Close to Call*, Little, Brown, 1995, p. 59.

4. Ibid., p. 58.

5. David Butler et al, *Failure in British Government*, p. 182.

6. Thatcher, *Downing Street Years*, p. 663.

7. Ibid., p. 597.

8. Leslie Bash and David Coulby, eds., *The Education Reform Act*, Cassell, 1989, p. 17.

9. *Public Finance*, 5 August 2005.

10. Paul Meredith, *Education and the Law*, Longman, 1994, p. 126.

11. 'Managing the NHS', Department of Health and Social Security, 1994.

12. See David Marsh and R.A.W. Rhodes, eds., *Implementing Thatcherite Policies*, Open University, 1992, p. 116.

13. Rupert Darwall, KPMG/Reform, *Financial Times*, 19 April 2006.

14. Robert Reiner, *The Politics of the Police*, Harvester Wheatsheaf, 1992, p. 61.

15. Robert Mark, *In the Office of Constable*, Collins, 1978, p. 200.

16. Simon Jenkins, *Accountable to None*, p. 99.

17. House of Commons, 23 March 1993.

18. House of Lords, 15 February 1994.

19. 'Police Reform', Home Office, 1993.

20. *Political Quarterly*, April, 1995.

21. *Independent*, 11 November 2000.

22. Cmnd 8092, 1981, para. 6.3.

23. *Criminal Law Review*, 1994, p. 903.

24. House of Commons, 26 April 1994.

25. Home Office bulletin, 2 July 2002.

26. Kenneth Baker, *Turbulent Years*, p. 464.

13 The Treasury and the Cult of Audit

1. Nigel Lawson, *View From No 11*, p. 586.

2. Leo Pliatsky, *The Treasury under Mrs Thatcher*, Blackwell, 1989.

3. Hugo Young and Anne Sloman, *'But Chancellor'*.

4. Hugh Heclo and Aaron Wildavsky, *The Private Government of Public Money*, Macmillan, 1981.

5. Sarah Hogg and Jonathan Hill, *Too Close to Call*, p. 5.

6. Lawson, *View From No 11*, p. 391.

7. Simon Jenkins, *Accountable to None*, pp. 232–3.

8. Michael Power, *The Audit Explosion*, Demos, 1994.

9. Major, *Autobiography*, p. 257.

10. Ibid., p. 245.

11. Anthony Seldon, *Major*, p. 193.

12. Major, *Autobiography*, p. 253.

13. Colin Crouch and David Marquand, *The New Centralism*, Blackwell, 1989.

14. Major, *Autobiography*, p. 257.

15. Ibid., p. 726.

14 A Cuckoo in the Nest

1. *The Times*, 17 July 1995.

2. Anthony Seldon, *Blair*, Free Press, 2004, p. 450.

3. *Sunday Times*, 25 May 1997.

4. Personal correspondence from a contemporary.

5. Seldon, *Blair*, p. 227.

6. Ibid., p. 70.

7. Ibid., p. 53.

8. John Rentoul, *Tony Blair*, Little, Brown, 2001, p. 69.

9. Ibid., p. 72.

10. Ibid., p. 84.

11. Ibid., p. 102.

12. Tom Bower, *Gordon Brown*, HarperCollins, 2004, p. 13.

13. *Woman* magazine, 10 March 1997.

14. *The Times*, 13 June 1987.

15. Rentoul, *Tony Blair*, p. 14.

16. *The Times*, 1 July 1987.

17. Rentoul, *Tony Blair*, p. 142.

18. Ibid., p. 149.

19. Ibid., p. 120.

20. Philip Gould, *The Unfinished Revolution*, Abacus, 1999, p. 143.

21. Major, *Autobiography*, p. 307.

22. Clare Short, *An Honourable Deception? New Labour, Iraq and the Misuse of Power*, Free Press, 2004, p. 36.

23. Later to form the basis of *The Unfinished Revolution*.

24. Peter Riddell, *The Unfulfilled Prime Minister*, Politico's, 2005, p. 24.

25. Private information.

26. Seldon, *Blair*, p. 123.

27. Quoted in Rentoul, *Tony Blair*, p. 197.

28. *Marxism Today*, October 1991.

29. Tony Blair, 'Introduction', in Chris Bryant, ed., *Reclaiming the Ground: Christianity and Socialism*, Hodder and Stoughton, 1993, p. 12.

30. Robert Peston, *Brown's Britain*, Short Books, 2005, p. 34.

31. Ibid., p. 35.

32. Ibid., p. 42.

33. Bower, *Gordon Brown*, p. 96.

34. *Sunday Express*, 6 September 1992.

35. 'Labour and the Economy', *Tribune*, 1993.

36. *Tribune*, 1 January 1993.

37. BBC Radio 4, 10 January 1993.

38. Rentoul, *Tony Blair*, p. 160.

39. *New Statesman*, 18 November 1994.

40. *On the Record*, BBC Radio 4, January 1993.

41. Quoted in Rentoul, *Tony Blair*, p. 216.

42. Gould, *Unfinished Revolution*, p. 182.

15 Granita Rules

1. Robert Peston, *Brown's Britain*, p. 50.

2. For roughly consistent accounts of Granita, see Donald Macintyre, *Mandelson*, HarperCollins, 1999; Paul Routledge, *Gordon Brown*, Simon and Schuster, 1998; James Naughtie, *The Rivals*, Fourth Estate, 2001; Peston, *Brown's Britain*; Anthony Seldon, *Blair* and Tom Bower, *Gordon Brown*.

3. Peston, *Brown's Britain*, pp. 66–8.

4. Seldon, *Blair*, p. 194; Peston, *Brown's Britain*, p. 67.

5. *Guardian*, quoted in Peston, *Brown's Britain*, pp. 66–7.

6. *Breakfast with Frost*, BBC1, 12 June 1994.

7. Philip Gould, *Unfinished Revolution*, p. 216.

8. In *New Yorker*, 5 February 1996.

9. House of Commons, 25 April 1995.

10. *Sun*, 2 April 1997.

11. Meg Russell, *Building New Labour: The Politics of Party Organisation*, Palgrave Macmillan, 2005.

12. Anthony Seldon, ed., *The Blair Effect 1997–2001*, Little, Brown, 2001, p. 555.

13. Seldon, *Blair*, p. 34.

14. *Daily Mail*, 30 June 1995.

15. John Rentoul, *Tony Blair*, p. 261.

16. See Gould, *Unfinished Revolution*.

17. Cm 4310, 1999.

18. *Guardian* lunch, 27 March 2006.

19. William Keegan, *The Prudence of Mr Gordon Brown*, Wiley, 2003.

20. Speech at the Queen Elizabeth II Centre, London, 20 January 1997.

21. Peston, *Brown's Britain*, p. 165.

22. Paddy Ashdown, *Diaries, 1988–1997*, p. 280.

23. Ibid., p. 348.

24. Seldon, *Blair*, p. 269.

25. *Observer*, 5 May 1996.

26. *The Times*, 17 July 1995.

27. Rentoul, *Tony Blair*, p. 277.

28. *Sun*, 2 April 1997.

29. Gould, *Unfinished Revolution*, p. 240.

30. Quoted in Leo Abse, *The Man Behind the Smile*, Robson Books, 1996, p. 71.

31. Quoted by Peter Hennessy, *Prime Minister*, p. 476.

16 Something of Napoleon

1. Andrew Rawnsley, *Servants of the People*, Penguin, 2001, p. 27.

2. See Peter Mandelson and Roger Liddle, *The Blair Revolution*, Politico's, 2003.

3. Valedictory lecture, 26 July 2005.

4. Peter Riddell, in Anthony Seldon, ed., *Blair Effect, 1997–2001*, p. 32.

5. Christopher Foster, *British Government in Crisis*, Oxford University Press, 2005.

6. Riddell, in Seldon, ed., *Blair Effect, 1997–2001*, p. 23.

7. Rawnsley, *Servants*, pp. 29–30.

8. James Naughtie, *The Rivals*, p. xxi.

9. J.H. Grainger, *Tony Blair and the Ideal Type*.

10. Ibid., p. 84.

11. Anthony Seldon, *Blair*, p. 276.

12. *Sun*, 29 July 1997.

13. *Fabian Ideas*, No. 598.

14. See Graham Allen, *The Last Prime Minister*, Politico's, 2003.

15. Peter Riddell, *Unfulfilled Prime Minister*, p. 159.

16. Seldon, in Anthony Seldon and Dennis Kavanagh, eds., *The Blair Effect, 2001–5*, Cambridge University Press, 2005, ch. 18.

17. John Rentoul, *Tony Blair*, p. 405.

18. Christopher Meyer, *DC Confidential*, Weidenfeld and Nicolson, 2005, p. 88.

19. Peter Riddell, *Hug Them Close*, Politico's, 2003, p. 62.

20. Meyer, *DC Confidential*, p. 95.

21. John Kampfner, *Blair's Wars*, Free Press, 2003, p. 22.

22. Seldon, *Blair*, p. 449.

23. Kampfner, *Blair's Wars*, pp. 28–9.

24. *Financial Times*, 23 April 1999.

25. Kampfner, *Blair's Wars*, pp. 53, 57.

26. Ibid., p. 85.

27. Seldon, *Blair*, p. 486.

28. Press reports, 3 October 2001.

29. Kampfner, *Blair's Wars*, p. 130.

30. Riddell, *Hug Them Close*, p. 2.

31. Skidelsky, in Seldon and Kavanagh, eds., *Blair Effect, 2001–5*, p. 443.

32. See Bob Woodward, *Plan of Attack*, Simon and Schuster, 2004, and Meyer, *DC Confidential*.

33. See Barbara Tuchman, *The March of Folly*, Abacus, 1990.

34. Lord Butler, *Review of Intelligence on Weapons of Mass Destruction*, The Stationery Office, 2004, p. 159.

35. See Anne Deighton, in Seldon, ed., *Blair Effect, 1997–2001*, p. 319.

36. Naughtie, *The Rivals*, pp. 129–31.

37. Philip Stevens, in Seldon, ed., *Blair Effect, 1997–2001*, p. 202.

38. House of Commons, 7 December 2005.

17 Gordon Brown, Thatcherite

1. James Naughtie, *The Rivals*, p. xiii.

2. *Prospect* magazine, May 2005.

3. Speech to the London Chamber of Commerce, 5 April 2000.

4. Anthony Seldon, *Blair*, p. 194.

5. Derek Scott, *Off Whitehall*, Tauris, 2004, p. 24.

6. Robert Peston, *Brown's Britain*, p. 167.

7. Philip Stephens, in Anthony Seldon, ed., *Blair Effect, 1997–2001*, p. 196.

8. Peter Riddell, *Unfulfilled Prime Minister*, p. 75.

9. William Keegan, *The Prudence of Gordon Brown*, p. 183.

10. Scott, *Off Whitehall*, p. 20.

11. See Seldon, ed., *Blair Effect, 1997–2001*, pp. 217, 319.

12. Speech to TUC conference, September 1997.

13. OECD, 2005.

14. *Daily Telegraph*, 16 July 2005.

15. Christian Wolmar, *Wrong Line*, p. 332.

16. Cm 4310, 1999.

17. Alan Smithers, in Anthony Seldon and Dennis Kavanagh, eds., *Blair Effect, 2001–5*, p. 273.

18. 'Private Finance Initiatives', HM Treasury, 2003.

19. House of Lords, 10 March 2004.

20. *Public Finance*, 27 May 2005.

21. House of Commons Research Paper, 21 October 2003.

22. Philippa Roe and Alistair Craig, *Reforming the PFI*, Centre for Policy Studies, 2004, p. 17.

23. Ibid., p. 15.

24. *Financial Times*, 11 January 1997.

25. *Public Finance*, 1 July 2005.

26. *The Times*, 31 December 2005.

27. Wolmar, *Wrong Line*, p. 333.

28. *The Times*, 10 April 2006.

29. Stephen Glaister, in Seldon and Kavanagh, eds., *Blair Effect, 2001–5*, p. 212.

30. *Today*, BBC Radio 4, 2 January 2006.

31. *Public Finance*, 22 April 2005.

32. See league table published in *The Times*, 9 May 2006.

33. *The Times*, 12 August 2005.

34. *Times Educational Supplement*, 26 September 2003.

35. *Guardian*, 10 March 2003.

36. *Public Finance*, 28 April 2006.

37. *Guardian*, 28 December 2005.

38. David Craig and Richard Brooks, *Plundering the Public Sector*, Constable, 2006.

39. *The Times*, 26 September 2005.

40. Private information.

41. Tom Bower, *Gordon Brown*, p. 241.

42. Smithers, in Seldon and Kavanagh, eds., *Blair Effect, 2001–5*, p. 275.

43. Bower, *Gordon Brown*, p. 368.

44. *The Times*, 3 March 2005.

45. Bower, *Gordon Brown*, p. 366.

46. Kitty Stewart, in Seldon and Kavanagh, eds., *Blair Effect, 2001–5*, p. 318.

47. Geoffrey Howe, *Conflict of Loyalty*, p. 37.

48. *Guardian*, 27 July 2005.

49. Private conversation in 2005.

50. Polly Toynbee and David Walker, *Better or Worse: Has Labour Delivered?* Bloomsbury, 2005, p. 50.

51. Published by the Office of National Statistics.

52. *Public Finance*, 29 October 1999.

53. *Guardian*, 5 April 2006.

54. Julian le Grand, *Motivation, Agency and Public Policy*, Oxford University Press, 2003.

55. Kenneth Morgan, in Seldon, ed., *Blair Effect, 1997–2001*, p. 587.

18 Tony Blair and the Commanding Heights

1. Speech to Venture Capital, 6 July 1999.

2. Anthony Seldon, *Blair*, p. 429.

3. Sir Andrew Turnbull, Valedictory lecture, 26 July 2005.

4. Derek Scott, *Off Whitehall*.

5. Private information.

6. Quoted in Seldon, *Blair*, p. 629.

7. See John Micklethwait and Adrian Wooldridge, *The Witch Doctors: Making Sense of the Management Gurus*, Times Books, 1998.

8. *Sunday Times*, 16 April 2006.

9. *The Economist*, 23 July 2005.

10. *Sunday Times*, 13 November 2005.

11. *Guardian*, 5 July 2005.

12. Patrick Dunleavy and Helen Margetts, *Guardian*, 3 March 2006.

13. *The Times*, 3 March 2005.

14. Examples gathered from various issues of *Public Finance* magazine.

15. Peter Riddell, *Unfulfilled Prime Minister*, p. 61.

16. Lord Wilson, in *Political Quarterly*, 76, 2005.

17. Turnbull, Valedictory lecture.

18. Andrew Povey, paper for the Centre for Policy Studies, 1999.

19. *Hansard*, 17 March 2002.

20. *Sunday Times*, 30 April 2006.

21. *Guardian*, 16 September 2005.

22. *Public Finance*, 27 May 2005.

23. *Guardian*, 17 November 2005.

24. *Public Finance*, 17 March 2006.

25. See Simon Jenkins, *Big Bang Localism*, Policy Exchange, 2005, p. 61.

26. *Daily Telegraph*, 14 December 2005.

27. *Guardian*, 14 February 2005.

28. *Observer*, 26 March 2006.

29. Howard Glennerster, in Anthony Seldon and Dennis Kavanagh, eds., *Blair Effect, 2001–5*, p. 284.

30. *British Medical Journal*, June, 2004.

31. *The Times*, 10 May 2006.

32. *The Economist*, 16 October 2004.

33. *The Times*, 8 December 2005.

34. *Guardian*, 17 January 2006.

35. *Public Finance*, 17 March 2006.

36. *Guardian*, 28 December 2005.

37. *The Times*, 9 October 2004.

38. *Guardian* survey, 13 December 2004.

39. *Sunday Times*, 12 March 2006.

40. Barry Loveday and Anna Reid, *Size Isn't Everything*, Policy Exchange, 2003.
41. Ibid.
42. Report from Save Britain's Heritage, February 2006.
43. Barbara Tuchman, *March of Folly*.
44. Christopher Foster, 'Why Are We So Badly Governed?' Public Management and Policy Association, 2005, p. 32.
45. Jenkins, *Big Bang Localism*, pp. 10, 68.
46. *Guardian*, 1 September 2005.
47. *Public Finance*, July 2005.
48. *Guardian*, 28 September 2005.
49. *Guardian*, 10 May 2006.
50. Peter Hyman, *One Out of Ten*, Vintage, 2005, p. 384.
51. Private interview.

19 The New Localism

1. Jean-Benoit Nardeau and Julie Barlow, *Sixty Million Frenchmen Can't Be Wrong*, Robson Books, 2004.
2. See Linda Weisse, in Colin Crouch and David Marquand, *The New Centralism*.
3. Robert Putnam, *Making Democracy Work*, Princeton University Press, 1993.
4. John Laughlin and Steve Martin, Balance of Funding review papers, Office of the Deputy Prime Minister/Cardiff, 2004.
5. Ibid.
6. Crouch and Marquand, *The New Centralism*.
7. Study by Elias Mossialos for the London School of Economics, Ashgate, 1999.
8. Council of Europe returns, 1998–2000; see also Simon Jenkins, *Big Bang Localism*, p. 13.
9. John Rentoul, *Tony Blair*, p. 45.
10. *Observer*, 24 July 1997.
11. David Willetts, *Blair's Gurus*, Centre for Policy Studies, 1996.
12. Jeffrey Jowell and Dawn Oliver, *The Changing Constitution*, Clarendon Press, 2004, p. 306.
13. 'Mayors Make a Difference', New Local Government Network, 2006.
14. Paddy Ashdown, *Diaries*, II, p. 446.
15. *Public Finance*, 12 November 2004.
16. *Spectator*, 12 July 2003.
17. 'Devolved Decision Making', HM Treasury, December 2004.
18. *The Times*, 8 September 2005.
19. Council of Europe and other sources; Jenkins, *Big Bang Localism*, p. 13.

20. 'Total Politics', Conservative Political Centre, 2003, p. 2.

21. *The Times*, 26 January 2006.

22. Hugo Young lecture, HM Treasury, 13 December 2005.

23. *Financial Times*, 2 September 2003.

24. Hazel Blears, *Communities in Control*, Fabian Society, 2003.

25. *Localising the NHS*, New Local Government Network, 2004.

26. *Daily Telegraph*, 12 December 2003.

27. In Dan Corry, et al., eds., *Joining up Local Democracy*, New Local Government Network, 2004.

28. *Financial Times*, 7 February 2003.

29. David Walker, *In Praise of Centralism*, Catalyst, 2002.

30. 'Local Delivery of Central Policy', Cabinet Office, 2002.

31. *The Times*, 2 January 2006.

32. Tony Travers, in Anthony Seldon and Dennis Kavanagh, eds., *Blair Effect 2001–5*, p. 73.

33. 'Future of Local Government', Office of the Deputy Prime Minister, 2004.

34. 'Sustainable Communities', Office of the Deputy Prime Minister, 2005.

35. Edmund Burke, *Reflections on the Revolution in France*, Penguin, 1982, p. 140.

36. Travers, in Seldon and Kavanagh, eds., *Blair Effect, 2001–5*, p. 83.

37. *Observer*, 26 February 2006.

20 The Third Revolution

1. A model for police decentralization, set out by Barry Loveday and Anna Reid, *Going Local*, Policy Exchange, 2003.

2. Simon Jenkins, *Big Bang Localism*, Policy Exchange, 2005.

3. Thatcher, *Downing Street Years*, p. 684.

4. Tony Travers and Lorena Esposito, *Nothing to Lose But Your Chains*, Policy Exchange, 2004.

5. Douglas Carswell, *Paying for Localism*, Adam Smith Institute, 2004.

6. *Making Sense of Localism*, John Smith Institute, 2004.

7. Iain McLean and Alistair McMillan, *New Localism, New Finance*, New Local Government Network, 2003.

8. See cases cited by Simon Jenkins, *Sunday Times*, 1 April 2006.

9. Commission for Local Democracy, 'Taking Charge', *Municipal Journal*, 1995.

10. McLean and McMillan, *New Localism*.

Conclusion

1. YouGov survey for the *Guardian*, 2 February 2006.

2. Michael Oakeshott, *The Masses in Representative Democracy*, 2000.

3. Robert Worcester, Roger Mortimer and Paul Baines, *Explaining Labour's Land-slip*, Politico's, 2005, p. 189.

4. See the 'Power Report', Joseph Rowntree Foundation, February 2006.

5. Onora O'Neill, *A Question of Trust*, Cambridge University Press, 2002.

6. Keiron O'Hara, *After Blair*, Icon Books, 2005.

7. John Gray, *The Undoing of Conservatism*, Social Market Foundation, 1994, p. 106.

8. David Runciman, *The Politics of Good Intentions*, Princeton University Press, 2006.

9. Ulrich Beck, *Risk Society*, Sage, 1992.

10. William Waldegrave, *The Binding of Leviathan*, Hamish Hamilton, 1978, p. 118.

11. R.G. Collingwood, *New Leviathan*, Clarendon Press, 1999 (first published 1942).

12. There is an extensive review of the Norwegian Study of Power and Democracy in the *Times Literary Supplement*, 13 February 2004.

13. Jonathan Freedland, *Bring Home the Revolution*, Fourth Estate, 1998.

Index